✧✧✧✧✧✧✧✧✧

Culture and Politics
in Indonesia

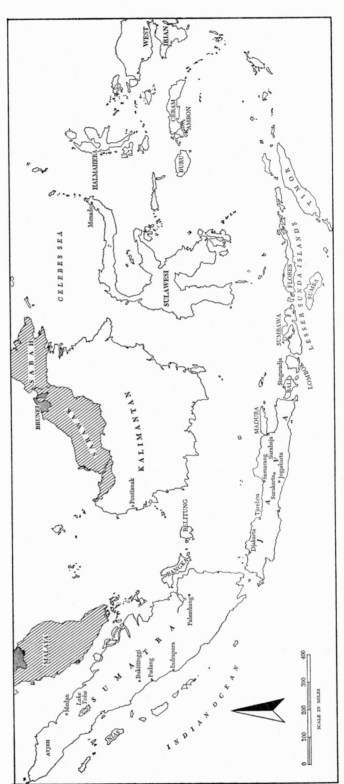

Map 1. INDONESIA

Culture and Politics in Indonesia

◇◆◇◆◇◆◇◆◇◆◇◆◇◆◇◆◇◆◇◆◇◆◇◆◇◆◇◆◇◆◇◆◇◆◇◆◇

Edited by CLAIRE HOLT

with the assistance of

Benedict R. O'G. Anderson

and James Siegel

Cornell University Press

ITHACA AND LONDON

First published 1972 by Cornell University Press.
Published in the United Kingdom by Cornell University Press Ltd.,
2–4 Brook Street, London W1Y 1AA.

Prepared under the auspices of The Asia Society

This book has been published with the aid of a grant from
the Hull Memorial Publication Fund of Cornell University.

International Standard Book Number 0-8014-0665-X
Library of Congress Catalog Card Number 78-162538

PRINTED IN THE UNITED STATES OF AMERICA
BY VAIL-BALLOU PRESS, INC.

Librarians: Library of Congress cataloging information
appears on the last page of the book.

Contents

Maps

Figure

Tables

Acknowledgments

The editors would like to express their gratitude to The Asia Society, particularly its Indonesia Council, for the financial and other assistance which made the preparation of this volume possible. They wish to convey their special thanks to His Excellency Ambassador Soedjatmoko, Professor Harry Benda, and Professor Clifford Geertz, who served as consultants and gave detailed criticisms of each of the essays. Special thanks are also due Miss Mildred Wagemann and Mrs. Elizabeth Witton, who assisted the editors at various stages in the growth of this book; and to Mrs. Tazu Warner and Mrs. Elizabeth Thorn, who typed the manuscripts.

B. R. O'G. A.
J. T. S.

Ithaca, N.Y.

Preface

"Culture" and "politics" are Western concepts that have no precise Indonesian analogues. The authors of this book have tried two complementary methods to show what can be learned about Indonesia through use of these Western concepts. Lev, Liddle, and Sartono demonstrate how much can be gained from presenting Indonesian life in Western terms, while Abdullah and Anderson contrast Indonesian and Western ideas.

Daniel Lev and William Liddle, both political scientists, work in sociological traditions. Liddle analyzes the process by which traditionally self-contained village communities are incorporated into a nation-state and shows how this amalgamation stimulates the growth of new ethnically and regionally defined identities. He explores the ways in which these new identities are given political expression, and the "crisis of participation" that confronts the nation's leadership as a result. He demonstrates how different types of political parties, to be successful at the local level, have to adapt themselves to local socioeconomic and cultural configurations, and he portrays the characteristic pattern of this adaptation. Lev analyzes the rapidly changing role of law in Indonesia since the end of the colonial period. He treats the decline of the Western-style legal profession both in terms of the decay of its necessary economic and political underpinnings and in terms of the persistence and even reinforcement of patrimonial values and local ethnic and religious traditions. At the same time, he shows how powerful forces of secularization and integration, deriving from nationalism and the bureaucratic imperatives of the nation-state, counteract these trends. He shows, too, how under such conditions, some of the most important functions performed by law and legal specialists in

certain Western societies have come to be performed by very different institutions and groups in contemporary Indonesia.

Sartono Kartodirdjo, a historian, continuing his work published
as *The Peasants' Revolt of Banten of 1888*, gives us an overview of
Javanese peasant movements. He uses a category, millenarianism,
which first gained prominence among social scientists when it was
used to describe certain medieval European social movements. The
picture he draws is of continuous and varied movements, revealing
a history of the peasantry that previous scholars have largely missed.
We are given an impression of peasants who act in terms they
themselves generate and who make their own history rather than
merely reacting to the pressures of colonialism.

Benedict Anderson, a political scientist, raises a question that
comes out of Western political theory—he asks what the Javanese
notion of power is. The meaning of power and its place within
society are so different from what they are in the West, that one
could conclude that the Javanese have another notion altogether.
Anderson's method is very suggestive. Although the initial question
comes out of Western political theory, he proceeds not by the application of Western ideas, but by making contrasts with them. His
is the most purely cultural essay in the book; part of its value may
be to demonstrate one method of cultural explication.

Taufik Abdullah as a historian believes that the narration of past
events can reveal the ideas which rule people's lives. He writes
about the leader of a conservative movement in Minangkabau (West
Sumatra). In doing so he is aware that the Indonesian word for
culture does not contain the notion of tradition. For Abdullah,
Minangkabau development from the past does not come from the
social products of the past as they are reformed in the present.
Rather, it results from the dialectic of men and governing ideas of
society. These ideas have a timeless logic which expresses itself
differently in different circumstances.

The essays in this book are of more than regional significance. For
instance, Liddle's description of the formation of new group identities among the Batak may be applicable to other parts of the world,
and Lev's study will certainly be of interest to those concerned with
the development of law anywhere in the world. Moreover, Sartono's
and Abdullah's essays indicate another sort of relevance of regional

studies for Indonesia. These two historians are themselves full members of Indonesian metropolitan culture, yet they write about their regions with no sense of discontinuity. Not only do they find sources of cultural continuity in movements that have failed by conventional standards, they also write with little indication that they feel themselves distant from the cultures they examine. There is nothing in tone or perspective which betrays estrangement from regional traditions. This suggests a source of continuity in metropolitan cultural life which deserves further study.

In his afterword Clifford Geertz discusses the contrast between Indonesian political institutions and power relationships and the cultural frameworks in which they exist. It was he who initiated the study of culture and politics in Indonesia. Moreover, his writings on Indonesia have been an indispensable background for any scholar concerned with the nation. His reflections on the questions raised by these essays are therefore especially pertinent.

JAMES SIEGEL

Ithaca, N.Y.

Foreword

We dedicate this volume to the memory of Claire Holt, who died on May 29, 1970, as her work on the manuscript was nearing completion.

This foreword was conceived originally as conveying to Mrs. Holt the thanks of the Asia Society and its Indonesia Council, under whose auspices this work is published, for the design of the symposium and for assuming a central and crucial responsibility in its preparation for publication. Our debt to her must now be acknowledged in mourning.

Her earlier volume, *Art in Indonesia,* and the present work stand as monuments to her scholarship, her love for her Asian friends, and her desire that people everywhere shall share her understanding of Asia.

She had known many of the facets of Asia's civilizations, and she moved from one culture to another, Asian, European, American, with ease, elegance, and effect. Other scholars have investigated the political and military structures and functions, the economic patterns, and the social systems of Indonesia. In this, many have repeated the one-dimensional approaches of the journalists, who seemed to know much about Asia but often little enough about Asians. A few writers did relate concepts of power and politics to religious belief and traditional visions of a spiritual world. But none was so aware as she of the Indonesian's connection of unseen worlds with the realities of everyday life and politics.

Mrs. Holt was one of the forces which have made the Asia Society an increasingly useful instrument of trans-Pacific discourse. Sensitive and resourceful, she designed brilliant Indonesian-American projects for the Society to undertake and worked hard for their achievement. Her loss is deeply felt.

We must express warm thanks to Professors Benedict R. O'G. Anderson and James Siegel, both of Cornell University, for preparing the manuscript for publication and for gallantly bringing this project to completion. To other friends of Claire Holt, at Cornell, in New York, in New Haven, in Washington, in Indonesia, and elsewhere, who helped with this volume, the Society and its Indonesia Council must add further words of gratitude. Two recent chairmen of the Council, Karl J. Pelzer and Michael Harris, in whose terms of office Mrs. Holt gave shape and body to the symposium, and Miss Mary Ann Siegfried, Mrs. Jordan Getz, and Mrs. Betty Holtz, who have provided the Council with the Society's staff assistance, also deserve very cordial thanks. Special acknowledgment is due the Rockefeller Foundation, whose grant to the Society's country councils program made this study possible.

The Society is obliged to add the traditional disclaimer and to assert that the views of the authors of these essays are theirs and not the Society's. As a nonpolitical educational organization, it cannot take any stands in the political sphere. It can hope to enlighten; it cannot assume a position or counsel one.

LIONEL LANDRY

The Asia Society
New York, N.Y.

❖❖❖❖❖❖❖❖❖

Culture and Politics
in Indonesia

The Idea of Power
in Javanese Culture[*]

✦✦✦✦✦✦✦✦✦

Benedict R. O'G. Anderson

INTRODUCTION

In spite of the considerable body of scholarly work that has been done on Indonesian, and especially Javanese history and culture, few attempts have been made at a systematic analysis either of traditional political conceptions or of their powerful, continuing impact on contemporary Indonesia.

The first deficiency can in part be attributed to the fact that Indonesia's classical literatures, unlike those of China and India, contain no full-fledged expositions of any indigenous "political theory." A contemporary reconstruction of such a theory has therefore to be abstracted from scattered historical sources and then synthesized with fragmentary insights drawn from field experience.

The second deficiency stems clearly from the first. The absence of a systematic exposition of a political theory in the classical literatures of Indonesia has fostered the assumption that no such theory, however implicit, exists and thus has hindered an awareness of the actual coherence and logic of traditional political conceptions. This lack of awareness has, in turn, hampered the analysis and evaluation of the influence of such conceptions on contemporary political be-

[*] The final form of this essay owes much to the insights and critical comments offered to the author by: Harry Benda, Lance Castles, Herbert Feith, Clifford Geertz, the late Claire Holt, George Kahin, Daniel Lev, Lionel Landry, Denys Lombard, Ruth McVey, Soemarsaid Moertono, Onghokham, James Siegel, John Smail, Soedjatmoko, Mildred Wagemann and Oliver Wolters. The author wishes to express his deep appreciation for all this help, while taking full responsibility for the content of the text.

1

havior. The tendency has been to select discrete elements from traditional culture [1] and correlate them in an arbitrary and ad hoc manner with particular aspects of present day politics. Cultural factors are typically brought in as a sort of *deus ex machina* when the combination of social, economic, and historical variables seems not completely to account for particular forms of political behavior. These cultural elements are thus introduced essentially to "save the phenomena." The implicit assumption of a lack of coherence in the cultural tradition has, it seems to me, inevitably led to a lack of methodological coherence in developing an over-all approach to contemporary Indonesian politics.

The present essay is an effort to remedy at least the first of the two basic deficiencies that I have pointed out. By offering a systematic exposition of traditional Javanese conceptions [2] about politics and demonstrating their inner coherence, I hope to take a preliminary step toward a fuller investigation of the interrelationships between culture and social action in Indonesia.[3] Such a presentation should make it evident that traditional Javanese culture did have a political theory which offered a systematic and logical explanation of political behavior quite independent of the perspectives of modern political science and in many ways in fundamental opposition to them. In effect, the same objective political phenomena can be, and have been, interpreted in quite different but equally consistent ways by observers from within each intellectual tradition. To use a time-worn but convenient simile, the two traditions provide strikingly different lenses for charting the political landscape.

My intention, then, is to describe the picture of social and

[1] In this essay the terms tradition, cultural tradition, and traditional culture are used interchangeably.

[2] My focus throughout is on Javanese tradition, partly for reasons of economy and clarity, but also because of my greater ignorance of the political traditions of other Indonesian ethnic groups

[3] In many respects this essay tries, however haltingly, to follow the program for the development of a "scientific phenomenology of culture" suggested by Geertz in his brilliant analysis of Balinese cultural tradition. See Clifford Geertz, *Person, Time and Conduct in Bali: An Essay in Cultural Analysis*, Southeast Asia Studies, Cultural Report Series no. 14 (New Haven: Yale University, 1966), p. 7. The second chapter of his study gives an excellent outline of the reasons why such a program is urgently required and the intellectual problems involved in its implementation.

political life seen through traditional Javanese lenses, and to draw explicit contrasts with the picture seen through the lenses of modern social science. Yet these lenses obviously not only structure the perceptions (and thus the interpretations) of those who wear them but, in so doing, influence their behavior. The pictures which filter through the lenses are, after all, approximately what Weber called the subjective meanings attached to social action by its participants, meanings which, as he amply demonstrated, are essential for any full understanding of such action by an observer.[4] Only a deciphering of the meaning attached by traditional (and partly detraditionalized) Javanese to such objective phenomena as sexual activity or the accumulation of wealth, will open the way to a general comprehension of the workings of politics in both traditional and present-day Java. But I can not undertake here a detailed analysis of the complex interplay of meaning and action within either traditional or contemporary Javanese society. For ideas must be systematically presented before their practical influence on objective phenomena can be studied in an orderly fashion.

I should also stress at the outset that I in no way assume that Javanese conceptions about politics are, in their separate elements, peculiarly Javanese—although I do believe that, in their totality, they form a unique amalgam. Many of these elements derive historically from the influence of Indic civilization; others have parallels in a wide range of Asian and non-Asian traditional cultures.[5] If an unwarranted uniqueness seems to be attributed here to Javanese conceptions, this stems mainly from the wish to avoid constant, irritating qualifications. Indeed, the similarities between Javanese and other traditional conceptions of politics are so integral a part of the assumptions behind this exposition that they form the basis of its theoretical conclusion: the possibility of a useful simplification and revision of the conventional concept of charisma and its historical emergence.[6]

---

[4] See the discussion of Weber's use of the term *Sinn* as a key theoretical concept in Reinhard Bendix, *Max Weber, An Intellectual Portrait* (Garden City: Doubleday Anchor, 1962), p. 474.

[5] Compare, for example, the excellent discussion of comparable Japanese concepts in Masao Maruyama, *Thought and Behaviour in Modern Japanese Politics* (London: Oxford University Press, 1963), chap. 1.

[6] See the Conclusion to this essay.

CONCEPTS OF POWER

Study of classical Javanese literature and present-day political behavior suggests that one key to understanding the Javanese theory of politics may be the traditional interpretation of what social science refers to as power.[7] For the Javanese conception differs radically from the concept of power which has evolved in the West since the Middle Ages, and from this difference there logically follow contrasting views of the workings of politics and history.[8]

[7] It is important to bring out from the start an inherent linguistic and conceptual problem in the analysis that I am about to develop. Because this essay is written in English, by a native English-speaker, primarily for native English-speakers, and also because my own intellectual perspective is irremediably Western, I see no choice but to use words and concepts like "power," which are drawn from a Western analytical and interpretative framework, in dealing with the problem of contrasting that framework with the Javanese. There is clearly a fundamental bias inherent in such a method of work. But without a superordinate language and conceptual framework in which to place both Western and Javanese terms and concepts, all that one can do is to recognize and remain constantly aware of this bias. When I say that the Javanese have a radically different idea of power from that which obtains in the contemporary West, properly speaking this statement is meaningless, since the Javanese have no equivalent word or concept. Conversely, speaking from within the Javanese framework, one could say that the West has a concept of kasektèn radically different from that of the Javanese, while in fact modern English does not really have such a concept at all. (The old usage of the word power, which survives in such phrases as "The Great Powers" or "the Power went out of him," approximates the Javanese idea, but by no means coincides with it.) Thus in strict intellectual principle the whole discussion of differing concepts of power in the ensuing section should be accompanied by a parallel discussion of differing Western concepts of kasektèn, as seen from the Javanese viewpoint. This parallel discussion might begin: "Westerners have a concept of kasektèn quite different from ours: they divide it up into concepts like power, legitimacy, and charisma." A full development of this line of analysis is indispensable in principle, but for the reasons given above I have not attempted here more than a pointer as to how it should be approached. Probably only a Javanese could do it effectively.

[8] In the ensuing discussion of Javanese political ideas, I am attempting to map out a pure model for analytical purposes. Traditional Javanese political culture was an extremely complex phenomenon, in which, as in any other culture, it would be naive to try to discern complete consistency or mathematical logic. In that traditional culture an indigenous matrix was imperfectly compounded with heterogeneous Brahmanic, Buddhist, and Islamic elements. Nonetheless, the slow process of absorption and synthesis over the centuries prior to the "coming of the West" permitted the crystallization of a relatively

It is perhaps useful to recall that the concept of power became an explicit problem for Western political thinkers only after the waning of the Middle Ages. The first philosophers to devote serious and extended attention to it were Machiavelli and Hobbes. The fact that, particularly since the time of Hobbes, the nature, sources, and use of power have been a major concern of Western political thinkers is surely no historical accident. It parallels more or less directly the tide of secularization which has swept over Europe since the Renaissance and the Reformation. The contemporary concept of power arose historically from the need to interpret politics in a secular world.

Clarification of the Javanese idea of power may be facilitated by a schematic contrast with the more significant aspects of the modern European concept, which can be summarized under four main headings: [9]

1. *Power is abstract.* Strictly speaking, it does not "exist." Power is a word used commonly to describe a relationship or relationships. Like the words authority or legitimacy, it is an abstraction, a

---

high degree of internal consistency. The model I am trying to delineate is thus an "ideal type" of precolonial Javanese political thought, deliberately simplified and exaggerated, which should not be taken as a historical reality.

Java's subjection to Western political, economic, and cultural domination has, particularly in the last hundred years, set in motion an irremediable process of decrystallization. Contemporary Javanese political culture is therefore a heterogeneous, disjunctive, and internally contradictory complex of traditional and Western elements, with a lower degree of internal logic and coherence than in the past. A start at understanding this complex requires a preliminary model of the pre-Western framework of reference—a model which this essay tries to provide.

[9] I use "modern European concept" as a convenient shorthand term. The four basic notions about power that I am proposing did not spring into existence all at once; their emergence was a slow, uneven process. Although some of these notions may be evident in Classical philosophy, they were largely submerged in the Middle Ages and only developed fully during later periods. Explicit theorizing about the relationship of power and legitimacy emerged historically from the long conflict between the Papacy and the rulers of mediaeval Europe. The modern concept of power as something abstract goes back at least as far as Machiavelli. The idea of the heterogeneous sources of power came into full philosophic flower with Montesquieu and his successors of the Enlightenment. What one might call the "non-zero-sum" view of power probably did not arise until the Industrial Revolution. (These datings are of course no more than rough marking-points.) Thus the "modern European concept" of power outlined here is essentially the culmination of a long process of intellectual evolution.

formula for certain observed patterns of social interaction. Thus we normally infer the "existence" of power in a wide variety of situations in which some men appear to obey, willingly or unwillingly, the wishes of others. We do not usually assert that a particular individual or group has power except by demonstrating the causal linkage between an order, explicit or implicit, and its execution.

2. *The sources of power are heterogeneous.* Since power is ascribed to or inferred from certain patterns of behavior and certain social relationships, a great deal of Western political thought has been devoted to the classification and analysis of these patterns and relationships, and thereby to the distinguishing of different sources of power. Thus we have come to accept such various sources of power as wealth, social status, formal office, organization, weapons, population, and so forth. Though in practice each of these sources of power may be, indeed usually is, linked with others, in everyday political analysis they are treated as separate variables influencing behavior.

3. *The accumulation of power has no inherent limits.* Since power is simply an abstraction describing certain human relationships, it is not inherently self-limiting. Moreover, insofar as we regard the sources of power as including weapons, wealth, organization, and technology, we recognize that at least in theory there are no limits to its accumulation. To put it another way, one could suggest that the total amount of power in the world today is significantly larger than it was thirty years ago (as the result, for example, of the invention of the hydrogen bomb), and that this sum of power will probably continue to increase in the thirty years to come. In this sense our concept of power is directly conditioned by the accelerating development of modern technology.

4. *Power is morally ambiguous.* It follows logically from the secular conception of political power as a relationship between human beings that such power is not inherently legitimate. This moral ambiguity is, of course, enhanced by our view of power as deriving from heterogeneous sources. This heterogeneity has accentuated the prominence and complexity of a question which continues to preoccupy political theorists: What kinds of power are

legitimate? Or, more pointedly, what is the relationship between the positivist concept of power and the ethical concept of right?

Briefly, then, the contemporary Western concept of power is an abstraction deduced from observed patterns of social interaction; it is believed to derive from heterogeneous sources; it is in no way inherently self-limiting; and it is morally ambiguous.

In essence, each of these premises about power runs counter to an equivalent premise in the Javanese tradition, and it is from the interrelations between these contrasting premises that the coherence and consistency of that tradition derive.

1. *Power is concrete.* This is the first and central premise of Javanese political thought. Power exists, independent of its possible users. It is not a theoretical postulate but an existential reality. Power is that intangible, mysterious, and divine energy which animates the universe. It is manifested in every aspect of the natural world, in stones, trees, clouds, and fire, but is expressed quintessentially in the central mystery of life, the process of generation and regeneration. In Javanese traditional thinking there is no sharp division between organic and inorganic matter, for everything is sustained by the same invisible power. This conception of the entire cosmos being suffused by a formless, constantly creative energy provides the basic link between the "animism" of the Javanese villages, and the high metaphysical pantheism of the urban centers.[10]

2. *Power is homogeneous.* It follows from this conception that all power is of the same type and has the same source. Power in the hands of one individual or one group is identical with power in the hands of any other individual or group.

3. *The quantum of power in the universe is constant.* In the Javanese view, the cosmos is neither expanding nor contracting. The total amount of power within it, too, remains fixed. Since power simply exists, and is not the product of organization, wealth, weapons, or anything else—indeed precedes all of these and makes them what they are—its total quantity does not change, even though the distribution of power in the universe may vary. For political

[10] Thus the well-known mystical formula *Tuhan adalah Aku* (God is I) expresses the concreteness of the Javanese idea of power. The divine power is the essence of I, of the self.

theory, this has the important corollary that concentration of power in one place or in one person requires a proportional diminution elsewhere.

4. *Power does not raise the question of legitimacy.*[11] Since all power derives from a single homogeneous source, power itself antecedes questions of good and evil. To the Javanese way of thinking it would be meaningless to claim the right to rule on the basis of differential sources of power—for example, to say that power based on wealth is legitimate, whereas power based on guns is illegitimate. Power is neither legitimate nor illegitimate. Power is.

In summary, then, the Javanese see power as something concrete, homogeneous, constant in total quantity, and without inherent moral implications as such.[12]

THE QUEST FOR POWER

The central problem raised by this conception of Power, by contrast with the Western tradition of political theory, is not the exercise of Power but its accumulation. Accordingly, a very considerable portion of the traditional literature deals with the problems of concentrating and preserving Power, rather than with its proper uses. In the orthodox tradition, the quest for Power is pursued through yogaistic practices and extreme ascesis. Although these yogaistic practices in various parts of Java take different forms, including fasting, going without sleep, meditation, sexual abstinence, ritual purification, and sacrifices of various types, one central idea underlies them: all are designed to focus or concentrate the primordial essence. The best guide for sensing the contours of the conception is perhaps the image of the burning-glass or the laser-beam, where an extraordinary concentration of light creates an extraordinary outpouring of heat. The analogy is especially apt since, in the classical imagery of Javanese literature, extreme ascesis has precisely this quality of generating physical heat. The legendary

[11] At least not in the form to which we are accustomed. For a fuller discussion, see the section "Power and Ethics."

[12] This contrast is discussed from a slightly different point of view in Maruyama, chap. 9 ("Some Problems of Political Power"), especially the section (pp. 269–275) on "substantive and functional concepts of power." Henceforward, when the word power is used in the Javanese, rather than European sense, it will be capitalized.

kris-makers [13] of the past were supposed to be able to forge the iron blades with their exquisite inlay by the heat concentrated in their thumbs alone. In the typical *gara-gara* section of the *wajang* plays,[14] where an unknown ascetic is practicing meditation, the most signal expression of his concentration is that, in the words of the *dalang* (puppeteer), the ocean begins to boil and bubble.[15]

The inward significance of such ascesis is in no sense self-mortification with ethical objectives in mind, but solely and singly the acquisition of Power. In the orthodox tradition, ascesis follows the law of compensation that is fundamental to the Javanese sense of the balance of the cosmos. Thus self-deprivation is more or less equivalent to self-aggrandizement within the ascetic mode; and, as we shall see, by a typical Javanese paradox, self-aggrandizement (in the sense of personal acquisitiveness or personal indulgence) comes to mean self-deprivation (in the sense of loss of Power or loss of concentration). The conception of *concentration* which underlies the practice of asceticism is also correlated closely with the idea of purity; conversely the idea of impurity is intimately related to *diffusion* and *disintegration*. The world, the flesh, and the devil are not necessarily conceived as evil or immoral in the first instance, but rather as distracting and diffusing, and thus as leading to the loss of Power. One finds many examples of this line of thought in the traditional literature. Not only heroes indulge in ascetic practices—some of the most notable practitioners come from the

[13] The kris is the short dagger traditionally a basic possession of every male Javanese. Many are believed to contain deposits of Power and are eagerly sought after even if their workmanship is not of the first quality. For a full discussion of the symbolic and social significance of the kris, see W. H. R. Rassers, *Pañji, the Culture Hero, A Structural Study of Religion in Java* (The Hague: Nijhoff, 1959), pp. 219–297.

[14] *Wajang* is the generic name for a variety of types of Javanese drama, the best known of which is the shadow-play. The *gara-gara* is a climactic section of the play in which the order and tranquillity of the cosmos is disturbed.

[15] Cf., e.g., Ki Siswoharsojo, *Pakem Pedhalangan Lampahan Makutharama* (Jogjakarta: n.p., 1963), pp. 44–45; J. Kats, *Het Javaansche Tooneel*, 1 (*Wajang Poerwa*) (Weltevreden: Commissie voor de Volkslectuur, 1923), p. 52; and for a historical parallel, in which Panembahan Sénapati's ascetic practices have the same effect, see Soemarsaid Moertono, *State and State-craft in Old Java*, Cornell Modern Indonesia Project Monograph Series (Ithaca, N.Y.: Cornell University, 1968), p. 19, citing J. J. Meinsma, ed., *Babad Tanah Djawi* (The Hague: Nijhoff, 1941), p. 77.

ranks of the demons and giants who in the wajang stories are the
traditional enemies of gods and men. Accordingly, their Power is
often enormous, on occasion even exceeding that of the gods. The
essential difference between the heroes and their adversaries, however, is that the latter eventually permit their Power to be diffused
by indulging their passions without restraint, whereas the former
maintain that steadfastness, that tense singleness of purpose which
assures the maintenance and continued accumulation of Power.[16]

Besides this orthodox view of the road to Power, another, heterodox tradition exists in Java, historically best exemplified in the person of the last ruler of Singhasari, King Kertanagara. In this
Bhairavist (Tantric) tradition, Power is sought through a kind
of Rimbaudian *dérèglement systématique des sens*—drunkenness,
sexual orgies, and ritual murder.[17] But even this tradition, which
still finds more or less clandestine adherents in contemporary
Indonesia, ultimately aims at the same objectives as the more
orthodox tradition. For in the Bhairavist belief-system, the systematic indulgence of the sensual passions in their most extreme form
was believed to exhaust these passions, and therefore to allow a
man's Power to be concentrated without further hindrance. Thus in
both traditions the ultimate aim was concentration for the sake of
Power, although the paths chosen to reach this purpose radically
diverged.

While personal ascesis was generally regarded as the fundamental
way to accumulate and absorb Power, traditional Javanese thinking
also recognized that this process of absorption or accumulation
could be furthered both by certain rituals, often containing a core
of asceticism, such as fasting, meditation, and so forth, and by the
possession of certain objects or persons regarded as being "filled"
with Power. Since C. C. Berg has written at length about the ritual

[16] It may be suggested that a kind of moral judgment about Power is
implicit in this difference between heroes and demons. My own inclination,
however, is to believe that insofar as a moral judgment is made, it is not
about the use of Power but about its retention or dispersal. Criticism of the
demons is leveled at their inability or unwillingness to conserve the Power
they have accumulated.

[17] On this topic, see W. F. Stutterheim, *Het Hinduisme in de Archipel*,
3d ed. (Djakarta and Groningen: Wolters, 1952), pp. 63, 67, and 138; and
W. F. Stutterheim, *Studies in Indonesian Archaeology* (The Hague: Nijhoff,
1956), pp. 107–143.

mobilization of Power through "verbal magic" in the chronicles of Old Java, further exploration of the subject here is unnecessary.[18] But it is difficult to understand the great importance attached to ceremonies of state in the contemporary period without bearing this part of the tradition clearly in mind. This obsession with ceremony has commonly been interpreted either as simple love of ideologizing, as manipulative sleight-of-hand, concealing political and economic realities from the population, or as a way of formally integrating conflicting groups and interests in a nation where institutional devices for this purpose have always been exceedingly weak. Such judgments are doubtless partly valid (although opinions may well differ over the extent to which Indonesian political leaders were consciously motivated in this way). But it would be unreasonable to deny that the importance attached to ceremonies may also have a more traditional basis, certainly in the minds of the spectators and probably, if to a lesser degree, in the minds of the leaders themselves. One should not underestimate the dynamic and aggressive aspect of these ceremonies and the degree to which they represent to the participants the conjuring of Power.[19]

Some ceremonies are quite openly of this conjuring character: for example, the holding, at the President's palace, of wajang shows, with plots specifically chosen for their relevant political symbolism; the summoning of leaders of various spiritualist or mystical groups to participate in the war campaign against the Dutch during the Irian crisis of 1961–1962; and in the National Monument the erection of a modernized *lingga* (sacred phallus). But many other typical aspects of modern Indonesian public political behavior—mass rallies, symbolic marches, hortatory speeches, evocations of the Revolution —while overtly having little connection with tradition, and indeed deriving formally from Western political practice, in the esoteric sense are strongly Power-oriented, intended to concentrate and display Power absorbed from various sources—Power-ful words

[18] A large part of C. C. Berg's writings center on this theme. For a good, brief, and comprehensive formulation, see his "The Javanese Picture of the Past," in Soedjatmoko *et al.*, eds., *An Introduction to Indonesian Historiography* (Ithaca, N.Y.: Cornell University Press, 1965), pp. 87–117

[19] For a rather different interpretation of the political function of ceremony, defining it as more or less an end in itself under the rubric of the Doctrine of the Theater State, see Clifford Geertz, *Islam Observed* (New Haven: Yale University Press, 1968), p. 38.

(*Pantjasila, Revolusi, Sapta Marga*),[20] Power-ful experiences (the Revolution) and Power-ful collectivities (the People).[21] In effect, many of Sukarno's political rallies, ostensibly designed to convey a particular message to the population or to demonstrate the President's popular backing, were no less important as methods of accumulating and demonstrating Power from the willing submission of so many thousands of persons. The greater the extent to which different and even hostile political groups could be brought into these ceremonies, the greater the real and the perceived Power of the master of ceremonies. Sukarno's highly traditional style of incantatory rhetoric naturally added to the political impact of the ceremony as a whole.[22]

Moreover, it was an old tradition in Java that the ruler should concentrate around him any objects or persons held to have or contain unusual Power. His palace would be filled not only with the traditional array of *pusaka* (heirlooms), such as krisses, spears, sacred musical instruments, carriages, and the like, but also various types of extraordinary human beings, such as albinos, clowns, dwarves, and fortunetellers. Being in the palace with the ruler, their Power was absorbed by, and further added to, his own. Their loss, by whatever means, was seen as an actual diminution of the king's Power and often as a sign of the impending collapse of the dynasty. The extent to which this tradition survives even in elite political

[20] The *Pantjasila* are the Five Principles—Belief in God, Nationalism, Humanism, Democracy, and Social Justice—first formulated by Sukarno in a historic speech on June 1, 1945, and later accepted as a key element in the national ideology. *Revolusi* is self-explanatory. The *Sapta Marga* (The Seven Principles) is the code of the Indonesian Armed Forces, formulated by Colonel Bambang Supeno in the early 1950's.

[21] It may be pointed out that marches, rallies, and so forth, are used to gain power or demonstrate it in the West as well. My point here is that the power gained and demonstrated is seen very differently in the two cultures.

[22] Mohammad Roem, in talks with the writer in Ithaca early in 1968, remarked that prior to the rise of the nationalist leader H. O. S. Tjokroaminoto in the 1910's, political speech-makers borrowed their oratorical style from the *bangsawan* stage-plays, which in turn derived largely from the European theater. Gesture and imagery tended to be mechanical and formal. The great innovation of Tjokroaminoto, which was picked up and developed by Sukarno, was to base his oratorical style on the dalang's manner of recitation. This allowed for the skillful use of traditional imagery and traditional sonorities by these two master orators to build up unprecedented rapport with their audiences.

circles is no secret to observers of the Indonesian scene, both under Sukarno and his successor. It should perhaps be noted, however, that being thought to have such objects or persons at one's disposal is just as politically advantageous as actually having or making serious use of them. A striking illustration of this phenomenon has been the tendency for many prominent non-Javanese politicians to let it be known that they too have some of the regalia of Power.[23]

THE SIGNS OF POWER

The Javanese tradition of political thought thus typically emphasizes the signs of Power's concentration, not the demonstration of its exercise or use. These signs are looked for both in the person of the Power-holder and in the society in which he wields his Power. The two are, of course, intimately related. In the words of one of Indonesia's most prominent contemporary intellectuals, "A central concept in the Javanese traditional view of life is the direct relationship between the state of a person's inner self and his capacity to control the environment." [24]

The most obvious sign of the man of Power is, quite consistently, his ability to concentrate: to focus his own personal Power, to absorb Power from the outside, and to concentrate within himself apparently antagonistic opposites. The first type of concentration we have already dealt with briefly; it suffices to say here that the image of asceticism is the prime expression of concentrated Power. The ability to absorb external concentrations of Power is a frequent theme in both the wajang legends and historical tradition.[25] One typical image, which links this type of absorption with the concentration of opposites, is a battle between a hero and a powerful adversary, in which the defeated adversary in death enters the hero's body, adding to his conqueror's strength. A famous example in the wajang literature is the story of King Parta entering the body of Ardjuna

[23] Some of them, of course, are sufficiently Javanized to make serious efforts actually to acquire Javanese types of regalia.

[24] Soedjatmoko, "Indonesia: Problems and Opportunities," *Australian Outlook*, 21, no. 3 (Dec. 1967), 266.

[25] One familiar aspect of Old Javanese historical writing, namely references to historical kings as being incarnate deities can be interpreted in this light to signify the absorption of external Power into the person of the ruler. See, for example, Berg, pp. 93, 112.

after defeat in battle.[26] But other stories, such as those describing the spirit of Begawan Bagaspati descending into Judistira to enable him to kill King Salya, or the fusion of Srikandi and Ambalika to encompass the destruction of Resi Bisma at the outset of the Bratajuda War, reveal parallel patterns in which Power is absorbed from external sources.[27]

But no less striking and in the historical perspective of perhaps more enduring significance is the ability to concentrate opposites. The classical iconographic symbol of this is the combination of male and female. In ancient Javanese art this combination does not take the form of the hermaphrodite of the Hellenistic world, an ambiguous transitional being between the sexes, but rather the form of a being in whom masculine and feminine characteristics are sharply juxtaposed. One finds, for example, in the *ardhanari* type of image that the left side of the statue is physiologically female, the right side male.[28] The essential characteristic of this combination of opposites is not their merging but their dynamic simultaneous incorporation within a single entity. Thus the ardhanari image expresses the vitality of the ruler, his oneness, and his center-ness. He is at once masculine and feminine, containing both conflicting elements within himself and holding them in a tense, electric balance.[29]

[26] See the plot of the play *Arimba*, summarized in Kats, p. 282.

[27] See the plots of the plays *Pedjahipoen Soejoedana* and *Pedjahipoen Bisma lan Seta*, summarized in Kats, pp. 436 and 428.

[28] A beautiful example of a *hari-hara ardhanari* image can be found in Claire Holt, *Art in Indonesia* (Ithaca, N.Y.: Cornell University Press, 1967), p. 81.

[29] My interpretation here derives in part from J. M. van der Kroef's essay on "Transvestitism and the Religious Hermaphrodite," in his book *Indonesia in the Modern World* (Bandung: Masa Baru, 1956), pp. 182–195, though clearly my analytic method differs markedly from his. One can perhaps see another version of the male-female conjuncture as an image of Power in an interesting institution of the Central Javanese *kraton* (court). Among the various types of royal regalia, thus part of the ruler's emblems of Power, one finds the *bedaja*, a special group usually composed of women, responsible both for guarding the other regalia and for performing the most sacred of the court dances. The interesting thing is that when the king went off to battle, the bedaja were always brought along; and many of the texts of the songs accompanying bedaja dances celebrate royal victories. Significantly, it was not the *permeswari* (senior queen) or other official consorts of the ruler who thus performed the function of representing the female component of his Power, but rather the bedaja. A further involution of this juxtaposition of male and female elements may be revealed by the fact that at least in

Although in the world of art the masculine-feminine combination remains a vivid representation of Power, in the world of politics, for obvious reasons, the dynamic syncretism of Javanese thinking expresses itself in other ways. The most striking recent expression was the so-called *Nasakom*-politique of former President Sukarno.[30] When Sukarno proclaimed himself at once nationalist, religious man, and Communist, he was frequently interpreted by observers outside the Javanese political tradition to be talking the language of manoeuvre and compromise. The Nasakom formula tended to be seen either as an irresponsible and intellectually incoherent slogan or as a subtle device for weakening the anti-Communist prejudices of powerful nationalist and religious groups. Such interpretations, however, failed to place the Nasakom-politique within the context of Javanese political thinking. In this world-orientation, Sukarno's formula could be interpreted not as a compromise or stratagem, but as a powerful claim to the possession of Power by the ruler. By its terms all other political actors were condemned to subordinate roles as parts of the system: Sukarno alone was whole, *sembada,* absorbing all within himself, making the syncretic conquest.

But it is not only in the overt symbolism of Nasakom that one finds the unity-in-opposites formula of Power.[31] The same relationship can also be found in the powerful appeal made in the prewar

---

Jogjakarta, up to the reign of Sultan Hamengku Buwana VII, the bedaja dances were performed by pubescent boys dressed in female garments.

The traditional guardians of the regalia of the Buginese and Makassarese rulers of Southwest Sulawesi were the so-called *bissu,* men who dressed in a special combination of male and female garments. For an excellent description of these bissu, with photographs, see Claire Holt, *Dance Quest in Celebes* (Paris: Les Archives Internationales de la Danse, 1939), pp. 27–36, 87–89, and plates 15–18, 94–97.

[30] *Nasakom* is an acronym formed from the words *Nasionalisme* (nationalism), *Agama* (religion), and *Komunisme* (Communism). The Nasakom-politique, pursued by Sukarno during the period of Guided Democracy, was designed to encourage mutual trust and cooperation between the groups and parties normally classified under each of these three rubrics.

[31] Interestingly enough, this formula is most succinctly expressed in the Indonesian national motto *Bhinneka Tunggal Ika.* This motto is usually translated as "Unity in Diversity" and is often regarded as equivalent to the American national motto *E pluribus unum.* There is an important difference of nuance, however, between the two. The American motto implies a process of unification out of divergent elements, while the Indonesian suggests the inseparability of unity and diversity.

period by the PNI (Indonesian National Party) and in the 1960's especially by the PKI (Indonesian Communist Party)—an appeal at once to modernity and to tradition, or perhaps more exactly a mediation of tradition through modernity. Ruth McVey has given a subtle account of the development of Indonesian cultural nationalism in the Taman Siswa school system before World War II.[32] She has shown how the Taman Siswa's founder, Ki Hadjar Dewantara, was able to combine what at the time were ultramodern humanist educational theories with traditional elements in Javanese education to provide, for that period at least, a particularly effective dynamic combination of new and old, radical and conservative. Whereas Dutch sympathizers attributed Ki Hadjar's ideas to Froebel and Montessori, Javanese adherents saw them as emerging from the formulations drawn up by the traditionalist *kebathinan* (meditation) group, Pagujuban Selasa-Kliwon, led by a group of Ki Hadjar's friends. This typical two-sided quality of radical nationalism has, of course, a clear sociological and historical explanation. But this doubleness can also be seen as reflecting the dynamic Power-orientation of Javanese thinking.[33]

If the ability to contain opposites and to absorb his adversaries are important elements in a leader's claim to have Power, one key public sign of it has traditionally been what the Javanese call the *wahju* (divine radiance). Of this emanation Moertono writes: "It was visualized in different shapes and forms—bright luminescence, a 'star,' but most often it was seen as a dazzling blue, green or white ball of light (*andaru, pulung*), streaking through the night sky."[34] (This imagery reveals the pervasive identification of Power and light in Javanese thought.) The movement of the wahju typically marked the fall of one dynasty and the transfer of the light-source to another. The everyday presence of Power was more usually marked by the *tédja* (radiance) which was thought to emanate softly from

[32] Ruth McVey, "Taman Siswa and the Indonesian National Awakening," *Indonesia*, 4 (Oct. 1967), 128–149.

[33] In the 1960's the Indonesian Communist Party was particularly successful in reviving, developing, and adapting traditional forms of popular art and theater. By presenting these adaptations of traditional art as ultimately more modern and progressive, as well as more *asli* (indigenous) than the uprooted, derivative, bourgeois culture of the cities, the party played successfully on Javanese sensibilities about the nature of Power.

[34] Moertono, p. 56.

the face or person of the man of Power. The psychological grip of this image can be glimpsed in a remarkable speech given by Sukarno in 1963, on the occasion of receiving an honorary doctorate at the University of Indonesia in Djakarta.[35] On that occasion he spoke at length about the tédja, noting that various European figures had possessed it, among the most notable of whom was Adolf Hitler. Sukarno's discussion of Hitler and his tédja evoked dismay among some Western observers present, who judged it within the frame of reference of European history. But seen within the Javanese tradition, Sukarno's references were calmly analytical. Nowhere in his references to Hitler was there any mention of the moral qualities of the Fuehrer's rule. The reason for this omission was not that Sukarno lacked appreciation for moral questions, but rather that within the categories of Javanese political theory, the specific morality of a government is quite secondary (both in historical and in analytical terms) to its Power aspects. The *fact* that Hitler had the tédja was central and formed the starting-point of any analysis of his regime.[36]

The glow of the tédja was traditionally associated with the public visage of the ruler. Moertono cites the case of Amangkurat III (1703–1708), of whom it was said, when he was about to be deposed, that having "lost his *tjahja* (radiance), he looked pale as a Chinese with a stomach-ache." [37] By contrast, of Amangkurat II (1677–1703), at the moment of his resolve to resist the incursion of Trunadjaja and to defend the crumbling empire of Mataram, it was related that his followers "did not recognize their lord; formerly his expression was wan and without expression, now his countenance became bright and of a stately gravity." [38]

But since the tédja was merely an external manifestation of the inner creative energy of the universe, it could appear not only in the ruler's visage but also in his sexual power. The following re-

[35] Soekarno, *Ilmu Pengetahuan Sekadar Alat Mentjapai Sesuatu* (Djakarta: Departemen Penerangan Republik Indonesia, Penerbitan Chusus 253, 1963). The speech was delivered on February 2, 1963.

[36] As we shall see below, a ruler can lose his tédja by indulging in evil actions, but the tédja comes first and is not acquired by good actions as such.

[37] Moertono, p. 40, citing *Babad Tanah Djawi*, p. 273. My translation differs slightly from Moertono's, both here and in the two notes following.

[38] Moertono, p. 57, citing *Babad Tanah Djawi*, p. 174.

markable anecdote, which refers to the succession crisis after the death of Amangkurat II in 1703, was designed to indicate why Pangeran Puger, who with Dutch assistance usurped the throne from his nephew Amangkurat III, was the deceased sovereign's legitimate successor. "The story is told that the [dead] king's manhood stood erect and on the top of it was a radiant light (tjahja), only the size of a grain of pepper. But nobody observed it. Only Pangeran Puger saw it. Pangeran Puger quickly sipped up the [drop of] light. As soon as the light had been sipped, the manhood ceased to stand erect. It was Allah's will that Pangeran Puger should succeed to the throne." [39] Indeed the sexual fertility of the ruler is one essential sign of the Power that he holds, for his seed is the microcosmic expression of the Power he has concentrated. The fertility of the ruler was seen as simultaneously evoking and guaranteeing the fertility of the land, the prosperity of the society, and the expansionist vitality of the empire. The Sukarno period once again provides a striking modern parallel to this old idea. Outside observers of the Indonesian scene frequently remarked that Sukarno's well-publicized sexual activities appeared to do him no political harm. It was even said that the Javanese indulgently expect their rulers to act in this way. But if the foregoing analysis is correct, the political aspects of Sukarno's personal life are overlooked in such a perspective. For signs of the ruler's virility are political indicators that he still has the Power. Conversely, any marked decline in sexual activity could be taken as sign of waning Power in other respects. More sophisticated observers of late Guided Democracy were indeed inclined to suspect that Palace officials deliberately spread exaggerated stories about the President's personal life as part of a continuing effort to maintain his authority.

The social signs of the concentration of Power were fertility, prosperity, stability, and glory. As the dalang of the *wajang bèbèr* puts it in the classical imagery of the ancient Javanese kingdom of Kediri:

The land of Kediri may be described as stretching far and wide, with long shores, high mountains, rich, fertile, prosperous, tranquil and well-ordered. If fertile, it was the villages which were fertile; if prosperous, it was the Kingdom which was prosperous, food and clothing were very

[39] Moertono, p. 58, citing *Babad Tanah Djawi*, p. 260.

cheap. Even the lowliest widow could keep her own elephant with its mahout. Such was the richness and prosperity of the Kingdom. . . . There were no men who begged from one another; each had possessions of his own. All this was because of the richness and good ordering of the Kingdom.[40]

The two fundamental ideas behind these conventional images are creativity (fertility-prosperity) and harmony (tranquillity-order), expressed in the age-old motto so often on the lips of the contemporary elite, *tata tentrem karta rahardja* (order, peace, prosperity, good fortune). Both fertility and order are simply expressions of Power. Power is the ability to give life. Power is also the ability to maintain a smooth tautness and to act like a magnet which aligns scattered iron filings in a patterned field of force. Conversely, the signs of a lessening in the tautness of a ruler's Power and of a diffusion of his strength are seen equally in manifestations of disorder in the natural world—floods, eruptions, and plagues—and in inappropriate modes of social behavior—theft, greed, and murder.[41] Again, one should bear in mind that in Javanese thought there is no reciprocal effect between declining power and the appearance of these undesirable phenomena. Antisocial behavior arises from a ruler's declining Power but does not in itself further diminish that Power. It is a symptom but not a cause of his decline. Therefore, a ruler who has once permitted natural and social disorders to appear finds it particularly difficult to reconstitute his authority. Javanese would tend to believe that, if he still had the Power, the disorders would never have arisen. They do not stem ultimately from autonomous social or economic conditions, but from a looseness or diffusion of Power within the state.

POWER AND HISTORY

How does the idea of Power affect the traditional Javanese view of the nature or structure of the historical process? Sartono has

[40] The citation is drawn from an unpublished transcription and translation of a *wajang bèbèr* performance recorded in Donorodjo, Central Java, in 1963, made by the writer. On the wajang bèbèr, see Holt, *Art in Indonesia*, pp. 127–128.

[41] For a good, detailed list of the undesirable natural and social phenomena which appear in a time of decline, see Tjantrik Mataram (pseud.), *Peranan ramalan Djojobojo dalam revolusi kita*, 3d ed. (Bandung: Masa Baru, 1954), pp. 29–31.

argued that the essential difference between the traditional Javanese view of history and the modern Western perspective is that, in the modern view, history is seen as a linear movement through time, whereas Javanese traditionally tended to see their history as a series of recurrent cycles. He suggests that while Western historians and political scientists differ on the direction of history's linear movement and the degree to which it is determined by objective factors, all share the sense, essentially derived from the technological revolution of the last 200 years, that history is noniterative, a series of unique events linked by a complex causality. By contrast he believes that traditional Javanese historical thinking, influenced in part by Sanskrit cosmological writings, saw history as a cycle of ages (*Yuga*) moving from the Golden Age (*Krtayuga*) through successively less happy epochs (*Tretayuga* and *Dyapara Yuga*) to the evil *Kaliyuga*—before the wheel turned again and brought back a renewed Krtayuga.[42] My own interpretation, however, would be that while the Javanese may have utilized elements from Indic cosmology for formal classificatory purposes, their intuitive sense of the historical process was fundamentally a logical corollary of their concept of Power. In popular Javanese thought today and in the rich eschatological literature of the past, one finds little sense of cycles and of orderly decline and rebirth; instead one sees a sharp contrast drawn between the *djaman mas* and the *djaman édan,* the golden age and the mad age.[43] These two types of historical epochs were seen typically as times of order and times of disorder. The critical point, I think, is that the Javanese view of history was one of cosmological oscillation between periods of concentration of Power and periods of its diffusion. The typical historical sequence is concentration-dif-

[42] See Sartono Kartodirdjo, *Tjatatan tentang segi-segi messianistis dalam Sedjarah Indonesia* (Jogjakarta: Gadjah Mada, 1959). My comments on Sartono's subtle work by no means do it justice. Its main theme is actually to show how the prophetic *Serat Djojobojo* marks a decisive shift from a cyclical to a linear historical perspective under the influence of Islamic eschatology. Cf. also Moertono, pp. 81–82; and Heinrich Zimmer, *Myths and Symbols in Indian Art and Civilization* (New York: Harper Torchbooks, 1962), pp. 13–19, 35–37.

[43] Even Hindu cosmology points in this direction since the pattern of change is not strictly circular; the change from the Kaliyuga to the Krtayuga does not pass through gradual stages of reintegration symmetrical to the process of disintegration.

fusion-concentration-diffusion without any ultimate resting-point.[44] In each period of concentration new centers of Power (dynasties, rulers) are constituted and unity is recreated; in each period of diffusion, Power begins to ebb away from the center, the reigning dynasty loses its claim to rule, and disorder appears—until the concentrating process begins again. The historical necessity of diffusion is no less compelling than that of concentration, since Power is immensely hard to retain and has perpetually to be struggled for. The slightest slackness or lack of vigilance may begin the process of disintegration, which, once it sets in, is irreversible. (The loosening of cosmological tautness stems from *pamrih,* which essentially means the use of Power for personal indulgence or the wasting of concentrated Power on the satisfaction of personal passions).[45]

This conception of history helps to explain two notable but apparently contradictory features of Javanese political psychology: its underlying pessimism and at the same time its susceptibility to messianic appeals. The pessimism derives from the sense of the impermanence of concentrated Power, the difficulty involved in its accumulation and retention, and the inevitability of disorder on the far side of order. The susceptibility to messianism in times of disorder, however, arises from the sense that a new concentration of Power is always preparing itself within that disorder, that one must be alert for portents of its imminent appearance and then approach

[44] I would like to stress that what I am saying here is meant as an interpretation of the Javanese view of *history* in a quite specific sense. It is not an interpretation of the Javanese concept of *time,* which I think is probably closely comparable to the Balinese concept based on the combinatorial calendar, so brilliantly elucidated by Clifford Geertz. (See Geertz, *Person, Time and Conduct in Bali,* pp. 45–53.) My feeling, essentially intuitive, is that the calendrical, "punctuational" concept of time is in Java the framework within which everyday social life takes place, and applies primarily to familial and local contexts. Perhaps because of the long imperial history of Java, the dramatic rise and fall of dynasties whose names are familiar even to illiterate peasants through the oral wajang tradition, and the long period of colonial subjugation, there is a distinct view of what one would call political history, which is not calendrical at all. This *historical* perspective comes out very clearly in the chronicles (*babad*) of the courts, and the long tradition of messianic and millenarian beliefs among the peasantry, discussed by Sartono in the present volume. To my limited knowledge, Bali shows a relative lack of both dynastic historiography and peasant millenarianism.

[45] See the section "Power and Ethics," for a fuller discussion of the meaning and significance of *pamrih.*

the germinal center as rapidly as possible, attaching oneself to the new order as it emerges. This messianism clearly has little of the linear quality of many European millenary movements, which saw the world coming to an end with the arrival of the Messiah. Traditional Javanese sense that history does not come to an end, that messiahs are only for their time, and that the primordial oscillations of Power will continue as before.

UNITY AND THE CENTER

It may be useful to begin discussion of the traditional polity not with its concrete structures but with its ideal symbolic form. Perhaps the most exact image of the ordered Javanese polity is that of a cone of light cast downwards by a reflector lamp. This image conveys, I think more accurately than more conventional terminology, some of the nuances of Javanese political thought. The good society is not strictly hierarchical, since a hierarchy presupposes a certain degree of autonomy at each of its various levels. The movement of traditional Javanese thought implicitly denies this, seeking ideally a single, pervasive source of Power and authority. As we shall see, the gradual, even diminution of the radiance of the lamp with increasing distance from the bulb is an exact metaphor for the Javanese conception not only of the structure of the state but also of center-periphery relationships and of territorial sovereignty. While the undifferentiated quality of the light expresses the idea of the homogeneity of Power, the white color of the light, itself the "syncretic" fusion of all the colors of the spectrum, symbolizes the unifying and concentrating aspects of Power.

The core of the traditional polity has always been the ruler, who personifies the unity of society.[46] This unity is in itself a central symbol of Power, and it is this fact as much as the overt goals of statist ideologies that helps to account for the obsessive concern with one-ness which suffuses the political thinking of many contemporary Javanese. The popular hostility expressed toward the Federal Republic of Indonesia (1949–1950) reflected, I would argue, not simply the explicit suspicion that its component states were pup-

[46] Cf. Geertz, *Islam Observed*, p. 36, on the Doctrine of the Exemplary Center.

pets of Dutch creation, but also the sense that one-ness is Power and multiplicity is diffusion and weakness.[47]

Sukarno's constant appeals for national unity can in part be attributed to traditional anxiety about a dispersion of Power. Within a traditionalist Javanese framework the multi-party system, the constitutional separation of powers, and federalism were easily interpreted to mean the decline of Indonesia's international Power and that of Sukarno himself as its political focus. The Sumpah Pemuda (Oath of Youth) of 1928—One Country, One Flag, One Language—reiterates the same theme. One can detect it also in the program and strategy of the PKI (Indonesian Communist Party) in the period before its destruction; there the traditional Marxist formulas of class struggle were transformed into a style of propaganda in which essentially one *Rakjat* (People), with all its deserving components, was arrayed not so much against an adversary *class* as against small clusters of foreign elements, who by their reactionary or compradore character endangered the wholeness and the unity of the nation.[48] One can find the same style of thought in the defense speech of Sudisman, secretary-general of the PKI, before the Extraordinary Military Tribunal, in July 1967, where the deeply emotive Javanese word *manunggal* (to become one) occurs again and again. As he put it, the leadership of the party consisted of five men—Aidit, Lukman, Njoto, Sakirman and himself—but these five

---

[47] Javanese hostility to the concept of federalism has continued long after the departure of the Dutch and the political destruction of their federalist allies. What I am suggesting here is not meant to devalue the sociological and historical reasons for this hostility. The Javanese imperial tradition and the concrete material interests of Java vis-à-vis the Outer Islands in themselves would lessen Javanese enthusiasm for federalism. What I am pointing out is the mutual reinforcement of interests and perceptions involved in this question.

[48] At the risk of irritating repetition, I should say that I am not trying to suggest that the PKI leaders adopted this strategy because they were Javanese traditionalists. One could, from a Western vantage-point, suggest that the crucial influences on the PKI leadership were the history of the Popular Front, their experiences in World War II, the example of Mao, and practical calculations of advantage in political manoeuvre. I would argue here, however, that for much of the PKI's traditionalist constituency, and perhaps for some of its more traditionalist leaders, the national united front line was "culturally comfortable."

manunggal djadi satu (were united as one) in life and in death.[49]

The urge to one-ness, so central to Javanese political attitudes, helps to explain the deep psychological power of the idea of nationalism in Java. Far more than a political credo, nationalism expresses a fundamental drive to solidarity and unity in the face of the disintegration of traditional society under colonial capitalism, and other powerful external forces from the late nineteenth century on. Nationalism of this type is something far stronger than patriotism; it is an attempt to reconquer a primordial one-ness.

The same sense of the polity helps, I think, to explain the psychological malaise experienced by the Javanese under the system of multi-party parliamentary democracy in the early 1950's. Herbert Feith has written acutely about this uneasiness as a sense of letdown after the élan of the Revolution, a sense of what both the left-wing politician Sudisman and the right-wing journalist Rosihan Anwar have referred to as *sleur* (a rut).[50] Feith connects this feeling with the impotence of the governments of that period, the inability of weak cabinets to sustain themselves in power, to carry out their programs, indeed to make their weight felt in the community at large. But I suspect that this argument possibly reverses the intellectual sequence in many Javanese minds; for, seen through a traditional lens, it is less that the various parties *in practice* were unsuccessful in cooperating to carry out a program, than that the very structure of parliamentary government, with its formal divisions between opposition and government, and between executive, legislature, and judiciary, expresses a looseness at the center. In this perspective, inflation, factionalism, and regionalism would be interpreted as consequences rather than as causes of the diffusion of Power, which was the inner reason for the rapid demise of parliamentary government. Not only were the parties by definition segmental, but nothing in the structure of the state promised to

[49] Speech of Sudisman before the Extraordinary Military Tribunal, July 1967 (unpublished document in my possession), p. 8. There is little doubt in my mind that Sudisman was also alluding very consciously to the five Pandawa brothers, the heroes of the wajang stories, and identifying the PKI leaders with them.

[50] Herbert Feith, *The Decline of Constitutional Democracy in Indonesia* (Ithaca, N.Y.: Cornell University Press, 1962), pp. 221–224. See also the speech of Sudisman cited above, pp. 17–18; and Rosihan Anwar's column in *Kompas*, Aug. 7, 1968.

resolve this cluster of partialities into a higher unity. It was surely Sukarno's—and presumably General Suharto's—intuition of this problem that led both men to what some observers have described as a "centrist" politique; an apt enough term, if understood to mean not "in the middle" but "of the center." [51]

ACCESSION AND SUCCESSION

I have suggested that the logic of the Javanese traditional conception of Power required a center, syncretic and absorptive in character, and that this center was usually realized in the person of a ruler. How was the ruler discovered or recognized? In the historical tradition, the ruler emerged typically in one of two ways. If he represented the first ruler of a new dynasty, he emerged as the man believed to have received the wahju, the divine radiance which passed from the disintegrating Power of one kingdom to the founder of its successor. Very often, the new ruler would be a parvenu of relatively humble origins—such as Kèn Angrok, Panembahan Sénapati, Sukarno, Suharto—coming to power after a period of turmoil and bloodshed usually instigated by the new ruler himself. Though Javanese history is replete with stories of rebellions, the leaders of these rebellions were never said to have the wahju unless they succeeded in establishing a new dynasty. Failure in itself meant retrospectively that the rebel leader did not have the Power; if he had, he would have succeeded. The main claim to legitimacy of the founder of a new dynasty rested on his successful destruction of a previous center of Power and the belief that in so doing he had received the divine wahju. But it is typical of the Javanese urge toward the center, toward the accumulation of all pools of Power, that the parvenu ruler frequently tried to associate himself through court chronicles with the residues of previous centers of Power and greatness. Schrieke, Berg, and Moertono have amply demonstrated the concerted attempts to link parvenu founders of dynasties with their predecessors through complicated (and often falsified) lines

[51] For an explication of this point, see, e.g., Benedict Anderson, "Indonesia: Unity against Progress," *Current History* (Feb. 1965), pp. 75–81; Donald Hindley, "President Sukarno and the Communists: The Politics of Domestication," *American Political Science Review*, 56, no. 4 (Dec. 1962), 915–926; Daniel S. Lev, "Political Parties of Indonesia," *Journal of Southeast Asian History*, 8, no. 1 (March 1967), 52–67, esp. 61–64; and Herbert Feith, "Suharto's Search for a Political Format," *Indonesia*, 6 (Oct. 1968), 88–105.

of descent.[52] This characteristic, of course, is not exclusively Java-nese. But the most interesting feature of Javanese "falsification" of history is that it does not primarily involve the establishing of ances-tral links with previous dynasties to demonstrate legal, inherited legitimacy—in which case almost any ancestor would do. Typically, ancestral links are made with the most powerful and celebrated representatives of those dynasties.

Thus in the modern period one finds Javanese claiming descent from the great Sultan Agung of the Mataram dynasty (1613–1646), or the possession of potent relics (gongs, krisses, and so forth) of the same ruler. A claim to descent from his no less polyphiloprogeni-tive but considerably less politically adept successors Amangkurat I, II, III, and IV is virtually unknown. The point here is not simply the historical glory of Sultan Agung's rule, but also the character of traditional Javanese cosmological thought which makes no sharp distinction between the living and the dead. The dead may have Power as well as the living. A ruler of such preeminent Power as Sultan Agung retains in death at least some residue of the great con-centration of Power that was his in life. Thus the typical linkages with Sultan Agung are in part for the sake of historical continuity, but more significantly for the sake of coopting and absorbing a recognized pool of Power. In this same tradition one finds Sukarno claiming direct descent from, not just any royal ancestors, but a celebrated king of Singaradja, North Bali; the legendary, prophetic King Djajabaja of Kediri; and the greatest of the early Moslem proselytizing saints, Sunan Kalidjaga.[53] Contemporary rumors that President Suharto is really the son of the late Sultan Hamengku Buwana VIII of Jogjakarta, fall into the same conceptual framework. Conversely, of course, the fall of a ruler gives wide currency to underground oppositionist stories that the ruler is not

[52] B. Schrieke, *Indonesian Sociological Studies*, 2, bk. 1 (The Hague and Bandung: van Hoeve, 1957), chaps. 1, 2; Moertono, pp. 52–54, 63–64; C. C. Berg, "Javaansche Geschiedschrijving," in F. W. Stapel, ed., *Geschiedenis van Nederlandsch Indië* (Amsterdam: Joost van den Vondel, 1938).

[53] For the first two claims, see Cindy Adams, *Sukarno: An Autobiography* (Indianapolis: Bobbs-Merrill, 1965), p. 19. The last claim is referred to in *Sin Po*, April 13, 1958. Sukarno revealed this part of his ancestry after a visit to Kadilangu, near Demak, where Sunan Kalidjaga's grave is reputedly located. We need not concern ourselves with the genealogical truth or falsity of these claims. What is important is why they were made.

really the son of this or that potentate, but, for example, the son of a Dutch planter or a Eurasian.

The fact, however, that ultimately the link sought is a genetic one points again to the linking of sexuality and Power in Javanese thought, and the idea that the human seed, and especially the seed of a man of Power, is itself a concentration of Power and a means of its transmission.[54] Indeed in normal times, when a dynasty was in assured control, succession to political power ran through the royal descent group. But this conception of succession differed markedly from that of European dynastic inheritance, where the predominant considerations were legal and bureaucratic. In the Javanese tradition each successive generation removed from a particular ruler dropped one degree in rank until, after the seventh generation, the lineal descendants merged back into the wide group of commoners, unless in the meantime they had established newer, fresher descent links with succeeding rulers. In this process one can see clearly the immanent conception of the royal seed as a source of Power that progressively diminishes in concentration through increasing his-

---

[54] One should note here that at least one reason for the stress on sexual abstinence for the accumulation of Power is that a man thereby retains his seed within himself, and does not permit its wasteful outflow. It may be asked how the Javanese reconciled this stress on sexual abstinence with their emphasis on the sexuality of the ruler as a sign of the vitality of the kingdom and society. There are various answers possible. One is that they are not fully reconcilable, but derive from the orthodox and heterodox traditions about the acquisition of Power that we have discussed previously. Another is that the ruler has such an extraordinary superabundance of Power within himself that he can "afford" to dispense some of it in extensive sexual activity. My own inclination is to believe that the apparent contradiction resolves itself if sexuality is linked directly to fertility. The Power of the dynast is revealed by his ability to create successors and transmit his Power to them. The ordinary Javanese has no means of gauging the ruler's virility except by the number of children that he produces. Should the ruler be impotent or sterile, it would be taken as a sign of political weakness. The ruler's intermittent periods of asceticism become that much more credible if his sexual vitality is otherwise so conspicuously evident. Significantly, in the wajang stories there is very little mention of sexual intercourse between heroes and their women which does not produce instant pregnancy. This fertility in sexual intercourse is taken to farcical extremes in some comic plays in which the Gods themselves become pregnant when they bathe in a pool in which the Pandawa hero Ardjuna is having submerged relations with a *widadari* (heavenly nymph). Sexuality without pregnancy then would have no political value.

torical distance from the original source and growing admixtures of nonroyal seeds. Thus the essential link to the ruler is measured in terms of proximity, whether through genetic descent or, as we shall see, along other axes of royal power. The successors to the dynasty's founder derived their original Power from the initial impulse provided by the founder himself. But this Power tended to grow diffuse over generations; unless it was renewed and reintegrated by the personal efforts of a particular descendant, the dynasty would fall of its own enfeebled lack of weight.

POWER AND EMPIRE

The Javanese concept of Power has implications also for conceptions of sovereignty, territorial integrity, and foreign relations. Moertono and others have pointed out the almost invariable rule both in Javanese wajang stories and in the historical tradition that the names of Empires and Kingdoms are those of the capital cities. Among the well-known examples are Madjapahit, Singhasari, Kediri, and Demak.[55] Indeed the Javanese language makes no clear etymological distinction between the idea of capital city and that of kingdom. In the word *negari* both are included. Thus the state is typically defined, not by its perimeter, but by its center. The territorial extension of the state is always in flux; it varies according to the amount of Power concentrated at the center. Certain frontiers were generally recognized in practice, formidable geographical obstacles like mountains and seas, which, however, tended to be regarded as the abodes of powerful unseen forces. Otherwise the kingdoms were not regarded as having fixed and charted limits, but rather flexible, fluctuating perimeters. In a real sense, there were no political frontiers at all, the Power of one ruler gradually fading into the distance and merging imperceptibly with the ascending Power of a neighboring sovereign.

This perspective brings into relief the fundamental difference between the old idea of a Southeast Asian kingdom and the modern state, which derives from totally contrasting views about the meaning of frontiers. Implicit in the idea of the modern state is the conception that a frontier marks a critical fall in the power-voltage of the state's rulers. Ten yards this side of the frontier, their power

[55] The same seems to be true of Burma, Siam, and Cambodia.

is "sovereign"; ten yards the other side, it is in theory negligible.[56] Moreover, within the perimeter of the state, the power of the center is theoretically of uniform weight. Citizens at the periphery should share status equally with citizens at the center, and legal obligations should apply uniformly throughout the territory. Since the traditional idea of power is totally different in character, and the idea of the uniform lateral application of power is meaningless, the concept of the frontier assumes very limited importance: the traditional state is defined by its center, not by its perimeter.[57]

The highly centripetal character of traditional Javanese thought is strikingly illustrated by the division of the world into two types of states: Java and Sabrang (an undifferentiated word meaning "overseas" but essentially applied to all non-Javanese groups and political entities). Although contemporary politesse and the ideological requirements of Indonesian nationalism make this kind of division no longer publicly acceptable, one finds in private discussion with many Javanese strong and obvious residues of this intellectual conception. Indeed, so strongly imbedded was the idea that the Dutch more or less unconsciously adopted it, dividing their own colonial territories terminologically into Java and the Outer Regions. Many Javanese still find it extraordinarily difficult to accept fully the idea of Indonesia's being composed of a cluster of equal, interacting islands—Sumatra, Sulawesi, Kalimantan, Java, and the rest. All tend

[56] The recognition of spheres of influence extending beyond legal-cartographic frontiers is a partial modification of this idea, but it is striking that the word influence is used, partly in deference to the idea of the sovereign national state, to mark a qualitative shift from the idea of internally organized power.

[57] Compare the case of Siam, where the problem of "regionalism" in the Northeast, for example, only becomes meaningful in the context of the nation-state. Regionalism implies recognition of the center but political disaffection toward it, rather than an autonomous center in an antagonistic relationship with another center. Prior to the twentieth century, Thai rulers had at different times varying degrees of control over the Northeast, but the problem was never defined as a regional one, since disaffection with, say, Bangkok resulted either in the formation of new centers or the drift of parts of the area into the kingdom of, say, Laos, without any implication of historical permanency either way. This fluidity was significantly enhanced by the rulers' preoccupation with control over populations rather than land. In a sense, then, we can date the inception of the regional problem in Siam to the intellectual shift in the Siamese view of the political entity they lived in from a kingdom to a nation-state.

to be seen in their relationship to the center (Java). Similarly, many Javanese find it hard to conceive of the existence of two negari, at least in Java. Thus, although the principalities of Jogjakarta and Surakarta have led separate existences for more than 200 years and are situated less than 40 miles apart, most Javanese will use the word negari—for instance in the phrase *kulo badé dateng negari* (I am going to the negari)—to mean one capital and will refer to the other by its name, as they would any other city in Indonesia.[58]

The centripetality of Javanese political thinking, combined with the conceptions of graduated sovereignty sketched out briefly above, leads logically to a specific perspective on foreign relations. In the first place it implies a stress on the control of populations rather than of territory. Historically, there were practical reasons for this emphasis. Only the concentration of large populations made possible by intensive rice cultivation could provide the economic surplus and reserve of manpower necessary for building monuments or armies. But the concentration of large populations around a ruler was also the best sign of his having the Power, the magnetic attraction of which revealed the continuing possession of the wahju. This idea may help to account for one well-known aspect of inter-dynastic conflict, not merely in Java but also in mainland Southeast Asia— wholesale deportations of populations by victorious rulers. Bringing these conquered populations near to the center augmented royal Power that much more. One can perhaps discern this importance attached to density of population behind Sukarno's consistent opposition to birth control, partly perhaps out of personal conviction, but evidently also from political considerations.[59]

In the second place, a certain logic in the *pattern* of foreign relations becomes evident. Moertono describes this pattern well in his discussion of the concept of *mandala*, which derives from Indian political theory, but which finds itself very comfortably at home in Java.

The *mandala* (circle, namely of influence, interest or ambitions) can be described as a complex of geopolitical relations, relating to boundaries

[58] Similarly the Thai refer to their capital as Krung Thep (City of the God [Indra]): Bangkok is a name used only by and to foreigners.

[59] Cf. Louis Fischer, *The Story of Indonesia* (New York: Harper, 1959), p. 165. One should note the pride with which Sukarno frequently referred to Indonesia's population as the fifth largest in the world.

and to contact with foreign countries. The doctrine emphasized the cult of expansion, a necessary spur to the struggle for existence, self-assertion and world domination, and the dynamic factor calculated to disturb the equilibrium of inter-state relations. A state's belligerence is in the first place directed towards its closest neighbour(s), thus making necessary the friendship of the state next to the foe, which, because of its proximity, is also a natural enemy of the foe. But if the mutual foe should be conquered, the two allies would become close neighbours, which would create a new enmity. So this circle of alignment and alienation would steadily expand until a universal peace is reached by the establishment of a world-state with a sole and supreme ruler (*chakravartin*).[60]

Several important points emerge from this description of the mandala as the basis for international or rather inter-kingdom relations. The first is that the a priori enemy of the ruler is his closest neighbor. Moertono does not elaborate on the reasons why this pattern should exist. But if our general line of argument is correct, the logic is quite clear. We have seen how in Javanese thinking the Power of the ruler is by no means equally distributed throughout his realm but tends to diminish evenly toward the periphery, so that he is weakest just at the point where his sphere of Power merges into the perimeter of his neighbor's. Thus if his control is not to be diminished and weakened by the pull of his neighbor's Power, he must first exert his own Power against the neighbor. We may recall how the idea that the total quantum of Power in the universe is constant implies that any increase of Power in one place means an exactly equivalent diminution elsewhere. Since Power is also fluid and unstable, always ready for dispersal and diffusion, inter-state aggression necessarily becomes a basic assumption about interstate relations.

There are three possible methods of dealing with the threat posed by proximate concentrations of Power—destruction and dispersal, absorption, or a combination of the two. Destruction of the opponent, as for example practiced by Sultan Agung in his murderous campaigns against the trading city-states of the Javanese *pasisir* (north coast), has its disadvantages. On the purely practical level, massive destruction leads to local depopulation, disorder, and economic decline, and possibly later to rebellions or guerrilla resistance. (Deportation of populations may partly prevent this latter problem, but,

[60] Moertono, p. 71, n. 207.

insofar as the deportation is not total, it may not do so decisively.) [61]
On the more theoretical level, destruction of others does not in itself
automatically mean any enlargement or renewal of the ruler's
Power, merely the dispersal of his rival's, which may be picked up
or absorbed by other rivals. Moreover, destruction itself is the most
blatant and *kasar* (crude, rough) means of subduing a rival, and
on this account the least desirable. More satisfactory is the method
of absorption, which in practice involves diplomatic pressure, and
other *halus* (smooth, civilized) methods of inducing recognition of
superiority or suzerainty.[62] In theory, absorption is seen as the
voluntary submission of neighboring kingdoms to the supreme
Power of the ruler. One finds thus in the classical description of the
great kings of the past that *radja séwu negara nungkul (sujud)*—
the kings of a thousand kingdoms offer submission to them. Significantly, the glorification of the ruler does not mention his prowess in
battle, as might be the case with a European mediaeval monarch.
That the ruler has to use the methods of warfare is a theoretical
admission of weakness. The idea of "a thousand kings offering their
submission" also implies the absorption of their smaller centers of
Power into the Great King's, and thus a directly proportional increase in his majesty.[63]

Thirdly, the logical end-result of inter-mandala relationships is the
emergence of the chakravartin—in Javanese, *prabu murbèng wisésa
anjakrawati* (world-ruler). The ideal form of temporal power is a
world-empire, in which all political entities are combined in a
coherent unity, and the ebb and flow of Power implied in a universe
of multiple mandala locked in conflict with one another for a time
no longer exists. One striking illustration of the centrality of this
universalism in Javanese political thought is that words meaning
universe (*buwana*) or natural world (*alam*) occur in the titles of
three of the four rulers in contemporary Java—Paku Buwana (Nail
of the Universe), Hamengku Buwana (Sustainer of the Universe),
and Paku Alam (Nail of the World).

Finally, it is perhaps more than a coincidence that the typical pat-

[61] Sultan Agung did in fact deport large numbers of people to Mataram.
[62] Cf. Schrieke, p. 142.
[63] One can speculate that in a period when administrative control over
distant regions was difficult, formal submission combined with practical
autonomy was for both parties a convenient form of interstate relations.

tern of political relationships between Java and the Outer Islands has tended to resemble the "leapfrogging" relationship described by Moertono in his discussion of the mandala. In the period of independence alone, one finds striking examples of this pattern in the close connections between the center and the subordinate Karo Batak against the dominant Toba Batak of East Sumatra; between the center and the inland Dayak groups against the Bandjar of South Kalimantan; and between the center and the upland Toradja against the Buginese and Makasarese in South Sulawesi. Although this "leapfrogging" pattern can perfectly well be understood in the light of Western political theory, it is also quite consistent with a very different intellectual framework.

RULER AND RULING CLASS

If we now turn to the traditional relationship between the ruler and the governmental structure through which he ruled, the concept of Power may help to throw light on the perspective in which this relationship was viewed. Schrieke has drawn a detailed picture of the administrative structure of the precolonial Javanese kingdom, which admirably fits Max Weber's model of the patrimonial state.[64] According to this model, the central government is essentially an extension of the ruler's personal household and staff. Officials are granted their positions and the perquisites that go with them as personal favors of the ruler, and they may be dismissed or degraded at his personal whim. No feudal caste exists as such. Payment of officials is essentially in the form of specified benefices allotted by the ruler for the period of tenure of each particular office. Within the central government latent or overt tension persists between the royal descent group, or the ruler's extended family, and the *ministeriales*, high-ranking officials of common origin who have risen to power on the basis of their administrative capacities and personal loyalty to the ruler. Since commoners have no hope of succeeding to the throne, barring the complete collapse of the dynasty, they are not regarded as a political threat by the ruler, and insofar

[64] See B. Schrieke, *Indonesian Sociological Studies,* 1 (The Hague and Bandung: van Hoeve, 1955), 169–221; and Bendix, chap. 11. Cf. Th. Pigeaud, *Java in the Fourteenth Century,* 4 (The Hague: Nijhoff, 1962), 521–536.

as he is a powerful, strong-minded man, the ministeriales tend to be assigned to key positions at the expense of the royal descent group.

While the power of the ruler in the immediate environment of his capital is unquestioned, the poor quality of communications and perennial financial difficulties in a largely nonmonetary economy make it difficult for him, in spite of periodic and impressive military expeditions, to maintain tight administrative control as his empire grows in size. He must inevitably attempt to coopt regional notables and to devolve a great deal of informal power to them.[65] He is not in a position to "hire and fire" them as he may his own ministeriales. Though he will try to replace such local notables as he can with personal aides, these notables will naturally resist his centralizing encroachments. The ruler has also to face the danger that a ministerialis assigned to govern some remote province may develop such roots there that he assumes leadership over, or is coopted into, the group of local notables and in effect joins the latent opposition. The ruler has constantly to shift such men to prevent them losing their ultimate dependency on himself.

The administrative structure, while formally hierarchical, is in effect composed of stratified clusters of patron-client relationships. Both in the regions and in the center, officials gather around them clusters of personal dependents, on the model of the ruler himself. These dependents' destinies are linked with the success or failure of their patrons. They work as administrative and political aides, and have no real autonomous status except in relation to him. They are financed by portions of the benefices allotted to their patron by his patron, or by the ruler himself if their master is highly enough placed. Just as the power of the ruler is measured by the size of the populations he controls, so the power of the subordinate official (patron) is gauged by the size of the clientele that he heads.

In the case of Java, Schrieke pointed out the constant tug of war between provincial notables, who often had lineages older than the ruler's, and the ministeriales of the court; and between the ministeriales and the royal descent group. He stressed the arbitrary and personalistic features of the personnel and public policies of the

[65] This may be done by arranging marriages with prominent regional families, by insisting on periodic residence at the royal court, and by the delivery of hostages to the center.

rulers of Mataram, and the financing of the state administration through both royal monopolies and the appanage system of benefices, whereby officials were assigned the usufruct over specified (and often dispersed) lands, including the labor of the peasants living on them.

It should be readily apparent that the traditional concept of Power in Java provides a coherent perspective within which to view the structure and operations of the patrimonial state. In the first place, the image of the proportional fading of the lamp's radiance with increasing distance does not merely correspond to the decline of a ruler's Power vis-à-vis a neighboring ruler at the periphery of his domains. It can be applied with equal aptness to the center-province struggle to which Weber and Schrieke attach such importance. Indeed within the traditional perspective no clear analytical distinction can be made between a powerful provincial notable and a rival sovereign. Each is potentially the other, depending on the Power that the center can accumulate. The cone of light's luminosity expands as the ruler is able to force the submission of rival rulers and demote them to the status of provincial notables; it contracts as provincial notables free themselves from the center and establish their own independent areas of rule. The dreaded "looseness" at the center corresponds then to successful pressures for decentralization, and the admired "tautness" to the successful imposition of centralization.

Secondly, what Weber and Schrieke note as the highly personalistic character of patrimonial rule, in which the corps of officials is regarded as an extension of the person of the ruler, implies that proximity to the ruler, rather than formal rank, is the key to power in such a state. The commoner ministeriales owe their ascendancy over the royal descent group under powerful dynasts precisely to this proximity. Ultimately everything depends on the personal Power of the ruler. The emanation of this Power reveals itself in a quite undifferentiated way along three separate axes: the center-periphery axis, which we have already discussed; the "ascriptive" axis, or the diachronic diffusion of a powerful ruler's seminal Power through seven generations of descendants; and the patron-client or administrative axis, whereby the Power of the highest patron (the ruler) seeps down through descending strata of patron-client

clusters till it reaches the peasant base of the society. Thus although sharp distinctions were made between the ruler's immediate family and high-ranking ministeriales of common origins, these
distinctions tended to be less politically significant than might
otherwise have been expected; they were subordinate in importance to the crucial factor of proximity to the ruler.[66]

These points may be useful for understanding some aspects of
political behavior in contemporary Indonesia. What we have seen,
in effect, is the marked consonance of the traditional Javanese concept of Power with the political structures and behavior of the
patrimonial state. We can further take note that the "indigenization" of bureaucratic structures and behavior in Indonesia [67] that
was so marked after the middle 1950's can be usefully viewed as a
reemergence of the patrimonial model. A full analysis of the reasons
for this reemergence of patrimonialism would take us too far afield.
Doubtless the major cause was the fact that the rational-legal
bureaucracy bequeathed by the Dutch proved economically un-
sustainable in this period of secular economic decline.[68] But the
holding-power of patrimonialism was probably also accentuated by
the persistence of traditional perspectives so consonant with it.

The signal unwillingness of the *pusat* (center) to accede to demands for decentralization and regional autonomy in the late parliamentary period (1956–1958), while clearly stemming from fears
for the national exchequer if the foreign-exchange-producing areas
in Sumatra and Sulawesi increased their power, can also be attributed in part to the continuing impact of old conceptions about
relationships between center and provinces as indicators of the
"health" of the realm. The subsequent triumph over the regional
rebellion in 1958 and the consolidation of Guided Democracy were
marked by a great increase in the appointment of ministeriales to

[66] Compare Maruyama, pp. 12–20. On page 13 he writes: "The standard
of values, then, that determined a person's position in society and in the
nation was based less on social function than on relative distance from the
Emperor."

[67] This process of "indigenization" is excellently treated in Ann Ruth
Willner, *The Neo-Traditional Accommodation to Political Independence:
The Case of Indonesia,* Center of International Studies, Research Monograph
no. 26 (Princeton, N.J.: Princeton University, 1966).

[68] I am indebted to Daniel Lev for this important insight.

key military and civilian positions in the regional bureaucracy, and the absorption of the office of *Kepala Daerah* (elective regional head) into the centrally appointed administrative positions of governor and *bupati* (regent).[69] These ministeriales were, in the old tradition, appointed largely on the basis of their loyalty to Djakarta rather than of any special administrative competence.

A parallel line of argument can be pursued for patterns of administrative behavior at the center, particularly after the restoration of the 1945 Constitution in 1959. This Constitution provides explicitly that cabinet ministers are to be the assistants of the President and responsible to him alone. While its models are to be found in Kuomintang China, post-Meiji Japan, and perhaps the United States, one can discern the influence of the old patrimonial style in the sense of comfort with which many Javanese accepted it and abandoned the liberal parliamentary constitution of 1950. The psychological unwillingness of many cabinet ministers to accept any kind of autonomous responsibility, particularly responsibility to parliamentarians and the general public, was quite evident in the liberal period but was out of kilter with the ethical norms implicit in a parliamentary constitution. Under the 1945 Constitution, formal norms and traditional propensities tended to coincide. Insofar as real Power is seen to flow out of the concentrated center and not from the diffuse perimeter, ministerial behavior should reflect the wishes of the former rather than the latter.[70] The same argument helps to explain the ease with which many Javanese accepted the emergence under both the authoritarian Sukarno and Suharto regimes of informal power-groups outside the "rational-legal" structure of the bureaucracy. The so-called *golongan istana* (palace group) under Guided Democracy and the President's SPRI (private staff) under the New Order represented the kitchen cabinet of the ruler, his

---

[69] On the decentralizing and centralizing trends of the period 1955–1959, and the creation and virtual abolition of the independent office of *Kepala Daerah*, see J. D. Legge, *Central Authority and Regional Autonomy in Indonesia: A Study in Local Administration, 1950–1960* (Ithaca, N.Y.: Cornell University Press, 1961), chaps. 4 and 9.

[70] Ultimately, personal responsibility must be based on autonomous personal power; this is a difficult norm to sustain in combination with the traditional view that the assistants of the ruler have no Power of their own independent of their master.

personal agents and confidants. The enormous power they in fact wielded depended solely on the fact that their proximity to the center was recognized by the entire politico-administrative elite.[71]

POWER AND ETHICS

Although the ruling class of traditional Java could be defined in structural terms as the hierarchy of officials and their extended families, like any other ruling class they were also marked off—indeed marked themselves off—from the rest of the population by their style of life and self-consciously espoused system of values. Today, the word *prijaji*, which is the most common appellation for this class, primarily connotes ethical values and modes of behavior rather than official position. Yet these values and modes of behavior are linked closely with the traditional functions of this class; and the concept of Power reveals the nexus very clearly.

The quality which the prijaji have traditionally stressed as distinguishing them from the rest of the population is that of being halus. The meaning of this term, which eludes precise definition in English, though some notable efforts have been made by Clifford Geertz [72] and others, is to a certain extent covered by the idea of smoothness, the quality of not being disturbed, spotted, uneven, or discolored. Smoothness of spirit means self-control, smoothness of appearance means beauty and elegance, smoothness of behavior means politeness and sensitivity. Conversely, the antithetical quality of being kasar means lack of control, irregularity, imbalance, disharmony, ugliness, coarseness, and impurity. Since being kasar is the natural state of man, in which his energies, thoughts, and behavior lack all control and concentration, no effort is required to achieve it. Being halus, on the other hand, requires constant effort and control to reach a reduction of the spectrum of human feeling and thought to a single smooth "white" radiance of concentrated energy. The connection between halus-ness and Power here is readily evident; Power is the essential link between natural

---

[71] SPRI is a standard acronym for *Staf Pribadi* (Private Staff). Though it was Suharto who first created this official nomenclature, his example has been widely followed. Today, almost anyone of any importance in the Indonesian government has his own SPRI.

[72] See Clifford Geertz, *The Religion of Java* (New York: Free Press, 1964), p. 232.

man and the halus *satria* ("knight") of wajang mythology and Javanese prijaji etiquette. In the minds of traditional Javanese, being halus is in itself a sign of Power, since halus-ness is achieved only by the concentration of energy. In Javanese legends and folk-history the slight, halus satria almost invariably overcomes the demonic *raseksa* (giant), *buta* (ogre), or wild man from overseas. In the typical battle-scenes of the wajang plays the contrast between the two becomes strikingly apparent in the slow, smooth, impassive, and elegant movements of the satria, who scarcely stirs from his place, and the acrobatic leaps, somersaults, shrieks, taunts, lunges, and rapid sallies of his demonic opponent. The clash is especially well symbolized at the moment when the satria stands perfectly still, eyes downcast, apparently defenseless, while his demonic adversary repeatedly strikes at him with dagger, club, or sword—but to no avail. The concentrated Power of the satria makes him invulnerable.

This smooth invulnerability is the much-prized hallmark of the satria, both as military man and as statesman. But it is achieved only by the self-discipline that we have seen as the key to the accumulation of Power. The single most imminent threat to this invulnerability is not the satria's adversary, but pamrih.

Pamrih is a complex term perhaps best translated as "concealed personal motive." It means doing something, not because the act has to be done, but because one's personal interests or desires are thereby satisfied. The traditional motto of the Javanese administrator, *sepi ing pamrih, ramé ing gawé*, still frequently quoted by contemporary politicians and officials, means that the correct attitude of the prijaji official should be to refrain from indulging personal motives, while working hard for the good of the state. At the level of everyday morality, pamrih is the socially undesirable quality of selfishness and personal aggrandizement. But on a deeper level, the pamrih of the administrator or the military man is really a threat to his own ultimate interests, since the indulgence of personal, and therefore partial, passions or prejudices means interior imbalance and a diffusion of personal concentration and Power. The idea of pamrih is a constant motif in the "morality" of the wajang plays. It forms the essential contrast between the Pandawa and the Kurawa in the Bratajuda-cycle, and between Rama and Dasamuka in the Ramajana-cycle. In each case the "evil" party is destined to be defeated, not so much because of his "evilness," as because "evil" means the indulgence of personal passion, which ultimately undermines the concentration of Power.[73]

This theme is strikingly illustrated in two critical episodes of the Bratajuda-cycle. The first instance is the final dialogue between Sri Batara Kresna and Adipati Karna on the eve of the war between the Pandawa and Kurawa, in which Kresna tries to persuade Karna to abandon the cause of the Kurawa and fight on the side of his half-brothers, the Pandawa. The heart of Karna's eloquent refusal is his rejection of pamrih. He tells Kresna that he knows perfectly well that the Kurawa have done wrong and that the Pandawa will win the war. But everything that he is he owes to Sujudana, the eldest of the Kurawa, and disinterested loyalty is the first quality of the satria. Moreover, should he go over to the side of the Pandawa, he would not only be "climbing on the bandwagon," but would also lower the prestige of the Pandawa's ultimate victory. Without Karna on their side, the Kurawa would be no match for their cousins, and the destined Great Bratajuda War would be an inglorious one-sided military operation. Thus, vis-à-vis both the Kurawa and the Pandawa, he will fulfill his dharma by siding with King Sujudana, though he knows it will cost him his life.[74]

In an even better known passage of the epic, Ardjuna and Karna face each other on the field of battle. Confronted with his own half-brother, Ardjuna "weakens." Turning to Kresna, he says that he cannot bring himself to kill his brother and cannot face the prospect of so much suffering and death. Kresna's classic response is that this humane sentiment is essentially a form of pamrih. Personal ties should not be permitted to sway a satria from the responsibilities laid upon him. The satria goes into battle ready to die, if necessary, but he fights not out of personal hatred or passion, but because of dharma. Ardjuna should be no less a satria than Karna, who is per-

---

[73] The prototypical example of this is the rape of Rama's wife Sita by the demonic Prabu Dasamuka. One could almost say, however, that the act of abduction itself is less "evil" than Dasamuka's self-indulgence in executing it. In this sense the evil is done to Dasamuka rather than to Sita.

[74] Dharma is usually translated "duty," a word which has unfortunate Christian overtones. It is really a caste or status-obligation. Being a satria, one acts as a satria. In a more general sense, it has some of the connotations of "justice."

forming his dharma though foreseeing his own death. The purposes of destiny are above those of individual mortals. Recalled to his responsibilities, Ardjuna reenters the fray.

Only in the light of the concept of pamrih can the attitude of many Javanese toward the accumulation of wealth properly be understood. Personal acquisitiveness, like sexual indulgence and political ambition, is one of the most obvious types of personal indulgence or pamrih. Accordingly, the overt pursuit of wealth that is characteristic of the merchant or businessman shows a lack of Power and therefore lack of status. This judgment should not be taken to suggest that the typical high-status Javanese is not a man of wealth or that the Javanese tradition does not conceive of riches as an important attribute of the ruler and his closest associates. But money in itself should never be the object of active pursuit. Wealth should flow to the holder of Power, as a consequence of that Power, in the same way that pusaka, large populations, wives, neighboring kingdoms or states flow toward the ruler, as it were, magnetically attracted to the center. The vast wealth that the great rulers of the Javanese past are described as possessing is always an attribute of Power, not the means for acquiring it. Thus in the Javanese political tradition wealth necessarily follows Power, not Power wealth.

One important reason for widespread anxiety about the regime of late Guided Democracy (and, incidentally, of the New Order) was that some of the highest figures in the state were believed to be bent on the acquisition of personal wealth. The issue of corruption has wider resonances than simply the lack of personal probity among high officials or the waste of national resources, since personal corruption is interpreted as a sign of a regime's decay. A most significant element in the 1966–1967 campaign to drive Sukarno from public life was the publicity given to evidence of the President's pamrih in the matter of corruption and other forms of abuse of power for personal advantage. Conversely, one of the most powerful cards in the PKI's hands under both liberal and Guided Democracy was its largely deserved reputation for incorruptibility. This lack of corruption in the PKI not only appealed to the "modern" desire for rationality, probity, and discipline in public life, but also to the traditional respect for the man without pamrih, the potential source of new-rising Power. Thus, among the first steps taken by the military propaganda apparatus in the anti-Communist campaign of late 1965 was an attempt to demonstrate that the PKI leaders were secretly sexual libertines (Njoto) and embezzlers (Aidit), because of the powerful images thereby evoked.[75]

The same argument helps to clarify one well-established tradition of Javanese administrative behavior—the so-called *perintah halus*. This phrase is generally understood to mean the giving of orders in polite and indirect language, sometimes even in the form of a request rather than a command; the request is nonetheless understood by both parties to be a command. The nuances of the concept have been sensitively treated from the political and sociological perspective by Ann Willner and Donald Fagg, who see the perintah halus as the result of a highly formalized pattern of inter-personal relations among the Javanese or as a necessary device to conceal the bargaining and bluffing which characterizes Javanese power relationships.[76] But within the context of traditional Javanese thinking, the perintah halus is by no means a weak or indirect command designed to cover the uncertainty of the order-giver as to how far his authority will be obeyed. On the contrary, it is a more powerful command than an express order because it is necessarily given by a halus person, one of higher power and status and closer to the center of Power. Moreover, we should bear in mind the symbolism of the satria in battle. The man of Power should have to exert himself as little as possible

[75] One can speculate in passing that the strategy of the PKI in the period 1963–1965 of trying to create a sense of an irresistible tide flowing in their direction, a snowballing accumulation of adherents, was a partly conscious harnessing of traditional ideas about the flow of Power from a decaying to a rising center.

[76] See Donald R. Fagg, "Authority and Social Structure: A Study in Javanese Bureaucracy" (Ph.D. thesis, Harvard University, 1958), pp. 362–368, 372–429, and Willner, especially pp. 44–57. In both Fagg's and Willner's analysis there is a certain lack of historical and cultural perspective. The *perintah halus* in the post-independence period was necessarily in part a bluff. Not only was the belief-system out of which the perintah halus arose being eroded by conflicting norms derived from the secular, sceptical West, but the monolithic power of the Dutch and Japanese colonial governments, which had previously been present to reinforce the perintah halus with indisputable physical coercion, no longer existed. The weakness and multiplicity of authorities in post-independence Indonesia exposed the hollowness of the perintah halus, which had been caused by the colonial experience but concealed by the total domination of the colonial government.

in any action. The slightest lifting of his finger should be able to set a chain of actions in motion. The man of real Power does not have to raise his voice and does not have to give overt orders. The halus-ness of his command is the external expression of his authority. The whole Javanese style of administration is therefore marked by the attempt, wherever possible, to give an impression of minimum effort, as through the perintah halus. The ethics of halus-ness are at bottom the ethics of Power.

POWER AND KNOWLEDGE

If halus-ness is the hallmark of the prijaji, the focus of his ethics, and the expression of his Power, how is it attained? In one sense, the answer has already been given: since halus-ness is a manifestation of Power, it can be achieved by the traditional road of asceticism and spiritual discipline. Yet this spiritual discipline can not be achieved by haphazard methods; its attainment is only possible through education in certain specific forms of knowledge. In this perspective, knowledge becomes the key to Power.

Traditional Javanese education can fairly be described as an initiation into a more or less permanent arcane lore. Samudja Asjari has described in detail the process of traditional education in the rural *pesantrèn* under the leadership of the *kjai*.[77] In these pesantrèn the *santri* (pupils) go through a carefully graded series of levels of knowledge, starting from the simplest, most earthly type, through increasingly esoteric studies till they reach the stage of the *ngèlmu makripat* (the secrets of being, of divinity).[78] The progress of the santri is seen as a long process of moving closer and closer to the ultimate secrets of the cosmos, finally attainable only through illumination.[79] Only a few of the santri ever reach the final stage—one can envisage them spread out like planets in ever-narrowing orbits

---

[77] Samudja Asjari, "Kedudukan Kjai Dalam Pondok Pesantrèn" (M.A. thesis, Gadjah Mada University, Jogjakarta, 1967), especially pp. 120–136. *Pesantrèn* are rural Islamic schools. *Kjai* is a general Javanese term of high respect, which may refer to human beings or to inanimate objects. In this instance it refers to the venerated Islamic teachers who head the pesantrèn schools.

[78] Cf. Geertz, *Islam Observed*, pp. 36–37, on "graded spirituality" in a slightly different context.

[79] At a cruder level, the santri may also gradually learn the secrets of *ngèlmu kedotan* (invulnerability).

around an inner sun. Education thus provides a key (*kuntji*) to the door separating ignorance from knowledge, and that knowledge is access to an ontological reality.[80]

But this pattern of education has not been (and is not) confined to the rural Islamic schools; it underlies the education of the traditional elite as well. In the wajang stories and in the historical chronicles, a critical period in the life of a young satria is a period of isolation and training in a hermitage or mountain grotto. There, under the tutelage of a *resi* (seer) he undergoes an initiation into the esoteric sciences. The initiation may include studying the arts of combat (*ngèlmu kadigdajan*) but is mainly devoted to magico-religious introspection. Perhaps the best-known of the wajang plays, *Déwa Rutji,* is an exact dramatic representation of this process.[81]

In this play, the young hero Brataséna asks his teacher, Pandita Durna, how to learn the secret of life and is told to seek it at the bottom of the sea. In the depths of the ocean he is attacked by a monstrous serpent (*naga*) but finally wins the day. Then there appears before him a tiny divinity, Déwa Rutji, a miniature replica of himself, who tells Brataséna to enter his ear. Brataséna obeys this impossible command and, passing through the ear of Déwa Rutji, reaches the unattainable. Common folk-interpretations of the play stress that the serpent and the sea represent the distracting human passions, and that therefore the struggle with the naga means the struggle to master these base impulses. Déwa Rutji represents the *Aku,* the divine inner essence, only to be encountered after victory over the serpent. The paradoxical entry of the gigantic Brataséna into the miniature deity's ear symbolizes the idea that inner knowledge is not reached by ordinary study but by a suprarational moment of illumination. Only after going through this test does Brataséna emerge from the sea with altered visage and his full adult name of Wrekudara.[82]

[80] For an elaboration of this theme and its implications, see B. R. O'G. Anderson, "The Languages of Indonesian Politics," *Indonesia,* 1 (April 1966), 89–116, esp. 93ff.

[81] For a fuller account of this play, and a detailed, highly authoritative analysis of its mystical significance, see K. G. P. A. A. Mangkunegara VII, *On the Wayang Kulit (Purwa) and Its Symbolic and Mystical Elements,* translated from the original Dutch by Claire Holt, Southeast Asia Program Data Paper no. 27 (Ithaca, N.Y.: Cornell University, 1957), esp. pp. 16–19, 23–24.

[82] The prestige of learning of this kind is well illustrated by the fact that

The traditional image of the acquisition of knowledge is that of a search for a key which opens the door between ignorance and knowledge, making possible the qualitative leap from one to the other. Such a learning process contains nothing in the slightest degree heuristic or pragmatic. The residual power of this old conception is not hard to detect in contemporary Indonesian thinking. Bearing it in mind does much to render comprehensible the typical division of the population by the political elite into two radically separate groups, those who are *masih bodoh* ("still stupid, still unenlightened") and those who are *insjaf* or *terpeladjar* (aware, educated).[83]

Such a viewpoint possibly also helps to explain the immense appeal of explicitly ideological thinking in Indonesia today. The most powerful ideological currents in Indonesia—Communism, radical nationalism, and Islam (both reformist and orthodox)—are all seen as keys for explaining the complexities and confusions of the contemporary world. The adepts of each of these *aliran* (currents) feel themselves to have acquired, through a process of politico-religious initiation, an esoteric but comprehensive picture of the universe and its workings.[84] While each aliran contains within it powerful expansionist and proselytizing elements, nonetheless each retains a highly introverted character. The hermetic quality of the aliran has been noted by many observers. The general lack of congruence between them, the rarity of intimate social contact, the virtually total absence of intellectual exchange, and the sharp dividing line

the highest type of ruler is referred to as the *pandita ratu* (Sage-King), of whom the classical model is the eldest of the Pandawa brothers, King Judistira of Ngamarta.

[83] See Anderson, "The Languages of Indonesian Politics," p. 110.

[84] For an extended discussion of the *aliran,* see Clifford Geertz, "The Javanese Village," in G. William Skinner, ed., *Local, Ethnic and National Loyalties in Village Indonesia: A Symposium,* Southeast Asia Studies, Cultural Report Series no. 8 (New Haven: Yale University, 1959), pp. 37–41. Geertz offers two definitions of aliran: "a political party surrounded by a set of voluntary social organizations formally or informally linked to it," and "a comprehensive pattern of social integration." My own sense of what an aliran is would be closer to the second definition: a distinctive, integrated cultural outlook, together with its organized and unorganized (but potentially organizable) adherents. For a highly sophisticated discussion of the relationships of aliran, class, and political organization, see the introduction by Ruth McVey to K. Warouw and P. Weldon's translation of Sukarno's *Nationalism, Islam and Marxism,* Cornell Modern Indonesia Project Translation Series (Ithaca, N.Y.: Cornell University, 1969).

between adherents and nonadherents, at least in the minds of the adepts, can be seen as similar to the structures and values of the pesantrèn and other traditional institutions concerned with the acquisition of knowledge.[85]

Here we come full circle to the intimate relationship between knowledge and Power. It is not simply—as the history of the Republic shows—that ideologies offer a ready means to local and national power through the mechanism of political parties or that within each aliran those who claim greater knowledge of and deeper initiation into the aliran's inner lore have obtained positions of high respect and authority. Ideologies have developed deep roots precisely because they may be seen as giving Power. The more closely the "initiation" into a particular ideology approximates traditional educational practices and conceptions, the more effective the ideology is in developing a powerful psychological hold on the new adherent. This factor certainly contributed to the striking success of PKI educational work under the Aidit leadership. For the period of candidacy and the clear-cut conception of the party as a hierarchical educational pyramid reveal strong similarities with the structure of pesantrèn education. One should also not underestimate the powerful appeal which the discipline and secrecy demanded of party members exerted in traditionalist milieux.[86] The radical nature of the party's criticism of the existing order might be thought to be an obstacle to successful proselytization. But in fact it proved in many instances quite the opposite, since the criticism was seen to provide a coherence of vision and an implied renewal of order from within the confusions and antagonisms of everyday life. A more partial, piecemeal critical approach, more ready to accept major elements of the existing situation, would and did find it difficult to match the unity, certainty, and centripetalism of Indonesian Marxism-Leninism.

One should not, in this connection, overlook the peculiar political

---

[85] For a good description of this "closed" aspect of pesantrèn society, see Samudja Asjari, pp. 130–155, 160–166.

[86] Compare the character of the tarékat (Sufi brotherhoods) so excellently described in Sartono Kartodirdjo, *The Peasants' Revolt of Banten in 1888, Its Conditions, Course and Sequel: A Case Study of Social Movements in Indonesia* (The Hague: De Nederlandsche Boek- en Steendrukkerij v/h Smits, 1966?), pp. 157–165.

power of literate men in a largely illiterate traditional society. Where illiteracy is the rule, writing has an enormous power-creating potential both because of its esoteric character and because it allows mysterious and rapid communication between its adepts. Significantly, in the wajang stories the single most powerful weapon in the hands of the favored Pandawa is not an arrow, club, or spear, but a piece of writing, the Serat Kalimasada, the special pusaka of the eldest Pandawa brother, King Judistira. What is actually written in this pusaka is never made clear, indeed in one sense the power of the pusaka rests in its opaqueness to all but the initiated.[87] Seen in this light, literacy is simply an external sign of the possession of knowledge. Although in practice by no means all prijaji were functionally literate, the prijaji as a status group tended in the traditional world to be identified as the literati. The literacy of the ruling class was a symbol of Power largely because it presupposed the ability to make the qualitative leap out of illiteracy. The literati were not just better educated—they were the educated in a society of uneducated. Their power derived not from their ability to disseminate new concepts through society, but from their ability to penetrate to and conserve old and secret knowledge.

RULERS AND RULED

The centripetal propensities of traditional political thought naturally affected Javanese conceptions of the proper relations between ruler and ruled, between patron and client, and between prijaji and peasant.

Traditional thought clearly did not allow for any form of social contract or conceptualized system of mutual obligations between superior and subordinate. Any such system would have had to admit a formal reciprocity in political relationships fundamentally alien to Javanese thinking. It would have necessitated the recognition that being halus and powerful imposed obligations toward others less favored *because* they were kasar and unpowerful. As we shall see, the halus and powerful did recognize certain social duties, but the rationale for such obligations had a logic of its own, quite uncon-

[87] Note the prestige and strategic advantage of those in a village who can read the newspaper to the rest. *Koran bilang* (the newspaper says) was, at least until quite recently, a special kind of invocation of authority in the village sphere.

nected with ideas of contract or even, strictly speaking, of noblesse oblige.

If we turn first to relationships within the ruling class itself we find a conspicuous absence of the contractual element implicit in the European feudal institution of vassalage. This absence can be explained empirically by the centralizing tendencies and financial structure of the patrimonial state, which Weber contrasted with classical feudalism. The economic base of the prijaji ruling class was not independent landownership but the system of appanage bene-fices previously discussed. And part of the patrimonial ruler's policy was to prevent such appanages from becoming hereditary (and thus ultimately the basis for a more strictly feudal social structure) and to scatter the appanages attached to a particular position in order to prevent local consolidations of economic power which might ultimately give rise to a type of entrenched landlordism.[88]

The appanage system in effect meant that the land of the realm "belonged" to the ruler and its economic surplus (including the labor of the peasants who tilled it) was in his gift, to be distributed at his discretion to deserving officials. Between such a system and the concept of Power a clear harmony exists, since the former natu-rally encourages ideas that we have already encountered: wealth (or property) is an *attribute* of Power, not its provenance; and socio-economic status is a quality which derives from the center and has no meaning except in relation to that center. Such a system also suggests that the wealth of the state is in the gift of the ruler and may be distributed downward through officialdom as the perquisites of office, but this distribution is not to be conceived as an obligation of the ruler to his officials, but rather as a mark of his favor.

In view of what we have described as the reemergence of patri-monialism in independent Indonesia, the residual influences of the appanage system in contemporary administrative behavior can be clearly seen, particularly in the morphology of corruption. If one leaves aside the petty corruption-of-necessity arising from critical

[88] For a good account of the gradual evolution of the appanage system in Java from precolonial through colonial times, see Selosoemardjan, *Social Changes in Jogjakarta* (Ithaca, N.Y.: Cornell University Press, 1962), pp. 25–27, 31–33, 216–220, 272–275.

economic conditions, inflation, and low government salaries, and focuses on the large-scale corruption which assumes quasi-official form, it is striking how little evidence there is of the classical European buying and selling of offices. Millionaires (entrepreneurial or landed) usually cannot buy themselves administrative positions of power and prestige. Indeed this inability is a habitual cause for complaint among certain members of this tiny group. Corruption on a large scale typically takes the form of the allotting of the "surplus" of certain key sectors of the economy to favored officials or cliques of officials, whether civilian or military.[89] Rice-collection, tin mining, oil production and distribution, and tax collection are only some examples of the areas in which officially supervised venality occurs. In most cases the corruption is not chiefly for the immediate personal advantage of the official assigned to supervise a particular sector of the economy (though such an official is rarely in straitened circumstances). The corruption is typically used to finance a whole subsector of the administrative apparatus. That is to say there is a system of parallel financing of favored sectors of the bureaucracy through the invisible flow of corruption running alongside the formal salary-structure. The flow, channeled down through an informal pyramid of patron-client clusters on a typical patrimonial model, serves to reinforce the cohesion of such clusters. Cuts and commissions are often standardized enough to be called benefices in the traditional sense. Thus in many sectors, corruption has become an essential element in the stability of bureaucratic organization.

To the degree that corruption provides a predominant part of an official's earnings and takes the form of quasi-official benefices, his bureaucratic orientation tends to shift increasingly toward immediate patrons or the rulers at the center. A more or less genuine "service" ethic toward the public, which is sustainable in a system dominated by adequate, fixed salaries and rational-legal norms, is naturally difficult to preserve under reemergent patrimonialism. One could also suggest that this orientation toward patrons and rulers on the part of corrupt officials is even heightened by the dubious legal-

---

[89] This system of organized corruption has of course been enormously extended since the Indonesian state took control of the economic resources of the country in the anti-Dutch campaign of 1957–1958.

ity or even open illegality of such corruption today. Under such conditions the protection of one's superiors is especially necessary, and one's dependence on them is enhanced.[90]

While the structures of patrimonialism and the traditional concept of Power work in the same direction, focusing the loyalties of the ruling class inward and upward, this fact alone does not adequately account for the striking lack of *prise* of social contract ideas on modern Indonesian political elites. Insofar as such ideas form a central part of the Western conservative and liberal thought to which these elites were exposed in the colonial educational system, some further explanation seems necessary. In part this phenomenon can be explained by the wide influence of Marxism, in however diluted and distorted a form. The Marxist critique of social contract theory was particularly telling under a colonial regime which, for all its pronouncements of ethical aims, in practice made a mockery of any theory of mutual obligations between ruled and ruler.

We may note, however, that in the postcolonial era, particularly the so-called liberal period (1950–1959), social contract ideas acquired very little new influence or prestige. The PKI was naturally impervious to such notions. But the remaining power groups in Indonesian politics tended typically to cling to holistic conceptions of Indonesian society, thus denying theories both of class contradictions and also of class obligations.

In general, little thinking was devoted to the sociology of Indonesian politics, and insofar as there was any sociological perspective at all, it centered on an elite-mass dichotomy, symbolized by the words *pemimpin* and rakjat. The word pemimpin (leader, big shot), like its synonyms *tokoh, orang gedé* and *pembesar*, is quite undifferentiated in character and is applied without any sense of disjuncture to officials, generals, and politicians alike. At the bottom of the political system are the rakjat (often translated as "the people" or "the common people"), again a term without any precise sociological contours. The rakjat are those who are masih bodoh (nonelite

[90] The extent to which this quasi-official corruption is dependent on the tenure of particular bureaucratic positions is striking. Little evidence exists that control of such benefices gives the particular official an independent basis of power within the political system, which would prevent his relatively easy removal.

or nonleaders). Obvious parallels can be drawn with the older divisions prijaji and *wong tjilik* (little man), and literati and illiterates.

Yet, at the same time, the rakjat has all along been a central symbol of Indonesian nationalism. Ideologically speaking, the national revolution of 1945 was to secure the liberation of the rakjat; in more radical minds, indeed, the national revolution was the work of the rakjat. We find here an attitude which is ostensibly a complete intellectual reversal of the older viewpoint that the people are quite peripheral to the political system, which is oriented toward the powerful center.

But in many respects this reversal is more apparent than real. The formal contradiction was resolved without difficulty in much of contemporary Indonesian political thinking.[91] One well-known solution was Sukarno's claim that he was the *penjambung lidah rakjat*— literally, the "extension of the people's tongue," perhaps more concisely, *vox populi*. Although some sceptics have felt that Sukarno and most of his generation in practice kept the people's tongue rather short, in itself the formula represents an interesting mélange of modern populism and traditional ideas. The populism appears in the negation of any liberal theory of representation and thereby of the complex ideas of social contract or obligation implicit in such theories. A traditional theme appears in the close similarity of the concept of an undifferentiated, silent rakjat to the old idea of massed populations as an essential attribute of Power. In such a framework the penjambung lidah rakjat turns out to be less an extension of the people's tongue than the concentrated focus of the Power of the community as a whole. Sukarno's claim thus appears less as a statement of commitment than a claim to the possession of Power.

Thus, while the formally populist aspect of Sukarno's title contains an element of obligation—the obligation of the penjambung to express the demands of the people—its informal traditionalist character implies nothing of the kind. The humility implied in the self-bestowed title should not disguise its essential similarity to the many other glory-building titles—Great Leader of the Revolution, Supreme Boy-Scout, and the like—which the President assumed.

---

[91] While Sukarno is used here as the prime example, lesser political figures revealed patterns of thought very similar to his.

All such titles were claims to having Power, by the association of its symbols with his name.

It would nonetheless be a mistake to infer from what has just been said that there is no inherent sense of obligation and responsibility in the traditional Javanese world-view. But this sense of obligation was and is an obligation to Power itself. We have seen that the well-being of the community is regarded as depending on the center's ability to concentrate Power, and the external sign of a decline of that Power is the decay or disruption of the community. There is thus no inherent contradiction between the accumulation of central Power and the well-being of the collectivity, indeed the two are interrelated. The welfare of the collectivity does not depend on the activities of its individual components but on the concentrated energy of the center. The center's fundamental obligation is to itself. If this obligation is fulfilled, popular welfare will necessarily be assured. So, while traditional Javanese writers frequently devote long passages to discussing the proper conduct for a king and the art of statecraft, to suppose that the behavior required of the ruler is predicated on the stated or unstated needs of his subjects would be an error. The ruler must behave properly or his Power will ebb and vanish, and with it the good ordering and smoothness of the social system.

THE RULER AND HIS CRITICS

Although the great majority of what could be defined as the intelligentsia in traditional Java were incorporated into the structure of administration, there remained on the fringes of society one important type of "intellectual" with a special role to play.[92] This group is represented in pre-Islamic traditional literature by hermits and sages (resi, *begawan, adjar*), usually residing in isolated caves, or lonely mountain sides, remote from society. Their physical isolation expressed a fundamental separation from the interdependencies of community life. The adjar (with his *tjantrik* or pupils) was self-sufficient, outside the political order. He withdrew from society to

---

[92] In a general sense, the intelligentsia can be thought of as referring to the whole of the literate official class. In a narrower sense, it can be confined to the group of *pudjangga* (court poets and chroniclers), astrologers, and unofficial policy advisers to the throne. In the wajang literature the preeminent example is Pandita Durna, brahmin, educator of princes and *éminence grise* of the Kurawa.

cultivate clairvoyance, study the secrets of the cosmos, and prepare himself for death. The wajang stories and chronicles are filled with descriptions of these revered figures whose asceticism gives them special insight into the inner state of the world and into the future flow of Power within it. The typical role of the seer is to diagnose decay within the kingdom and warn of the impending downfall of the dynasty. The usual recorded reaction of the ruler is violent: the seer is beaten, tortured, or put to death. But the violence done is itself a sign that the seer's predictions are being fulfilled. The ruler's resort to violence clearly shows that he is dominated by personal passions. On the other hand, precisely because the seer has withdrawn from society for good, there can be no question of his being infected by pamrih. Indeed, since the seer was held to possess the gift of clairvoyance, his blessing was usually thought essential to the success of a pretender to the throne or the ambitious would-be founder of a new dynasty. No blessing would be forthcoming unless the seer was certain that the recipient would succeed. It was he who detected the first signs of the shifting of the wahju and located its ultimate destination.

The withdrawal of the adjar from society and politics was an essential element in his prestige, and, in our sense of the word, his power; and his criticism of the ruler depended for its authority on this condition. The seer was not an emanation of the center and not dependent upon it. His political disinterestedness made him a respected (and feared) barometer of the fortunes of the rulers, both in the eyes of the rulers themselves and also of interested third parties (rebels, subjects, and others).

The classical adjar largely vanished from the scene with the penetration of Islam and the later superimposition of bureaucratic colonial authority. But his social and political role, if we can speak paradoxically, by no means disappeared. Samudja Asjari has explicitly made the linkage between the adjar and the rural Islamic kjai of the late precolonial and colonial periods. In his description of the pesantrèn we find essentially the same features that marked the adjar-tjantrik community of an earlier era: physical separation from civil society, asceticism, the search for knowledge, and virtual isolation from the politico-administrative structures of the state.[93] The normal withdrawal of the kjai from political life made their

[93] Samudja Asjari, pp. 84, 101–105.

intervention, when it occurred, of great psychological importance. The fact that the kjai were now Islamic religious figures made no fundamental change; for the Islam of the kjai was of a kind in which traditional elements remained exceedingly powerful; intuitive, personal, and mystical in character, it inherited much of the pre-Islamic religion.

Although the rulers maintained Islamic officials (the *penghulu* and his subordinates) in their entourage as part of the court intelligentsia, with the function of contributing to the glory and Power of the center, these religious figures had little independent prestige. By contrast, the "wild" rural kjai, who were never absorbed into the state structure, built independent reputations, most often in villages remote from the court centers.

The kjai normally remained aloof from the political life of the state. Only in times of distress and confusion were they likely to emerge from their pesantrèn at the head of their faithful santri, to play brief but at times decisive roles in the collapse of an old order and the emergence of a new, before retiring once again to their former isolation. The contemporary sociologist would probably expect such charismatic leaders to emerge in times of social unrest; most writings about Javanese messianic movements stress this point.[94] But from within the traditional intellectual framework, once again causality must be reversed. It is the abrupt emergence of such figures into the political arena which reveals the inner decay or disruption of the social order, indeed precipitates it. The kjai has thus appeared to have inherited much of the role and status of the adjar before him.

In the colonial period, the rural kjai, not the urban penghulu, were the ones who remained an abiding preoccupation of the alien rulers. Like the traditional kingdoms, the bureaucratic colonial polity found no structural place for the kjai and their pesantrèn. The colonial authorities might repress the insurgence of the kjai when it occurred, but the repression scarcely augmented the prestige and authority of the government. Just as the violence done to the adjar did not disprove his foresight, but signaled the pamrih-filled char-

[94] Cf. Sartono Kartodirdjo, *The Peasants' Revolt of Banten in 1888*, especially pp. 154–175; G. W. J. Drewes, *Drie Javaansche Goeroe's. Hun Leven, Onderricht en Messiasprediking* (Leiden: Vros, 1925); J. M. van der Kroef, "Javanese Messianic Expectations: Their Origin and Cultural Context," *Comparative Studies in Society and History*, 1, no. 4 (1959), 299–323.

acter of the regime, so the repression of the kjai could be taken as a sign of the inner turpitude and decay of the colonial government.

Can the adjar's intellectual lineage be traced to our own time? The kjai have by no means vanished from the rural scene. Their massive intrusion into politics in the last three decades has only occurred twice—in 1945 and in 1965.[95] In both cases their intervention presaged and indeed helped bring about a fundamental change of regime—from Japanese to Republican authority in 1945, from Guided Democracy to the New Order in 1965–1966. In both instances they acted outside the established political framework and in many important respects outside the control of both declining and ascending ruling groups. (In neither case did they remain to take part in the new central authority.) But in addition, the roles played by parts of the modern urban intelligentsia[96] and the attitudes displayed toward them by the rulers and by certain sections of contemporary society, reveal striking morphological similarities to the tradition we have been discussing.[97]

In the later colonial period, one finds clear structural parallels with the older dichotomy between the official literati of the patrimonial center and the isolated adjar and kjai. Whereas the bulk of the indigenous literati formed part of the colonial bureaucracy or became appendages of it, the small nationalist intelligentsia was,

[95] For some material on the 1945 period, see B. R. O'G. Anderson, "The Pemuda Revolution" (Ph.D. thesis, Cornell University, 1967), pp. 7–12, 209, 234, 316–324.

[96] I use the term "intelligentsia" as a translation of *kaum intelek,* which roughly covers those who have received a higher Western-style education.

[97] This suggestion can be made without overlooking the fact that in any discussion of the conscious roles played by the urban intellectuals in contemporary Indonesia, Western antecedents and sociological imperatives are of central importance. The Western-educated intelligentsia have inherited that powerful tradition of dissent in modern Western history so eloquently described in Julien Benda's *La Trahison des Clercs.* The prestige attached to opposition and scepticism in Western intellectual history has certainly profoundly affected the Indonesian intelligentsia's conception of itself. See S. Tasrif, "Situasi Kaum Intelektuil di Indonesia," *Budaja Djaja* (Sept. 1968), for an extended discussion of Benda's book and its implications for the intellectuals under the Sukarno and Suharto regimes. Moreover, the ever-growing disproportion between the numbers of the intellectuals and of available administrative and political positions, has necessarily created a large body of educated or semi-educated people who cannot be incorporated into the government apparatus.

partly by choice and partly by necessity, excluded from the colonial power structure. It, too, depended for its prestige on an ostensible absence of pamrih—insofar as it claimed to speak, not for itself, but for the whole oppressed rakjat. It, too, claimed, largely on the basis of the Leninist critique of imperialism which it had absorbed from the West, a special, esoteric insight into the course of historical development and the inner decay of the existing order.

With the ascendance to power of the nationalist intelligentsia after 1945, one might have expected such structural similarities to disappear. Yet, particularly with regard to the behavior and attitudes of the nontechnical intelligentsia, one could argue that the same traditions are still at work: the dominant tradition of service to and glorification of the center; and the secondary tradition of isolation and criticism (as opposed to participatory opposition). During Sukarno's ascendancy, when the attractive power of the center was very great, particular ministers, such as Subandrio, Ruslan Abdulgani, and Prijono, as well as certain well-known Islamic politicians, were perceived by many observers as fulfilling ancient functions in modern guise. It is not entirely in jest that they were sometimes referred to as the *pudjangga* (court poets) or penghulu of Guided Democracy.[98]

On the other hand, among the critics of the regime, there were significant numbers who played, or were perceived to play, something of the role of the adjar or kjai. Around certain of these isolated figures there collected devoted tjantrik, young men from the provinces, who depended on them for intellectual education and spiritual guidance.[99] Such figures, standing outside the authority structure, depended for their following on their charisma, their moral disinterestedness, and their reputation for insight into the destiny of the center and the identity of its potential successors.[100]

[98] The New Order has found men to fulfill a similar role. Among those who were opposed to Guided Democracy there were not a few who aspired to play pudjangga and penghulu to a different leadership and in a new center.

[99] Such men are often regarded by their young followers as possessing the key (*kuntji*) to political and other types of problems, which will eventually be revealed to the most deserving among them. *Kuntji-ism* is also a marked feature of many students' attitudes to aspects of formal university education.

[100] Since the onset of the New Order, a similar dichotomy may be said

The political impotence of such intellectuals may paradoxically reveal their real power. This is not to say that the authorities, whether Sukarno or the military, will refrain from suppressing their critics. But repression will tend not to augment the authorities' power, insofar as the role of the critic is felt or perceived in more or less traditional terms. Thus, it may ultimately be at least as dangerous for the authorities to repress these impotent critics who stand more or less outside the political system as to suppress a potent opposition within it. For while suppression of the latter may be seen as revealing and augmenting the Power of the center, the crushing of the former may be taken as a sign of the center's impending disintegration. By doing violence to its powerless critics, the regime confirms their criticism and reinforces the authority of their predictions. Once again, in altered form, we find a restatement of an earlier paradox: the grasp for Power may mean its loss and the withdrawal from Power its conquest.

A NOTE ON ISLAM

Having carried the argument thus far, we can turn briefly to explore the relationship between this tradition of political thought and that of Javanese Islam. Such an analysis may throw additional light on the growing antagonism between important Islamic groups and the main bearers of the Javanese tradition, which has become a central theme of contemporary Indonesian politics. Moreover, from the rise of what Clifford Geertz has aptly referred to as Islamic "scripturalism" [101] in twentieth-century Java, significant implications can be drawn concerning the general phenomenon of charisma, implications which I shall point out in the conclusion to this essay.

It has been suggested that in the early days of its penetration of Java, Islam took over certain pre-Islamic traditional roles, such as court adviser, astrologer, brahmin, and hermit-sage. This assimila-

---

to have divided the student movement. Some student leaders have associated themselves with the hierarchy of the center—advising the government, speaking for it, and committing themselves to active participation in its structures. Others have insisted on remaining aloof and isolated. This is the group that wishes to see the students and intellectuals remain a moral force, committed not to the regime but to the ideas that the regime claims to practice.

[101] Clifford Geertz, *Islam Observed*, esp. pp. 56–74.

tion would have been unlikely had there not existed a large element of congruence and compatibility between the types of Islam that entered Java in the fifteenth and sixteenth centuries and the cultural tradition that they encountered. The "orthodox" stream in Javanese Islam sufficiently demonstrates this point. In popular folklore, the rivets linking the new religion to the old tradition are still conspicuous—especially in the association of Islam with the Power symbols of the preceding era. One obvious illustration of this is the body of legends which attributes the invention or development of such key elements of the pre-Islamic culture as wajang or the *gamelan* orchestra to the *wali*, the proselytizing saints of old Javanese Islam. Another well-known example is the common interpretation of the name of King Judistira's pusaka, the Serat Kalimasada, as the Kalimah Sahadat, the Koranic confession of faith.[102]

That the penetration of Islam was more assimilative than revolutionary can be attributed to the fact that Islam came to Java "on the heels not of conquest but of trade."[103] It was first brought by traders and has never lost the marks of its provenance, developing its strongest hold in the intermediate, commercial, rather than the upper, official or lower, peasant strata. After an initial period of zealotry, the devout Islamic groups were more or less absorbed into the patrimonial state. On the one hand, an Islam which had passed to Java through Persia and India was already patrimonialized and thus generally congruent with the traditional Javanese world-view (particularly with regard to the role and significance of the ruler). On the other hand, after the fifteenth century, the rulers assumed Islamic titles, kept Islamic officials in their entourage, and added Islam to the panoply of their attributes. Yet this overt Islamization of the rulers does not seem to have caused major alterations in their

---

[102] See, for example, Solichin Salam, Sekitar Wali Sanga (Kudus: Menara Kudus, 1960), pp. 35–51, for the culturally innovative role of the *wali*. Solichin Salam actually uses the words *assimilasi kebudajaan* (cultural assimilation) in describing the work of Sunan Kalidjaga (p. 48). For the Kalimasada-Kalimah Sahadat fusion, see p. 66 of the same work. For a detailed account of the reputed role of the *wali* in developing the wajang into its modern forms, see L. Serrurier, *De Wajang Poerwa* (Leiden: Brill, 1896), pp. 98–107. Much of Serrurier's information is based on an unpublished manuscript from R. Adipati Sasranegara, the Patih of Surakarta, sent to Amsterdam in 1883.

[103] Geertz, *Islam Observed*, p. 12.

way of life or outlook. The penetration of Islam scarcely changed the composition and the recruitment of the Javanese political elite or affected the basic intellectual framework of traditional political thought.[104] To use Gramsci's term, at no point did a "hegemonic" Islamic culture develop in Java. The self-consciousness of pious Moslems remained strictly "corporate."[105] Political and cultural subordination went hand in hand.

In the last quarter of the nineteenth century, both the socio-economic position and the world-view of devout Moslem elements in Java began to change. The opening of the Suez canal in 1870 vastly increased Javanese contact with the Near East at a time when the so-called Islamic Reform movement was in its heyday. Returning pilgrims transmitted to highly receptive audiences in colonial Java the central idea of this movement: the need to regain the "uncorrupted" and "progressive" Islam of the time of the Prophet, and to discredit the "non-Islamic," heterodox accretions of the intervening centuries.

The reasons for the great receptivity to "scripturalist" ideas must ultimately be traced to the deepening impact of Dutch capitalism

---

[104] Denys Lombard has pointed out to me, however, that in the nineteenth century, at least one important example of Islamic political thought was studied in court circles in Central Java. This was the Tādj us-Salātīn, allegedly written by Imam Buchārī ul Djauhārī in 1603, which Hooykaas aptly describes as "Arabic in title, Persian-Moslem in content, Malay in language, and composed in Atjeh" (C. Hooykaas, *Over Maleise Literatuur* [Leiden: Brill, 1947], p. 166). According to Soebardi, "The Book of Tjabolèk" (Ph.D. thesis, Australian National University, Canberra, 1967), pp. 69–70, the Tādj us-Salātīn was translated and adapted into Javanese verse by the great pudjangga of Surakarta, Jasadipura I (1729–1803), most likely in 1759. According to R. M. Ng. Poerbatjaraka, *Kapustakan Djawi* (Djakarta: Djambatan, 1952), pp. 143–144, Jasadipura composed this work in 1726, which seems improbable given his date of birth; the situation is further confused by Th. Pigeaud, *Literature of Java*, 1 (The Hague: Nijhoff, 1967), 100, who quotes Poerbatjaraka's view, but refers to Jasadipura as an early nineteenth century poet! In any event, Jasadipura's version was frequently printed in book form from the end of the nineteenth century, editions appearing in Semarang in 1873 and 1875, and in Surakarta in 1905 and 1922 (Poerbatjaraka, p. 144). Presumably, then, its major impact came at a time when the influence of Islam in general was increasing rapidly in Java as a result of the Reform movement in the Middle East.

[105] Antonio Gramsci, *The Modern Prince and Other Writings* (New York: International, 1957), pp. 154–156, 168–173.

and technology on traditional social and economic life and of secularizing rationalism on traditional beliefs. Reform Islam, as it grew and spread in twentieth-century Java, represented a rationalist religious response to the challenges created by these developments. Almost every component of traditional Islam, except the fundamental articles of faith, was subjected to this rationalizing tendency. In the process, many traditional elements were discarded, including those which had permitted the longstanding accommodation between Islam and traditional Javanese political thought. The result was ever-increasing self-consciousness and hostility between pious reformist Moslems and their fellow Javanese. In this conflict, the reformists were not only handicapped by their sociologically intermediate and economically weak position but also by the intellectual problems involved in abandoning assimilationist traditionalism. For since the fundamental assumptions of reformist Islam departed drastically from traditional Javanese assumptions, its adherents faced the need to find new answers to political questions which the older tradition had answered more or less satisfactorily for its time.

In the modernist Islamic cosmology, the older Javanese conception of divinity as something formless and intangible suffusing the whole universe, is replaced by a divinity sharply separated from the works of His hand. Between God and man there is an immeasurable distance. God is all-powerful, all-knowing, and all-merciful; man is nothing more than His creature. Thus power is, in a sense, removed from the world, since it lies with God, who is not of this world but above and antecedent to it. Furthermore, since the gulf between God and man is vast and God's power is absolute, all men are seen as equally insignificant before His majesty. But this very equality poses problems for any political theory and any permanent legitimation of political inequality and power. If all men are equally abject in the eyes of God, what is the religious basis for the political rule of one man over another?

Since Javanese cosmology made no sharp division between the terrestrial and the transcendental world, there was no extramundane referent by which to judge men's actions. For the traditionalist Javanese, possessed with the idea of divinity immanent in the world, virtually all aspects of behavior had, as it were, a "political" content insofar as they might affect the distribution and concentration of that Power which alone made the society they lived in well ordered, prosperous, and stable. The edicts of the ruler had no inherent, fixed ethical content; they were judged by the degree to which, in any given situation or period, they enhanced or undermined the concentration of Power. Hence the relativism of traditional Javanese thought, which has been so much commented upon.

By contrast, the newer currents in Islam particularly stressed the idea that Islamic law was based on God's prescriptions to the faithful, transmitted through the person of the Prophet. These prescriptions had a permanent transcendent value and served as a fixed basis for judging any man-made, political law. Such law had no inherent status. Ethics and terrestrial power were thus radically separated.

The logic of this rationalist perspective would appear to point toward a political and legal structure in strict conformity with the tenets of purified Islam. The question arises as to the status, in reformist eyes, of political and legal structures not so constituted. The problem is posed in particularly acute form in a highly pluralistic society like Indonesia and lies at the heart of the controversy over the "Islamic State." Pursuing the logic of Islamic rationalism to its conclusion under such conditions must inevitably arouse antagonism on the part of "statistical" Moslems, Christians, secularists, and others. Failure to pursue it is bound to create frustration among the Islamic devout.

We have already noted the close connection between Power and status in the Javanese world-view. It is therefore not surprising that traditional Javanese usually regard the politician as a man of high prestige—unless he abuses his Power through pamrih, in which case his Power will decline. In the modernist Islamic world-view, however, we have seen that little status is attached to terrestrial power precisely because all real power is in God's hands. Accordingly, the Islamic politician has no inherent claim to power, except, perhaps, insofar as he speaks for God. Yet any politician who sets himself up as God's spokesman is in a highly vulnerable position. In the Islamic community (*ummat*) the highest status is accorded to the religious scholar, the man with a deep knowledge of religious law and the teachings of the Prophet. This status derives exclusively from within the community. The politician, on the other hand, particularly in a heterogeneous society like contemporary Indonesia, is constantly faced with the need to deal with non-Moslem and barely Moslem groups. Where these dealings are not purely coercive in character, they tend to be seen as both blurring the boundaries between "we" and "they" and as contaminating the purity of Islamic teaching.[106] With a few rare exceptions, the modernist Islamic politician is caught in a critical dilemma. To the extent that he authentically represents the claims of Islam, he will have high prestige within his own community but little purchase on the nation as a whole; to the degree that he succeeds in working out relationships with non-ummat groups and spreading his effective influence in the society at large, his prestige within his own community may be weakened. The dilemma arises from the absence in modernist, rationalist Islam of any acceptable justification for the kind of dynamic syncretism typical of traditional Javanese thought. A Sukarno's prestige with traditional Javanese might be all the greater to the extent that he could successfully absorb the symbols of Islam into his regalia. A Natsir could not afford to absorb the symbols of non-Islam, for fear of destroying his influence and authority within his own community.[107]

CONCLUSIONS

If the overall argument of this essay has any validity, two very general considerations emerge. The first involves the relationship between the intellectual structure of traditional culture and the acceptance, transformation, or rejection of various institutional and ideational aspects of so-called modernization. The second concerns the extent to which the analysis of the Javanese conception of power may be of help in thinking about forms of domination outside the

[106] The centripetality of Javanese thought connotes a lack of strong concern for external boundaries and the outer perimeters of society. By contrast, Islam, as one of the great proselytizing religions of the world, has always, I think, been conscious of its perimeters and the line between the "we" of the *ummat* and the "they" of the *kafir* (unbelievers). In twentieth-century Indonesia, this sense of "we-ness" has, of course, been powerfully heightened by Dutch colonial policies of manipulation and repression, competition with aggressive and wealthy Christian missions, and the spread of secular ideas. One could almost suggest that precisely because of a growing lack of a sense of the center, the modernist Islamic community has increasingly tended to define itself by its frontiers.

[107] Natsir, former Prime Minister and leader of the reformist Islamic political party Masjumi, was probably the most prestigious Moslem politician of the post-independence period.

Javanese world, both in other preindustrial societies and in the industrial nations of the West.

I have tried to demonstrate the intellectual coherence of the traditional Javanese perspective on Power and politics, and to show how various political institutions and processes look when seen through this lens. I have argued that in spite of Dutch colonialism, the Japanese occupation, the nationalist revolution, and the socioeconomic changes they brought about, the cultural grip of this traditional perspective remains very strong. Such apparently discrete aspects of Javanese political thought and behavior in the contemporary period as the rejection of parliamentary democracy, the characteristic traits of Djakarta's inter-ethnic and international politics, the patterns of administrative organization and internal bureaucratic relationships, the styles of post-independence leadership, the forms of corruption, and the ambiguous political position of the urban intelligentsia can and indeed should be seen as inextricably related to one another, and that the link is precisely the continuing cultural hold of traditional conceptions, including conceptions about Power.

If, then, a radical transformation of Javanese politics and society is to take place, in what perspective should traditional political ideas be regarded? From one perspective one could argue the need for a frontal attack on these ideas, insofar as they were the linchpin of the traditional order and continue to reinforce powerful conservative tendencies in Indonesian society. In this view, if the linchpin can be displaced, overcoming resistance to a whole spectrum of social changes may be greatly facilitated. Clearly, in a sense the thrust of modernist Islam and the political propaganda of the New Order intellectuals is in this direction. But the success of this "strategy" will depend in the first instance on a clear conception of the nature of the "adversary" and the strength of his defenses. In the second instance, success will depend on the ability to provide a coherent and persuasive alternative to a deep-seated traditional orientation. As of now, my impression is that the self-styled modernizers are paying little attention to either problem. In spite of a large volume of abuse leveled at what is frequently called *mental lama* (the old mentality), scarcely any attempt is being made to understand this mentality and assess its strengths and weaknesses.

From another perspective, one could argue that the mode of social transformation must be adapted to traditional ideas. But such a strategy presupposes a leadership sophisticated enough to be deeply familiar with these ideas, yet not bound by them, and disciplined enough to use them without succumbing to them. The career of Sukarno is instructive in this respect. No one in modern Indonesian history used traditional ideas with greater success for mobilizing populations and enhancing his own personal authority. Yet Sukarno's ultimate failure, the growing conservatism of his regime and the internal impasse to which his policies led, can in part be attributed to his inability to liberate himself sufficiently from the hold of the ideas he manipulated. Too often the concepts of the center, of dynamic syncretism, of power as an end rather than a means, dominated his own innermost thinking as well as his public posture and private manoeuvrings. Guided Democracy was a very Power-ful state in the traditional meaning of the word but not at all a power-ful state in the sense of an organization capable of carrying out sustained and planned change. Yet it is doubtful to what extent the former President in his own mind clearly distinguished between the two.

I suggested at the start of this essay that a careful analysis of the Javanese conception of Power and politics might be of some value for political analysis outside the restricted geographical limits of Java or Indonesia. This value, I think, may lie in helping to elucidate the much-vexed problem of "charisma." The enormously wide range of personality types among the "charismatic leaders" of our time, their contradictory ideologies, the vastly differing socio-economic, religious, and ethnic character of their clienteles, the great variety of the types and "levels" of political organization in which they have appeared, pose in themselves difficult questions of analysis and conceptualization.[108] Continuing difficulties have been encountered in classifying "charisma" with more conventional sources of power, such as wealth, arms, population, and so forth. The apparent instability and fluidity of "charisma" as reflected in the meteoric rise and fall of such men as Nkrumah, Ben Bella, and Sukarno suggests

---

[108] For an interesting recent discussion of these difficulties and some suggestions for their resolution, see Ann Ruth Willner, *Charismatic Political Leadership: A Theory,* Center of International Studies, Research Monograph no. 32 (Princeton, N.J.: Princeton University, 1968).

that this type of power is in some way *sui generis*. But what the genus may be, is by no means clear.[109]

Today the prevailing view is that "charisma" lies in the eye of the beholder. It is less a real quality of the leader than a quality attributed to him by his followers, who see him as someone extraordinary, sometimes with a historic mission, sometimes with the grace of God, in any case with preternatural capabilities. What is the explanation of this perception? I would argue that this perception derives from ideas analogous to the Javanese conception of Power, and that the charismatic leader has Power in much the same sense that the traditional rulers of Java had it. He is regarded as the center from which Power radiates, and the believer attaches himself to this Power, rather than submitting to it as one might to rational-legal authority. His Power is revealed rather than demonstrated. The difficulty facing a charismatic leader trying to make a political comeback is exactly that of the weakened center, as the Javanese think of it. If he really still had the Power, he would never have lost it; if he had had the answer to disorder, the problem would never have come up. (We can also note that modern charismatic leaders, precisely like the figures of Power in Javanese legend and history, are often associated with asceticism, syncretic dynamism, and conjuring ceremonial.) [110]

If what has been said so far is correct, I would propose, very tentatively, that we have the basis for a useful simplification of Max Weber's description of "charisma." [111] In the first place, I believe that the difficulties and imprecisions of Weber's concept of "charisma" stem from the fact that he tended to view it primarily from

[109] These uncertainties help to account for the constant, almost unconscious tendency toward reification of the concept of charisma both in popular literature and scholarly writing. To avoid the dangers of reification, I have resorted to the irritating typographical device of putting the word charisma in quotation marks.

[110] Compare the description of charismatic leadership given by Weber, in H. H. Gerth and C. Wright Mills, trans. and eds., *From Max Weber: Essays in Sociology* (New York: Oxford University Press, 1958), pp. 245–252; cf. also Bendix, pp. 298–328.

[111] In the discussion which follows, I give a somewhat one-sided view of Weber's thinking. Weber's discussion of charisma is often rather confusing, not least because of repeated reification of his concept. Weber's ideas are here deliberately simplified for the purpose of clarifying the essential point that I want to make.

the sociological and psychological, rather than from the cultural anthropological perspective. That is to say, he focused his attention on the social, economic, and political conditions in which charismatic leaders emerged and on the personalities of such leaders, rather than on the culture of their followers. He was inclined to show the extraordinary *qualities* attributed to these leaders, without being able to define what these qualities were or had in common.

I would suggest that these discrete qualities can be reduced to a common denominator: the belief on the part of followers that their leader has Power. The *signs* of this Power—namely, particular qualities—will be determined by the contingent idiosyncratic character of particular cultures.[112] One might suggest asceticism in Southeast Asia, and virility (*machismo*) in Latin America, as examples. Asceticism in the one cultural area, machismo in the other, signify the same thing—Power.

In general, Weber was inclined to view "charisma" as something short-lived, spontaneous, unpredictable, and revolutionary, although under certain conditions it could become depersonalized and institutionalized.[113] Political "charisma" typically emerged when a given patrimonial, feudal or rational-legal bureaucratic system entered a period of stress. Later, "charisma" tended to undergo a process of routinization and bureaucratization—until crisis produced a new charismatic leader. The implication of this view is that there is an endless historical oscillation between charismatic and traditional or bureaucratic rule; like the chicken and the egg, neither can be said definitely to precede the other.

If, however, we can accept that "charisma" involves belief in Power, it should be clear that in both the historical and analytical sense, "charisma" precedes rational-legal domination.[114] Study of the Javanese political tradition demonstrates that in Old Java, all rule was charismatic insofar as it was based on belief in Power. Bureau-

[112] Cf. Willner, *Charismatic Political Leadership*, pp. 81–87, for an informative discussion of the way various contemporary charismatic leaders evoke the folk-heroes of their respective cultures.

[113] Cf. Bendix, pp. 309–314.

[114] One could probably also say, depending on one's precise interpretation of "traditional domination," that it is subsumed under charismatic domination.

cracy there was, but it drew its legitimacy and authority from the radiant center, which was seen to suffuse the whole structure with its energy. In such a society, "charisma" was not a temporary phenomenon of crisis, but the permanent, routine, organizing principle of the state. This suggests that the short-lived, unpredictable, revolutionary character which Weber attributed to "charisma" may be purely contingent and time bound and, with an important modification shortly to be discussed, all presecular societies may be said to be under charismatic domination. The question arises as to why Weber limited his use of the idea of "charisma" largely to situations of stress and crisis. It seems to me that the answer lies in a rather untypical absence of historical perspective. While Weber drew his general theory of the rise of rational-legal bureaucracy from what he saw as the *historical* spread of rationalism and secularism, in his discussion of "charisma" the historical element is largely absent.

If the historical component is restored, the argument shifts in the following direction. In the later historical evolution of the West the relatively rapid pace of economic, technological, and social change has been paralleled by a cultural transformation of unprecedented extent. This development can be seen, from the contemporary social science perspective, as the movement from magical religion through religious rationalism to secular rationalism, as traditional ontologies have been challenged by scientific discoveries, technological innovations, and the immensely increased complexity of social and economic life. This movement has, of course, by no means been confined to the West, although it has gone further there than elsewhere. In Geertz's description of Islamic evolution in Morocco, for example, the rise of the scripturalists at the expense of the marabouts can be seen as the ascendancy of religious rationalism vis-à-vis magical religion. One could perhaps argue a comparable evolution in China from the magical religion of the Shang era to the marginally religious rationalism of Confucian thought. In Indonesia, the spread of reformist Islam in the twentieth century is probably a comparable phenomenon.

As the West moved toward secular rationalism, a new conception of power was crystallized bit by bit, at the start by political philosophers like Machiavelli and Hobbes, and later by the proliferating apparatus of scientific-industrial education and research.[115] In its final form this concept of power is at radical variance with its ancestor, as I have tried to indicate in the introduction to this essay. Nonetheless, as Marx pointed out, the culture of a society, while following the general trajectory of technological and social development, always tends to change more slowly and in a more piecemeal, fragmentary fashion. In all societies whose cultures are dominated by religious or secular rationalism, one can expect to find residues of previous cultural modes. Older and newer cultural elements will exist in contradictory juxtaposition.

I would suggest that this is the case with so central a component of any culture as its ideas about power. In most contemporary cultures, including our own, the two polar conceptions of power that I have outlined exist side by side, with one or the other more or less predominant.[116] In our society the older conception of power appears residually in the interstices of legal-scientific culture—in faith healing, psychiatry, prayer, and what is referred to as "charisma." Although the older idea of Power may be residual in societies dominated by religious or secular rationalism, it is likely to emerge into prominence under conditions of severe stress and disturbance of routine assumptions—when institutions explained and legitimized in terms of the hegemonic cultural mode appear to be breaking down or to be in decay.[117] Such circumstances evoke not so much

[115] The decline of traditional European ideas of Power in late mediaeval and early modern times under the impact first of religious and later of secular rationalism is beautifully described in Marc Bloch, Les Rois Thaumaturges (Strasbourg: Librairie Istra, 1924). Bloch focuses particularly on the healing Power attributed to the monarchs of France and England (in the former case up till the French Revolution, in the latter up to the reign of Queen Anne), but, especially on pp. 51–79, he discusses in more general terms the cultural roots of the European monarchical idea. Curiously enough, on pp. 52–53 he makes explicit comparisons with cultural conceptions prevalent in Polynesia, drawing his data from Frazer's Golden Bough. For this reference, I am indebted to Denys Lombard.

[116] By stressing the crystallization process in the development of the modern Western concept of power, I mean to indicate that between the two polar ideal types, various intermediate types can be envisaged.

[117] It should come as no surprise in this perspective that the religious rationalism of the scripturalists in Morocco was superseded, during the crisis of decolonization, by the more ancient "maraboutic" tradition in the person of Sultan Muhammed V (cf. Geertz, Islam Observed, p. 81, where the author observes that "French rule had produced what, left to itself, the

new types of leaders or new forms of domination as ancient conceptions and ancient sources of authority.

---

dynasty was almost certainly no longer capable of creating—a maraboutic
king")—nor that the secular rationalism of the West was for a time successfully challenged, in the aftermath of the Great War and during the World
Depression, by charismatic leaders like Adolf Hitler and Benito Mussolini.

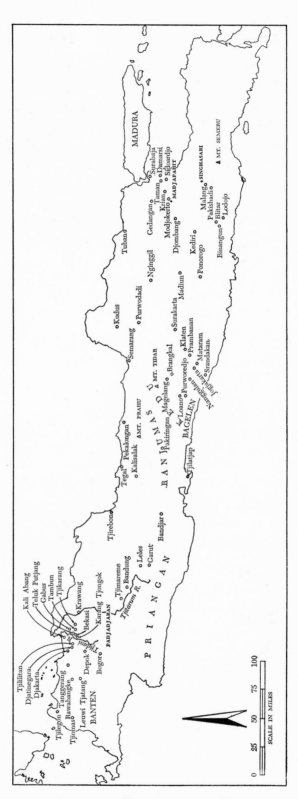

Map 2. Java

Agrarian Radicalism in Java:

Its Setting and Development *

❖❖❖❖❖❖❖❖❖

Sartono Kartodirdjo

INTRODUCTION

It might be asked whether students of Indonesian politics have really been concentrating their attention on the most significant sectors of the society. Studies of Indonesian political developments since Independence contain scarcely any sustained analysis of the politics of the rural population. Only very recently have a few scholars begun to evince some interest in the study of rural society from a political point of view.[1] Yet the detraditionalization and the politicization of rural life have exerted an increasingly important influence on the political process in independent Indonesia. Events of the last few years have shown that the rural population is far from being politically inert and indeed that political competition has been at

* The limited store of data available on millenarian movements outside Java does not permit us to include them for intensive study.

I should like to acknowledge my indebtedness to Abdurrachman Surjomihardjo and Lukman for valuable research assistance; to R. Mohammad Ali for providing documentary source materials from the National Archives, Djakarta; to H. G. Wondaal of the State Archives at Schaarsbergen for his assistance in collecting documents; to the staff of the District Attorney's office of Jogjakarta for assistance in data collection; and to Verne H. Fletcher for correcting the English text of my original draft.

[1] See Robert R. Jay, "Local Government in Rural Central Java," *Far Eastern Quarterly,* 15 (1956), 215–227; Peter R. Goethals, *Aspects of Local Government in a Sumbawa Village (Eastern Indonesia),* Cornell Modern Indonesia Project Monograph Series (Ithaca, N.Y.: Cornell University, 1961); G. William Skinner, ed., *Local, Ethnic and National Loyalties in Village Indonesia: A Symposium,* Southeast Asia Studies, Cultural Report Series no. 8 (New Haven: Yale University, 1959).

least as intense in the countryside as in the towns.[2] Nonetheless, these examples of political mobilization of the peasantry are only the most recent and dramatic expressions of persistent agrarian unrest in Indonesian society. From the archives of the Netherlands Indies government and the newspapers and magazines of the colonial period we learn of repeated clashes between groups of peasants and the colonial government. Cumulatively, these sources make it clear that the colonial authorities were faced with widespread and deep-rooted rural discontent. The sporadic agrarian uprisings of the past two centuries, all, whatever their stated objectives, expressed a fundamental protest against the existing conditions of rural life. In almost every instance this protest manifested itself in millenarian radicalism.[3] A map of such millenarian radical movements—social movements in the Hobsbawmian sense [4]—would show that they have appeared not only in nearly all areas of Java but also in various parts of the other islands.[5] Movements of this kind outside Indonesia

[2] There are many instances which could be cited. Perhaps the most striking of these would be the fourteen-year Darul Islam guerrilla movement in rural West Java; the so-called *aksi sepihak* movements in 1964–1965, which were unilateral attempts by Communist-led peasant organizations to force proper implementation of the laws on land-reform and share-cropping; and the political upheaval following the Gestapu coup on September 30, 1965.

[3] The history of Banten contains so many instances of millenarian agrarian uprisings that we can speak of a tradition of revolt. (For a discussion of this concept and for historical instances, see Sartono Kartodirdjo, *The Peasants' Revolt of Banten in 1888: Its Conditions, Course and Sequel. A Case Study of Social Movements in Indonesia* [The Hague: De Neder-landsche Boek- en Steendrukkerij v/h Smits, 1966], chap. 4.) In West Java there is a long-established millenarian tradition predicting the return of a King of Sunda. In Central and East Java we also find an age-old tradition of millenarian thought, particularly in the form of messianic prophecies. (J. A. B. Wiselius, "Djaja Baja, zijn leven en profetieen," *Bijdragen tot de Taal-, Land- en Volkenkunde* [hereafter *BKI*], 19 [1872], 172–217; A. B. Cohen Stuart, "Eroe Tjakra," *ibid.*, pp. 285–288; J. Brandes, "Iets over een ouderen Dipanegara in verband met een prototype van de voorspellingen van Jayabaya," *Tijdschrift voor Indische Taal-, Land- en Volkenkunde* [hereafter *TBG*], 32 [1889], 268–430.)

[4] E. J. Hobsbawm, *Primitive Rebels: Studies in Archaic Forms of Social Movements in the 19th and 20th Centuries* (Manchester: Manchester University Press, 1963), chap. 1.

[5] See Justus M. van der Kroef, "Messianic Movements in the Celebes, Sumatra, and Borneo," in Sylvia Thrupp, ed., *Millennial Dreams in Action* (The Hague: Mouton, 1962), pp. 80–121.

have been studied from various points of view and in terms of various disciplines. But, although there have been a number of philological and Islamological studies [6] of the verbal expressions of agrarian protest movements in Indonesia, there has hitherto been a marked lack of historical research on these movements themselves. Since such movements have been regarded as having no permanent or substantial impact on the course of "grand" history, they have usually been considered unworthy of the historian's attention.[7] A similar predisposition to disregard social movements in Indonesian historiography is found in the work of political scientists concerned with Indonesia, which has been largely focused on constitutional forms, governmental institutions, organizational conflict, and policy-making at the national level.

In order to comprehend the political process at the village level, we shall have to adapt our concepts to the setting of peasant society. Any coherent analysis of agrarian radicalism in Indonesia must take into account the composition and hierarchy of rural values, the specific allocation of authority in peasant communities, and the characteristic symbols, goals, and action-patterns of agrarian politics.

For the purposes of this essay I propose to regard as "radical" any social movement which totally rejects the existing social order [8] and is characterized by strong moral indignation against, and hostility toward, the privileged and powerful.[9] Understood in this sense, radicalism becomes simply a convenient label for millenarianism of

[6] Here the literature is overwhelming, and only a few titles will be cited: D. A. Rinkes, *Abdoerraoef van Singkel. Bijdrage tot de kennis van de mystiek op Java en Sumatra* (Heerenveen: Hepkema, 1909); B. J. O. Schrieke, *Het boek van Bonang* (Utrecht: den Boer, 1916); G. W. J. Drewes, *Drie Javaansche Goeroe's. Hun Leven, Onderricht en Messias-prediking* (Leiden: Vros, 1925).

[7] For examples of this "conventional" historiography, see F. W. Stapel, ed., *Geschiedenis van Nederlandsch Indië* (Amsterdam: Joost van den Vondel, 1939); H. J. de Graaf, *De Geschiedenis van Indonesië* (The Hague: van Hoeve, 1949); B. H. M. Vlekke, *Nusantara: A History of Indonesia* (The Hague: van Hoeve, 1959).

[8] Hobsbawm, p. 57; cf. Alfred McClung Lee, ed., *Principles of Sociology* (New York: Barnes and Noble, 1955), p. 197; see also R. Heberle, *Social Movements: An Introduction to Political Sociology* (New York: Appleton-Century-Crofts, 1951), p. 6.

[9] See Horace M. Kallen, "Radicalism," *Encyclopedia of the Social Sciences*, 13 (1954), 51–54.

a revolutionary character. The membership of such radical social movements has generally been restricted to the lower social strata,[10] the oppressed,[11] or the underprivileged.[12] Where such movements draw their following from peasant communities, we can speak of agrarian radicalism.[13]

Millenarianism is not always combined with manifest expressions of aggression and protest. For the colonial period, data is far more plentiful on aggressive millenarianism than on peaceful variants, since the former constituted a direct menace to the authorities and, for obvious reasons, rigorous inquiry into the causes of the resulting insurrections was usually made. Since independence, this imbalance has been partly corrected; the public media give considerable space to the many quietist millenary movements which flourish in contemporary Indonesian society, as well as to the occasional more violent varieties.

For the contemporary scholar, the causation of millenarian movements in Indonesia is as complex and difficult to disentangle as it was for the colonial authorities. The variety of factors which must be considered should obviously include economic deprivation, cultural disintegration, and political oppression. But these factors do not suffice to account for the phenomenon of agrarian radicalism as manifested in recurrent disturbances. The recorded instances suggest that, at least in Indonesia, the historical appearance of rural disturbances is powerfully conditioned by a long-established tradition

[10] See E. Werner, "Popular Ideologies in Late Medieval Europe: Taborite Chiliasm and Its Antecedents," in *Comparative Studies in Society and History* (hereafter *CSSH*), 2, no. 3 (1960), 344ff.

[11] V. Lanternari, *The Religions of the Oppressed: A Study of Modern Messianic Cults* (New York: Knopf, 1963).

[12] Max Weber, *The Sociology of Religion* (trans. E. Fischoff) (Boston: Beacon Press, 1963), pp. 95ff.

[13] In order not to create more confusion in the use of terms, my usage will be mainly based upon previous works on the subject, with some clarification where I try to categorize various social movements. For the term "messianism," see W. D. Wallis, "Quelques aspects du messianisme," *Archives de Sociologie des Religions*, 5 (1956), 99–100; also G. Balandier, "Messianismes et Nationalismes en Afrique Noire," *Cahiers Internationaux de Sociologie* (hereafter *CIS*), 14 (1953), 41–65; for "millenarism," see Norman Cohn, "Medieval Millenarism: Its Bearing on the Comparative Study of Millenarian Movements," in *Millennial Dreams in Action*, pp. 31–45; for "nativism," see R. Linton, "Nativistic Movements," *American Anthropologist*, 45 (1943), 230–240.

of millennial beliefs. I shall try to show that such millennial beliefs have enormous insurrectionary potential.

A major pitfall in the study of Indonesian millenarianism has been the tendency to derive it from colonialism and to associate it exclusively with the process of "modernization." Since most of the millenarian movements examined by recent writers indeed appeared in colonial areas, they have too often been looked upon simply as products of colonial rule itself.[14] In the case of Indonesia, we know that there were precolonial millenarian movements. However, the paucity of information about them has led us to focus on the better-documented movements of the colonial period, thus overemphasizing Western impact as the major, if not the sole, precipitating factor. What I would suggest, in fact, is that the main effect of Western domination during the colonial period was to undermine irremediably the traditional economic and political system. Accelerating social change and the forcible imposition of Western valuesystems detonated a disintegration of traditional culture. Under such conditions, millenarian movements, which in the precolonial era might appear at relatively rare intervals in times of dynastic upheaval, became increasingly persistent and marked a chronic state of crisis in society.

It is also important to set Indonesian agrarian radicalism within the context of traditional social structures, since it was and still is frequently stimulated by conflict between existing power groups. Deep-rooted millennial beliefs have long been used by counter-elites for agitation and insurrection against the established wielders of power, particularly at the local level. Because the cultural identity of peasants is inseparably bound up with their religion, they were and are predisposed to reassert this sense of identity in religious terms when threatened by alien values, ideas, and practices. Traditional religious leaders, controlling the symbols of identity and hope, are thus particularly well placed, not only to maintain the loyalty of their peasant followings, but also to stir them into active resistance and even to inspire armed insurrection. Agrarian radicalism must

[14] See T. Bodrogi, "Colonization and Religious Movements in Melanesia," *Acta Ethnographica Academica Scientiarum Hungarica*, 2 (1951), 259–292; G. Balandier, pp. 41–65; also Peter Worsley, *The Trumpet Shall Sound: A Study of "Cargo" Cults in Melanesia* (London: MacGibbon and Kee, 1957).

therefore be analyzed in the light of competition for peasant allegiance. The charismatic authority of religious leaders has always been a potential threat to the dominant bureaucratic elite. In recent times, with the secularization of the latter, the norms and values of these two groups have tended increasingly to diverge, and the peasants have often been mobilized in the increasingly bitter conflict between them.

The history of nineteenth and twentieth century Java provides a remarkably clear picture of traditional peasant society disintegrating under the impact of colonial domination. It reveals a wide range of millenarian movements which represent the classic response of threatened traditionalism.[15] Confining our study to the period of colonial rule gives us a stable frame of reference within which to analyze agrarian radicalism. Within this framework the large number of cases available for study makes a start at serious comparative analysis both practicable and instructive.

THE TRADITIONAL SETTING

The Village and Its Social System

Since millenarian movements in Java have been an overwhelmingly rural phenomenon, any discussion of them must begin with an analysis of the internal structure of the village community and its place within the framework of traditional society.[16] The basic political unit of peasant society in Java is the village (*désa* or *dukuh*), which consists of a relatively large cluster of houses with gardens attached. Within the village, economic and social life centers around the nuclear family, though a bilaterally extended kinship system still performs important residual functions. As a small, close-knit and often isolated community, the village has a strong

[15] In analyzing the characteristics of Indonesian millenarian movements, further study should be given to the prevailing cultural traditions of local or regional societies. Agrarian protest is often shaped by the patterns of local millenarian beliefs, especially in its ideological content, and such beliefs provide a political culture extremely well adapted for expressing protest, rejecting externally imposed change and encouraging hopes for successful action under otherwise exceedingly adverse conditions. In the absence of more in-depth regional studies I cannot undertake a systematic treatment of regional variation here.

[16] R. Redfield, *Peasant Society and Culture* (Chicago: Chicago University Press, 1956).

interest in maintaining internal harmony and cooperation. This interest is expressed in the village social system by a rather formalized concentric set of obligations imposed on every peasant—to his kin, to his neighbors, and to his fellow villagers. These obligations, taken as a whole, form a stable and deep-rooted system of reciprocity, which has been described as *tulung tinulung* or *sambat sinambat* (mutual help). These practical bonds are further cemented by some of the central moral values of the Javanese village, particularly the values of *gotong-rojong* (cooperativeness), *pada-pada* (equality) and *tepa-slira* (consideration). The effect of this value-system and the basic conditions of village life have been to make the Javanese peasant highly appreciative of smooth personal relationships and strongly desirous of acceptance as a good member of the community.

As in other agrarian communities, landownership is the prime determinant of status, and community responsibilities are distributed accordingly. Within the status hierarchy we find various classes of peasant proprietors (*kuli kentjeng*), tenants (*kuli karang-kopèk* or *kuli ngindung*), and wage laborers (*kuli ngindung tlosor, manumpang,* or *budjang*).[17] Social stratification is also partly based on length of settlement in the village, with the highest status being awarded to descendants of the founders of the village, the *tjikal-bakal*. More generally, the status and role of long-established families (*sikep ngarep*) are clearly distinguishable from those of more recent arrivals (*sikep buri*).

Age elicits a high degree of deference, reflected in the existence, alongside the official structure of local government, of a powerful council of village elders (*kasepuhan*).[18] Lastly, as we shall see below, religious office often commands a high status in the village community.

Village government is led by a headman (*lurah*), who is assisted by a staff of village officials (*prabot désa*). Somewhat separate from this secular leadership group are the religious officials (*kaum*), whose functions are largely confined to the religious sphere. Out-

---

[17] R. M. Koentjaraningrat, "Tjelapar, a Village in South Central Java," in R. M. Koentjaraningrat, ed., *Villages in Indonesia* (Ithaca: Cornell University Press, 1967), pp. 244–280.

[18] *Ibid.*

side any official governmental structure stand such powerful natural leaders as the local *kjai* (religious sage), the *hadji* (returned pilgrim), the *guru* (spiritual teacher), and the *dukun* (magician, healer, seer). These figures, who form an unofficial religious elite, are supported neither by the state nor the village budget, but often have large and devoted personal followings. They tend, by the nature of their role and clientele, to be much wealthier and more mobile than the average peasant. The more prestigious among them often develop contacts over a wide area. In times of crisis, indeed, when a special premium is put on contact with the supernatural, the authority of the kjai, guru, hadji, and dukun may often far exceed in scope and intensity that of the official government of any one village or group of villages. Accordingly, these unofficial, but charismatic religious leaders have always been regarded with suspicion by government authorities, who see their ability to mobilize mass support as a potential danger to the regime. Before we explore further the political role of this informal religious elite and its latently antagonistic relationship to the authorities, however, we must examine more closely the place of magic and religion in traditional village society.

The Web of Magic and Religion

Traditional Javanese culture was suffused by a strong sense of the supernatural. Human life existed in a cosmological context of sacred time and sacred space. It was surrounded by spirits and dominated by cults and rituals. An elaborate corpus of multifarious magico-religious beliefs, shared by lord and peasant alike, provided the whole society with a common framework of symbols, norms, and values. In spite of this framework, village society and the ruling literati (*prijaji*) of traditional Java developed variants on the basic matrix in accordance with their respective ecological environments and levels of sophistication. Whereas the elite variant tended to create a kind of highly personalized and power-oriented magico-mystical individualism, the peasant variant was shot through with magic and millenarian prophecy. The political powerlessness of the individual peasant and his consciousness of his position at the bottom of the social pyramid made him particularly attached to the magical elements (belief in charms, amulets, and so forth) in the traditional belief-system, for these magical devices provided super-natural armor against danger from above and outside his familiar world. Without hope of changing his life condition through individual prowess, the lowly peasant was particularly susceptible to those prophetic elements in the magico-religious belief system which promised a general transformation of the collectivity in which his personal destiny would naturally be subsumed. Thus the affinity of the peasantry for magic and millenarian beliefs was solidly based in a profound awareness of their condition.

In studying the development of any particular social movement in Java, one almost invariably comes across practices of an essentially fetishist type. The most common and significant of these is the distribution of *djimat* (charms) that offer protection from danger, illness, and death, or the ability to become invisible or invulnerable.[19] These djimat usually consist of *radjah*—sacred texts or compounds of characters, figures, and designs—inscribed on paper, earthenware, or other material. The frequent use of djimat, even today, shows the tenacious strength of the belief in their magical efficacy. To participants in rebellious social movements, facing the threat of violent government repression, the djimat cult gave enormous spiritual security and encouragement.[20] Even better than the acquisition of djimat was initiation into the esoteric arts (*ngèlmu kadigdajan, ngèlmu kawedukan,* or *ngèlmu kaslametan*) which gave their practitioners superhuman powers. Again, the history of nineteenth- and twentieth-century Javanese social movements reveals the widespread belief among the peasantry in the attainability of such powers. The main sources of both the djimat and the esoteric arts have always been the charismatic, unofficial, religious leaders we have previously discussed. These men are commonly referred to as *kramat* (holy men or saints), and their supernatural help is frequently invoked for such problems as barrenness, loss of valuables,

[19] These *djimat* often serve other purposes as well. (C. Geertz, *The Religion of Java* [Glencoe, Ill.: Free Press, 1960], p. 87; Th. Pigeaud, *Literature of Java,* 1 [The Hague: Nijhoff, 1967], 265–273.) They can be used to gain wealth, success in love, and so forth. They may also be used as dangerous weapons in the hands of people who wish to inflict suffering or death on their adversaries.

[20] On *djimat,* see E. Gobée and C. Adriaanse, eds., *Ambtelijke adviezen van C. Snouck Hurgronje, 1889–1936,* 2 (The Hague: Nijhoff, 1959), 1222–1236.

and sickness. Among the peasants, it is a matter of faith that the prayers of the kramat are heard; their blessings and curses are equally powerful. These holy men are credited with the power of transcending the ordinary limitations of time and space and with the ability to foresee the future. After death they continue to be venerated, and pilgrimages are made to their graves in the hope of gaining their help and intercession.

The kramat vary widely in the degree of their reputed powers, and in the spread of their fame. In Java, the term *wali* is commonly used to designate the kramat of greatest repute.[21] To this day the most highly venerated are the so-called *wali sanga*, the nine legendary saints, who first brought Islam to Java.[22] Their tombs have for centuries been crowded with pilgrims from all walks of life, seeking spiritual and temporal blessings. The *tarékat* (Sufi brotherhoods) have also contributed to these cults by fostering the tradition of holy guru (tarékat leaders).[23] Although the great wali have always had a Java-wide following, every region of Java has its own traditional cults of dead local religious leaders.[24] Their tombs have special symbolic and magical significance to the surrounding population, who often tend to regard these dead saints as peculiarly their own. Accordingly, it is readily understandable that pilgrimages (*njadran*) to such holy places (*pundèn*) in order to seek blessings (*njuwun pangèstu*) were often made before undertaking preparations for rebellion.

A word should be added on the veneration of kramat who are still alive. A man of this nature is recognized primarily by his disposition to ecstasy and visions and his ability to perform miracles. A few of the more interesting miracles [25] include traversing long dis-

---

[21] *Ibid.*, p. 1228; see also John A. Subhan, *Sufism: Its Saints and Shrines* (Lucknow: Lucknow Publishing House, 1960), pp. 111–112.

[22] For the hagiography of prominent saints in Java, see Rinkes, "De Heiligen van Java," *TBG*, 52 (1910), 556–589; 53 (1911), 17–56, 269–300, 435–581; 54 (1912), 13–206; 55 (1913), 1–200.

[23] On saintly *guru*, see *ibid.* (1909 and 1910); Drewes; Sartono Kartodirdjo, pp. 177–184; Pigeaud, pp. 89–91.

[24] In Banten it is Hadji Mangsur, see *Sedjarah Hadji Mangsur* (MS. in Snouck Hurgronje Huis, Leiden); in North Banjumas it is Sèh Djambu Karang, see J. W. van Dapperen, "Plaatsen van vereering op de zuid-helling van de Slamet," *Djawa*, 4 (1935), 24–32; for other regions, see Rinkes (1910–1913); see also Pigeaud, pp. 315–317.

[25] Subhan, pp. 110–111.

tances in a moment of time,[26] walking on water, flying in the air, and predicting future events.[27] Being credited with such powers, the kramat were bound to play a powerful role in many millenarian insurrectionary movements. Their extraordinary charismatic authority appeared to lend supernatural support to the rebel enterprise, while their predictions could stir the population into a state of frenetic expectancy.[28]

The kramat not only offered djimat and magico-religious formulae (*surat wasijat, djampé,* radjah), but also frequently revived and gave contemporary application to ancient legends and prophecies. Sometimes such legends provided the kramat with a justification for assuming names or titles associated with celebrated figures from the heroic past. This practice, when connected with prophecies of an imminent cataclysmic change in society, has invariably been regarded by governmental authorities with deep suspicion and has often been the signal for repressive action. We shall find examples of this in the description of some historical cases in the latter part of this essay.

One other important source of power for these unofficial religious leaders is the traditional belief in the complex Javanese prognostical system for personal success and community advantage. Javanese society has always made great use of *primbon*—books which contain esoteric formulae (radjah) and intricate numerological systems (*pétungan*) for calculating lucky days to hold a ritual feast, to build a house, to undertake a journey, and which in short deal with all kinds of basic activities of both the individual and his community.[29] Since the illiterate peasant does not usually possess the skills

[26] For the story of Sajid Abdallah Attas, who appeared to many people in different places while he was imprisoned, see Gobée and Adriaanse, p. 1229; for Hadji Mangsur's miracles, see *Sedjarah Hadji Mangsur;* for more instances, see Rinkes (1910–1913).

[27] For predictions made by Hadji Abdul Karim, see Sartono Kartodirdjo, pp. 177–183; predictions concerning the "Last Days" are usually known as the "last admonitions of the Prophet" or the so-called *wasijat,* see C. Snouck Hurgronje, in *Verspreide Geschriften,* 1 (Bonn and Leipzig: Schroeder, 1923), 134–139.

[28] For the dissemination of eschatological prophecy as stated in the *wasijat* in the eighties, see Sartono Kartodirdjo, pp. 167–168; cf. Gobée and Adriaanse, pp. 1222–1225.

[29] On Javanese numerology, see Geertz, pp. 30–35; also Gobée and Adriaanse, pp. 1222–1236. For an extensive study of Javanese numerology,

to decipher and utilize this numerological system, he turns for help
to the local experts, namely the dukun or the kjai.[30]

Such magico-religious beliefs, then, can be regarded as forming
the core of so-called *abangan* culture to which the majority of the
peasants in Central and large parts of East Java belong. It is a culture formally Islamic but at heart shaped by many pre-Islamic elements, such as those described above. In more sophisticated form,
this culture also commands the loyalty of the bulk of the prijaji
elite.[31]

Standing opposed to this dominant cultural viewpoint from the
beginning of the Islamic penetration of Java, however, has been an
outlook much more deeply impregnated with Islam, and in many
cases actively hostile to the "idolatrous" magical elements in abang-
gan culture. Adherents of this minority viewpoint, to be found in
both the villages and the towns, are usually referred to as the
kaputihan or *santri*. As a group, the santri are marked off from the
rest of the society by their strict observance of daily prayer and their
close attachment to the other institutions of Islam.

It is impossible here to do more than suggest the historical conditions which have hardened the corporate self-consciousness of the
santri. In the latter part of the nineteenth century the development
of modern means of communication greatly facilitated closer relations with Egypt and Arabia, the intellectual centers of Moslem
civilization. The strengthening of these ties had its effect on both
political and religious life in Java. In the religious domain, a strong
reformist and antitraditional Islamic revival developed steadily
deeper roots in the rural areas.[32]

---

see H. A. van Hien, *De Petangan's of tellingen der Javanen* (Batavia, Solo, and
Amsterdam: Rusche, 1894).

[30] For an extensive treatment of the *dukun*, see Geertz, pp. 86–118; cf.
Gobée and Adriaanse, pp. 1226, 1233: see also Snouck Hurgronje, 4, pt. 1,
passim.

[31] This is particularly true of areas where the population is less ardently
Moslem. Here we have to refer to the dichotomy of prijaji and *wong
tjilik* on the one hand, and that of abangan and *santri* (devout Moslems)
on the other. See my criticism of Geertz's prijaji-santri-abangan trichotomy,
Sartono Kartodirdjo, p. 50; cf. R. M. Koentjaraningrat, "The Javanese in
South Central Java," in G. P. Murdock, ed., *Social Structure in Southeast
Asia* (Chicago: Quadrangle Books, 1960), pp. 88–115.

[32] See my discussion of religious revivalism in the nineteenth century,
Sartono Kartodirdjo, esp. chap. 5.

This new self-consciousness among the santri was certainly a central, if by no means the only, factor in the growing and open antagonism between two types of Javanese leadership, long latently hostile to one another. As we shall see, the Western impact was to aggravate this antagonism further, since one major effect of colonial policy was to co-opt the largely abangan prijaji elite into the civil bureaucracy, while more or less isolating the santri leadership, as representing a new militant Islam believed dangerous to colonial hegemony. Discriminatory treatment by the colonial government thus exacerbated basic divergencies of cultural orientation which ultimately expressed themselves in growing suspicion and occasionally violent hostility between the two groups. More significantly still, an increasingly overt competition for the allegiance of the peasantry began to develop, with the prijaji depending on their traditional political and cultural prestige, and the religious leaders on their religious authority. To understand this competition, and the reasons why the prijaji elite in many cases found the peasants turned against them, we must begin with some analysis of peasant-prijaji relationships in traditional, and later, in colonial society.

Peasant and Lord in Traditional Javanese Society

The relationship of the peasantry to the ruling elite contained powerful latently contradictory elements of allegiance and alienation. There was always a wide socio-economic gap between lord and peasant, but they were strongly linked together by various political and cultural institutions. The strongest institutional link in traditional Javanese society was *suwita*, a system of client relations extending throughout society from top to bottom. The essence of this institution was an asymmetrical exchange of services, with the client providing products or labor in return for physical protection, chances for advancement, and enhanced status. The villages supplied the productive base of the state and were protected, at least in theory, by the ruler. Personal services (*tjaos*) to the courts (*kraton*) were performed on the basis of the client relationship. Military duties could also often be subsumed under this rubric. This system of clientship was not confined to the royal court but extended throughout the bureaucratic hierarchy. Every official was a client of his superiors, and at the same time had a group of clients under his own wing. Administrative returns—taxes, labor, services, and the like—were allocated symmetrically according to this proliferating structure. Each official distributed part of the share he received from his patron among his own clients. Thus the hierarchy of the state, and the bureaucracy in particular, was integrated not by formal institutional or organizational means, but by the myriad dyadic linkages of the client system.[33] Since the traditional state had no functionally specialized political and economic organizations separate from these particularized pyramids of patrons and retainers, political relationships were always preponderantly particularist, ascriptive, and diffuse in character.

But what kinds of advantages did the client, whether the lower official or peasant, gain by entering into a client relationship with a patron? In addition to the protection of his patron and to land grants (*sawah gandjaran*), given in return for service, the client expected to receive opportunities for upward mobility, and increased personal power and status.[34]

As a whole, the personalized, particularistic character of the social-political hierarchy undoubtedly helped to prevent too rigid and conspicuous a dichotomy between the ruling prijaji elite and its mass base. The client relationship was an elastic one, permitting some recruitment out of the peasantry into at least the local elite. The client system provided a conception of the state which combined a stable hierarchical order of relationships with fairly wide possibilities for mobility and change within it. The system also prevented too sharp a cultural differentiation of the elite from the mass; the client at each level took his patron as his cultural model, and accordingly a common matrix of values tended to be diffused throughout the society, within the wider framework of abangan culture. The flexibility of the system thus served to maintain a relatively low level of tension and conflict between the peasants and their overlords.

[33] As Lucy Mair has pointed out, client relationships may well be the germ from which state power springs. (Lucy Mair, *Primitive Government* [Baltimore: Penguin Books, 1964], p. 166.) The origins of traditional clientship must be traced back to the very foundation of a new kingdom. (Sartono Kartodirdjo, pp. 34–35.)

[34] These advantages were usually extended to the client's entire family.

In a more general sense, the patron-client relationship was also expressed in the interaction between urban and rural society. There was a continuing, if asymmetrical, exchange of services and commodities between town and countryside: the town had cultural and administrative services to offer, whereas the countryside provided agricultural products and labor.[35] The interaction of urban and rural populations was typically mediated through bonds of clientship and kinship, with the main contacts being sustained through markets and religious festivities.

Yet in spite of these interrelationships, there have always been important areas of tension between the largely urban prijaji and the peasantry. The clearly recognized differences between the urban and the rural ways of life are epitomized in the old saying *Nagara mawa tata, désa mawa tjara,* the city has its order and the village its custom. This dualistic concept, implying, at least in prijaji minds, the superiority of sophisticated urban (court) civilization and the inferiority of peasant culture, provides some justification for the literati's privileged status in society.

Built into prijaji values there is a deep contempt for village life. The term *wong désa* literally means villager but is used by the urban elite to denote an uncivilized person. *Ndésani* (acting in a rustic manner) is used to describe crude and vulgar behavior; its opposite, *mrijajèni* (behaving like a prijaji), implies polished and civilized manners. The synonyms *désa* and *dusun* symbolize limited mental horizons. On the other hand, especially during the colonial period, the term prijaji, no less than *walonda* (Dutch) and *tjina* (Chinese), was used to arouse feelings of contempt among adults and fear among children. The prijaji's privileged position, emphasized by their lordly style of life, conspicuous consumption, specialized speech patterns, and other external status symbols, while largely

---

[35] In actual fact the cultural relationship of village to court has always been a complex one, involving a two-way flow of innovation and imitation. Many types of peasant cultural performances were crude, inexpensive versions of kraton models. On the other hand, it was essentially the villages which supplied the constant stream of talented *dalang* (puppeteers), maskmakers, *gamelan*-players, singers, and batik-designers who actually created and developed court art. Furthermore some kraton art forms, for example, the *topèng* dance-drama, are clearly inspired by village models.

accepted in the precolonial age, now became, as a result of their close collaboration with the foreign colonial government, increasingly detested.

Whatever the pattern of latent allegiance and alienation between lord and peasant, their relatively infrequent contact was a factor which helped to mitigate potential hostility between them. Geertz has pointed out that the prijaji as a cultural elite owed their power ultimately to their control over the central symbolic resources of the society.[36] Yet this stress on cultural hegemony should not be exaggerated or misinterpreted. By and large, peasants were only marginal participants in the traditional political process, at least at the level of the state. Supravillage levels of authority were also by no means the main focus of village attachments; loyalties to kin and locality took priority over any allegiances to the wider political system. Though by no reckoning isolated from the larger society, local peasant communities stubbornly retained their own identity, which was bound up with attachment to the soil and to age-old village cults. Moreover, as we have seen, the central village virtues of cooperation and reciprocal help were prized because they allowed the village community to function as a more or less self-contained unit and were thus without outside referent. Where peasants did participate in the political process, their activities were generally confined to local matters and were neither very articulated nor very extensive. The two primary dimensions of the villager's social identification were membership in a nuclear family and participation in the village community. Usually, neither served as a basis for political mobilization or organization. Only in the case of descendants of the tjikal-bakal does one find kinship groups playing a significant political role in village political life.

The sole supravillage ties of real emotional depth were those linking the peasant to the informal religious leaders. Such ties generally cut across more institutionalized village loyalties and on occasion competed with them. Nonetheless, the wide contacts maintained by some of these charismatic leaders gave them the potentiality of mobilizing their village-oriented peasant clientele into a supravillage type of political activity. In most of the social movements we shall be looking at, the peasants were active on a small scale and strictly

[36] Clifford Geertz, p. 227.

within the confines of their own immediate locality. Only occasionally, when other, wider loyalties, particularly of religious inspiration,
were evoked, could local peasant groupings be integrated into large-
scale political action.

RESISTANCE AND CONFLICT IN THE PROCESS OF SOCIO-CULTURAL CHANGE

Although the impact of Dutch rule on Javanese society was not
felt at once in all its magnitude, from its very beginnings in the
seventeenth century it set in motion fundamental and irreversible
political change. The East India Company worked out a relatively
simple but convenient relationship with the regional Javanese elites
over which it had gained control; while upholding the principle of
minimum interference, the Company employed these native ruling
groups as the key intermediary link in developing the structure of
indirect rule. Given the hierarchical structure of Javanese society,
the top-level authorities were a potential instrument for extracting
products and services from the peasantry. For, although the colonial
government could impose its physical control, it was unable to
establish moral ties with the people. Consequently, the Javanese
elite's mediating role was obviously crucial in securing more or less
voluntary cooperation from the population.

During the nineteenth century, colonial administration was gradually expanded and rationalized in conformity with Western notions
of government. This process involved the imposition upon Javanese
society, particularly upon its prijaji elite, of the Western values and
bureaucratic norms that the Dutch set for themselves. Besides novel
administrative forms, the colonial government introduced new concepts of property, new views of morality, new social roles, and new
sources of status, all of which inevitably worked to weaken the
bonds of the traditional order.

As a consequence, a slow shift from traditional-patrimonial to
rational-legal patterns of authority was effected. The growth of a
body of legal rules delimiting the increasingly specific functions of
the *bupati* (regents) was only the beginning of an intensive bureaucratization which took place throughout the century. An important
step in this development was the differentiation and partial separation of economic from political power. For the bupati were not

only turned into officials of a specific rank, with duties and powers clearly prescribed; they also lost their economic independence when they were put on fixed salaries. Recruitment for office was based more and more on rational-technical qualifications.[37]

Under Westernization, with its concomitant secularization, new, externally imposed patterns of role definition tended to replace the traditional roles of the bupati and their subordinates.[38] The introduction among the prijaji bureaucratic elite of a new prestige order, based on Western performance criteria, successively severed the cultural arteries of the traditional body politic and created a pronounced cultural discrepancy between this elite and the rest of Javanese society. While the increasingly secularized prijaji developed strong allegiance to Western-style institutions, the traditional religious leaders, official and unofficial, remained largely oriented toward tradition.

Secularization opened a clear breach between religious belief and political authority, with the former unable to maintain its dominant influence over the latter. Consequently, segments of the religious elite emerged as the strongest of the forces opposed to Western penetration. We have already noted the conflict between prijaji and religious elites, based on differences of ideology and socio-economic status. The colonial co-optation of the prijaji exacerbated this opposition into open hostility, since the religious elites regarded those who were working as agents of the Dutch with hatred and contempt.[39]

Islamic leaders, whether hadji or kjai, usually enjoyed high social prestige among the rural population. Conversely, white men always, and the prijaji increasingly, were labeled *kafir* (unbelievers), in-

[37] Max Weber, *The Theory of Social and Economic Organization* (Glencoe: Free Press, 1964), pp. 328–336.

[38] See Talcott Parsons, *The Social System* (Glencoe: Free Press, 1951), pp. 180–200. For the implications of this process of modernization, see Bert F. Hoselitz, "Main Concepts in the Analysis of the Social Implications of Technical Change," in Bert F. Hoselitz and Wilbert E. Moore, eds., *Industrialization and Society* (Paris: UNESCO, 1963), pp. 11–29.

[39] Harry J. Benda, *The Cresent and the Rising Sun, Indonesian Islam under the Japanese Occupation, 1942–1945* (The Hague and Bandung: van Hoeve, 1958), p. 16; though non-Islamic religious leaders reacted similarly within their own cosmological tradition, in the following discussion we shall focus on the Islamic leaders because the ideological conflict with the secular Westernized bureaucratic elite was much more sharply pronounced.

herently sinful and deserving the contempt and abhorrence of the *ummat* (the community of Islamic believers).[40] Since most prijaji were afraid of falling foul of the colonial ruler, they carefully avoided any signs of Islamic zeal, a fact which accelerated their estrangement from the rural population.[41] The prijaji were in effect placed in an insoluble dilemma. Two incompatible sets of claims— those of the colonial government and those of the Islamic religion— could not be integrated; the fulfillment of both was impossible. In the face of this choice, the prijaji's instinct for self-preservation impelled them toward the normative structure imposed by the colonial power.

The colonial order, which exerted a massive secularizing impact, was a direct challenge to the fundamental principles upon which Islamic civilization is based. Within the colonial state religious and political roles were sharply separated. Religious leaders were no longer needed to support the authority of the government. Indeed, the spread of secular thinking threatened to undermine the very basis of their authority. Not surprisingly, their reaction was implacable opposition to the changes wrought by the colonial order.

For a better understanding of the political role that the Islamic kjai played in stirring up the peasants' hatred of the colonial rulers and their prijaji agents, we must briefly deal with the changing nature of their leadership and the character of the chief institutional devices for recruiting their following, the *pesantrèn* (rural Islamic schools) and the tarékat.

As a result of the growing impact of Westernization and secularization, the kjai lost much of their political influence and credibility at the elite level of Javanese society. Conversely, they largely displaced that elite in exercising political authority over the peasantry. Popular belief in their supernatural attributes and their magical capacities gave them great charismatic power, particularly in times of distress, when the peasants had no one else to turn to. Their authority was especially great in the peculiarly Islamic institutions of the pesantrèn and the tarékat. A prestigious kjai could recruit young

---

[40] For a good description of anti-*prijaji* sentiment among the *santri*, see Achmad Djajadiningrat, *Herinneringen van Pangeran Aria Achmad Djajadiningrat* (Amsterdam and Batavia: Kolff, 1936), p. 21.
[41] Benda, pp. 16–18; see also Sartono Kartodirdjo, pp. 89–90.

males from a wide variety of villages into his school. The traditional discipline of these pesantrèn demanded total and unquestioning obedience to the teacher on the part of the pupils in return for initiation into esoteric religious lore. A similar discipline was demanded in the tarékat, which indeed had very much the character of secret societies. Both institutions, constituted largely of young unattached males, inculcated an intense internal solidarity, overriding existing kinship ties and local loyalties. Their control over the pesantrèn and tarékat gave the kjai great influence in many areas to which they had no personal access, since their pupils spread their fame and message when they returned home to their native villages. These institutions were also very effective instruments for conducting political agitation, since their closed character permitted intense religious exaltation and hostility toward the prijaji and the foreign rulers to be built up.[42] On occasion, religious enthusiasm could be channeled into violent political action by citing the doctrine of the Holy War, which promised immediate salvation to all those dying in battle against the infidel.

It should now be clear why there was a strong propensity among the rural religious elite to propagate subversive political ideas and to lead radical political movements in which peasants were mobilized through networks of tightly disciplined religious educational institutions. But their success depended in large part on the power of certain sacred symbols associated with the pre-Islamic and Islamic traditions to arouse and sustain peasant hopes of radical changes in their lot.

CHARACTERISTIC FEATURES OF AGRARIAN RADICALISM

Before discussing some historical types of agrarian radicalism in detail, we should first consider four characteristic symbolic or ideological features which can be found in all such movements: millenarianism, messianism, nativism, and belief in the Holy War.

These ideological elements are not sharply distinguishable in the agrarian radicalism of nineteenth- and twentieth-century Java. It is impossible to categorize the peasant uprisings of this period as definitively and exclusively millenarian, messianic, nativist or "Holy War"; almost all were characterized by a typically Javanese syncre-

[42] Djajadiningrat, pp. 21–23; also Benda, pp. 16ff.

tism. Indeed, the coalescence of traditional symbols is so conspicuous as to suggest that the mingling of diverse ideological elements actually strengthened the appeal of these social movements by a process of mutual reinforcement.

We find social movements, for instance, which express a longing for the millennium and expect the coming of a Messiah to bring it about. Others show the development of a millenarianism primarily associated with nativist tendencies. In peasant communities undergoing detraditionalization, the millennium was often envisaged as the restoration of the indigenous traditional order in more or less idealized form. In this reassertion of traditional identity, the linkage of millenarianism and nativism is clear. In other instances, nativist rejection of foreign values, white domination, and externally imposed social change expressed itself ideologically in the call for Holy War. As for the devout Moslems, they could see the Holy War as the gateway to a millennium in which society would be governed by Islamic values once and for all.

Thus, while theoretical distinctions can (and should) be drawn between these symbolic elements, it is far from easy to estimate their relative impact in specific cases, or to demonstrate trends favoring one element over another. Nonetheless, it may be suggested that the history of the social movements of nineteenth- and twentieth-century Java reveals the rising importance of the Holy War idea. We have seen how Westernization and secularization served to alienate many traditional religious leaders, especially the Islamic kjai. Under their influence, traditional millenarianism became more and more associated with the Holy War (*djihad*). The core doctrine of the djihad is the sacred obligation imposed on all pious Moslems to wage war against the unbelievers in order to preserve or extend the Islamic community and restore true religion. An essential element of the idea is that those who die in the Holy War enter paradise directly. Although this faith was clearly in one sense revivalist in character, its millenarian aspects can certainly not be ignored.

In general, one can discern a continuing reworking of the Javanese cultural inheritance in accordance with changing circumstances. Successive social movements shifted the main emphasis within the complex of traditional symbols in the face of new challenges. By the time that Dutch intervention in rural life had become direct and intensive in the late nineteenth century, the Holy War idea with strong millenarian overtones loomed large in the ideology of agrarian radicalism.

In conclusion, then, we must try to avoid explaining the ideology of Javanese social movements in terms of one characteristic alone; each movement shows a blending of traditional symbols, one of which, however, is usually predominant. At the present stage of investigation, the data are far too incomplete to permit the construction of any rigid typology. In the following section, I shall try to discuss millenarianism, messianism, nativism, and the Holy War separately, for analytical purposes, in the hope of providing a rough guide for the overview of historical cases which concludes this essay.

Millenarianism

Several recorded millenary prophecies refer to a Golden Age in which all injustices will be ended and universal harmony will be restored. But this millennium of perfect happiness and peace will be presaged by natural catastrophes, moral decadence, and misery among the people. Inherent in this millenary idea is the expectation that the coming upheaval will bring a settling of scores and a reversal of existing roles; the dominant group (the Dutch) will be driven out and the traditional state and society will be restored.

The idea of a final cataclysm is to be found in several versions of the Javanese messianic tradition, popularly known as the Pralambang Djajabaja (alleged prophecies of a twelfth-century king of Kediri, East Java). The eschatologism evident in these prophecies has unmistakably Islamic origins. One version has it that because of the general laxity in religious life, Djamadjudja will break free from his chains and bring about floods, violent winds, earthquakes, and a universal darkness which will cause great calamity. Djamadjudja will dominate the whole world, except Mecca, Medina, Baitulmukadas, and Egypt. Then Dabatul Arli will rise from the dead and subdue Djamadjudja, thus restoring justice and welfare for the people.[43]

[43] A translation of Javanese eschatological literature is to be found in W. Hoezoo, "Het Javaansche geschrift 'Achiring djaman'," *Mededeelingen van wege het Nederlandsche Zendeling-genootschap* (hereafter *MNZ*), 27 (1883), 1–42. Various versions of this "Achiring djaman" tremendously contributed to the fervent intoxication of the people; see Gobée and Adriaanse, pp. 124–125.

The moral message of the millenarian beliefs is that misery, degradation, and misfortune are punishments for deviations from proper conduct, whether sexual indulgence, laxity in religious practice, conversion (of Moslems) to Christianity, humiliation of people of high rank or noble origin, and so forth.[44] Millenary prophecies also frequently include ominous references to changes taking place under Western domination such as the appearance of horseless carriages, taxation levied on every piece of land, the abandonment of holy places, and the winding of iron hoops around Java.[45] The prophecies almost invariably refer to these changes as signs of a deep underlying malaise.

Since the transformation of the existing situation into the Golden Age was conceived in cataclysmic terms, the faithful who wished to survive the cataclysm were usually warned to adhere strictly to the prescriptions of the leader in undertaking revolutionary action. These prescriptions were usually accompanied by threats of severe punishment for anyone refusing to take part in the movement.[46]

The idea of an apocalyptic cataclysm in itself exerted a powerful psychological hold and instilled a deep sense of urgency and anxiety. When the cataclysm was conceived as imminent, the tensest expectations were aroused among the faithful. It is no wonder that they became totally committed to the cause, and that the millenarian movements they joined had such a radical character. Implicit in the idea of cataclysm was the prediction that only a chosen few would be fortunate or virtuous enough to survive. The leaders of millenarian movements either urged their followers to take elaborate precautions or assured them that loyalty would ensure their salvation. In the Bekasi affair of 1869, to be described later, Bapa Rama referred to a total darkness in which only the faithful would be able to see.[47] Kjai Wirasendjaja of Tambakmerang foretold a great flood

---

[44] Hoezoo; cf. Tjantrik Mataram, *Peranan ramalan Djojobojo dalam revolusi kita* (Bandung: Masa Baru, 1954), pp. 28–31.

[45] Hoezoo; Tjantrik Mataram.

[46] Defection was naturally considered a serious crime, since it endangered the prestige of the leader. For an instance of this, see Sartono Kartodirdjo, p. 199.

[47] See State Archives, The Hague (hereafter SA), Missive of the Resident of Batavia, March 5, 1870, Lª B.B.B., Z.G. (These letters and those occurring in similar citations refer to archival codes.)

and warned that only those in his vicinity would be saved.[48] Aside from correct beliefs and proximity to the leader, the carrying of djimat was commonly believed to be the faithful's best safeguard against various evils.[49]

Lastly, it is of interest to note how the promises contained in many millenarian prophecies were oriented specifically to the common people. The belief that the ideal world envisaged in millennial tradition would be of especial benefit to the common man, was a logical reflection of daily frustrations and material needs.[50] Some typical examples are predictions of "an abundance of food and clothes" (*murah sandang pangan*),[51] an end to crushing taxes and labor services, and an equal distribution of cultivated land.

Messianism

Insofar as the idea of a Messiah implies a Golden Age, most messianic movements tend also to be millennial in character. In large parts of Java, millennial hopes were often focused on messianic leaders. According to age-old popular tradition, the Messiah expected is a king who will establish justice and peace in a land of great abundance. The best-known Javanese messianic myth refers to the appearance of the Ratu Adil, the Righteous King, who will deliver people from illness, famine, and all kinds of evil. During his reign righteousness will prevail. His coming will be preceded by natural disasters, degradation, misery, and suffering. One version of the old Djajabaja prophecies assigns a messianic role to King Tandjung Putih, destined to reign in the year 1700, and to King Erutjakra, whose rule would come to pass in the year 1900.[52] Together with the name of a mythical kingdom Katangga, these names of mythical Kings are found in various other versions of the

[48] A. C. Harjaka Hardjamardjaja, *Javanese Popular Belief in the Coming of Ratu Adil, a Righteous Prince* (Rome: Pontificia Universitas Gregoriana, 1962), p. 34.

[49] Drewes, p. 47.

[50] Some cases of unrest caused by excessive taxation are, for example, the Tjiomas affair (1886), the Banten revolt (1888), the Sidoardjo affair (1904), and the Garut case (1919).

[51] Tjantrik Mataram, pp. 22–23.

[52] See a version of the Djajabaja prophecy in J. J. de Hollander, *Handleiding bij de beoefening der Javaansche Taal- en Letterkunde* (Breda: Koninklijk Militaire Academie, 1848), pp. 173–183; Pigeaud, pp. 155–156.

Djajabaja prophecies. Their popularity in the Javanese millennial tradition goes far back into the past and has remained vivid until recent times.[53]

The last two centuries have witnessed the rise of a number of leaders of millenarian movements who have made conscious use of these legendary names. Many adopted the name of Erutjakra as an indication of their claims to be the Messiah or his messenger.

The first recorded rebel leader to assume the name of Panembahan Erutjakra was Prince Dipanegara, son of Paku Buwana I, during the reign of Amangkurat IV (1719–1727). It was prophesied that he would have his residence in Katangga, while extending his sway east of Mt. Prahu, south of Mt. Semeru, and west of Mt. Sampora, dominating Java, Madura, Patani, and Palembang.[54]

About one hundred years later, another, better known Prince Dipanegara also adopted the name Erutjakra. In his autobiography he claimed to be the recipient of a divine revelation from the Ratu Adil himself, who appeared to him at the top of Mt. Rasamuni. The mission he was given was to lead the reconquest of the island of Java from the hands of the Dutch.[55]

A third such leader, Mangkuwidjaja, appeared in Klaten, Central Java, in 1865.[56] An important element in his ability to attract followers was the belief in the imminent coming of Tandjung Putih, who would reside in Prambanan, while all foreigners would be killed. Over the space of four years Mangkuwidjaja's movement gained a wide following, spreading as far as Tegal and Pekalongan on Java's north coast. When he was arrested, manuscripts were found in his possession containing Djajabaja prophecies, originating, some would have us believe, from one of the children of Kjai Madja, the great ally of the second Prince Dipanegara. A certain R. M. Mohamad,

---

[53] For the oldest historical case on record with millenarian undertones, see Brandes, "Iets over een ouderen Dipanegara in verband met een prototype van de voorspellingen van Jayabaya," *TBG*, 32 (1889), 265–430; one of the more recent cases of millenarian movements is the Erutjakra movement subdued by the government in April 1967.

[54] Drewes, pp. 186–187; cf. Brandes, pp. 386–387.

[55] *Serat Babad Dipanegaran* (Surakarta: Rusche, 1917), pp. 98–100.

[56] L. E. Gerdessen, "De Zamenzwering in de Vorstenlanden," *Tijdschrift voor Nederlandsch Indië* (hereafter *TNI*), 1871, no. 2, p. 207; cf. SA *Verbaal* (minutes, filed by date and number), Oct. 18, 1865, E[15] *Kabinet* (minutes of cabinet sessions, filed by date and number, and also by a special code).

held by the movement to be the coming Messiah-King, adopted the name of Erutjakra.[57]

Messianic movements of a similar character can be reported from many regions of Java.[58] Sometimes the leader himself claimed to be the Ratu Adil—for example, Djasmani of Sengkrong (who adopted the name of Sultan Adil or Sunan Erutjakra), Sokadrana of Nanggulan, Jogjakarta,[59] and Imansudjana of Kenda, Surakarta. In other instances the leader merely claimed the role of divine messenger, as was the case with Malangjuda and Dulmadjid, while an intimate adherent of the movement or a person of noble birth assumed the role of Ratu Adil. Occasionally this role was imposed upon the leader by his disciples, as was the case with Kjai Tambakmerang.[60]

The coming kingdom of the Ratu Adil was almost always localized in a forest north of Madiun named Katangga. Thus, if an account of a social movement contains frequent references to Katangga or, as sometimes happens, of a pilgrimage to the forest, the movement almost certainly had messianic tendencies. Here we have in mind the visits of Sumasari Adikusuma, an adherent of Malangjuda, and of Imam Redja, the leader of the Srikaton movement, to the center of the mythical kingdom. Kramasedja, the self-proclaimed Ratu Adil of Srandakan (Jogjakarta), preached that his kingdom was descended from Katangga.[61]

Characteristically, the Javanese messianic prophecies recorded in various versions of the Djajabaja legends, although fundamentally

[57] Gerdessen. This prince seems to play an important role in the millenarian expectations of the people in Jogjakarta; see also the Ratu Adil movement led by Dulmadjid in 1889. For the disturbances around R. M. Mohamad, see *Babad Surjengalagan* (MS., Sanabudaja, Jogjakarta).

[58] Examples of such movements are the Imansudjana movement, the Achmad Suhada movement, and the Srikaton affair. See respectively: SA Missive of the Resident of Surakarta, Oct. 11, 1886, no. 32, in *Mailrapport* (copies of letters, reports, decisions of colonial authorities sent to Minister of Colonies, filed by year and number), 1886, no. 664; SA *Oost-Indisch Besluit*, May 10, 1890, no. 26; SA Report of the Resident of Surakarta of Nov. 1888, no. 1; also "Officieel relaas van de ongeregelheden in Solo," *De Indische Gids* (hereafter *IG*), 1889, no. 1, pp. 216–221; *ibid.*, 1889, no. 2, pp. 1768–1776.

[59] SA *Mailrapport* 1878, no. 452; SA Cable of the Resident of Jogjakarta, July 1, 1878, no. 68.

[60] Harjaka Hardjamardjaja, pp. 33ff.   [61] *Boedi Oetomo*, Aug. 5, 1924.

non-Islamic in character, include striking elements of Islamic eschatology. The Serat Djajabaja [62] predicted that in the year 2100 the *Kiamat Kubra* (Doomsday) would occur, marked by a great war initiated by Djamadjudja's attack on Arabia. The Imam Mahdi would then arise and, assisted by Umarmaja and Mohamad Hanafiah, would defeat the great usurper. According to another version of the same Djajabaja prophecies, the *Achiring Djaman,*[63] it was Dabatul Arli who would finally subdue Djamadjudja.

This kind of incomplete ideologic syncretism typifies many millennial movements. The Javanese messianic tradition which has come down to us through various records apparently absorbed the Imam Mahdi figure of the Arabic messianic traditions, without, however, identifying it with the Ratu Adil. One should note, too, the strikingly similar characteristics ascribed to both the premillennial period and the millennium, envisaged here as an age in which Islamic law will be enforced. The chronological structure of the prophecy reflects this incomplete assimilation, since the coming of Imam Mahdi is put after that of the Ratu Adil, to maintain the essence of Islamic eschatology. The millennium of the Ratu Adil's reign is thus denied any meta-historical status.

Although Islamic ideological elements plainly have been incorporated into the Javanese messianic tradition, specific information on the appearance of Mahdism in peasant uprisings is very rare. The best-known recorded instance occurred in Banten during the Tjilegon rebellion of 1888.[64] In this case the strongly Islamic culture of Banten must be taken into consideration. Through the adoption of Mahdist symbols, rural leaders enhanced the religious fervor of an already strongly devout population. In Central and East Java, where the peasants were and are less ardently committed to Islam, few Mahdist expectations can be reported, although in other respects as we shall see, Moslem traditions exerted conspicuous influence on older Javanese millenarian beliefs.[65]

[62] De Hollander, p. 173.

[63] Hoezoo; Pigeaud, pp. 97–98; see also Gobée and Adriaanse, pp. 1896–1912.

[64] Sartono Kartodirdjo, pp. 166–167.

[65] The Islamic elements, both eschatological and messianic, are quite conspicuous in various versions of the Djajabaja prophecies; for an analysis of these elements, see Sartono Kartodirdjo, *Tjatatan tentang segi-segi messianistis*

Nativism

Whereas millenarian and messianic beliefs were important in Javanese culture from very early times, the phenomenon of nativism clearly emerged only in the later colonial period as a specific reaction to alien white rule. The severe threat to the Javanese sense of identity posed by an increasingly heavy foreign political and cultural hegemony produced a powerful reaction in peasant society, expressed in an intense longing for a restoration of an idealized traditional order. The demand for a restoration of traditional values and ways of life was almost invariably coupled with violent hatred of the foreigners, who were blamed for all existing misery and degradation. Where nativist symbols dominated agrarian radical ideology, one finds typically that adoptions from foreign culture were denounced as sinful and polluting. More important still, Javanese officials employed in the Dutch colonial bureaucracy were regarded as decadent traitors who should be overthrown and punished. During periods of social disturbance, fierce verbal and physical attacks were launched on the native bureaucratic elite. The Tjilegon revolt and the Tjimareme affair speak volumes for this anti-prijaji sentiment.[66]

Nativist hopes typically envisaged the coming of a society from which white men would be expelled and in which their native allies would be overthrown. In 1843 an upheaval occurred in Kedu, Central Java, led by Achmad Daris, who adopted old royal titles and announced that the time had come to drive out all existing authorities.[67] The Mangkuwidjaja movement in 1865 aimed at wiping out all foreigners and destroying the Dutch-controlled principalities of Jogjakarta and Surakarta.[68] Kjai Nurhakim also intended to destroy the Europeans and collaborating native chiefs. He proclaimed himself king, assumed the name of Sultan Imam Mahdi, and announced that his residence would be established on Mt. Tidar near Magelang.[69] These examples show clearly that nativist aims included not

---

dalam Sedjarah Indonesia (Jogjakarta: Universitas Gadjah Mada, 1959). Cf. Gobée and Adriaanse, pp. 1222–1225.

[66] Sartono Kartodirdjo (1959), *passim*. For the Tjimareme affair, see *Het Vrije Woord*, no. 9 (1919), pp. 66–67.

[67] National Archives, Djakarta (hereafter NA), *Besluit*, no. 6, March 26, 1843.

[68] Gerdessen.   [69] Drewes, p. 47.

only the violent destruction of foreign rule but also of the existing Javanese ruling class.

Nativist social movements often expressed their desire for a revival of the precolonial order by proclaiming the return of an ancient kingdom or the establishment of a new dynasty. For a century and a half now, people in Banten have been periodically stirred by hopes for a restoration of the great realm of their long-vanished sultans.[70] In the Priangan region popular tradition maintains the dream of a return of the reign of Ratu Sunda.[71] Sometimes the leaders of social movements envisaged the founding not merely of one, but also of two or even three new kingdoms. In the case of the Nji Atjiah movement,[72] the story went round that two realms would be established, the kingdom of Sunda at Tegalluwar and the kingdom of Keling at Bandjar. In the Malangjuda affair, each of three prominent adherents was to be proclaimed king: Ipo in West Java, Sumasari in Central Java, and Santri in East Java.[73]

Nativism added a strong political element to existing millenarian beliefs, by attributing suffering and degradation specifically to foreign and collaborationist rule and to the corruption of traditional values and moral standards resulting from it. Nativism also tended to turn traditional millenarianism into politically revolutionary directions, by associating the Golden Age with the expulsion of the colonial rulers and their allies. This politicization of traditional millenarianism gained further momentum with the inculcation of the Holy War idea.

[70] Special reference should be made to the Njai Gumpara and Njai Perbata movements of South Banten in the thirties, aiming at the restoration of the sultanate; see SA *Political Report: 1839–1849*, in *Exhibitum* (incoming correspondence of the Ministry of Colonies, filed by date and number; hereafter *Exh.*), Jan. 31, 1851, no. 27 *bis*. In view of the latent hope among the people of Banten for a restoration of their sultanate, shortly before the outbreak of World War II the Dutch government approached a prominent member of an eminent family from Banten about becoming sultan of Banten; interview with Professor G. F. Pijper in Feb. 1966.

[71] For historical instances of the Ratu Sunda movement, e.g., in 1831, 1832, 1841, 1853, and 1863, see SA Missive of the Resident of Priangan, Dec. 20, 1871, L^a A^5, *Geh.*; for a more recent instance, see "Ratu Sunda," in *Weekblad voor Indië*, 2 (1905–1906), 22.

[72] SA Missive of the Resident of Priangan, Dec. 20, 1871, L^a A^5, *Geh.* in *Verbaal*, Jan. 30, 1873, no. 33.

[73] Drewes, p. 32.

The Holy War Idea

In nineteenth- and twentieth-century Java, millenarian and djihad or *perang sabil* (Holy War) movements have been closely linked, and have reinforced each other to produce an increasingly militant radicalism. Thus the growing popularity of the Holy War in part can be attributed to its absorption into many popular versions of the Djajabaja prophecies. One version, for instance, foretold that in the year 1970 of the Javanese calendar a great perang sabil would be waged against the white race. The *tjaping* (Javanese word for pointed hat; here, it refers to the Chinese) would be borne downstream. The river Tuntang would be stained red with blood. The Javanese would regain control of their own government, but only for a short period, for a king of the yellow race would reign over Java. According to the same version, the perang sabil would be preceded by the following omens: a thread being wound around the earth (the telegraph); people being able to talk to one another at great distance (the telephone); wagons being driven without horses (trains); and distances becoming unimportant (airplanes). During the year 2074, Java would be devastated by volcanic eruptions; part of it would sink into the sea, and the rest would break up into nine islands. Finally the *hari kiamat* (Doomsday) would dawn.

Although millennial hopes were rarely voiced in Islamic terms as such, their attainment via the expulsion or destruction of the white rulers was frequently conceptualized and justified in an Islamic framework, in other words in terms of the Holy War. The leading part played by the kjai and hadji in most social movements of the time certainly contributed largely to this development. In their hands the perang sabil idea became a powerful weapon for opposing the Dutch, since it made a strong appeal to all Moslems to unite in defense of their religion. Even the relatively low commitment of the abangan peasant to Islam was enough, given the identification of Javanese-Dutch hostility with antagonism between Moslem and infidel through the idea of the Holy War, to rally many of them behind the kjai. Accordingly, religious enthusiasm for the djihad was inseparable from violent hatred against foreign rulers and against prijaji officials, who were alleged to have dishonored their religion by cooperating with the infidel.

Apart from earlier great wars led by kings and princes under the banner of Islam, [74] from the 1840's onwards, zealous preachers intermittently instigated hostility against foreign and kafir rulers. One could mention here the movement led by Baudjaja of Semarang in 1841, the Achmad Daris affair of Kedu in 1843, and the Hadji Djenal Ngarip affair of Kudus in 1847, all of which aimed at exterminating the Europeans. It may be recalled that the Tjikandi Udik affair in 1845 was strongly antiwhite in purpose. [75]

Similar movements occurred in other parts of the island, notably the Tjiomas affair (1886), the Tjilegon rebellion (1888), the Gedangan affair (1904), the incident of Pak Djebrak in Brangkal (1919), and the Hadji Hasan affair of Tjimareme (1919). Each of these movements proclaimed the perang sabil and was directed against the infidel rulers and their native collaborators. The history of some of these movements, however, for example, the Tjilegon uprising and the Gedangan affair, shows that perang sabil agitation served to channel a wide range of hostilities and grievances into insurrectionary activity. Like the nativist conceptions, the idea of the Holy War not only increased the peasants' awareness of their position under alien (infidel) rule, but accelerated the development of millenarian movements in politically radical directions. [76]

---

[74] E.g., the Trunadjaja rebellion (1676–1678); the Surapati revolt (1686–1706); the "Pakepung" war (1792), and the Dipanegara war (1825–1830). See Vlekke, p. 182; *Babad Pakepung* (MS., Sanabudaja, Jogjakarta) and *Babad Dipanegara* (MS., Sanabudaja).

[75] For an extensive account of this case (Tjikandi Udik affair), see "De Opstand en Moord van Tjikandi Oedik in 1845," *TNI*, 1859, no. 1, pp. 139–168; see also NA *Besluit*, April 21, 1841, no. 3; NA *Besluit*, March 26, 1843, no. 6; NA *Besluit*, Dec. 20, 1847, no. 5.

[76] In addition to dealing with resurgent native kingdoms and the Holy War, some Javanese prophecies treated the problem of Dutch domination in positive ways. According to a version of the Babad Padjadjaran, Brawidjaja predicted that after defeat by the Moslems, the power of Madjapahit would be restored through seafaring merchants who would settle in Djakarta. This prediction unmistakably refers to the Dutch. Another prophecy, attributed to Sjeh Lemah Abang, foretold that "people with white skin and blue eyes will come to Java; the people will be sifted like rice and they will not till the fields voluntarily; there will be a time of prosperity, righteousness and order." Sjeh Bela-Belu's predictions also referred to the rule of people with white skins and blue eyes. One of the versions of the Djajabaja prophecies also makes mention of the coming of merchants from abroad, who would settle down, wage war, and finally rule the country. Then there would be

SOME HISTORICAL CASES

I propose now to discuss certain manifestations of agrarian radicalism recorded in various parts of Java, showing not only their common features, but the relationship of their ideological expressions
to the particular subcultural setting and the period in which each
movement took place. Regrettably, great gaps in our information
preclude a full comparative analysis.

These movements can be divided into three broadly defined
groups. The first includes agrarian uprisings in which particular,
local socio-economic grievances assumed prime ideological importance, because the social environment in which they took place
provided little in the way of a cultural tradition through which
protest could be given a more inclusive religious or political content.

The second group covers cases in which social and economic
grievances can still be detected but are largely subsumed within
the terms of religious revivalism or puritanical Islamic reformism.

In the third group of cases, concrete particularistic grievances are
quite difficult to locate. In these more politicized social movements,
the ideology of protest is overwhelmingly millenarian, messianic,
nativist, or "Holy War," according to the social and cultural environment in which they arise.

This division may be vulnerable to the charge of arbitrariness.
What limited advantages it has are: first, it avoids the immensely
difficult tasks of determining the complex *causation* of the particular
social movements and of classifying them in terms of such causation;
second, it provides a simple (perhaps overly simple) approach to
the problem of linking political action and cultural tradition, by
focusing on the way local cultural traditions contribute to determin-

---

no evildoers any more. (See J. Kreemer, "Onze heerschappij over Java en
de aloude Javaansche profetieen," *MNZ*, 35 [1891], 101–108.)

It is remarkable that in these cases Dutch domination is shown in a favorable light and no hostility is expressed toward the Dutch. This contrasts
sharply with the so-called Baron Sakendar story in which both the inferiority
of the Dutch in Mataram's eyes and latent but significant popular hostility
toward the Dutch are clearly revealed. (Cf. J. M. van der Kroef, "Javanese
Messianic Expectations: Their Origin and Cultural Context," *CSSH*, 1, no.
4 [1959], 309–310.) These legends can thus be regarded as devices either for
rationalizing or legitimizing foreign domination of Java.

ing the goals and clienteles of agrarian radicalism. The groupings, nonetheless, are highly tentative, and one should bear in mind that a classification into only a few types obscures a view of the whole spectrum of these movements.

Into the first group falls the so-called Bekasi insurrection in West Java (1869).[77] The movement started at the beginning of 1868 in the village of Rawabangke in the district of Bekasi. The story goes that a certain Arpan, the son of Hadji Arsad, discovered that his forefathers had a claim to the area of Pamingkis. As evidence of this claim, Arpan referred to a copperplate in the possession of Ambu Maria in Tjipamingkis. Arpan later happened to meet a certain Bapa Rama of Leuwi Tjatang, who also laid claim to the land, alleging that it had originally belonged to his ancestors. The two men agreed to share the land between them. To give weight to their claim, they called in the assistance of the well-known painter Raden Saleh, through the mediation of a certain Bapa Kollet. It turned out, however, that the copperplate had nothing to do with the land they claimed. Thereafter Arpan dropped out of the picture, while Bapa Rama and Bapa Kollet worked closely together to enforce the former's claim. For this purpose, they made a journey to Surakarta to meet Raden Saleh himself, and also to receive a gold medal—as they put it—from the *radja* of that city. The story of their visit to Surakarta was widely circulated among the local peasantry and much enhanced their prestige.

In the meantime they met a certain Djungkat Bapa Nata of Karang Tjongak in the district of Bekasi. Although he was over seventy, his memory was still excellent, and he easily recalled the events of forty years before, including the original opening up of the land in Tambun, Karang Tjongak, and Gabus. His recollections appeared to reinforce Bapa Rama's claims. By the end of 1868, Bapa Rama and Bapa Kollet had gathered a considerable number of followers who believed and proclaimed that the land between the rivers Tjitarum and Tjidani belonged by right to these two men and that the government's lease of this land had already run out.

[77] See Report of the Assistant Resident of Meester Cornelis, in his SA Missive of Sept. 15, 1869, no. 1464; see also Report of the Resident of Batavia, in his Missive of Sept. 25, 1869, no. 5, SA in *Exh.*, May 30, 1871, no. 34.

Frequent meetings were held to discuss what to do about the claim. The people who gathered for these meetings, the most prominent of whom were Bapa Rama, Bapa Kollet, Dris, Bapa Nata, Aleng, Raden Mustafa, Bapa Basirun, and Bapa Tunda, finally agreed that the land should be taken back from the government. Meanwhile, the number of their followers continued to increase and the time for decision drew closer.

On March 14, 1869, a *sedekah* (religious feast) was held in Ratu Djaja, attended by about five hundred men. After a wedding celebration at which a *wajang* (shadow play) was performed and a musical band from Krawang added lustre, Bapa Rama was proclaimed leader of the movement and assumed the name of Pangeran Alibasa. The group decided that Bapa Tunda would lead the movement in Gedong Gedeh, Bapa Nata in Tjikarang, Dris and Bapa Selan in Tambun, Bapa Basirun and Raden Mustafa in Teluk Putjang, Arsain and Bungsu in Bogor, and Bapa Kollet in Depok. Two days later, another sedekah was held in Bapa Rama's home, where further important decisions were taken. The group attending solemnly pledged to take back the land between the rivers Tjitarum and Tjidani by force. All adherents to the movement were promised exemption from compulsory services (*kerdja kumpeni*) and taxes (*tjukai*). The plan was not to be revealed to outsiders, and djimat were distributed among the followers. Titles were granted to other prominent leaders: Pangeran to Bapa Tunda and Bapa Selan, and Raden to the others. These men were led to believe that they possessed supernatural powers which would enable them to put people to death simply by pointing at them. Anyone who dared to turn informer would be punished in this way. Bapa Rama prophesied that total darkness would cover the earth for seven days; the government's soldiers would not be able to see the faithful, although the faithful could see them.

It was decided to make simultaneous assaults on the towns of Tambun, Bogor, and Depok. The main insurgents would attack Tambun, set free any prisoners held there, and head for Bekasi. From there they would proceed through Teluk Putjang to Meester Cornelis (Djatinegara) where they would wait for the other rebel groups from Bogor and Depok, headed by Bungsu, Arsain, and

Bapa Kollet. Then they would all head straight for Batavia and overrun the city.

The week preceding the outbreak of the revolt was a period of intense activity during which secret meetings were held and last-minute arrangements made. As we shall see, only the assault on Tambun could actually be carried out, since prior word of the mustering of people began to reach the authorities in Bekasi, who passed it on to Batavia. Alarmed by these reports, the Assistant Resident of Meester Cornelis, accompanied by the local *djaksa* (prosecutor), the local chief of police, and a police squad, hurried off to Tambun to head off the insurgents.

Meanwhile, a large rebel band about one hundred strong, led by Bapa Selan, Bapa Tunda, and Raden Mustafa, proceeded toward Tambun. During a halt at Kali Djali to get something to eat and drink, Bapa Selan said prayers and burned incense to strengthen the spirit of his men. At the head of the procession walked Bapa Selan, Dris, and Raden Mustafa, swords in hand, while two men blew trumpets. Bapa Tunda brought up the rear, keeping an eye on stragglers. On reaching their destination, they learned that the frightened Assistant Resident and his following had taken refuge in the country-house of Tambun and barricaded the entrance with five carts.

The band immediately marched on the house, encircled the barricade and raised the battle-cry: "Madju" (Onward), "Bunuh" (Kill). The local *kampung* guards ran for their lives. While Bapa Selan, Raden Mustafa, and Bapa Tunda guarded the gateway, the main body of the insurgents launched their assault on the house. A police sergeant tried to force his way out through the band but was driven back and fatally wounded. The Assistant Resident was also attacked; mortally injured, he was taken out to die in a *tjabé* (hot pepper) garden nearby. Thereafter, the rest of his entourage, including a *dokter djawa* (native physician) and the *tjentèng* (watchman) of the house, attempted to escape but were caught and slaughtered. Only the djaksa succeeded in eluding death by changing his clothes and passing as a commoner. After their victory, the rebels set the house on fire and marched off in the direction of Bekasi. On the way they met a trader heading for Krawang who told them that military forces were moving in the direction of Teluk Putjang, Gedong Gedeh, and Karang Tjongak. After setting fire to a rice-barn, the band veered toward Kali Abang. The alarmed village mobilized about sixty men in its defense, but these people were eventually forced to join the insurgent movement.

With the prospect of an imminent confrontation with the government's military arm, dissension arose among the leaders. Bapa Delang called on the whole population to resist the government troops; Bapa Selan commanded only the members of his own band to defend themselves against the army; Bapa Tunda, however, abandoned his men and ran for his life.

The eventual encounter with the army at Kali Abang did not end in bloodshed because most of the rebels were disinclined to fight and simply surrendered. During the next few weeks the fleeing rebel leaders were captured one by one and the movement died out.

The official report on the affair makes it clear that the peasants who took part in the revolt were protesting very real local grievances. Bapa Bairah, one of the big landlords in the area, was believed to have exploited the peasants mercilessly by lending out paddy at exorbitant interest rates, at times amounting to over 50 per cent. He was also suspected of having bought up stolen water buffaloes from Krawang and the vicinity of Batavia.[78] Both the leaders and the rank-and-file of the movement, on the other hand, were ordinary peasants, either small farmers or agricultural laborers.

What is most notable about the Bekasi affair is its relative barrenness of millenarian, nativist, or other ideological motifs. The peasants involved reacted to specific injustices in a highly specific way. In part this can perhaps be attributed to the diverse origins of its leaders—some, like Bapa Rama and Bapa Kollet, came from Tjirebon and others came from the Priangan. These regions represent very different traditions, the Priangan being the inland heart of Sundanese society, while Tjirebon forms a special culture area as the seat of the oldest sultanate in Java, with its own idiosyncratic language and ancient Islamic *pasisir* (coastal areas) tradition. Possibly diversity of cultural background made it difficult to draw on complex ideological motifs. But one can also suggest that the protest was concrete and specific in character because Bekasi, like Tanggerang,

[78] Report of the Assistant Resident of Meester Cornelis.

Tjiomas, and Tjililitan, lay within the area of the so-called *particu-liere landerijen*, in which oppression of the peasantry was more gross and notorious than anywhere else in Java. These particuliere landerijen were huge private estates whose owners were granted virtually feudal rights over their tenants, including the privilege of exacting private taxes and heavy compulsory labor services. The colonial government rarely interfered in the internal affairs of the estates, thus permitting the most outrageous abuses to continue for long periods without remedy.

With these factors in mind, we should not be surprised that many features of the Bekasi uprising reappeared in the Tanggerang affair of 1924.[79] Once again claims were laid to land alleged to belong to the leaders' forefathers; the belief was spread that momentous events would be preceded by a period of total darkness; and the top leaders were credited with supernatural powers. The main difference lay in the fact that, in legitimizing his cause, Kjai Bapa Kajah of Tangger-ang was more sophisticated than his predecessors in Bekasi. For ex-ample, he appealed to Sundanese nativism by evoking the legend of Prabu Siliwangi.

In the incident of Tjiomas, an area of leased land near Bogor, we know that one rebel leader named Apan claimed the role of Imam Mahdi and raised the battle-cry of the Holy War, "Sabilillah." [80] Another of the rebel chiefs, Mohamad Idris, adopted the title of Panembahan, which we have seen as a typical sign of messianic tendencies in Javanese social movements. Yet the participants in the Tjiomas incident of 1886 gave two very concrete reasons for their actions: that existing conditions "hanja bikin mati orang ketjil" (destroy the little man) and "sebab hati sudah terlalu panas djadi seberang sadja" (because we were so enraged we simply attacked). There is little indication here that scattered millenarian motifs effectively synthesized particular, bitterly felt acts of exploitation. Nor apparently were these grievances incorporated into any general-ized attack on colonial rule.

A similar protest movement, again in the area of the particuliere

[79] For the data on this movement, see "Rapport over de Tangerangsche Ratu Adil" of March 1924 (MS., Sanabudaja, Jogjakarta).

[80] See Report of the Assistant Resident of Buitenzorg in his SA Missive, June 26, 1886, L⁰ V.; see also SA *Kab.*, Sept. 9, 1886, L⁰ A¹⁰.

landerijen was the rebellion led by Entong Gendut at Tandjung Oost (Tjililitan) in 1916.[81] As in the Tjiomas affair, the local peasants were enraged by the ferocity of a landlord whose excessive exactions had left many of them homeless. Again a number of features, such as the use of djimat, and collective prayers at the mosque, gave the movement a marginal religious tinge.

In the second group of cases, we find protest being generalized from specific economic grievances into a broader critique of cultural and moral decline, framed in terms of religious revivalism and a return to strict observance of orthodox teaching. Although movements of this type can be found as early as the eighteenth century, they still appeared as late as the first quarter of the twentieth. Perhaps the most illustrative example is the case of Hadji Rifangi.

Hadji Rifangi of Kalisalak inaugurated his puritanical Moslem revivalist movement in the strongly santri Pekalongan area in the 1870's.[82] Unlike the other radical leaders we have discussed, Hadji Rifangi aimed at the regeneration of society by fighting against internal decay and abuses of Islamic law. In his intense desire for a Moslem revival, strong millenary elements are evident, for he was convinced that the restoration of the pristine purity of Islam would bring about a just and prosperous society in Java. Hadji Rifangi began his movement by attacking "sinful" native chiefs, such as the bupati, demang (middle-ranking Javanese official), and lurah, whom he accused of drifting into worldly secularism and wallowing in vices of every kind. He criticized their cooperation with the infidels, their indulgence in forbidden worldly pleasures such as gambling and unlimited polygamy, their mistreatment of underlings, and their laxity in religious practice. He insisted that such chiefs be rejected by the people and went so far as to forbid his followers to obey them. At the same time, he also urged all such chiefs to seek continuing guidance on religious matters from the envoys of the

[81] See "De Opstootjes boven Meester Cornelis" in Weekblad voor Indië (1916), pp. 390–394; see also Java Bode, April 10 and 11, 1916; for documentary sources, see Ministry of Overseas Affairs, The Hague (hereafter MOA), Verbaal, April 28, 1916, no. 39.

[82] On the Rifangi movement, see SA missives of July 15, 1859, no. 37; of Nov. 13, 1858, Lᵃ, K, ZG; also of May 7, 1859, Lᵃ, N. For an account from the Javanese side, see K. R. A. P. Soerjokoesoemo's writing on a theological debate between Hadji Rifangi and the Penghulu of Batang, Serat Tjabolèk (Semarang: van Dorp, 1885).

Prophet. While Hadji Rifangi's teachings, as expounded in his book *Nilam Wikajah,* were primarily religious and revivalist in character, it is interesting that they evidently included some reference to the Holy War idea.[83]

The specific character of Rifangi's teachings cannot be separated from the cultural environment in which the revivalist leader appeared. Pekalongan has long been one of the most important centers of the santri community. Like other cities of the north coast (pasisir) of Java, Pekalongan forms part of the santri belt, with a tradition of antagonism toward the abangan villages and aristocratic ruling class of the interior. In such an environment, the symbols of the Just King and the revival of Old Javanese (read abangan) values would have relatively little appeal.

The third group of cases shows the development of a more politicized type of agrarian protest, in the sense that specific peasant grievances and a deeper cultural malaise are given a wider frame of reference through the increasing tendency to utilize the complex of messianic, nativist, and Holy War traditions as the ideological focus of resistance. All these traditions incorporate clear political elements—the creation of an ideal social order, the appearance of a just ruler, and the declaration of war against infidel and alien hegemony. Some of the early cases in which this process of generalization is still only rudimentary could perhaps more properly be assigned to our first group. Nonetheless it seems fruitful to place them here to try to establish a sort of genealogy of the growth of a political ideology of protest out of age-old traditional beliefs.

During the second half of the nineteenth century, when these movements arose, wholesale changes were occurring in colonial policy and law on landholding, which had a deep impact on peasant life. Their main effects were to break up communal land, make rural taxation increasingly an individual burden, and open the way for landlordism in the villages. Some of the social movements of the time responded to these conditions with hopes or demands for the general abolition of taxes and the equitable redistribution of arable land. What is notable, however, is that, by contrast with earlier

[83] A translation of the text by Cohen Stuart is included in SA *Verbaal,* July 15, 1859, no. 37. For Hadji Rifangi's works, see Pigeaud, pp. 95–96; Gobée and Adriaanse, pp. 1930–1943.

cases, these demands are generalized and placed in the context of a millenarian program. The political change involved in moving from demands for specific redress to demands for a total change in social and economic conditions is highly significant.

In the movement led by Kjai Nurhakim,[84] *badal* (envoys) were instructed to spread the word that the advent of the Ratu Adil was to be preceded by a week-long eclipse of the sun and moon; water in the rivers would run red for three days; and a plague would cause much sudden death. Kjai Nurhakim would then be proclaimed king, assume the name of Sultan Imam Mahdi, and reside on Mt. Tidar. Europeans and native chiefs would be destroyed. There would be only one religion. Land taxes would not exceed one *reaal* (silver coin) per *djung* and land would be divided equally.

The Malangjuda movement showed many similar features. Its leader, Malangjuda, acquired considerable prestige on the basis of his claim to the position of Demang of Pakiringan, justified by his alleged lineal descent from Makdum Wali Perkosa, a revered local kramat whose grave was located in the region.[85] His visit to Katangga may be regarded as an indication of messianic intentions, an indication confirmed by his subsequent promise to set up three kingdoms in Java, when the Prophet revealed to him the proper time for so doing. Malangjuda promised his four village-chief adherents that the Tjahjana region would be divided equally among them, and that sufficient land would be granted to the faithful to enable them to live in peace and prosperity.[86] He is also reported to have insisted on a strict and literal observation of the precepts of Islam and a restoration of religious discipline. More generally, the Malangjuda movement was openly hostile to the infidels, preached the Holy War, and aimed at overthrowing, or, as its followers put it, *bikin hilang* (eliminating) or *bikin bersih* (purifying) the government.[87]

In the late 1870's, distinctly anti-European features developed in

[84] Drewes, pp. 46–47.

[85] On the holy graves of Gunung Lawet, see Drewes, pp. 19ff.; see also van Dapperen; also *Babad Djambukarang* (Jogjakarta: Soemowidjojo Mahadewa, 1953).

[86] In this case, the charismatic leader's appeal was strengthened by popular resentment at the exploitation practiced by chiefs of the local *perdikan* (tax-free) villages.

[87] Drewes, p. 32.

agrarian radicalism, as exemplified by the movement led by Amat Ngisa and Djumadilkobra.[88] Djumadilkobra himself, originally a certain Hasan Achmad, was a powerful charismatic leader, who proclaimed to his followers that during a visit to the holy graves on Mt. Lawet he had received a message that Erutjakra would soon appear at the head of an army of demons and poisonous animals.[89] This army would attack the whites and drive them from the land. Three rulers would then arise, one from Madjapahit, another from Padjadjaran, and the third from Kalisalak (Pekalongan). His associate, Amat Ngisa, meanwhile preached repentance and ordered *slametan* (ritual meals) to be held. The faithful were required to wear djimat consisting of pieces of the clothes of Djumadilkobra. The movement gradually assumed ominous forms, and at several meetings predictions were uttered, prophesying an insurrection which would break out all over Java. Many people from Tjilatjap, Kedu, Semarang, and Jogjakarta were affected by Djumadilkobra's teachings and joined the movement, among them lower level officials and even some noblemen. Alarmed by these rumors of an impending uprising, local government authorities stepped in and put an end to the whole affair.

In the messianic movements that sprang up among the peasantry of the southern part of East Java, one finds similar melanges of basic pre-Islamic beliefs and Islamic motifs, most of them with a strongly political character. Two movements typical of the area were those of Djasmani of Blitar and of Achmad Suhada of Ponorogo, both of which appeared in 1888.

Djasmani was a renowned religious teacher and healer (dukun), believed to possess the power of fulfilling wishes for such things as good harvests, riches, and children.[90] On one occasion, at a large gathering at the house of his own guru, Amat Mukiar, Djasmani prophesied the imminent ousting of foreign rulers, of the Chinese, and of the native civil servants; the return to one religion; and the coming of the kingdom of Sultan Adil which would be established at Birawa in the district of Lodojo (Blitar) at the end of the

[88] On the Kobra movement, see SA Missive of the Resident of Pekalongan, Aug. 21, 1871, no. 4081, *Geh.*

[89] On the Amat Ngisa movement, see SA *Verbaal*, March 25, 1872, no. 52.

[90] For data on the Djasmani movement, see SA Missive of the Resident of Kediri, Oct. 18, 1888, no. 52, *Geh.*

Javanese year Wawu. Amat Mukiar would then assume the role of
regent, while Djasmani would be proclaimed Ratu Adil Igama.
Djasmani's precepts to those who would follow him included the
wearing of djimat, the gathering of weapons, the abolition of the
ritual washing of the dead (*ngèlmu pasutjèn*), and the wearing of a
"uniform" consisting of blue jacket and trousers, and a black head-
cloth. Djasmani announced that he himself would appear in Javanese dress on the top of a hill in Birawa. On that spot he would set
up a banner bearing Arabic religious texts, and under this standard
he would march out at the head of his army. At the time of his
arrest, the movement had already spread to Banjumas, Bagelen, Jogjakarta, Surakarta, Madiun, and Malang. According to Djasmani's
plans, his army and that of Amat Mukiar would march on Surakarta
and Jogjakarta to overthrow the native rulers there.[91]

Achmad Suhada's movement [92] appeared on the scene almost
simultaneously with Djasmani's. During the previous few years he
had gone with several companions to various holy places to fast
and pray, in the hope of receiving a revelation. While in retreat
on Mt. Grana, he had a vision in which he met the daughter of the
Sultan of Rum. It was revealed to him that a pure Islamic kingdom
would soon be established and be ruled by the Ratu Adil. On
descending from the mountain, Achmad Suhada proclaimed that he
himself would rule the new kingdom, a certain Karmidjan would be
appointed *patih* (grand vizier), and Karmanawi *sénapati* (com-
mander-in-chief). In the meantime, he and his followers prepared
for war against the white infidels. The violently anti-European aims
of this movement were made clear by slogans such as "ngetok
walonda" (behead the Dutch) and "ngusir kumpeni" (oust the
Company).

In the ideology of these movements, Islamic motifs played a
relatively minor role, but by the turn of the century, these motifs assumed great importance. This development was partly a response
to the growing political awareness of the peasantry and the felt need
for a more complex ideological framework capable of linking together

[91] SA Cable from the Resident of Kediri to the Governor-General, Aug. 15,
1888, no. 492.
[92] On the Achmad Suhada movement, see SA Missive of the Resident of
Madiun, Oct. 13, 1888, no. 3017.

and subsuming localized centers of discontent. The potential following of earlier social movements was, as we have seen, limited by their particularized demands and the narrowing effect of reliance on regional cultural traditions. At a time when increasing communication was broadening the horizons of the peasantry and making localized groups aware of their common sufferings, common aims, and common adversaries, the time had come to develop an intellectual or ideological definition of this wider community. Since a modern-style nationalist ideology did not exist, it was natural that Islam should fulfill this need. Solidarity was thus increasingly defined for the peasant masses in Islamic terms, and the white adversaries were conceived as the kafir against whom the Holy War could appropriately be waged.[93] For an important period in the history of Java, then, Islam was seen not as marking off one segment of society from the rest, but as supplying the political definition of "national" identity and the focus of resistance toward the colonial ruler. The long-established network of rural religious institutions provided a ready-made system of communication for the spread of this new political role for Islamic concepts and traditions. Accordingly, in the two movements next described we shall find a complex blend of political and moral appeals, in which attacks on the infidel rulers are combined with revivalist efforts to remedy the social evils caused by kafir domination.

The inaugurator of the Gedangan movement in 1904 was Kjai Kasan Mukmin of Samentara.[94] His father was reputed to be a

[93] In particular, the years of the second decade of the twentieth century saw an extraordinarily rapid spread of Islamic modernist organizations, many of which became vehicles for the expression of every kind of discontent. The most celebrated instance, of course, was the wildfire expansion of the Sarekat Islam. In its early days especially, the Sarekat Islam central leadership's modernist political goals were scarcely understood by its mass following, who tended to regard it and participate in it as if it were a conventional millenarian movement. The initial success of the Sarekat Islam was the first instance in Indonesian history of the successful mobilization of popular support for modern political purposes through the use of millenarian traditions. The ultimate failure of the movement to maintain its momentum and support must be attributed to inadequate organization, strategy, and tactics.

[94] On the Gedangan affair, see J. F. A. C. van Moll, "De Onlusten in Sidhoardjo (Mei 1904)," *Archif Java Suikerindustrie*, 13 (1905), Bijblad, no. 33, pp. 579–607; see also Gobée and Adriaanse, pp. 1965, 1969ff., 2093; for documentary sources, see MOA *Verbaal*, Aug. 13, 1904, no. 30, and April 28, 1906, no. 33.

religious teacher who had been exiled from Jogjakarta and later
founded a pesantrèn at Binangun in the district of Pakishadji. Kasan
Mukmin himself was sent to school in Cairo but was forced to
break off his education there upon his father's death. Subsequently,
he turned up as a guru in Samentara, in the district of Krian, Surabaja. Like his father, he was a guru tarékat, of the Kadirijah-Naq-
sjabandijah brotherhood.[95]

Evening prayer meetings of tarékat members at the home of Kjai
Kasan Mukmin came to be gatherings for mapping out a rebellion
against the colonial government. Among the concrete grievances
nurtured by Kjai Kasan Mukmin and his followers were the forced
cultivation of second crops, such as corn and cassava, the introduction of the so-called Hindu plough, the compulsory placing of
peasant land and labor at the disposal of the sugar factories, and
the maldistribution of irrigation water. Religious enthusiasm rose to
such an extent that the members of the movement became impatient
for action. Eventually, the date of the revolt was determined as the
twelfth day of Maulud of the year Wawu, or May 27, 1904.[96]

On the appointed day, following the afternoon prayer, the insurgents began to perform their purification rites. Then they assem-
bled in an open rice-field where a white-blue-white flag was un-
furled, to which klaras (dry banana leaves) were attached, as a
symbol of barrenness, sadness, and impermanence. Meanwhile, the
dikir (repeated recitation of short religious phrases praising Allah)
was performed and djimat were distributed. The idea of the Holy
War was preached. Insurgents from the neighboring villages Samentara, Taman, and Damarsi flocked to join the ranks. Adherents from
Modjokerto and Djombang, however, did not show up.

When the wedana (lower-level district official) of Gedangan received the message that a mustering of insurgents was taking place
in Keboan Pasar, he hurried off to meet them, accompanied by
armed policemen. In the encounter with the rebel band, he and the
police soon found themselves taken prisoner.

The government authorities now directed a full military force

---

[95] His father had been persecuted and expelled from Jogjakarta for this
reason; as a prominent adept of this tarékat, he had been held responsible
for political disturbances in the area.

[96] On Kjai Kasan Mukmin, see Gobée and Adriaanse, pp. 1969–1973.

against Keboan Pasar. The insurgent band, perhaps one hundred men in all, advanced into the fray, dancing *pentjak*-style, holding krisses and uttering the prayer "La illaha illaha" (the opening of the Moslem confession of faith). The battle was short and bloody. Thirty-three rebels were killed and thirty-seven wounded. Kjai Kasan Mukmin was wounded but managed to flee to his house. Shortly afterward, however, the building was besieged and its owner killed. The rebellion then broke up.

The Tjimareme incident in 1919 was initiated by Hadji Mohamad Hasan Arip, popularly known as Hadji Hasan.[97] Due to his wealth, age, character, and wide religious knowledge, Hadji Hasan was influential, not only in the circle of his large family, but also throughout the area where he lived. In fact he exerted a kind of broad patriarchal authority over both his disciples and his tenants. At the same time, he was believed to be greatly under the influence of his father-in-law, Hadji Gadjali, who was thought to possess magical powers. His relationship with government officials in the area had always been good until shortly before the incident developed.

The rift began in 1918 when the government compelled Hadji Hasan to cut down on planting tobacco in order to make room for rice cultivation. The following year his dissatisfaction grew more intense and was marked by his refusal to accept a monetary advance on the compulsory delivery of paddy, as the government required. In conveying the government's orders, the wedana of Leles reportedly muttered threats and made insulting remarks. On April 24, 1919, Hadji Hasan sent a letter to the Assistant Resident explaining his objection to fulfilling the requirement, namely, that he had to support a large family. No attention was paid to this letter, and his relations with the government authorities deteriorated markedly during the next two months.

Preparations were made for open defiance of the authorities, although at first Hadji Hasan seems not to have harbored any violent intentions. The wedana of Leles received warning, however, that

[97] See further the Hazeu report, "Het Drama te Tjimareme," in *Het Vrije Woord*, no. 9 (1919), pp. 66–67. For documentary sources, see Kern's private papers, in H. J. de Graaf, *Catalogus van de Westerse Handschriften van het Koninklijk Instituut voor Taal-, Land- en Volkenkunde* (The Hague: Nijhoff, 1963), no. H474, containing Hazeu's report and the report of the Resident of Priangan, Sept. 17, 1919, no. 138.

Hadji Hasan's sons and sons-in-law, twelve in number, were assembling to plot armed resistance to any attempt to seize their paddy.

On July 4, the government authorities, escorted by policemen, proceeded to Tjimareme. On the same day Hadji Hasan sent a second letter to the Assistant Resident, expressing his willingness to submit to the regulations. Meanwhile public opinion was solidifying against the wedana of Leles and the delivery of paddy to the government. No incident took place that day, nor was any punitive action taken by the authorities. But on July 7, the patih (deputy to the bupati) of Garut, the head penghulu (mosque official) of Garut, and several wedana, escorted by a squad of policemen, set out for Tjimareme to confront Hadji Hasan and his family. At this meeting the behavior of Hadji Hasan, Hadji Gadjali, and their following was quite orderly. The patih urged Hadji Hasan to go with him to Garut where the case could be properly investigated, but failed to persuade the Hadji to agree. When a policeman attempted to take away a sickle from one of Hadji Hasan's followers, they all stood up and took on a threatening attitude. The patih ordered his squad not to shoot, and then succeeded in persuading Hadji Hasan's men to leave their weapons inside the house. Thereupon the penghulu delivered an address to the people.

Panic suddenly broke out when news came that the Resident and the bupati were approaching, accompanied by military units. Hadji Hasan and his followers rushed to take refuge in his house; Hadji Gadjali, however, was seized before he could join them. The building was then surrounded and, when warning signals were ignored, the authorities opened fire. Among the dead was Hadji Hasan himself.

The incident at Tjimareme in itself attracted wide attention. Interest became still more intense when it was discovered that Hadji Hasan had affiliations with the Sarekat Islam, indeed that he belonged to the Guna Perlajan (sic) division, the organization's militant avant-garde.[98]

At the outset the incident had seemed an isolated phenomenon, but as the testimony of witnesses accumulated, the affair took on broader implications. It appeared that Hadji Hasan's ostensibly

[98] On the Garut incident, see, for instance, among the numerous articles, "Het Garoet Drama en de Afdeeling B," *IG*, 1920, no. 1, pp. 449–458.

personal act of defiance toward the government authorities was actually part of a general plan for the slaughter of Europeans, Chinese, and all natives who at the moment of the outbreak of the revolt were not members of the Sarekat Islam. It was also revealed that the Guna Perlajan was the core of the so-called *Afdeling B* (B Division), a regional subsection of the Sarekat Islam, which, contrary to the policy of the organization as a whole, apparently aimed at the violent overthrow of the Dutch.

In general, the relationship of the modern-style Sarekat Islam to agrarian unrest in this period is extremely interesting. As the organization developed mass roots, it was sometimes used by the peasantry, as in the Tjimareme affair, for purposes of their own, in some respects quite remote from those of its top leaders. For example, as the Sarekat Islam began to spread across Java in 1912, an outburst of religious frenzy occurred in Tuban.[99] Those who were unwilling to become members of the organization there were molested and even killed.

In the island of Madura, too, agrarian unrest developed rapidly after the Sarekat Islam had begun to penetrate in 1919.[100] Not only did the organization's local branch air grievances about excessive taxation, but it claimed that the peasants were no longer obliged to pay their taxes or to perform labor services, since their fields belonged to their ancestors. Weapons were reportedly purchased and preparations made for staging a revolt. But after the arrest of the local Sarekat Islam leader, Kjai Taman, the movement melted away.

In both these instances, agrarian unrest still took the form of localized, largely spontaneous outbreaks with a low level of organization and uncertain political intent. Although the leadership, or perhaps better the stimulus, was now coming from a modern-style movement such as the Sarekat Islam, the character of these outbreaks marks no very clear breach with the earlier traditions of agrarian protest.

[99] See "Verzetsbewegingen op Java en Madoera en de voorkoming daarvan," *Orgaan van den Nederlandsch-Indischen Politiek-Economischen Bond,* 5 (1924), 120–131. For documentary sources, see MOA *Verbaal,* April 9, 1919, no. 70.

[100] "Verzetsbewegingen op Java en Madoera"; for documentary sources, see MOA *Mailrapport,* 1919, no. 689.

While, in the course of time, agrarian protest increasingly came under the organizational control of modern political movements, the leaders of such movements continued to use traditional rural beliefs and aspirations for tactical purposes of mobilization. The Banten revolt of 1926 is a case in point,[101] and the pattern is clearly evident in the history of rural protest politics since independence.[102]

SOME NOTES ON RECENT CASES

Since so many of the rural social movements that we have been discussing apparently represented at bottom a deep-seated resentment at the colonial situation, it may at first seem surprising that the attainment of Indonesian independence did not bring the era of such movements to an end. In fact, the post-independence era has witnessed the emergence of considerable numbers of social movements, in many respects very similar to their predecessors. This suggests that the millenarian tradition has a strength of its own apart from specific social conditions.

While it is important to recognize that these post-independence movements have been enormously diverse in character, they can, nonetheless, be divided into two broad categories. One group of social movements seems to represent a complete rejection of what is conventionally thought of as politics; such movements are typically hostile to party activity and believe that a fundamental change in affairs can only come through some form of religious revival, whether of radical Islam or of old abangan values and customs. Many of these movements are retrogressive, desirous of a return to

[101] The Banten revolt of 1926 is an excellent example of attempts by secular political leaders to strengthen their position by appealing to traditionalist ideas. See Harry J. Benda and Ruth T. McVey, eds., *The Communist Uprisings of 1926–1927 in Indonesia: Key Documents*, Cornell Modern Indonesia Project Translation Series (Ithaca, N.Y.: Cornell University, 1960).

[102] No attempt has been made in this study to present an explanation of the Samin movement. This movement can be identified as one of passive resistance to authority or as a general self-defense against intrusion from outsiders, especially foreigners. The Saminists' ideal society was strongly egalitarian. Their economic thinking envisaged an equal distribution and ownership of land. Their rejection of any act of imposition or oppression from above found expression in an attitude of quietist denial toward government, particularly the regulations and taxes it imposed. (For an extensive discussion of Saminism, see Harry J. Benda and Lance Castles, "The Samin Movement," *BKI*, 125, no. 2 [1969], 207–240.)

an idealized past away from the difficulties of the present. Many are tinged with millenarianism and magic. Most are quietist in their approach to social and political life, indeed emphasize withdrawal from it.[103] They are rarely a danger to the existing order, though established governments, whether colonial or independent, have tended to regard them with a jaundiced eye, since they clearly reject the order over which such governments preside, and there is always the fear that ultimately they may be drawn into insurrectional activity.

The second group of cases includes social movements that are highly political in character. They do, however, stand outside the institutional framework of modern-style party politics and work for the attainment of their goals by unconventional, if quite traditional, means. Such movements represent no less basic a rejection of the existing order than the first group of movements, but this rejection takes the form of militant political or para-political activity, often with a strong messianic, nativist, or even Holy War character. Most such movements are inherently "revolutionary," and it should not surprise us that, as in colonial times, the government has tended to deal harshly with them.

In the description of some modern instances of social movements which follows, two cases are given from each category. The Hidup Betul and Agama Adam Makrifat [104] movements fall into the apolitical, revivalist group,[105] while those of Embah Sura and Semana are most easily fitted into the militant, para-political category. None of these movements has had any sustained success, at least in the sense of attaining wide influence, let alone of achieving substantial change, and all of them have eventually been suppressed by the authorities.

In the ideology of the Hidup Betul movement, clear millennial elements have apparently never led to direct political action. The

[103] The aim of individual salvation is obvious in the Pangestu movement; see R. T. Hardjoprakoso and R. Trihardono Soemodihardjo, eds., *Serat Sasangka Djati* (Surakarta: Pagujuban Ngesti Tunggal [Pangestu], 1964).

[104] For data on this movement, see Darmowasito, *Kitab Agung "Pandom-Sutji"* (Wonosari: Dewan Agama Pran Soeh, 1960).

[105] According to the list of the District Attorney of Jogjakarta, dated March 31, 1967, thirty-six movements are to be found in the Jogjakarta area, almost all of a pacifist and quietist character. Cf. the list of movements in *Pewarta P.P.K.* (July, Aug., Sept. 1953). At present many of them are banned.

core of this ideology is the belief that the perfect world will only come into being when Badan Allah (God's Institution) is treated in the right way by the authorities.[106] The faithful are mainly concerned with the sanctification of their lives and have no political ambitions whatever. They hope for the realization of a peaceful and prosperous world as soon as possible and for the attainment of *Kemerdekaan 100%* (100 Per Cent Independence) for Indonesia. The message of the Hidup Betul movement has strong nativist as well as utopian characteristics, as revealed by its nostalgia for the traditional (Javanese) way of life and its fears for the survival of Javanese customs, language, and alphabet. In spite of the Hidup Betul's quietist character, its leader, or Panatagama Kalipatollah, Iman Sliradiwisma, was arrested during a government purge in 1951 and exiled to Menado; [107] the organization itself was subsequently banned. Since then, the movement seems to have gone underground and has apparently managed to continue most of its activities.

Another movement of a primarily religious rather than political character is the Agama Adam Makrifat, founded by Rama Resi Pran-Suh Sastrasuwignja, better known as Den Tjarik (*tjarik*, village secretary). He preached a very elaborate doctrine, based on the following articles of faith: worship is due to Rama Pran-Suh, the Supreme Being; Rama Resi Pran-Suh Sastrasuwignja is an emanation of the Supreme Being and the Nabi (Prophet) of the Agama Pran-Suh movement; the divine trinity consists of Rama Pran-Suh, Rama Resi Pran-Suh, and Rama Resi Pran-Suh Sastrasuwignja.

Significantly enough, the movement emphasizes that concentration on the pursuit of salvation requires a virtually complete withdrawal from political activities. As Rama Resi Pran-Suh Sastrasuwignja put it, "I do not belong to any party, but I champion the poor, the sick and all those who suffer." Although it showed no signs of political activity, the movement incurred the suspicion of the authorities and was finally suppressed.

While not much detail is available on the Hidup Betul and the Agama Adam Makrifat, we are better informed in the case of the

---

[106] See the pamphlet issued by Wakil Badan Iman Betul, Ratu Adil (Hidup Betul) Ki Ageng Panatagama: I, Jogjakarta, Kartodjoemeno.

[107] See the letter to the Central Government in Djakarta sent by Pusat Wakil Badan Iman Betul (Ratu Adil) Paku Buwono I.

movement of Embah Sura.[108] Embah Sura himself was born in 1921. His father was a village chief, a position which Embah Sura himself subsequently occupied for about sixteen years. He was also a dalang and a dukun of some local repute. When he began to come into wider prominence, he was known as a guru who had gathered a band of followers around him at his headquarters in Nginggil, in the remote southeastern part of the district of Purwodadi. Among his many adherents, he formed an inner core of devotees (*putu,* grandchildren) by initiation through two rituals: first, *sungkem,* a traditional ceremonial act of homage to older people (in this case to Embah Sura), accompanied by the presentation of gifts such as clove cigarettes, incense, perfume, and petty cash; and second, *timbul,* a rite for receiving *kasektèn* (magical power).

Embah Sura proclaimed himself a *pandita* (hermit-sage) or wali (Islamic saint), with the power to foresee the future (*weruh sakdurungé winarah*). He prophesied that at the end of 1966 and the beginning of 1967 a terrible war would rage in Java, followed by mass slaughter and great bloodshed. In his preaching he referred to the name of Erutjakra and made use of such ancient magical symbols as the black head-cloth and the baton (wand). Almost without exception, inquiries made into the political orientation and activities of Embah Sura's movement described it as deeply devoted to former President Sukarno and his ideology. The names used by Embah Sura's bodyguards, such as Barisan Sarinah and Bantèng Utuh, unmistakably indicated their leader's loyalties. The great popularity of portraits of Sukarno and the use of the acronym APES, meaning *Aku Pendukung Sukarno* (I am a Supporter of Sukarno), point in the same direction. By early 1967 the movement had grown large enough to alarm the government, and on March 5, 1967 it was crushed by government paratroopers.

The Neo-Erutjakra movement [109] shows certain clear similarities to that of Embah Sura. The movement was started by a certain Semana from Loano, Purworedjo. He was born in 1900, the fourth child of Pak Kasandikrama. As a boy of three he is said to have

[108] We have to rely on one secondary source, a rather impressionistic work, Ramelan, *Mbah Suro, Nginggil* (Djakarta: Matoa, 1967).

[109] See Herman Pratikto, *Panggugah Hanané Manungsa,* 1 (Jogjakarta: Budiprajoga, 1965). This work is a collection of teachings of "Romo," i.e., Erutjakra himself; it is written as a kind of catechism.

already shown supernatural qualities, such as having two or even seven shadows, and his father thought that he must be an incarnation of Prince Surjengalaga, son of Sultan Hamengku Buwana V of Jogjakarta.[110] When he first came into national prominence, however, he was a retired captain of the Indonesian navy.

Semana gave out that he had received a divine revelation (*midjil*) on November 14, 1955. According to some witnesses, at that moment a golden coach was seen flying through the air; a luminescence was seen moving in the sky from southwest to northeast, which was taken to be the *andaru* (radiance of royalty) or *bradja teluh* (harbinger of pestilence); and Semana's house in Surabaja was seen as if in flames. After receiving his revelation, Semana adopted the name of Erutjakra. In 1961, he also claimed to be the Ratu Adil. In his preaching, he talked mysteriously of the coming of an era of tranquillity (*djaman ketentreman*) and the fall of the banyan tree. He also foretold a large-scale slaughter that would halve the population.[111] The events of 1966–1967 carried echoes of Semana's predictions. Whether for this or other reasons, the authorities decided to take action, by detaining him. At the time of Semana's arrest, his disciples (*putra manunggal*) numbered about 68,000, including some high officials and prominent political leaders.[112]

CONCLUSIONS

A few concluding remarks may be in order concerning the most significant dimensions of the agrarian radicalism manifested in the social movements described above. All have been dealt with sketchily, since the deficiency in our knowledge of source materials prevents us from devising a satisfactory scheme of causal explanation of these movements and from carrying out an in-depth analysis of the historical conditions in which they rose. A series of regional uprisings has been described in order to trace certain themes through different subcultural settings and at different historical periods.

A fact of considerable importance emerges clearly from a general review of such social movements as manifestations of agrarian radi-

[110] See n. 58; older people in the Jogjakarta area still know the story of the Surjengalaga affair, which was also related to the Hadji Istad rebellion; interview with Sugito in July 1967; cf. *Babad Surjengalagan.*
[111] Interview with Herman Pratikto in June 1967.   [112] *Ibid.*

calism; their specific symbolic forms are inevitably shaped by the cultural stock of the society. It has been shown that millenarian ideologies in Java have always drawn on age-old myths, indigenous and Hindu, as well as Islamic. The Ratu Adil response, for example, appears to be quite persistent through time and highly adaptive to new situations. Again and again in the study of Java's social movements, we find ourselves faced with a reworking of cultural inheritances. This creative adaptability means that millenarianism in Java can probably maintain its popular appeal indefinitely: the manifest content of Ratu Adil expectations is constantly being revised according to changing conditions. Our analysis of certain historical cases indicates that agrarian unrest expresses itself in such forms because only more or less traditional beliefs and practices have a genuinely strong and meaningful appeal to the rural population. In the face of the threat of detraditionalization, the most conspicuous forms of peasant reaction have been traditionalism and nativism. Of course, millenarian ideas can be and have been used to give new issues the sanction of tradition; for a full understanding of agrarian radicalism, one should always take this type of conscious traditionalizing into account. But it is surely of great significance that the historical pattern of millenarian movements in Java shows such marked ideological and institutional continuity, and that certain of their patterns of action have proved so persistent.[113]

One of the most interesting aspects of Javanese social movements is their political dimension. At bottom, all such movements are expressions of protest against unjust or disturbed social conditions, including extortion and oppression by the wielders of power. Yet their ideologies are suffused with religious symbolism, because the world-view of the rural people to whom they appeal is still dominated by religion. Charismatic religious leaders, who are able to stir up peasant political action by utopian propaganda, are thus always a potential danger to bureaucratic power-holders. Under the repressive authoritarian rule of the Dutch, political opposition and agitation could survive and spread only if couched in terms of religion. In the millenarian religious message, the peasantry certainly saw the

---

[113] For the continuities of ideologies and patterns of action in social movements, see Bryan A. Wilson, "Millennialism in Comparative Perspective," in *CSSH*, 6, no. 1 (1963), 93–114.

key to salvation from colonial oppression. At the same time one should be careful to avoid the interpretive danger of deriving these movements exclusively from the impact of colonial rule itself. There is some evidence, as we have indicated, suggesting that social movements of a millenarian type also occurred in the precolonial age.[114]

Millenarian movements in Java, even those apparently purely religious and apolitical in character, have almost invariably been regarded as provocative and dangerous by established government. The authorities have usually reacted violently to their expansion and suppressed them with great severity because such movements have proved capable of aggregating and channeling peasant loyalties along new and unofficial lines, cutting across existing ties and boundaries. Moreover, their partly spontaneous and wholly unbureaucratized nature makes them enigmatic and difficult to deal with on a routinized basis. The protest of such social movements is felt as an implicit or explicit accusation leveled at the rulers of the state, who receive it, because of its millenarian character, with impatience, resentment, and even contempt. Unfortunately, perhaps, official repression of millenarian movements has often turned them into consciously political movements, willing to resort to violence to achieve their aims.

Ultimately, the political radicalism that has grown up in the rural areas of Java has its roots in peasant millenarianism. This millenarianism cannot be divorced from traditional religious thought and still plays an essential role in rural politics. We have cited some examples of the use of millenarianism for secular political purposes by modernist organizations. In each case, these organizations had decidedly radical aims. Both the Sarekat Islam and the PKI (Indonesian Communist Party) presented their ideological goals very much in the manner of prophecies and appropriated major elements of traditional millenarian symbolism for this purpose.[115]

[114] For a religious movement during the Kartasura period, see Soerjokoesoemo; see further, D. A. Rinkes, "Ki Pandanarang te Tembajat," *TBG*, 53 (1911), 435–581; Th. Pigeaud, "Aantekeningen betreffende de Javaanschen Oosthoek," *ibid.*, 72 (1932), 215–313; H. J. de Graaf, *De Moord op Kapitein François Tack* (Amsterdam: Paris, 1935), esp. pp. 14–19.

[115] For the Banten revolt of 1926, see Harry J. Benda and Ruth T. McVey, esp. pp. 43–47; for a comparison with disturbances in Djambi which also showed both traditionalist and modern features, see "De Opstand in Djambi," *IG*, 1917, no. 1, pp. 640–653.

But by no means all peasant radicalism has been successfully channeled into modern-style organizations. It is very important to remember that in the mid-twentieth century traditional millenarian movements still flourish, alongside modernist secular and religious movements. Thus millenarianism, as the original expression of Javanese peasant radicalism, exhibits great staying-power, acquiring new significance by constant adaptation to changing circumstances.

Nonetheless, one can perhaps speculate that to the extent that modern mass organizations successfully take over the active representation of rural political and economic interests, there will be a growing tendency for new millenarian movements to assume a much more uniformly quietist stance, concentrating upon personal salvation and moral renewal. This is not to deny the fact that during recent upheavals political fanaticism expressing itself in large-scale violence and murder was aroused and sustained by conscious appeals to religious and quasi-millenarian beliefs. What is clear is that insofar as agrarian protest continues to be shaped by traditional religious symbols, the effectiveness of millenarianism as a basis for mass political action is likely to remain unimpaired.

Ethnicity and
Political Organization:
Three East Sumatran Cases *

❖❖❖❖❖❖❖❖❖
R. William Liddle

INTRODUCTION

One of the presumed common denominators of political life in the new states, distinguishing that genus from its counterparts elsewhere, is the prominence of primordialism as a variable affecting political loyalties and behavior.[1] Yet, despite the frequency with which its importance is asserted (and its influence decried), we have had little analysis specifying the arenas within which primordialism is a factor, the conditions under which it occurs, and the consequences which it produces. The absence of systematic knowl-

* Field work in East Sumatra in 1963–1964 was made possible by a Ford Foundation Foreign Area Training Fellowship. A more elaborate analysis of ethnic politics in this region is presented in my *Ethnicity, Party, and National Integration: An Indonesian Case Study* (New Haven: Yale University Press, 1970), from which sections of this essay have been adapted.

I would like to thank Benedict Anderson, Harry Benda, and James Guyot for their comments and criticisms.

[1] The term primordialism is taken from Clifford Geertz ("The Integrative Revolution, Primordial Sentiments and Civil Politics in the New States" in Geertz, ed., *Old Societies and New States* [New York: Free Press, 1963]), who defines a "primordial attachment" as one that derives from "the assumed givens . . . of social existence: immediate contiguity and kin connection mainly, but beyond them the givenness that stems from being born into a particular religious community, speaking a particular language, or even a dialect of a language, and following particular social practices. These congruities . . . are seen to have an ineffable, and at times, overpowering, coerciveness in and of themselves." (p. 109).

edge relating primordialism to political behavior is characteristic not only of cross-national comparative studies in new states' politics but of treatments of specific political systems as well. Indonesia is no exception to this common pattern of neglect.[2]

In a situation of relative ignorance—both theoretical and empirical—it seems most useful to begin an exploration of the role of primordialism in Indonesian politics by narrowing the focus of analysis as much as possible. Accordingly, this essay attempts to formulate some theoretically interesting questions concerning the relationship between primordialism—with special emphasis on ethnicity —and the development of political parties in post-independence Indonesia, and to suggest and apply a method for answering these questions.

As an initial assumption, it seems justified to consider the study of political parties and party systems as a worthwhile enterprise not only in those polities where there is relatively unfettered partisan competition and where parties play a major role in national decision-making, but also in systems (such as present-day Indonesia) where parties are only marginal or peripheral to the political process. This assumption is based on a functionalist conception of the political system which asserts that, in every polity, structures and processes exist through which demands emanating from various segments of the society are channeled and acted upon by the decision-makers.[3] In relatively simple, "premodern" political systems, demands typically originate from a narrow segment of the population—an aristocracy

[2] Studies most closely related to the problem include Herbert Feith, *The Indonesian Elections of 1955,* Cornell Modern Indonesia Project Monograph Series (Ithaca, N.Y.: Cornell University, 1957); G. William Skinner, ed., *Local, Ethnic and National Loyalties in Village Indonesia: A Symposium,* Southeast Asia Studies, Cultural Report Series no. 8 (New Haven: Yale University, 1959); Hildred Geertz, "Indonesian Cultures and Communities," in Ruth McVey, ed., *Indonesia* (New Haven: Human Relations Area Files, 1963); and Gerald S. Maryanov, *Decentralization in Indonesia as a Political Problem,* Cornell Modern Indonesia Project Interim Report Series (Ithaca, N.Y.: Cornell University, 1958).

[3] The following formulation is based on the work of members of the Social Science Research Council's Committee on Comparative Politics. See especially Gabriel Almond and G. Bingham Powell, Jr., *Comparative Politics: A Developmental Approach* (Boston: Little, Brown, 1966), and Joseph LaPalombara and Myron Weiner, eds., *Political Parties and Political Development* (Princeton, N.J.: Princeton University Press, 1966), Conclusion.

or body of village elders, for example—and are relatively few in number and limited in scope. Such polities have not normally developed functionally specific demand-channeling (or decision-making) structures. In most contemporary political systems, on the other hand, including those of only partially modernized Asian and African societies, the range and scope of demands and the proportion of the population which regards the polity as a problem-solving instrument are so vast that novel structures and processes must be created in order to cope with this new environment. Interest groups and political parties, whether in the form of the single party and its associated mass movements (whose principal objective is to manipulate and control from above the channeling of demands), competitive political organizations (which permit a less restricted channeling of demands from below), or some combination or modification of these, have been typical (although by no means the only) structural responses to the almost universal problem of heightened demands for participation. We assume, then, the existence of a common and critical "challenge of participation" in the new states, and suggest that political parties are worth studying as structures directly related to confronting and overcoming this challenge, regardless of whether they are or are not at any particular time or in any given political system central to the decision-making process.

Independent Indonesia began its career as a constitutional democracy characterized by unrestricted partisan competition in the framework of free elections and a powerful (relative to other structures) Parliament. Within a very few years, dissatisfaction with the achievements of representative democracy and more broadly with the whole style and tenor of parliamentary government had become widespread. There followed a period in which the general trend—still not reversed despite the upheavals of the mid-1960's—was toward the emasculation of the party system as the legitimate representative of public opinion and of party leaders as the central decision-makers in the polity. And yet, despite their declining role, the parties have in varying degrees continued their attempts to organize the population and to press demands upon the government. Given the persistence of the "challenge of participation" and the continued inability of the Indonesian government to find suitable alternative structures for the channeling and processing (or manip-

ulating) of demands, it is not overly hazardous to predict that political parties and other popular organizations will be around for
some time to come.

In what ways can a party and organizational system be affected
by primordial loyalties? At least four dimensions of party political
life would seem both to be related to primordialism and to have
considerable impact upon the capabilities of political organizations
to channel popular demands and to play an effective role in governmental decision-making. These dimensions are: the bases of partisan
choice, the reasons why individuals support one party rather than
another, and the resulting inclusivity or exclusivity of primordial
groups; the social origins of party leadership, i.e., recruitment from
either traditional or modernized elites; the firmness of partisan attachment; and the characteristics of internal party organization, i.e.,
"mass" versus "cadre" organizational types.[4]

Under what circumstances will a party system be affected along
these lines by primordialism? One central variable is modernization,
including such related processes of change as urbanization, modern
education, exposure to mass media of communications, participation
in a money economy, industrialization, and so on. Some students of
modernization and political development, taking a dichotomous approach to problems of system change, argue that primordial loyalties are a feature of premodern or traditional societies and tend to
be dissolved in new groupings based on socio-economic class or the
complex patterns of role differentiation and interaction produced by
modernization and industrialization.[5] On the other hand, there are

[4] Maurice Duverger, *Political Parties, Their Organization and Activity in
the Modern State* (New York: Wiley, 1954), Bk. 1. The mass party is constructed of branches and cells and is structurally complex and "strongly
articulated" (i.e., its various components are well coordinated). The basic
structural units of the cadre party are caucuses, small elite groups of "party
notabilities." This type of party is structurally simpler and more weakly
articulated. Duverger sees the mass party essentially as a product of universal
suffrage, which forced party leaders to concentrate on the development of
a mass membership, while the cadre party is a survival of nineteenth-century
elitist politics. He does not attempt—as we shall—to link differences in party
organization to primordialism and social change.

[5] An argument of this type has recently been made for Indonesia by
W. F. Wertheim, "From Aliran Towards Class Struggle in the Countryside
of Java," Paper No. 55, *International Conference on Asian History* (Kuala
Lumpur, Aug. 1968).

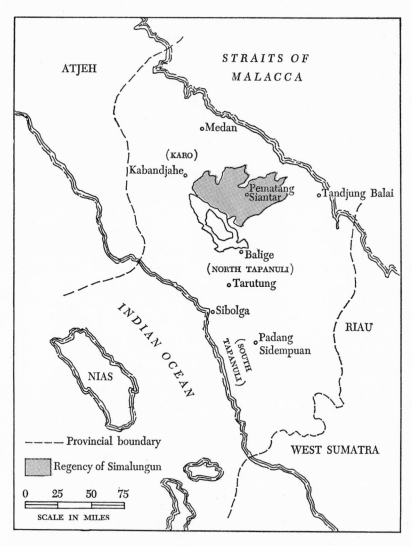

Map 3. Province of North Sumatra

those who argue that the forces of modernization—at least in the short run—are likely to turn culturally diverse states into centrifuges of primordial tension, making national integrity difficult or impossible to maintain.[6]

[6] See for example Karl Deutsch, "Social Mobilization and Political Development," *American Political Science Review,* 55 (1963), 493–514. It may be added that although in some respects diametrically opposed, both of the above formulations share a distaste for primordialism and its political consequences.

These comments suggest the utility of attempting a comparative analysis of the impact of primordialism on organizational development among populations which differ along the modern-traditional continuum. In order to keep the number of uncontrolled variables to a minimum, such comparison can perhaps most fruitfully be conducted by choosing localities within a single political system whose socio-economic characteristics vary along the specified dimension.[7] This method, which will be applied here to three Indonesian localities, should produce hypotheses suitable for further testing not only within the Indonesian context but in other new states as well.

THE LOCALITIES

The three localities chosen for comparison—Lower Simalungun, Upper Simalungun, and Pematang Siantar—are contiguous territories within the former East Coast Residency of Sumatra, now a part of the province of North Sumatra (see Map 2). Only one of the three—the municipality of Pematang Siantar—is an administrative subdivision of the province, whereas the other two are groups of subdistricts defined by the inhabitants of the region as distinct socio-economic areas.[8] The most modernized localities are Lower Simalungun, where a plantation economy and related developments have resulted in substantial social and cultural change, and the commercial and administrative urban center of Pematang Siantar. The least modernized region, Upper Simalungun, has experienced

---

For contrasting views, see Myron Weiner, *The Politics of Scarcity* (Chicago: University of Chicago Press, 1962); Lloyd I. Rudolph and Suzanne Hoeber Rudolph, "The Political Role of India's Caste Associations," *Pacific Affairs*, 33 (1960), 15–22; Immanuel Wallerstein, "Ethnicity and National Integration," *Cahiers d'Etudes Africaines*, 1 (1960), 129–138; and C. Geertz.

[7] The strategy of initial comparison within "culture areas" has been suggested by Lloyd Fallers, *Bantu Bureaucracy* (Chicago: University of Chicago Press, 1965), and A. R. Zolberg, *Creating Political Order: The Party States of West Africa* (Chicago: Rand McNally, 1966).

[8] The operative administrative levels of Indonesian government in 1964 were province, regency or municipality, subdistrict, and village. The first two of these levels were considered self-governing regions and possessed regional legislatures, the subdistrict was a purely administrative unit with an appointed head, and the village (at least formally) elected its own leadership. See J. D. Legge, *Central Authority and Regional Autonomy in Indonesia: A Study in Local Administration, 1950–1960* (Ithaca, N.Y.: Cornell University Press, 1961). The subdistricts discussed in this essay are all located in the regency (second-level self-governing region) of Simalungun.

comparatively little economic development or other change since the precolonial era.

Lower Simalungun

Lower Simalungun (*Simalungun Bawah*) is a relatively flat, low-lying, densely populated (160 inhabitants per square kilometer) region ecologically and geographically a part of the fertile plantation belt of East Sumatra. Its distinguishing characteristics are a heavily plantation-oriented economy—about 60 per cent of total arable land is under plantation concession—and a multi-ethnic population, consisting chiefly of Javanese (40 per cent), North Tapanuli Bataks (30 per cent), South Tapanuli Bataks (15 per cent), and Simalungun Bataks (10 per cent).[9]

The imposition of a plantation economy was the major engine of change in Lower Simalungun in the early decades of the twentieth century, bringing in its train large-scale immigration, a modernized communications system of roads, telegraph, and telephones, the provision of limited educational facilities for Indonesian children, the beginnings of a money economy and, as small towns grew up to serve the needs of the plantation population, a measure of urbanization. These developments resulted in turn in substantial modifications in culture, social structure, and patterns of social interaction. The most striking of these changes were the emergence of a pronounced sense of ethnic identity, buttressed by religious differences and occupational and residential separation, and the creation of new forms and patterns of social leadership within each of the migrant ethnic groups. Only in more recent times have cleavages based on ethnicity begun to be bridged, hesitatingly and partially, by the growth of nationalist sentiment and of common economic interests.

The first newcomers to Lower Simalungun were the Javanese, recruited as contract laborers to fill the gap created by local underpopulation and the unwillingness of the indigenous peoples of East Sumatra to work on the plantations. The greatest influx of Javanese began during the rubber boom of 1911–1912 and continued steadily through the 1920's, tapering off during the final decade of Dutch

[9] These are rough population estimates, based on census data concerning religious affiliation and place of birth and on informed guessing.

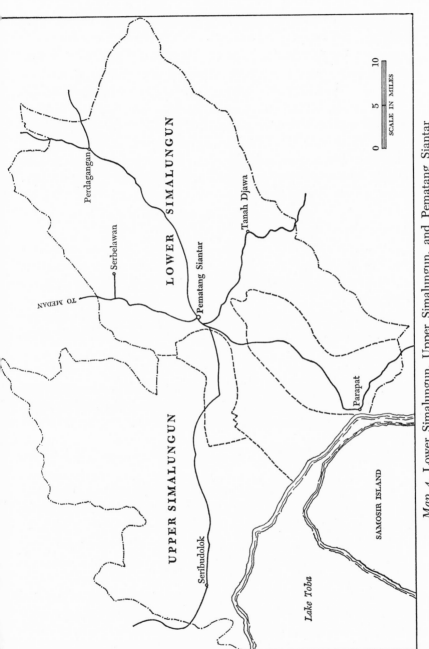

Map 4. Lower Simalungun, Upper Simalungun, and Pematang Siantar

rule. At the end of their contract period many Javanese remained in
Lower Simalungun, some continuing to work for the plantations and
others moving to nearby villages or to the growing market towns,
where they found employment as unskilled laborers or petty traders.

The North Tapanuli Bataks, skilled in wet rice agriculture but
lacking sufficient farmland in mountainous Tapanuli, also began to
enter Lower Simalungun in large numbers as soon as the Dutch
were firmly established in the region and could provide suitable
land and assure their safety.[10] They settled in the river valleys and
along the migration route from Tapanuli, where it was possible to
construct extensive irrigation systems.

For the most part the North Tapanuli immigrants came from the
regions of Toba, on the southern shore of Lake Toba around the
present town of Balige, and the Silindung valley, where the town
of Tarutung is now located. Many were Christians, as German missionaries from the Protestant Rheinische Missionsgesellschaft had
been working in Tapanuli since 1861 and had been particularly successful in the Toba and Silindung areas. The missionaries encouraged migration to East Sumatra, expecting the migrants to help
convert the peoples of the region to Christianity.

Not all of the North Tapanuli Bataks who came to Lower Simalungun in the colonial period were wet rice farmers. As a part of
their conversion efforts, the missionaries had been very active in
establishing village schools, a fortuitous development for the Dutch
government and the European planters who needed personnel
to fill a wide variety of white-collar jobs. Few positions requiring
education were available in Tapanuli, and many educated North
Tapanuli Bataks gravitated to Lower Simalungun.

South Tapanuli—the heavily Islamic regions of Angkola, Man-
dailing, and Sipirok along the west coast of Sumatra—also sent

[10] On the North Tapanuli Bataks in East Sumatra, see E. M. Bruner,
"Kinship Organization among the Urban Batak of Sumatra," *Transactions
of the New York Academy of Sciences*, series 2, 22 (1959), 118–125; E. M.
Bruner, "Urbanization and Ethnic Identity in North Sumatra," *American
Anthropologist*, 63 (1961), 508–521; and Clark Cunningham, *The Postwar
Migration of the Toba Bataks to East Sumatra*, Southeast Asia Studies, Cultural
Report Series no. 5 (New Haven: Yale University, 1958). Cunningham's is the
only recently published study which deals directly with Simalungun, and it
includes useful information on the Simalungun Bataks and the Javanese as well
as the North Tapanuli Bataks.

substantial numbers of migrants to Lower Simalungun. The South Tapanuli pattern of migration was rather different from that of their neighbors to the north. Whereas the latter were predominantly farmers seeking irrigable land, the former were strongly attracted by the prospect of trade and settled for the most part in the market and administrative towns. Only a few South Tapanuli farmers, who were not as beset by population pressure on the land as the North Tapanuli Bataks, joined in the migration.

Besides the trading element there was also a significant group of Moslem Bataks who became white-collar workers for the government, the plantations, and the traditional Simalungun kingdoms. In the last half of the nineteenth century South Tapanuli pilgrims in the Middle East had been strongly influenced by the Islamic reform movement, which stressed modern education. Moreover, German missionaries, whose work in South Tapanuli predated their entrance into North Tapanuli, had also established schools, and some of their students had been Moslems. Many migrants from South Tapanuli had thus acquired at least a rudimentary Western-style education.

Like the Christian North Tapanuli Bataks, the South Tapanuli Moslems were attracted by the possibilities of missionary work in East Sumatra. Many religious teachers came to Lower Simalungun, where with the assistance of the merchants and other educated Moslems they established schools and several educational and social organizations. The most important of these were Muhammadijah, founded in 1927, and Aldjam'ijatul Waslijah, founded in 1930 and today by far the largest Islamic organization in the region.

The indigenous people of Lower Simalungun, the Simalungun Bataks, were considerably disadvantaged by the growth of the plantations and the building of wet rice fields. Seeing the rapid decline in land available for slash-and-burn cultivation and unwilling to be assimilated into the cultures of the migrant groups, many of them moved into the highland areas of what is now called Upper Simalungun. By the 1930's they were a small minority in Lower Simalungun, located mostly in and around the central villages of their diminished kingdoms. Most of those who remained, including the traditional aristocracy, were converted to Islam by South Tapanuli and Coastal Malay traders and religious teachers.

Ethnic loyalties and hostilities, as far as one can determine, were not characteristic of precolonial East Sumatra. In those days of sparse population and limited communications, loyalties centered primarily on the village unit, localized kinship groupings, or at most the small traditional kingdoms. Only in the twentieth century, as individuals of a variety of backgrounds came into direct and prolonged contact and competition with each other, particularly in the towns, did feelings of ethnic exclusivity—the structuring of social relationships in terms of a "we" versus a "they" defined in ethnic terms—begin to emerge in Lower Simalungun.

Each of the major groups had its own cultural traditions, forms of social organization, and language, which served as the basis of ethnic differentiation. The Javanese, by virtue of their language, bilateral kinship system, and Hindu-Buddhist culture, were of course the most distinctive, while the various Batak groups shared a patrilineal kinship system and many common traditions and practices. Centuries of infrequent contact, however, had produced dialect, *adat* (custom and customary law), and other differences which, in the conditions of early twentieth-century Lower Simalungun, permitted each group to develop its own sense of a unique identity in contrast to all others.

Religion, on the whole, intensified ethnic exclusivity. The North Tapanuli Bataks were set apart from the other groups by their Christianity; indeed, in the absence of the Christian-Moslem cleavage between North and South Tapanuli Bataks there would have been little foundation for the development of separate identities, since in all other respects the two groups are quite similar. Although the South Tapanuli Bataks and the Javanese are both Moslem groups, there is a vast difference between them in terms of adherence to and practice of the Islamic faith. The great majority of the Javanese in the region are of the *abangan* persuasion, a more syncretistic, animistic, and Hindu-influenced variant of Islam, while the South Tapanuli people belong to the more devoutly Islamic *santri* element in Indonesian Islam.[11] It is largely this latter group which participates in religious activities, the Islamic educational system, and Moslem social organizations.

---

[11] The *abangan-santri* division is from Clifford Geertz, *The Religion of Java* (Glencoe, Ill.: Free Press, 1960), but it is applied here in a broader, Indonesia-wide context.

Residential segregation, a consequence both of occupational and religious differences, also encouraged the development of separate ethnic identities. Javanese contract laborers were housed on the plantations; South Tapanuli traders lived in the towns; and Simalungun Batak dry rice farmers tended to remain in their precolonial villages. North Tapanuli Batak settlements, whether in the rural areas or the towns, contained nearly as many pigs (pork being the principal ritual food of the North Tapanuli Bataks) as people, and were therefore avoided by the various Moslem groups.[12]

Table 1. Ethnic groups of Lower Simalungun

Ethnic group	Javanese	North Tapanuli Batak	South Tapanuli Batak	Simalungun Batak
Percentage of population	40 %	30 %	15 %	10 %
Religion	abangan Moslem	Protestant	*santri* Moslem	*santri* Moslem
Occupation	plantation and urban labor wet rice agriculture	wet rice agriculture white collar trade	trade religious education	dry rice agriculture
Place of residence	plantations	towns and villages	towns	traditional villages
Predominant leadership group	school-teachers petty traders	civil servants ministers and lay leaders	religious teachers association officials traders civil servants	traditional aristocracy

In this environment of ethnic exclusiveness there was no overarching social elite accepted by all of the people of the locality. Instead, each ethnic community developed its own elite which reflected the particular circumstances of the migration and the situation in which it found itself in Lower Simalungun.

[12] The explosiveness of pigs as a social issue was demonstrated in 1968 when dozens of pigs in the town of Serbelawan in Lower Simalungun, allowed by their North Tapanuli owners to wander freely, were slaughtered by irate Moslems. See *Suluh Marhaen* (Edisi Nasional), Nov. 27, 1968, p. 2.

The North Tapanuli Bataks in their homeland had lived in small villages (*huta*) coterminous with localized lineages and governed by lineage elders and adat specialists. Most of these leaders did not join in the migration, which generally attracted only the younger, more restless and pioneering spirits. In addition, the mixture of individuals of many different lineages in the new villages of Lower Simalungun necessitated the replacement of the localized lineage as the basic unit of social organization. New or modified structures, including the territorially based village association, the kinship-based clan (*marga*), and the local church (which in most cases linked several villages together in a single congregation), were pressed into service by the migrants. In each of these structures the best educated and most worldly individuals, expressing the pioneering aspirations of the migrants and best equipped to deal with the impinging non-Batak world, tended to assume the most prominent leadership roles. This was especially true of the church and church-related hierarchies and of town organizations, but the pattern set by these structures was widely adopted in the villages as well.

Among the South Tapanuli Bataks one effect of Islamization has been to reduce the importance of kinship and territorial affiliations in favor of allegiance to the wider community of Islamic believers (*ummat Islam*). This process was intensified in Lower Simalungun since, as in the case of the North Tapanuli Bataks, the more traditionally oriented adat leaders tended to stay at home. The Islamic social and educational organizations, particularly Aldjam'ijatul Waslijah, thus came to provide much of the structure of South Tapanuli social life in Lower Simalungun, and the teachers, traders, and civil servants associated with them became the uncontested leaders of the community.

The most painful and least successful adjustment to Lower Simalungun was made by the Javanese. With few exceptions, the Javanese migrants were from the poorest and most disadvantaged segment of peasant society. The social organization which they brought with them was relatively atomistic and poorly integrated, characteristics which were intensified by the rigors of plantation life.[13] Particularly in the early years, sanitary facilities were minimal

[13] On Javanese social organization, see the useful brief treatment by

and there was much overcrowding in the barracks-like *pondok* in which the workers were housed. As new migrants were constantly arriving and older hands were being transferred to other parts of the plantation, attempts to develop a sense of community within the pondok were not very successful.

Cut off from their traditional political and cultural leaders, it was difficult for the Javanese plantation workers to develop an indigenous elite. Their lives centered around the plantation and its activities and their affairs were regulated largely by the plantation managers, who even involved themselves in the selection of pondok heads. The pattern of social stratification which developed was also plantation-oriented, comprising two principal status groups, the ordinary workers and the *mandur* (foremen). Relationships between mandur and workers and between pondok heads and residents were at best uneasy, as these potential leadership groups were often seen as instruments of higher authority rather than as spokesmen for the workers.

For the children of most Javanese, whether in the pondok or the villages and towns, there were few educational opportunities which might have encouraged the development of a new elite group comparable to the North and South Tapanuli Batak leadership. A few individuals, principally the sons of mandur and town Javanese, became teachers in the so-called *wilde scholen* (unaccredited private schools) or moderately successful traders, but almost none received enough education to become civil servants. In the absence of alternative leadership, some Javanese turned for advice and assistance to the South Tapanuli Batak religious teachers to be found in many predominantly Javanese neighborhoods and villages, and at least a few were drawn into the santri orbit.

Ethnic exclusivity and separation, either at the mass or at the elite level, did not constitute the whole of social relationships in Lower Simalungun during or after the colonial period. As early as the 1920's, awakening Indonesian nationalism in its various ideological manifestations found adherents in the towns. In the 1940's national consciousness deepened as a result both of Japanese military training in ostensible preparation for the defense of the nation,

---

Hildred Geertz, "Indonesian Cultures," and also her *The Javanese Family* (New York: Free Press, 1961).

and of the events of the Revolution, when Lower Simalungun became a supply and staging area for troops sent to the Medan Area
front. Members of the various elite groups, in most frequent contact
with comparable individuals in the world beyond Lower Simalungun and convinced that their own ambition and their community's development were being stifled by colonial rule, were
among those most receptive to nationalism. By 1950, despite many
real differences among them, all local social leaders accepted, and
all but the Simalungun Batak aristocracy were positively committed
to, the concepts of Indonesian identity and an indivisible Indonesian
nation. Through the leaders, these ideas had percolated down, at
first gradually and then at a quickening pace, to the less sophisticated and less directly involved townsmen and villagers.

A developing sense of common economic interests among that
portion of the population most directly affected by the plantation environment has also been of some importance in fostering interethnic
relationships in Lower Simalungun. During the Japanese occupation large numbers of Javanese and North Tapanuli Batak farmers
and Javanese plantation workers began to grow rice and other crops
on formerly inviolable plantation land. Since the restoration of the
plantations in the postwar years, under both Dutch and Indonesian
government management, these squatters have fought a continuing
battle for expansion of their holdings and acceptance of their
claims.[14] In this effort both North Tapanuli and Javanese squatters,
together with Javanese workers, have shared a common enemy—the
plantation administrators and the government. The result has been
increasing agreement on the necessity of inter-ethnic unity to
achieve common goals. This lessening of ethnic separatism has not,
however, extended to other ethnic groups, whose members are not
so directly affected by the plantations, nor even to those North
Tapanuli Batak farmers whose villages are outside the plantation
environment.

Pematang Siantar

The municipality of Pematang Siantar (usually abbreviated to
P. Siantar or Siantar) has also experienced considerable social

[14] For a general treatment of the squatter problem, see Karl J. Pelzer,
"The Agrarian Conflict in East Sumatra," *Pacific Affairs*, 30 (1957), 151–159.

change in recent decades. At the turn of the century still an "insignificant Batak village," in the words of a contemporary Dutch observer, Siantar in 1961 had a population of over 114,000, and its annual growth rate of 6.5 per cent was the highest in Indonesia.[15] This remarkable growth may be attributed to the town's strategic position as a crossroads linking Tapanuli and the East Coast, and to its location in the areas of plantation and wet rice agricultural development. Under colonial rule, Siantar became the predominant commercial center in Simalungun, and also the principal locus of industrial development, government administration, and higher education. Today nearly half of the population is engaged in trade, a further 15 per cent are employed by government, and a similar proportion is enrolled in the city's numerous government and private schools. The nongovernmental labor force, about 10 per cent of the population, is employed in a variety of medium-sized and small industries, ranging from cigarette manufacture and textile weaving to cabinet-making and one-man tailor shops set up on the sidewalks.[16]

Because of Siantar's central location and the opportunities available in its expanding economy, the small indigenous Simalungun Batak community was soon inundated by migrants. Today the North Tapanuli Bataks, estimated at about 40 per cent of the total population, are the largest group in the city, followed by the South Tapanuli Bataks (20 per cent), the Chinese (12 per cent), the Javanese (10 per cent), and the Simalungun Bataks (10 per cent).[17]

A crossroads town culturally as well as commercially, Siantar was subjected with even greater intensity than Lower Simalungun to the winds of change sweeping Indonesia in the twentieth century. Dutch colonialism provided the physical appurtenances of a modern town, created a modern governmental administration, and established the conditions under which a commercialized, monetized economy could flourish. These developments unintentionally pro-

[15] Figures from Pauline D. Milone, "Contemporary Urbanization in Indonesia," *Asian Survey*, 4 (1964), 1005.

[16] Figures supplied by the census division of the city government and the Office of People's Industry.

[17] As in the case of Lower Simalungun, these figures are only estimates. The Chinese community in Siantar did not participate in partisan politics and is thus not included in our analysis.

moted the emergence of an urbanized style of life, dependent on success in the civil service or in commerce, to which increasing numbers of townspeople of all ethnic groups were drawn. Colonialism also brought to Siantar a European community attempting to live, as in other colonies, in splendid isolation, but in fact setting an urban cultural pattern which the Indonesians simultaneously emulated and hated. The turmoil that followed colonial rule—Japanese occupation, two often chaotic years of revolution (during which Siantar served briefly as the temporary Republican capital of Sumatra), followed by two years of Dutch reoccupation before independence was finally achieved—also made a deep impression on town residents. Much of the activity and many of the principal events of these periods occurred in or were organized from Siantar,

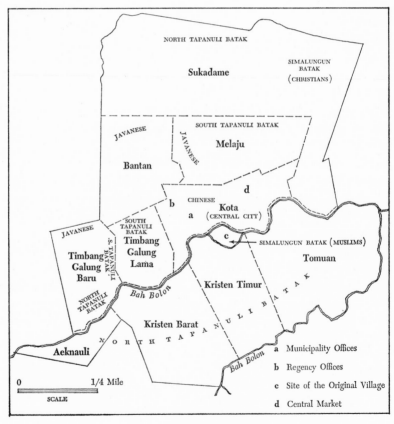

Map 5. Pematang Siantar

and it was the townsman, physically accessible, economically vulnerable, culturally and intellectually in flux, who was most affected by and responsive to changing circumstances.

These events promoted a national consciousness that penetrated ever more deeply and permanently throughout the locality, but none of them disturbed the basic paradigm of social interaction—intra-ethnic unity and inter-ethnic hostility—which had been established during the first wave of migrations. Cultural, linguistic, and religious differences provided the foundations of ethnic identity, and were reflected in the pattern of residential clustering (see Map 3). As in Lower Simalungun, each ethnic group developed separate leadership. Inter-ethnic communication and cooperation among the various elites, despite greater physical proximity, was minimal.

In an environment of constant conflict and competition, group relationships in Siantar resembled a boiling rather than a melting pot. Commerce and industry were major arenas of ethnic conflict, since particular groups tended to predominate in different sectors of the economy and were similarly challenged on a group basis. As educational opportunities became more equalized, ethnic competition also spread to the civil service, where it was intensified by Dutch preference for Christians and at least initial Japanese preference for Moslems.

The extent to which ethnic differences were reflected occupationally also promoted antagonisms during the revolutionary years, since an individual's support for various revolutionary policies and indeed for the Revolution itself depended in part upon his occupation or, more generally, his position in the social hierarchy. Most urban, working-class Javanese, for example, had little to lose in the Revolution and tended to join militant organizations. Civil servants (of whom the majority were North Tapanuli Bataks) had, potentially, a great deal to lose in a Republican, perhaps Moslem-dominated, Indonesia, and tended to waver or to have more moderate political views. As civil servants, too, they were less inclined by virtue of their education and administrative experience to favor either radical policies or militant action. At the other extreme, Simalungun Batak aristocrats and their supporters welcomed the return of the Dutch, whom they saw as the protectors of the traditional kingdoms.

Much of our description of Lower Simalungun, then, applies also to Pematang Siantar. Both localities are creations of the twentieth century, products of an intensive Dutch colonialism and profoundly affected as well by postcolonial events. Both are multi-ethnic, containing indeed the same groups in roughly similar proportions, and have undergone some urbanization and economic modernization. Both localities have also experienced growing ethnic consciousness and the emergence of separate elite groups within the various ethnic communities, and finally both have eagerly accepted their incorporation into an independent Indonesian nation. The essential difference between them is that much of Lower Simalungun's economic and social life is dominated by the plantations, whereas Siantar is a totally urbanized area, with an economy based on commerce and government administration. This contrast between a plantation and an urban economy in otherwise very comparable situations is reflected, as we shall see, in some interesting differences in political organizational dynamics as well.

Upper Simalungun

Upper Simalungun (*Simalungun Atas*) is the least modernized and most isolated of the three localities. The area is hilly to mountainous, without rivers suitable for navigation or wet rice cultivation, and land communication is generally difficult. The population is sparser than in Lower Simalungun (comparative densities of 50 per square kilometer versus 160 per square kilometer) and dispersed in small villages. There are no major population concentrations comparable to the towns of Lower Simalungun, with the partial exception of the town of Seribudolok located on the border between Upper Simalungun and the regency of Karo. Plantation agriculture is a very small part of the economy. Land available for village agriculture is thus much more extensive than in Lower Simalungun, and there is no squatter problem or other major conflict over land. Upper Simalungun is also ethnically homogeneous, as the great majority of the population consists of the indigenous Simalungun Bataks. The majority religion is Protestantism, although many Simalungun Bataks still adhere to traditional religious practices and beliefs.

In the precolonial period the Simalungun Bataks were organized politically into several formally autocratic but in practice loosely governed kingdoms. Each of these kingdoms was ruled by an aristocratic elite, its membership determined by birth and differentiated from ordinary villagers by the possession of magical powers. At the turn of the present century the kingdoms were subjected to Dutch overlordship and reorganization, but the rulers continued to hold office and to exercise authority over their Simalungun Batak subjects.

Social change was slow in coming and directly affected only a small segment of the population in Upper Simalungun. What change did occur was caused primarily by three factors: Christianity, brought by German and North Tapanuli missionaries; education, also provided by the missionaries; and the construction of a road from Pematang Siantar to Seribudolok, opening the region to contact with the more modernized outside world.

One important consequence of these developments was the creation of a new (albeit very small) class of educated and semi-educated individuals, mostly affiliated with the Christian mission. This group constituted an alternative, and potentially challenging, elite whose status was derived from educational attainments and acceptance of Christianity rather than aristocratic origin. The ministers and teachers were also the most mobile group in Upper Simalungun, and their contacts with other ethnic groups, particularly the North Tapanuli Bataks, were most frequent. Ethnic consciousness grew rapidly among the educated Simalungun Bataks, who disliked having to learn the North Tapanuli language and resented having North Tapanuli Bataks as their superiors within the church and educational hierarchies.

In addition to the educated elite incorporated into the religious and educational systems, there was a large group of primary school graduates whose limited education and partial exposure to urban life left them dissatisfied with village society but unable to advance in the city. Lacking funds, they could not acquire the further education (for the most part, only the sons of the aristocracy and individuals selected by the missionaries received more than three years of schooling) which would fit them for positions as teachers or clerks in government or plantation offices. Lacking already successful urban relatives who could give them a start in commerce, they were hesitant about moving to Siantar. As they were not members of the aristocracy, they could have little hope of entering the traditional structures of government. Frustrated at every turn, these young men spent their time in the coffee shops of Upper Simalungun, brooding over the barriers which inhibited their advancement but doing little to organize resistance to the traditional rulers or to the Dutch.

As in Lower Simalungun and Siantar, occupation and revolution brought further changes in the region. Provided with military training by the Japanese, the undereducated and underemployed youths became militant nationalists and were largely responsible for the Social Revolution of 1946 [18] and the dissolution of the traditional kingdoms. The church-affiliated elite, freed from Dutch- and Japanese-imposed restrictions, also became politically active, mobilizing the faithful against the youthful militants, the traditional rulers,

Table 2. The three localities: A simplified schematic comparison

	Upper Simalungun	Lower Simalungun	Pematang Siantar
Population	78,000	322,000	114,000
Population density	50/sq. km.	160/sq. km.	urban area
Ecology	dry rice cultivation	plantations wet rice cultivation	commerce government administration
Ethnic groups	Simalungun Bataks	Javanese North Tapanuli Bataks South Tapanuli Bataks	North Tapanuli Bataks South Tapanuli Bataks Javanese
Religious affiliations	Predominantly Protestant, with a substantial animist minority	Predominantly Moslem (*abangan*), with substantial *santri* and Protestant minorities	Predominantly Protestant, with a substantial Moslem (*santri*) minority

[18] The Social Revolution is a label applied to the wave of assassinations of traditional rulers and others which occurred in East Sumatra in early 1946. In Simalungun the rulers of four of the seven traditional kingdoms and many lesser aristocrats and their families were killed.

the Dutch, and, within the church, the North Tapanuli Bataks. The aristocrats, restored briefly to positions of prestige (if not of authority) during the Dutch occupation of 1947–1949 but soon flung again into political purgatory with the formation of the unitary state in 1950, began to regroup their forces and to plan a restoration of their influence within the framework of an independent Indonesia. As subsequent events were to demonstrate, the aristocracy still commanded more support in Upper Simalungun than either the religious elite or the youths, despite half a century of social change.

THE DEVELOPMENT OF POLITICAL ORGANIZATIONS

Specifically political organization in the three localities developed to its fullest extent only after the transfer of sovereignty in December 1949. During the colonial period there had been some embryonic nationalist activity in local branches of Partindo (Partai Indonesia, Indonesian Party), Indonesia Muda (Young Indonesia), and Gerindo (Gerakan Rakjat Indonesia, Indonesian People's Movement), but these were limited to Pematang Siantar, had very few members, and were effectively suppressed by the authorities. The Revolution witnessed an efflorescence of guerrilla groups, but these were for the most part short-lived, poorly organized above the level of the basic fighting unit, and not effectively controlled by the political parties to which they were presumably attached. Party and guerrilla leaders were often in fact the same individuals, and the requirements of the revolutionary situation were such that the tasks of fighting on the Medan Area front or providing supplies to the troops there took precedence over party-building.

With the successful completion of the Revolution, political leaders and party politicians turned their attention to the struggle for control of the government of their new nation. In 1950 Indonesia became a constitutional democracy and a unitary state, two events which had a profound impact on the development of a national party system. Constitutional democracy and the prominent position it gave to the new Parliament (Dewan Perwakilan Rakjat, People's Representative Council) encouraged the proliferation of political parties and assured them an important place in the governmental process. Elections for Parliament and a Constituent Assembly, whose seats were to be distributed on the basis of proportional representation, provided a further stimulus to party growth and the extension of party branches to all sections of the country. The years 1954–1955, immediately preceding the elections, were a period of intense campaigning throughout the archipelago.

With the rejection of the Dutch-imposed federal Republic of the United States of Indonesia and the establishment of the unitary state, Indonesian politics became in large measure Djakarta politics. Formal decision-making authority was highly centralized in national-level governmental structures such as the DPR and the central ministries. The chief goal of the political parties was thus to acquire a strong position in the DPR, from which most other benefits, and especially control of the ministries and of bureaucratic patronage, flowed.

The creation of a strong Parliament and the centralization of authority provided some but not all the conditions necessary for the development of a vigorous system of national political parties. In addition, each party with national pretensions was forced to seek popular support by devising policies and programs—or more broadly, by creating an image of itself—in accord with the wishes of a substantial segment of the population. The national parties active in our three localities had of necessity to come to terms with the patterns of interests, loyalties, and hostilities whose evolution we have described in the preceding section.[19]

This interaction between party and environment resulted in turn in different patterns of organizational development reflecting the special qualities of each locality. In Lower Simalungun the combination of economic differentiation, primordialism, new elite

[19] The replacement of parliamentary by Guided Democracy in the late 1950's of course altered the conditions for partisan growth and the objectives of party leaders. During the period of this research, local party leaders in Simalungun and Siantar spent much of their time in activities designed to influence regional bureaucrats and Army officers. The change was not, however, as drastic as might be expected. Party branch leaders in 1963–1964 were still oriented—perhaps due to an exaggerated optimism—toward a future situation of open partisan competition, elections, and enhanced governmental influence through legislative structures, and thus continued to be concerned with the maintenance and expansion of popular support. Their activities in this area were also influenced by the realization that, in the fluid, uncertain political climate of Guided Democracy, maximum popular support constituted an advantage in the test of strength which was sure to come.

groups, and some shared economic interests constituted an environment in which four parties, all of them nationally significant,
achieved popular success: PNI (Partai Nasional Indonesia, Indonesian National Party), PKI (Partai Komunis Indonesia, Indonesian
Communist Party), Masjumi (originally an abbreviation of Madjelis
Sjuro Muslimin Indonesia, Council of Indonesian Moslem Associations), and Parkindo (Partai Kristen Indonesia, Indonesian Christian [Protestant] Party).[20] In Pematang Siantar the absence of politically aggregable economic interests reduced the number of successful parties to three (Masjumi, Parkindo, and PNI), all of them
dependent on primordial loyalties for their mass support. Finally,
in Upper Simalungun ethnic homogeneity, the presence of a traditional elite, and a low level of economic differentiation all mili-
tated against national party success, producing instead a one-party
dominant system in which the major party was a purely local and
ethnic-motivated organization.

Lower Simalungun

The case of Lower Simalungun provides the most complex and
multi-faceted pattern of political organizational development. All
four successful parties in the locality were alike in that they were
national organizations and recruited the majority of their local
leaders from twentieth-century, nationally-oriented elites, many of
whose members had participated in the Revolution. There were,
however, substantial differences among them at the ideological
level, in the strategies which they adopted to win local support,
in the sources of support actually obtained, in the strength of the
attachment of members and followers to the party, and in organi-

[20] At the national level four parties won the bulk of the vote in the parliamentary elections: PNI (22.3 per cent), Masjumi (20.9 per cent), Nahdatul
Ulama (Moslem Scholars' Party) (18.4 per cent), and PKI (16.4 per cent).
Herbert Feith, *The Indonesian Elections of 1955*, p. 58. Parkindo, despite its
small national vote (2.6 per cent), had significant support in five of the
fifteen electoral districts and was also influential within the Djakarta political
elite.

Since Masjumi was banned in 1960, it had no formal organization in
Simalungun and Siantar during the years in which this research was conducted. The discussion of Masjumi here thus pertains to the pre-1960 period
only.

zational characteristics. These differences resulted in two party types: the secular, nonethnic, mass party based on economic interest, complex and strongly articulated organizationally but with only minimal membership attachment, represented by PNI and PKI; and the religio-ethnic cadre party, dominated by a single ethnic group, weakly articulated organizationally but with firm partisan attachment, represented by Masjumi and Parkindo.

At the national level PNI and PKI strategies were shaped by a conception of a modern Indonesia in which ethnic and religious cleavages and loyalties should play little or no role in political life. Party ideologies of Marhaenism and Marxism-Leninism denied the relevance of these loyalties for modern political organization, substituting for them either a rather simplistic notion of the commonality of all Indonesians, of whatever background or walk of life, as nationalists committed to the realization of a "just and prosperous" egalitarian society, or a conception of class conflict in which the farmers and workers were pitted against the capitalists and bureaucrats.[21] At the same time, it should be added, both parties were heavily Java-oriented, as the large majority of their total 1955 vote and much of their national leadership were from East and Central Java. Their ideologies, especially in the case of PNI, were deeply rooted in the world-view of the Javanese-aristocratic political culture, described by Herbert Feith as "contemptuous of economic pursuits . . . , associated with support for a secular or broadly theistic or pantheistic state," inclined toward nativism and

[21] The term Marhaenism was originally coined by Sukarno to apply to the Indonesian "common man." See Sukarno, *Marhaen and Proletarian*, Cornell Modern Indonesia Project Translation Series (Ithaca, N.Y.: Cornell University, 1960). Feith describes PNI's Marhaenism as "a political creed stressing national unity and national culture and socialist or collectivist economics. It affirmed the importance of democratic rights and opposed dictatorship, but condemned liberalism and individualism, declaring them to be offshoots of capitalism. Based on an eclectic selection of ideas from Western and Asian nationalists, Western socialists, and traditional Indonesian social thought, Marhaenism reflected both the PNI's attachment to the symbols of the nationalist revolution and the difficulties which the party faced in establishing a highest common factor of ideological orientation." (*The Decline of Constitutional Democracy in Indonesia* [Ithaca, N.Y.: Cornell University Press, 1962], pp. 139–140.) For a discussion of PKI ideology, objectives, and strategies, see Donald Hindley, *The Communist Party of Indonesia, 1951–1963* (Berkeley and Los Angeles: University of California Press, 1964).

opposition to Western influences, and sympathetic to socialist ideas.[22]

With this kind of ideological baggage both parties faced serious obstacles in Lower Simalungun, where ethnic and religious divisions are deeply rooted, the Javanese are only one of several groups, and class consciousness or abstract conceptions of the essential solidarity of all Indonesians are at best embryonic. To overcome these problems the two parties developed a basic strategy which relied primarily on appeals to the material interests of the most uprooted and detraditionalized groups in the region, the plantation and urban workers and the squatters on plantation land.

Organizationally, this strategy required PNI and PKI to create elaborate political machines, including not only party structures but also functionally differentiated subsidiary organizations directed to the specific needs of workers, squatters, and other groups. A party subbranch was maintained in each of the subdistricts of Lower Simalungun and there were dozens of village-level party and subsidiary organization units, located mostly in the immediate vicinity of the plantations. Under the supervision of regency-level party and organization leaders in Pematang Siantar, each of the subdistrict units operated at a fairly high level of activity in recruiting new members and leaders, increasing the number of village branches, holding mass rallies to explain party policy and to combat the propaganda of the opponent, making demands on government on behalf of worker and squatter members, and so on. Much of this work was carried out by youthful activists, on part or full stipend from the party, who had been recruited from the small towns of Lower Simalungun (often through party organizations in the schools) and given some ideological and organizational training before being assigned to party or organization offices in the sub-

[22] *The Decline of Constitutional Democracy in Indonesia*, p. 32. On the predominant position of Javanese in the vote for PNI and PKI, see Feith, *The Indonesian Elections of 1955*, p. 62. Some students of Indonesian politics would go further than this, arguing that PNI ideology is so heavily influenced by the Javanese world-view as to make the "secular" label inapplicable. My own view, shaped by close examination of the party only at the local level, is that neither the "secular" nor the "Javanist" view is wholly apposite. Both tendencies are present within the party, the latter stronger of course in East and Central Java and, perhaps, at the national level and the former more pronounced in East Sumatra.

districts. Competition between PNI and PKI for the same constituencies further intensified the development of elaborate organizations and the recruitment of semi-professional activists. When observed in the early 1960's both parties, despite some important differences in the intensity of training given new recruits, patterns of coordination among party and affiliated structures, and processes of local leadership selection, had fairly smooth-running and efficient organizations.

The organizational characteristics of the religious parties, Parkindo and Masjumi, differed in several important respects from those of PNI and PKI. Although formally similar to the latter, their party and subsidiary organizations were flaccid and weakly articulated, with no paid activists, few formally organized branches in the villages, often indeterminate leadership even at the subdistrict level, and no concerted drives to increase membership or to carry out any other policies or programs. The basic unit of party organization, formally the branch, in reality more closely resembled Duverger's caucus, "a grouping of notabilities for the preparation of elections, conducting campaigns and maintaining contact with the candidates." [23]

The most important reasons for these differences are related to the image which each party had of itself in relation to the national and local political processes and to the nature of the local support which each sought. PNI and PKI leaders regarded their parties as at least potentially representing all the people of the region and indeed the whole Indonesian people, irrespective of religion or ethnicity. Partisan appeals thus had to be made on nonprimordial grounds, by translating secular (and to a large extent Javanese-oriented) ideologies into positive programs which would strike a responsive chord at the local level. This in turn required, in the particular circumstances of Lower Simalungun, concentration upon the large and consciously disadvantaged worker-squatter population and continual organizational efforts.

Parkindo and Masjumi, on the other hand, had much more finite and clearly demarcated support bases in Lower Simalungun. Their potential constituencies were limited to particular religious segments of local society, the Protestant and santri Moslem com-

23 Duverger, p. 64.

munities. To win the support of their respective coreligionists, they adopted a strategy much less dependent on organizational skills and continuous effort. In the opinion of the leadership, the strength of local religious loyalties, which they believed could easily be transformed into partisan support, made such intensive activity unnecessary.

Prior to the elections the Parkindo-Masjumi strategy was simply to make the party organization's existence and its views as well known as possible among the people whom they sought to represent. In large part the local election campaigns of Parkindo and Masjumi were conducted via the established religious institutions of the locality. Christian ministers, for example, although they did not hold leadership positions in the party, inserted Parkindo propaganda into their Sunday sermons, and church lay leaders became party officials and active campaigners in their subdistricts. Similarly, Moslem religious leaders and teachers in Islamic schools were pressed into service by Masjumi, which was closely identified with Aldjam'ijatul Waslijah, the largest Moslem social and educational organization in Lower Simalungun. Most Masjumi leaders in the locality were in fact recruited from Aldjam'ijatul Waslijah, which served as the basic, though informal, organizational framework for the rather haphazardly developed party.

In the years following the elections both religious parties were relatively inactive in the villages, where there were in general no formal party leadership structures. At the subdistrict level, however, formal (but largely inactive) leadership councils were maintained so that periodic conferences to select new leaders at the regency and provincial levels could be held. In 1964 Parkindo had not held subdistrict branch conferences for three years and had no immediate plans to do so; Masjumi, outlawed for the preceding three years, had no formal organization, but most of its former leaders continued to be active in other Islamic organizations and were prepared to reestablish the party on short notice.

Partisan support actually obtained both in the 1955 elections and in more recent years fitted the hopes and expectations of the four parties rather closely, but with some important nuances. First, Parkindo and Masjumi in Lower Simalungun became the principal spokesmen not only for Protestants and santri Moslems respectively,

but also for particular ethnic communities, the North and South
Tapanuli Bataks. That the Parkindo vote (15 per cent) in 1955 was
almost entirely North Tapanuli Batak is easy to document, for the
overwhelming majority of Protestants in Lower Simalungun are
North Tapanuli Bataks. Moreover, according to the most recent
General Report of the regency party branch, all Parkindo subdistrict leaders in Lower Simalungun in 1961 were North Tapanuli
Bataks, as were most of the more than 12,000 (claimed) party
members.

The extent to which the Masjumi vote (19 per cent) can be attributed to South Tapanuli Bataks is impossible to establish without
precise (and unobtainable) data on the ethnicity of the Moslem
voters of the various subdistricts and of the locality as a whole.
The Masjumi vote, however, was highest in the two subdistricts
which, on the basis of personal observation, contain the highest
concentrations of South Tapanuli Bataks in the region. Among the
Moslems of Lower Simalungun, according to village informants, the
Masjumi versus PNI-PKI division followed closely the cleavage
between santri (mostly South Tapanuli Bataks) and abangan (Javanese).[24] Other evidence, including the dominant position of
South Tapanuli Bataks in Aldjam'ijatul Waslijah, the major constituent organization of Masjumi in Lower Simalungun, and the
apparent fact that most subdistrict Masjumi leaders were of South
Tapanuli origin, tends to confirm the argument of South Tapanuli
dominance of the party.

It is, of course, one thing to show that most Masjumi supporters
were South Tapanuli Bataks and Parkindo supporters were North
Tapanuli Bataks, and quite another to argue that there was a
specifically ethnic, rather than simply a religious, basis for partisan
affiliation. Some of the data presented in the discussion of party

[24] In some Javanese villages, however, a Masjumi vote of as much as
20 per cent was reported. At least part of this support may be attributed
to the fact that religious conflict between santri and abangan seemed rather
less intense in Lower Simalungun than in East and Central Java, despite the
added complication of ethnic cleavage. The few South Tapanuli Bataks
found in many predominantly Javanese villages often served as both the
spiritual and secular leaders of their communities, providing a nucleus for
Islamic political organization. A considerable proportion of the Javanese attracted to Masjumi may have been women, whose interest in Islam was
reported to be much greater than that of their husbands.

organization in Upper Simalungun and Pematang Siantar are relevant to this problem, and the reader is referred to those sections.

Briefly, if one examines the relationships between different Protestant ethnic groups and Parkindo and santri Moslem groups and Masjumi in the regency and municipality as a whole, it becomes clear that neither party had great appeal beyond the North and South Tapanuli Batak communities. Simalungun Batak Protestants had little use for Parkindo, and Simalungun Batak and Coastal Malay santri Moslems in Pematang Siantar were not attracted to Masjumi. Members of these ethnic groups saw the two parties as the monopolies of North and South Tapanuli Bataks who were not willing to share influence within the party. For their part, regency and municipality leaders of Parkindo and Masjumi were distrustful of the political aspirations of the other ethnic groups and were content to have them remain outside the party. In the villages, North Tapanuli Batak identification of Parkindo as the party of the ethnic as well as the religious community was quite high, while the ordinary South Tapanuli Batak, with a somewhat less developed sense of ethnic identity separate from his membership in the ummat Islam, viewed Masjumi in rather broader terms. In any event, each party was dominated by members of a single ethnic group and was closely identified, especially by others, with group interests.

PNI and PKI also came up to their own expectations, obtaining at least bi-ethnic support in Lower Simalungun as a direct result of their efforts among Javanese plantation workers and Javanese and North Tapanuli plantation squatters. PNI, because of a more diversified support base extending beyond the worker-squatter constituency, was the more successful of the two parties.

In the absence of sufficient data on the ethnic and socio-economic composition of the various subdistricts and villages in Lower Simalungun, it is difficult to document the argument of PNI-PKI bi-ethnicity and dependence on plantation support. One indirect indicator, the "Parkindo support ratio," provides some evidence with regard to the elections, as does more recent data concerning the ethnic affiliations of PNI and PKI membership and leadership.

The Parkindo support ratio (the percentage of the Parkindo vote divided by the percentage of North Tapanuli Bataks in a given subdistrict) was computed for the six Simalungun subdistricts with a large North Tapanuli Batak population. These ratios were then compared with the percentage of arable land under plantation concession in each subdistrict. The findings—two subdistricts with a low percentage of plantation land and a high Parkindo support ratio, two subdistricts with a high percentage of plantation land and a low support ratio, and two subdistricts intermediate on both scales (see Fig. 1)—clearly indicate an inverse relation-

Figure 1. "Parkindo Support Ratios" in six subdistricts with large North Tapanuli Batak populations, compared with plantation hectareage as a percentage of total arable land

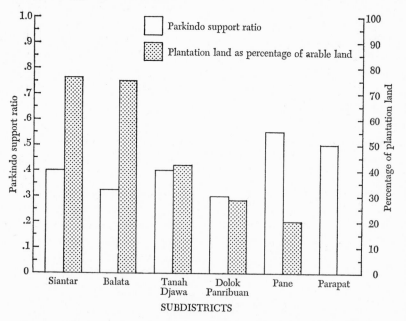

Sources: Electoral data from Pemerintahan Daerah tkt. II Simalungun, *Daftar: Perhitungan hasil-hasil pemungutan suara dalam daerah Kabupaten Simalungun/Pemilihan Anggota Dewan Perwakilan Rakjat* (A list: Calculation of the election results in the region of Kabupaten Simalungun, election of members of Parliament), Sept. 29, 1955. North Tapanuli Bataks as a percentage of subdistrict population estimated from interview data and a table on religious affiliation in Pemerintahan Daerah tkt. II Simalungun, *Lapuran Tahun 1963*, p. 115. Parkindo support ratio: Per cent Parkindo subdistrict vote divided by per cent of North Tapanuli Bataks in the subdistrict population. Plantation hectareage as per cent of arable land from Djawatan Agraria Kabupaten Simalungun, *Daftar: Nama2 Perkebunan di Kabupaten Simalungun* (P. Siantar, 1963), and *The general agricultural condition of Simeloengoen* (P. Siantar: Gunseibu-Keizaibu, 2602 [1942]).

ship between the two variables. In other words, in villages where many of the North Tapanuli Bataks were squatters, the vote for Parkindo tended to be small; conversely, in regions where titles to land were not in question, the Parkindo vote was greater. The North Tapanuli vote which did not go to Parkindo in the plantation subdistricts could only have been given to PNI or PKI, since the only other party with significant support in Lower Simalungun was the Moslem Masjumi. PNI and PKI were thus able to win North Tapanuli votes, to overcome the barriers of religious and ethnic loyalties to Parkindo, where the interest of the individual as squatter took precedence over his identification as a North Tapanuli Batak and as a Protestant.

More direct evidence for the bi-ethnic support obtained by PNI and PKI may be found in figures on the ethnic affiliations of party leaders and members in Lower Simalungun. According to almost

Table 3. The 1955 elections in the three localities

Lower Simalungun		Pematang Siantar		Upper Simalungun	
Party	% Vote	Party	% Vote	Party	% Vote
PNI	30.1	Masjumi	38.3	KRSST	43.7
PKI	20.0	Parkindo	29.3	PNI	19.8
Masjumi	19.3	PNI	13.9	Parkindo	9.3
Parkindo	15.4	PKI	2.7	Masjumi	7.2
Other	15.3	Other	15.8	PKI	4.1
				Other	15.9

Source: Computed from *Daftar: Perhitungan hasil-hasil pemungutan suara.*

certainly incomplete information obtained from government files, total PKI membership in Lower Simalungun in 1961 was 111.[25] Of this number, 75 were Javanese, 32 were North Tapanuli Bataks, and 4 were Simalungun Bataks. Comparable data were not available for the much larger (4,000 claimed members in 1963) PNI subdistrict branches, although interviews with subdistrict and village party leaders indicated a North Tapanuli-Javanese division approaching equality. Membership in the various PKI and PNI

[25] The small size of PKI membership did not reflect unsuccessful recruitment but rather a deliberate policy of emphasizing the development of subsidiary organizations rather than of the party itself.

subsidiary organizations was also divided primarily among the Javanese and North Tapanuli groups, the specific percentage varying with the organization (e.g., the farmers' associations having many more North Tapanuli Bataks than the plantation workers' unions). At the leadership level, North Tapanuli Bataks represented slightly more than a majority of all PNI subdistrict branch leaders in Lower Simalungun, while about two-thirds of the comparable PKI leaders were Javanese.

Data on the ethnicity of PNI and PKI subsidiary organization leaders below the regency level were difficult to obtain, since in most cases these organizations did not maintain subdistrict branches, and lists of village leaders were not available in party or government offices. In general, labor union leaders were Javanese, although there was some admixture of North Tapanuli Bataks (from among the white-collar employees of the plantations, and in the transportation unions where most members were North Tapanuli Bataks). Village-level leadership of both PNI and PKI farmers' organizations was divided roughly equally among members of the two ethnic groups.[26]

Although both parties seem to have received much of their support from workers and squatters responding to appeals to their material interests, PNI received a larger and more dispersed vote. PNI's 30 per cent of the total Lower Simalungun vote was distributed fairly evenly among all subdistricts, ranging from a high of 35 per cent to a low of 26 per cent, while PKI's 20 per cent was divided more unequally, ranging from 34 per cent to 14 per cent. This disparity, which probably continued without substantial change into the 1960's, is attributable not to the greater success of PNI in the immediate plantation environment (indeed there are some indications that PKI may have been more successful there)[27] but

[26] Parenthetically, bi-ethnicity did not necessarily mean inter-ethnic cooperation, particularly among the village membership. In both PNI and PKI, residential separation along ethnic lines meant that village party units consisted wholly or in very large part of members of a single group. For PNI this pattern was strengthened by the importance of ethnic-based support in subdistrict and regency party leadership contests. Ambitious party leaders each had their own ethnic constituency upon which they depended for votes at party conferences and to the cultivation of which they devoted much of their time and energy.

[27] PKI's largest vote percentages were in those subdistricts where the proportion of arable land under plantation concession is highest.

to its broader appeal throughout Lower Simalungun generally.

One compelling reason for PNI's greater and broader support was its unique identification with the nationalist movement and the struggle against the Dutch. The party was able to gain many supporters, irrespective of direct material interests, among those sympathetic to the goals of the Revolution. Although PKI guerrilla units also fought in the Revolution, the party did not share the special position of vanguard of the nationalist movement generally accorded to PNI. Moreover, PKI's nationalist credentials were considerably discredited by the party's role in the Madiun Affair of 1948 (in which PKI took up arms against the nationalist government), an event which was widely known among those who had been involved in the Revolution.

PNI was also the beneficiary of a certain amount of support based on ethnic-related loyalties. During the Revolution influential members of the Javanese community in Lower Simalungun had supported PNI, and in more recent years Javanese with roots in the region have been prominent in the party at both the subdistrict and regency levels. PNI thus became to some extent identified in Lower Simalungun as *the* party of the abangan Javanese. PKI, despite its Java-centrism at the national level, had little ethnic-related support among the Javanese in the locality, in large measure because the party lacked Javanese leaders comparable in stature to those of PNI.

Finally, the association of Communism with atheism, a frequent theme in religious party (and PNI) propaganda, severely hampered PKI's electoral campaign in 1954–1955 and continued to make the party (although not its subsidiary organizations) unattractive in subsequent years. Among those individuals who were neither workers nor squatters, for whom PKI had little appeal in any event, the stamp of atheism provided an additional deterrent. Despite long effort the religious parties were not able to use this weapon effectively against PNI.

Beyond the contrasts in strategies, structural elaboration, and bases of support, the two types of party differed significantly in the degree of partisan attachment felt by the ordinary member or supporter. Parkindo and Masjumi, both multi-ethnic at the national level, became in Lower Simalungun vehicles for the political aspirations of particular ethnic groups. The effect of this close bond between religion and ethnicity was that, despite minimal party activity, partisan support was deeply rooted and well-nigh indestructible. Thus the banning of Masjumi in 1961 produced no discernible shift in the political allegiance of South Tapanuli Moslems. Instead, the great majority of Masjumi supporters and leaders simply withdrew from politics to await more favorable conditions for a resumption of activity. Outside the immediate plantation environment, the North Tapanuli population continued to resist the blandishments of PKI and PNI and remained loyal to Parkindo. In a small town in subdistrict Tanah Djawa, for example, which had no squatter population, informants reported a large Parkindo vote in 1955; by 1964 both PNI and PKI had established subsidiary organization branches in the town, but these had few members.

Support for PNI and PKI was much less deeply rooted than that for Parkindo and Masjumi, particularly among subsidiary organization members. Organization leaders at the very local level were primarily oriented to their villages. They affiliated with PNI or PKI labor or farmer unions in order to further specific village interests or to enhance their own political influence among their followers within the village. Thus a local irrigation committee might become a branch of the PNI or PKI farmers' organization because these organizations had influence with the government or provided protection if the villagers decided to expand illegally their rice fields at the expense of the nearby plantation. Similarly, a plantation worker personally influential among his fellow workers would join the PNI or PKI labor union in order to gain the necessary political resources to make demands upon the plantation administration and simultaneously solidify his own local power by meeting the expectations of his followers. If the party was unable to meet their demands, these leaders were likely to seek support elsewhere. In the most extreme case related to the author, a local leader in Tanah Djawa who had a substantial following among bus company workers had been in and out of PSI (Partai Sosialis Indonesia, Indonesian Socialist Party), Masjumi, and PKI labor unions before he joined PNI in 1964.

Both parties were of course aware of the tenuous loyalties of village-level leaders and their followers and paid considerable attention to ideological indoctrination and to the placing of regular party activists in key positions on local leadership councils. These efforts met with only limited success, however, as an examination of the recent history of labor unions in the region vividly demonstrates.

Between 1961 and 1964 membership in the PNI plantation workers' union dropped from nearly 11,000 to a little over 4,000. The reason for this decline is to be found in the emergence in late 1962 of a new labor organization, SOKSI (Sentral Organisasi Karyawan Sosialis Indonesia, Central Organization of Socialist Functionaries of Indonesia), a corporatist "company union" led in East Sumatra by plantation administrators and retired army officers and unaffiliated with any political party. At least in part through such policies as providing gifts of clothing and other commodities to potential leaders and members and threatening the more intransigent with transfer to less attractive employment, SOKSI succeeded in a very short time in becoming one of the largest labor organizations in Simalungun, claiming a membership of over 11,000 in early 1964. Although membership figures for PKI's SOBSI (Sentral Organisasi Buruh Seluruh Indonesia, All-Indonesian Federation of Labor Unions) do not indicate a decline comparable to that of the PNI union, conversations with union leaders of all political persuasions and visits to various plantations (not to mention SOBSI's furious anti-SOKSI propaganda) suggest that its membership loss was at least as great.[28] Squatter support for the two parties was equally tenuous, although as of 1964 there had been no crisis to dramatize the situation.

Pematang Siantar

The mass support obtained in Lower Simalungun by parties appealing to economic interests reflected the impact of a plantation economy that had created large numbers of workers and squatters with substantial and specific grievances against that economy. These grievances were moreover amenable to aggregation and expression through subsidiary organizations of the type created by PNI and PKI, which could provide real assistance through collective action.

Pematang Siantar contains neither plantation workers and squat-

---

[28] SOBSI-Simalungun leaders stated that their 1964 membership (claimed to be 45,000) was about the same as it had been in 1963.

ters nor their functional equivalent. Petty trade is the predominant occupation in the city, and the culture of Siantar traders is individualistic, competitive, and distrustful of organized political activity as a means of achieving economic goals. In the local view the primary purpose of commercial organizations, usually established by fiat from above, has always been to control and limit rather than to promote the individual's pursuit of a livelihood. Collective security and individual assistance come not from organizations of merchants, who are to be trusted neither as a group nor individually, but from one's blood brothers and (to a lesser extent) fellow Christians or Moslems.

Even the labor segment of the Siantar population, especially in private industry, has been difficult to organize. There are few sizable factories in the city, most employing fifty or fewer workers. To build a union on such a fragmented base requires an intensive effort which, even if successful, produces only a limited gain, particularly in view of the inconstancy of member affection for the union. Certain industries have, moreover, presented special problems. The textile industry, for example, is dominated by North Tapanuli Bataks who tend to hire members of their own and related patrilineages. Unionization, predicated on the idea of a divergence of interest between the workers and their employers, has not been able to take hold among the family-oriented textile workers.

In this environment, political organizational development did not parallel Lower Simalungun's bifurcated pattern of one party type based on primordial loyalties, organizationally flaccid but with unwavering mass support, and a second type based on economic interests, multi-ethnic, organizationally complex but with shallow support. Instead, ethnic-religious or simply ethnic loyalties were the principal—almost the sole—ingredient of partisan success. The result was a single type of party comparable to the primordial, "cadre" party of Lower Simalungun.

The most successful parties in Siantar in 1955 were Masjumi (38 per cent) and Parkindo (29 per cent). Both followed essentially the same strategies as in Lower Simalungun, operating through the local religious leadership or cooperating closely with it, phrasing their appeals in mostly religious rather than ethnic terms, and exhibiting a confident disdain for organizational coherence and efficiency. Similarly, their success was based as much on the identification of the party with the corresponding ethnic as with the religious community.

Parkindo was closely tied to the predominant Protestant ethnic group, the North Tapanuli Bataks, who contributed all of the party's city-wide leadership, including its four representatives in the municipality legislature, and 85 per cent of the leadership at the ward level. These leaders were drawn primarily from the merchant and civil servant strata, and most of them were lay leaders in the largest North Tapanuli church (HKBP, Huria Kristen Batak Protestan). Of the two small Protestant ethnic minorities in the city, one, the Karo Bataks, had supported Parkindo in the 1955 election but had since lost their representative in the municipality-wide leadership council. Simalungun Batak Christians showed little interest in Parkindo from the start and were not active in the party at either the municipality or ward level.

Masjumi's voters, members, and leaders were predominantly South Tapanuli Batak to an even greater degree than in Lower Simalungun. Among the voters, the party was strongest in those wards with a large South Tapanuli population, although it also received some Javanese votes.[29] Among the leadership, all city-wide Masjumi officials and all party representatives in the municipality legislature were South Tapanuli Bataks, as were most ward leaders. With few exceptions these individuals were recruited from the two largest Moslem social and educational organizations in the city, Muhammadijah and Aldjam'ijatul Waslijah.

The almost total local dominance of Masjumi by the South Tapanuli Bataks was largely responsible for the establishment of a Siantar branch of Nahdatul Ulama (Moslem Scholars' Party), Masjumi's major national competitor for the support of Indonesian Moslems. In national politics NU has represented the more syn-

[29] The contrast between the South Tapanuli Batak percentage of the population (20 per cent) and Masjumi's percentage of the vote (38 per cent) is due not to the party's appeal beyond the South Tapanuli community but to differences in the composition of the 1955 electorate and the 1961 population. By the latter year the city limits had been expanded to include large numbers of North Tapanuli and Simalungun Bataks who had formerly been included in the Lower Simalungun population.

cretistic, conservative, rural, and Javanese element within Indonesian Islam, whereas Masjumi was the party of Islamic modernism and reform, strongest in the cities, among the merchant population, and in the Outer Islands. In Siantar these differences were overshadowed, although not totally eclipsed, by ethnicity. NU from its inception in 1953 was the special province of two disgruntled ethnic minorities, Simalungun Batak and Coastal Malay Moslems. Hostile to Masjumi because they felt unable to obtain high office or influence within it, leaders of these two ethnic groups preferred to establish a party which they could control, at least in the locality.[30] Because of the small size of its constituency, however, NU has never made much of an impact in Siantar.

Nonprimordial parties in Siantar have had a particularly difficult time adapting themselves to an environment which severely limits the effectiveness of partisan appeals framed either in terms of secular ideologies or pragmatic interests. The most rigidly nonprimordial, and thus least successful, party in Siantar was PKI. Communist strategy followed closely the pattern described for Lower Simalungun, with special emphasis on labor union and youth organization development. Because of its acknowledged predominance in the labor movement, extending as far back as the late 1940's, and the militancy of its younger members, PKI gave an impression of considerable strength in the municipality. This was a superficial impression, however, which did not take into account the inability of PKI to transform union membership or provocative slogan-painting into partisan support. In 1955 the party won only 445 votes (less than 3 per cent) in Siantar, and there were few indications of increasing strength in subsequent years.

PNI, which captured 14 per cent of the 1955 vote in Siantar (making it the third largest party in the city) was much more suc-

[30] Another factor of some importance was the close relationship between the future NU leaders and the rulers of the Simalungun kingdoms and the Coastal Malay sultanates in the prewar period. Modernist Moslem organizations, in particular Muhammadijah, had been among the chief antagonists of the traditional political systems, which they saw as too closely tied to adat and unresponsive to twentieth-century social change. These animosities were further intensified during the Revolution, when the traditional elite opposed and the modernist Moslems supported independence. See HAMKA (Hadji Abdul Malik Karim Amrullah), *Kenang2-an Hidup* (Kuala Lumpur: Pustaka Antara, 1966).

cessful than PKI. This success was due in a broad sense to PNI's greater flexibility and adaptability to the conditions of the local environment. Of special importance, however, was the party's ability —comparable to that of Parkindo and Masjumi—to monopolize the support of a particular ethnic group, the Javanese. Accompanying this monopolistic support were weakly articulated party and organizational structures and a firmness of partisan attachment that corresponded closely to the pattern which we have described as characteristic of the religio-ethnic party type.

PNI's public posture was much the same as in Lower Simalungun; it eschewed primordially-based appeals and claimed to be the party of the common Indonesian regardless of ethnic origin. Party propaganda—and indeed the personal commitment of the branch chairman and some other leaders—echoed the central party leadership's emphasis upon secular nationalism as a unifying force and the ordinary farmer and laborer as the pillars of the Revolution and of the just and prosperous society of the future.

In some measure the partisan support that PNI actually achieved was in accord with its chosen image of nonprimordialism. More than any other successful party in the locality, PNI had multi-ethnic leadership and membership, drawn primarily from the Javanese and North and South Tapanuli groups but including representatives of smaller communities as well. This diversity was attributable to some of the same factors which operated in Lower Simalungun. First, PNI was in the popular view preeminently the party of revolutionary nationalism and thus attracted support from more militant elements in all ethnic groups. It was also seen by many as the party of the Establishment and especially in the early 1950's had the active backing of many prominent civil servants and professionals.[31] Third, the party picked up some support from Moslems and Christians opposed to the pervasive influence of the religious leadership in all

[31] In view of PNI's position in Java as the party of the bureaucrats and, in general, the professional elite, it should be stated that the elite types attracted to PNI in Siantar never had a controlling voice in the party and became increasingly disaffected from it. The dominant municipality (and regency) leadership from the 1940's through the 1960's consisted of professional politicians. Civil servants, doctors, and others with advanced education were never comfortable in the party, although many kept nominal membership.

spheres of social life but unwilling to turn to the atheistic PKI, a step which would have led to ostracism from community activities. Finally, PNI in Siantar also had its share of pure opportunists, men with no firm political convictions who chose to make a career (or simply gain influence in city government) by joining an organization that was strong nationally and regionally but was weak and thus controllable in their particular wards.

Despite its undoubted multi-ethnicity, PNI was heavily dependent for its mass support in the city on the loyalty of the Javanese community. In 1955 the only solidly PNI ward in Siantar was Javanese-inhabited Bantan, with the Javanese in neighboring Melaju and Timbang Galung Baru also voting heavily PNI. By making some rather tenuous assumptions about the population of Siantar at the time of the elections and the likely percentage of PNI voters in the Javanese sections and extrapolating from election figures, it is possible to conclude that Javanese voters accounted for perhaps 1,000 of PNI's 2,310 votes, with the rest of the party vote probably distributed roughly equally (relative to proportion of population) among all other ethnic groups.[32] In the early 1960's nearly half the party membership also consisted of Javanese, followed by the North Tapanuli Bataks (27 per cent) and the South Tapanuli Bataks (about 15 per cent). These figures are all the more striking when it is recalled that the Javanese are only a small minority of the municipality population, whereas in Lower Simalungun they are the largest group.

Javanese support for PNI, while reflecting some of the factors described above, was firmly rooted in the notion that the party most closely reflected community interests. Not only was it in the local view the party of Sukarno, but also of the most eminent Javanese—schoolteachers, ward heads, ex-guerrilla leaders—in Siantar

[32] The 15,605 votes cast in the Siantar election represented a third of the total 1955 population of about 50,000. Assuming that the proportion of voters to population was reasonably consistent from ward to ward, there were roughly 1,000 to 1,500 voters in the major Javanese ward, Bantan. If Bantan's vote was only 60 per cent PNI, something like 600–900 of PNI's 2,310 votes came from that ward. Add to that another 200 or so votes from Javanese in other wards and one arrives at the figure of 800–1100, or one-third to one-half of the total PNI vote. Such an estimate is obviously not very reliable and is offered only as an indication of the ethnicity of PNI voters in Siantar.

itself, in the subdistrict of Siantar which surrounds the city, and in Simalungun regency as a whole. In supporting PNI the Javanese community was expressing its solidarity with its most respected members. PNI's only potential opponent among the Javanese, PKI, contained no individuals of comparable stature and was thus unable to win the community's support.

PNI-Siantar differed from its Lower Simalungun counterparts not only in the degree of ethnic-related membership support but also in structural development and selection of strategic priorities. The party had no office in the city, did not conduct membership drives, and had no paid activists. Party activity at the ward level was minimal and communications between municipality and ward leaders were intermittent at best. The party's labor union was in 1964 in a state of advanced decay, with dispirited, inactive leadership and a membership of fewer than 300. Most other affiliates were similarly weak and disorganized.

This pattern of organizational weakness and inactivity was a direct result of PNI's firm support among the Javanese and its limited ability to overcome the resistance of North and South Tapanuli Batak merchants and civil servants to political organizations neither dominated by members of their respective communities nor motivated toward the protection of community interests. Aware that the realistic limits of their potential constituency did not extend much beyond the Javanese community, PNI leaders did not stress the development of subsidiary organizations or make any concerted effort to organize the non-Javanese. Instead they directed most of their attention outward to city government and upward to influence within the provincial party organization. Siantar's social and cultural environment thus molded a PNI which in terms of strategy, organization, and support characteristics rather closely resembled the religio-ethnic parties Parkindo and Masjumi. There was, indeed, no other route to success.

Upper Simalungun

In Upper Simalungun political organizational development was similarly affected by the distinctive characteristics of the locality, including ethnic homogeneity and consciousness, the presence of a traditional ruling elite, and a slower and less penetrative pattern of social change. As in the case of migrant groups in the other regions, linguistic, cultural, and kinship uniformities among the Simalungun Bataks became the basis of a new and intense sense of ethnic awareness in the early decades of the twentieth century. In the post-independence period ethnic loyalty, complicated only by support for or opposition to the political leadership of the traditional aristocracy, has been the principal ingredient of partisan success in the region. Religious cleavages (among Christians, animists, and Moslems) have played only a very limited role, and socio-economic divisions, in the absence of extensive economic change, have been of no consequence.

The combined effect of these variables, in the conditions of open partisan competition which prevailed in Indonesia in the early 1950's, was the creation of a one party dominant system in Upper Simalungun. The major party in this system was KRSST (Kebangunan Rakjat Simalungun Sumatera Timur, The Awakening of the Simalungun People of East Sumatra), which won 44 per cent of the 1955 vote in the region. KRSST was an example of the primordial, "cadre" party type, sharing with its counterparts in Lower Simalungun and Siantar an ethnically-oriented mass base and a low level of organizational activity. As a purely local rather than a national party, explicitly committed to the protection of ethnic interests and dependent for its mass support upon the leadership of the traditional aristocracy, it was an extreme variant of the type.

KRSST was established just prior to the election campaign of 1954–1955 by a small group consisting mostly of former traditional rulers and their close relatives. The organization's purpose was to present an ethnic-group-oriented alternative to the ostensibly non-ethnic national parties. In the eyes of its founders it was not a political party in the sense of a continuing multi-purpose organization with a constitution, a hierarchy of branches, and an elected leadership. Instead, it was a "caucus" party to an even greater extent than Parkindo and Masjumi, with no more complex organization than was required to wage an electoral campaign among people who merely needed to be made aware of the party's existence in order to vote for it.

Most of KRSST's largely self-selected activists in Upper Simalungun were Protestants, as most Simalungun Bataks with a measure of education and organizational skills are Protestants, but animists and Moslems were also represented. In KRSST, a man's religious affiliation was irrelevant; those who worked for and supported the party were motivated by the goal of ethnic unity and by respect for the traditional aristocracy as the legitimate community leadership.

Despite heavy support in several of the subdistricts of Upper Simalungun, KRSST's vote was not sufficient to win a seat in the national Parliament (or even in the proposed provincial legislature). Shortly after the elections the party began to atrophy. Its leaders were aware that, at least for a group as small as the Simalungun Batak, a purely ethnic political organization was a road to nowhere in post-independence Indonesian politics. Unwilling to participate in political life on any other basis, they turned to private pursuits. In 1961, long after it had ceased to play a meaningful role in the locality, KRSST was banned under the provisions of a presidential edict (no. 7 of 1959) simplifying the party system.

Since the decline of KRSST there have been two attempts in Upper Simalungun to build successor political or quasi-political organizations. Both of these occurred in the special circumstances of the 1956–1957 North Sumatran Army rebellion, led by the North Tapanuli Batak Colonel Simbolon, and its aftermath of increased insecurity at the village level. The two organizations, Rondahaim (named for a former *radja*) and Bapost (Badan Penuntut Otonom Sumatera Timur, Body to Demand East Sumatran Autonomy) were created for special, short-term purposes. Rondahaim, with a fairly elaborate network of village organizations in a few subdistricts, was designed to provide security to villagers threatened by bandit activity and the feared incursions of rebels from North Tapanuli. It also engaged in various development projects, such as road and school construction. Its leaders, like those of KRSST, were close to the traditional aristocracy. Bapost's purpose was to promote the administrative separation of East Sumatra from Tapanuli, in the hope that Simalungun Bataks (and other indigenous East Sumatrans) could become masters in their own house if the house was smaller. Bapost's leadership was more broadly based than Rondahaim's, including traditionalists, Christians, Moslems, former revolutionaries, and also Karo Bataks and Coastal Malays, but was not

well organized even at the subdistrict level, where a few individuals
were active as propagandists for the idea of East Sumatran autonomy. Both Rondahaim and Bapost were short-lived, enduring
no longer than the circumstances which had called them into existence. By 1964, when the authority of the central government was
again established in Upper Simalungun and Simalungun Bataks
held important political and governmental positions in the regency
and, to a lesser extent, the province, no organization existed in
Upper Simalungun which represented, or could appeal to, the large
group of former KRSST supporters.

The most successful of the national parties which campaigned
in Upper Simalungun was PNI, with 20 per cent of the vote. It was,
however, a very different PNI from its counterparts in Lower Simalungun or even Siantar. First, of course, it was largely a Simalungun
Batak party. According to 1963 data, two-thirds of the PNI subdistrict leaders in Upper Simalungun were Simalungun Bataks, as
were most of the party's members and voters.

Secondly, PNI leadership in Upper Simalungun consisted mostly
of former revolutionary activists generally credited with a central
role in the assassinations of the aristocracy in 1946. These were the
brooders of the 1930's, men with enough education and exposure
to the outside world to desire change for themselves and their
people, but with too little opportunity to bring it about. They saw
the traditional leadership—the aristocracy of the colonial period
and the KRSST activists of 1954–1955—as "feudal," inegalitarian,
oppressive, and incapable of leading the ethnic group in modern,
independent Indonesia. While they differed in many respects from
the KRSST leaders—in social background, values, personal aspirations—Simalungun Batak PNI leaders in Upper Simalungun shared
with them a concern for the progress of the ethnic group in competition with other groups resident in Simalungun, a concern which
was strengthened by their realization that, if they were to rise
within the party at the regency or higher levels, they would need
substantial support from members of the ethnic community. Their
desire to make PNI the predominant party among the Simalungun
Bataks was limited, however, by the particular circumstances of
Upper Simalungun.

Organizationally, PNI in Upper Simalungun more closely resembled Parkindo, Masjumi, and even KRSST than it did its own branches in Lower Simalungun. There were no genuine PNI activists, in the sense of organization-building "full-timers," few subsidiary organization branches, and no intensive or continuing attempts to develop mass support. In large part these differences were related to the finite quality of the party's base in the locality. Since its leadership was closely identified with the militants of the revolutionary period, PNI could not hope to win the support of that large group of Simalungun Bataks who had kinship or other ties to members of the traditional aristocracy or who simply retained their respect for the memory of the traditional social order. On the other hand, the party had already obtained the firm support of those individuals estranged from the old order—whether they had participated in or merely approved the events of the Revolution—a support which did not need to be shored up by further organizational efforts.

There is little that needs to be said of the remaining parties in Upper Simalungun. Parkindo, which ran third in the elections, was hampered by the virulent anti-North Tapanuli attitudes of most Simalungun Batak Protestants and the concomitant identification of the party as North Tapanuli-dominated. Although many Protestant ministers declared themselves sympathetic to the national objectives of Parkindo, their support was less than wholehearted; many, in fact, overtly or covertly supported KRSST. Despite a population that was over 50 per cent Protestant, the Parkindo vote was, for the whole locality, less than 10 per cent. As of 1963–1964 Parkindo's branches in Upper Simalungun were its weakest and most poorly organized; in four of the seven subdistricts the party organizations were one-man operations, with no party councils and no activity at either the village or the subdistrict level.

The support of an ethnically-mixed Moslem electorate in two subdistricts located on the fringes of the locality made Masjumi the fourth largest party in Upper Simalungun in 1955 (7 per cent of the vote). Because of the small Moslem population, neither Masjumi nor Nahdatul Ulama campaigned extensively in Upper Simalungun and neither party was active there in 1964.

Finally, the weakest of the four major national parties in Upper Simalungun was PKI, which obtained only 4 per cent of the vote.

The party's difficulties in the locality were similar to those it experienced in Pematang Siantar. It was unable to overcome opposition based on religious loyalties and on the sense of ethnic unity, with which it would not compromise. In subsequent years PKI continued its almost total reliance on the worker-squatter strategy, inapplicable in largely plantation-less Upper Simalungun, refused to support—or to permit its one regency-level Simalungun Batak leader to support—the movement for East Sumatran autonomy, and made no serious effort to organize in the subdistricts of Upper Simalungun. Without roots in the locality comparable to those of PNI as articulator of the interests and aspirations of the former revolutionary militants, PKI in effect wrote off the Simalungun Bataks. In the early 1960's the party had one subdistrict branch, with nine members, in the locality.

Conclusions

Examination of three party systems in diverse circumstances of social change suggests several conclusions with regard to the impact of primordialism on patterns of political organization. First, primordial loyalties and hostilities are quite clearly not "traditional" in the three localities. Instead they are a response to an initially colonially induced process of modernization which introduced Christianity and Islam to the region, created a communications network, established the conditions for the growth of towns and cities, and provided wage employment for many people in both urban and nonurban areas. Competition for scarce values and material goods—land, certain kinds of employment, education, status— led individuals to begin to perceive themselves as members of distinct ethnic groups, based on common language, culture, clan membership, and to some extent religious affiliation, whose interests they defended against incursions from other groups. The conditions of contemporary Indonesian social life represent an intensification of this process, so that ethnic division today is at least as much of a reality as it was in the colonial period. It is, moreover, highly probable that ethnic loyalties will continue for a long time to come to be a major characteristic of individual self-identification in the context of local social life. This statement applies equally to Lower Simalungun and Pematang Siantar, where individuals from a variety of ethnic groups are in close proximity, and to Upper Simalungun, whose people feel a sense of unity vis-à-vis the migrant groups whom they consider usurpers in their homeland.

Second, ethnic loyalties have spilled over into partisan politics. Ethnicity has provided a focal point not only for the individual's sense of personal identity and his evaluation of others, but also for his conception of his relationship to the Indonesian polity. Belonging to a particular ethnic group has consequences for individual political attitudes and for the way in which the individual perceives the structure of political competition for scarce values. These perceptions led to the identification of Parkindo with the North Tapanuli Batak community, Masjumi with the South Tapanuli Bataks, and, to a lesser extent, PNI with the Javanese. Unable to aspire to an influential position in any of these parties or in PKI, Simalungun Bataks created an explicitly ethnic organization of their own, KRSST.

Third, ethnicity is not the only basis for political organization in the region. The role of religious affiliation is highly complex and difficult to separate from ethnic-derived attitudes, and indeed many supporters of Parkindo and Masjumi did not make any distinction. For them, the sense of being a North (South) Tapanuli Batak, a Protestant (santri Moslem), and a Parkindo (Masjumi) supporter were fused together in a single concept of cultural identity and political affiliation. At least some members of other groups, however, did make a distinction, as we have seen in the cases of Simalungun Batak Protestant opposition to Parkindo in Upper Simalungun, and Simalungun Batak and Coastal Malay santri Moslem opposition to Masjumi in Pematang Siantar. Religious loyalties *per se,* divorced from ethnic ties and antagonisms, have also been a factor of some importance, most notably among non-South Tapanuli (and also perhaps some South Tapanuli) supporters of Masjumi.

Socio-economic interest as an independent causal variable in determining political affiliation is more clear-cut. In the case of North Tapanuli Bataks in Lower Simalungun, both impressionistic evidence and some hard data demonstrate that proximity to the plantation environment (i.e., squatter status) produced a shift in partisan support from Parkindo to PNI and PKI. Somewhat more difficult to evaluate are the motivations behind Javanese support for PNI and PKI since both parties are Java-centric and might be expected, even in the absence of plantations, to appeal to the local Javanese. In the case of PKI, it seems clear that the plantation worker-squatter strategy was the crucial ingredient, since the party was largely unsuccessful among the Javanese of Pematang Siantar. For PNI, on the other hand, worker-squatter appeals were supplemented in both localities by reliance on locally influential Javanese and by the belief of many Javanese that PNI was identified with their interests as members of a particular ethnic group.

It is important in this context to emphasize that, among the socio-economic variables which might have been relevant, only the plantation environment was able to produce a real shift away from primordial patterns of voting and partisan support. Urbanization and the development of a peculiarly urban pattern of class stratification and of associations which cut across primordial lines are often cited as factors which can overcome primordial loyalties and produce a "modern," class- or economic-interest-oriented party and organizational system. In Siantar, however, and apparently in the towns of Lower Simalungun as well, the effect of urbanization —a further intensification of primordial cleavages closely reflected in the pattern of partisan support—was quite the opposite.

To complete this catalogue of explanations for party support one further factor must be added, the development among a substantial portion of the local population of a sense of Indonesian nationhood. Still embryonic during the colonial period, the positive acceptance of the concept of an Indonesian nation spread rapidly through the region during the Japanese occupation and the long years of Revolution. In each of the three major migrant communities, members of the dominant elite groups, whose leadership was based on their ability to interpret a changing environment and to represent the community to the outside world, were among those most deeply affected by the nationalist idea and oriented toward participation in national political life. The result was a post-independence social and cultural environment which readily accepted the organizational efforts of nationally significant political parties. PNI, which came closest to being the organizational expression of pure Indonesian nationalism in the localities, was able to obtain support from such groups as the urban, educated elite, minority segments of the North and South Tapanuli Bataks who were both nationalistically inclined and estranged from the dominant religious leadership of their communities, and the revolutionary militants among the Simalungun Bataks of Upper Simalungun. Although no other party could capitalize directly on the growth of nationalist sentiment, the prominence of the nationally important PKI, Parkindo, and Masjumi in the region clearly reflected a sense of membership and participation in the Indonesian nation, at the very least among local elites who in turn commanded popular support. Even KRSST's traditionalist and inward-looking leaders set as their principal goal representation in the national Parliament.

Within each of the major parties in the region, the relationship between primordialism and partisan affiliation had a powerful impact on party organizational structure and on the degree of commitment which the individual made to his party. Those parties not dependent or only partially dependent on ethnic and religious loyalties, i.e., PNI and PKI in Lower Simalungun, were highly active, complex, and strongly articulated organizationally, with a full complement of subsidiary organizations, paid cadres, and so on. At the same time, popular support for these parties depended largely on alliances made by village-level leaders for essentially pragmatic reasons. Such support could dissolve rapidly, as in the case of the creation of SOKSI. On the other hand, those parties based on ethnic or ethnic-religious ties, i.e., Parkindo, Masjumi, and KRSST, had minimal organizational elaboration but, because of the strength of the loyalties which bound the individual to his community and his party, nearly indestructible support. Perhaps the effects of the local environment on party organization may best be seen in a comparison of PNI branches in the three localities. Highly organized and active in Lower Simalungun because of the tenuousness of worker-squatter commitment to the party, less active in Siantar because of the firmness of Javanese support and the limits to its expansion set by ethnic-religious loyalties, still less well organized in Upper Simalungun where its support was limited to antitraditionalists, PNI branches in the region ran the gamut from Duverger's "mass" to his "cadre" party.

Finally, the data and conclusions reported in this essay have important implications beyond the purely local level. In the three localities—and, we suspect, in many other regions as well—there has been in the twentieth century a rather rapid and fateful transformation of some basic political attitudes. As recently as seventy-five years ago, the structures within which governmental decisions were made and the prevailing conceptions of the limits of the political community were no more extensive than the kinship group, the village, or at most the traditional kingdom. Today the predominant structure is the state and the predominant conception of the political community is the nation. Within this new framework the people of our three localities are attempting to develop new political relationships with each other and with the national elite responsible for decisions in many areas directly affecting their lives. They have seized upon political organizations, imported from Djakarta or created independently, precisely because they do not see themselves simply as members of particular village, ethnic, or religious communities, but rather as members of and potential participants in a national political system. The region of Simalungun and Siantar, its more modernized as well as its still relatively traditional localities, is increasingly beset by a "participation crisis" characterized by rising demands for participation in local and national political life through organizations heavily influenced by primordial loyalties. These developments create a problem of no mean dimensions for the national political and governmental elite, which must somehow decide on an appropriate response. Since 1958 the principal response to nearly all autonomous political organizations has been repression in one form or another. Whether such a policy can be maintained over a long period without serious damage to local-national relationships and to the individual's sense of membership in the nation is a complex and difficult question.

Since this essay has explored the particular but not, one may hope, the unique, it may be useful to restate—at the risk of repetition—some of its findings and conclusions in the form of general propositions and hypotheses.

(1) In many new states primordial loyalties of one sort or another—kinship, ethnic, racial, linguistic, religious, cultural—are of primary importance in determining political loyalties at the local level. Despite probably growing national consciousness it is these

loyalties which provide structure and coherence to many of the individual's roles, political and other, in his society.

(2) In a political system which encourages open partisan competition for votes and support, the successful political parties are those which are able to relate themselves to the conditions of local social and cultural environments.

(3) In localities such as those described in proposition (1) there is a high probability that the party system, whatever the nature of the conflicts which divide the parties at the national level, will take on the coloration of local primordial cleavages. Parties which do not do so will be unsuccessful in these localities.

(4) In localities in which some economic modernization has taken place, nonprimordial attitudes such as those based on common socio-economic interests may be utilized successfully to build partisan support. Even in such areas, however, primordially based parties are likely to be of continuing importance because of the uneven patterns and effects of processes of social change.

(4a) Nonprimordial parties are likely to have less firm support than primordial parties because of the continued hold of primordialism on the bulk of the population and the more weakly developed sentiments of common socio-economic interest or class. Nonprimordial parties are thus likely to be much more highly organized for the mobilization of support than are primordial parties.

(4b) There are different types of socio-economic change, and urbanization *per se* will not necessarily produce a stratification system cutting across primordial lines of cleavage. On the contrary, it may produce an intensification and a politicization of these cleavages in an atmosphere of competition for status, wealth, and values waged in large part among primordial groups.

(5) In still heavily traditional areas locally created political organizations without ties beyond the local community may gain considerable support and, as a corollary, national political organizations may be unable to adjust themselves to the special conditions of these localities. This would seem particularly likely where a traditional elite, oriented toward and seeking its legitimation in the

distinctiveness and unique past of the community, provides the post-independence political leadership. Modernization, on the other hand, may produce a new kind of leadership, rooted in primordialism but oriented toward the national community and eager to play a "broker" role on behalf of its constituency through participation in a national party system.

Modernization in the Minangkabau World:

West Sumatra in the Early Decades of the Twentieth Century *

✧✧✧✧✧✧✧✧✧

Taufik Abdullah

INTRODUCTION

A society's forced encounter with a stronger outside world creates unprecedented problems. Inability to cope with unintelligible and powerful pressures very often results in frustration and despair. The most obvious symptom of this condition is rebellion. A positive response, which is an effort to make some adjustment to the new environment, impels such a society to reexamine its own cultural treasury. In this sense, modernization—whether motivated by internal desire or outside pressures, or both—which is seen as a way out of the impasse created by the painful encounter, has to be constantly redefined. Increasing experience, growing awareness of the outside world, as well as accumulating discontent with the process of accommodation, indeed require continuing revision of the meaning of modernization. Problems of adjustment to the new environment involve not only the tension between tradition and moderniza-

* This essay is based in part on research conducted by the author in 1968 in Indonesia and in the Netherlands under a grant from the London-Cornell Project of Cornell University's Department of Asian Studies, herewith gratefully acknowledged. I would like to express my gratitude to the National Museum in Djakarta and the Library of the Koninklijk Instituut in Leiden for granting me access to their valuable documentary holdings. Special thanks are also due Oliver Wolters for his generous advice and criticism.

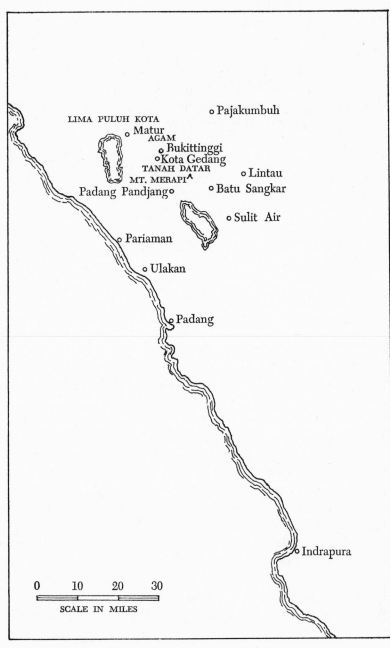

Map 6. West Sumatra

tion, continuity and change, but, more importantly, new attitudes toward tradition itself and the search for a suitable basis for modernization.

The history of West Sumatra, the home of the Minangkabau people, in the first two decades of the twentieth century, clearly reflects both the frustration of the people in the face of expanding Dutch political and economic domination and their attempts to adjust to the new environment. The former reaction manifested itself in numerous rural uprisings, such as the widely scattered rebellions in 1908, which were generally directed against the breakdown of the traditional social system and the threatened collapse of its basic assumptions. In the same period Minangkabau * began to experience economic change, expansion of religious as well as secular schools, and increasing urban influence in the rural areas. The religious and intellectual conflict which developed in the first two decades of this century at times polarized Minangkabau society.

In its secular forms this conflict started with the desire to enter the "modern world" (*dunia madju*) of the Europeans. This desire soon created the need for an appropriate ideological basis for modernization and for the framework for its proper realization. At the same time there developed an intense religious movement, which not only attacked traditional religious practices and local custom or *adat*, but also began to propagate the ideas of Islamic modernism. In its fundamentalist aspect, the movement strove to purify religion; in its modernist program it wanted to provide a sound religious basis for social change. Influenced by the new trends in the centers of the Islamic world, the Minangkabau reformist *ulama* (religious teachers) urged a return to the original sources of Islam in order to recover the true ethic of the religion, which in the past had brought Islam to the peak of spiritual enlightenment and temporal power. These two intellectual strands contributed to making Minangkabau a center of Islamic modernism and one of the most dynamic societies in Indonesia. But this position was achieved at the expense of social harmony. It was a period of social polarization and conflict of generations; advocates of change, religious or otherwise,

---

* "Minangkabau"—short form of the "Minangkabau World"–is used to designate not only the ethnic group but often the totality of the land and the people and their culture.

were impatient in their attempts to transform society, and the guardians of the old order were suspicious of any movement which threatened to undermine the traditional system of values.

How should these different responses to the new environment be understood? What was the attitude of Minangkabau society toward change instigated by the outside world? These questions lead us to inquire into Minangkabau conceptions of history and the world, which can reveal the Minangkabau view of their society and the outside world. Historical events can then be understood not simply within the framework of cause-and-effect but also within the context of the society's life-situation and its system of values.

In order to render a clear picture of the process of change in this period, this essay discusses the role and function of Islam and its network of schools within the social structure, as well as the colonial impact on Minangkabau society. The last part of the essay concentrates on some historical phenomena in the first two decades of the century, with a focus on the nature of intellectual and religious conflict and its effect on society. What were the issues and how did the different social groups perceive them? What was the mood of Minangkabau in facing its internal conflict? A convenient way to look at these historical events is through an intellectual biography of Datuk Sutan Maharadja (1860–1921), one of the first Minangkabau modernizers and a prominent adat ideologue. Known as "the father of Malay journalism" as well as "the Caesar of Minangkabau adat," he remained in the center of social and intellectual movements. He contributed to laying a foundation for the Minangkabau drive toward modernization, participated in religious conflict, and finally became the leader of the Kaum Kuno, the "Conservative Group." He was a great Minangkabau nationalist who, nevertheless, believed in the unity of the Malay race. Though a loyal subject of the Dutch government, he persisted in his belief in the inherent greatness of the Minangkabau World (Alam Minangkabau). From Datuk Sutan Maharadja's biography, the hopes and the disillusionments of Minangkabau in its attempt to update itself can be clearly traced.

THE MINANGKABAU WORLD

History of the World

In the beginning there was only the Light of Muhammad (Nur Muhammad),[1] through which God created this universe, "the sky and the earth." From the Light emanated angels and Adam, the first human being. Later God forced Adam and his offspring to live on earth, which was still undergoing the process of perfection. After some time Iskandar,[2] the ruler of the East and the West, descended to earth. He established the first kingdom and made the Land of the Sunset (*benua Ruhum*) [3] its center. In the meantime the face of the world expanded, hills and mountains appeared. When Iskandar decided to take a wife, God sent him a nymph from paradise. From this marriage three sons were born: Maharadja Alif, Maharadja Dipang, and Maharadja Diradja. After the death of Iskandar, the three princes journeyed to the Land of the Rising Sun (*benua Tjina*). Near Langkapuri, their boat ran aground. When three princesses from the kingdom under the sea emerged from the water, and informed the three princes that they each were destined to marry a son of Iskandar, the princes married them.

[1] There are several published versions of the Minangkabau traditional chronicle (*tambo*) in Dutch, Minangkabau, and Indonesian. One of the oldest Dutch versions is "Legende van de afkomst der Sumatranen en van hunne instellingen," *Tijdschrift voor Nederlandsch Indië* (hereafter *TNI*), 30, part 1 (1859), 378–389. Although its main theme is similar to that of other versions, there are a number of differences in its initial sections. The version used for this essay is a nineteenth-century manuscript belonging to the School of Oriental and African Studies (London), *Silsilah Melaju*, dated 1290 Hidjrah, MS. no. 3656. (I am indebted to Professor O. W. Wolters of Cornell University for introducing me to this manuscript.) A similar version is given in Datoek Batoeah Sango, *Tambo Alam Minangkabau* (Pajakumbuh: Limbago, 1955). See also Achmad Datuk Batuah and A. Dt. Madjo Indo, *Tambo Minangkabau dan Adatnja* (Djakarta: Balai Pustaka, 1956), pp. 11–42. On the concept of Nur Muhammad in Islamic mysticism, see Hadji Aboebakar Atjeh, *Pengantar Sedjarah Sufi dan Tasawwuf* (Bandung: Tjerdas, 1962), pp. 139–141. On the spread of this concept in Minangkabau religious schools in the nineteenth century, see C. Snouck Hurgronje, "Een en ander over het Inlandsche Onderwijs in de Padangsche Bovenlanden" (1883) in his *Verspreide Geschriften*, 4, part 1 (Bonn and Leipzig: Schroeder, 1924), 29–52.

[2] His full name was Iskandar Zulkarnain, Iskandar with the Two Horns, He is believed to be Alexander the Great.

[3] *Benua Ruhum* probably refers to Turkey, the new ruler of the Eastern Roman Empire.

The princes, however, lost the only crown left by their father. One of Maharadja Diradja's followers, a very fine goldsmith, made an exact copy of the crown and advised his master to proclaim his superiority over his brothers. Having established Maharadja Diradja's supremacy, the brothers parted. Maharadja Alif went to the Land of Sunset, Maharadja Dipang sailed to the Land of Sunrise, and Maharadja Diradja to the Land between Sunset and Sunrise. During the trip the boat of Maharadja Diradja sprang a leak, and the prince, who by this time had acquired three other wives,[4] announced that he would accept as sons-in-law those able to solve the difficulty. After the boat was repaired by his followers the journey was continued and the travelers finally landed on the Island of Pertja, at the top of Mount Merapi. This was the genesis of the Minangkabau World.

The heart of the *tambo* is a description of the mythical period of Minangkabau history, the period of the legendary adat givers and the establishment of the monarchy. The last sections of the tambo deal with the rise of the *rantau* or fringe kingdoms, whose rulers were related to the royal family in the heartland. The tambo gives mystical sanction to the existing order and provides categories for the perception of reality. As an attempt to conceptualize history and the world, the tambo also provides a model for interpreting observable historical events.

Gradually, according to the tambo, which sees the history of Minangkabau as beginning before its world emerged, the water surrounding Mount Merapi subsided, the face of the earth expanded, and the number of inhabitants increased. A period of continuing exploration for new lands began and new settlements were established. Finally the "three *luhak*" (districts),[5] which were to become the heartland of Minangkabau, were populated. In this stage, men were

[4] Symbolized in the tambo as a cat (*kutjieng Siam*), a tigress (*harimau Tjampo*), and a dog (*andjieng muallim*). For a hypothesis on totemist remains in Minangkabau, see P. D. de Josselin de Jong, *Minangkabau and Negeri Sembilan: Socio-political Structure in Indonesia* (Djakarta: Bhratara, 1960), pp. 101–102. Modern Minangkabau adat theoreticians usually interpret these animals as representing the different behavior of the three wives who were the ancestresses of the different regions in the Minangkabau heartland.

[5] *Luhak* refers to the major regions of the Minangkabau heartland, namely Tanah Datar, Agam, and Lima Puluh Kota. Thus this heartland is usually called "the three luhak" (*Luhak nan Tigo*).

only parts of nature; they spread just as the face of the earth enlarged. After the perfection of nature was completed, nature began to reveal its law to the Minangkabau ancestors, who had acquired the heartland.

Then, the wise Tjati Bilang Pandai established the heads of the oldest families in the various settlements as legitimate chiefs. This act was important because the early settlers in one way or another were related to Maharadja Diradja, the first king. At this juncture a prince came to Pariangan, near Mount Merapi, the first settlement of the Minangkabau ancestors. In the oldest tambo and in *pidato adat* (adat speech) he is usually described as "the deer with the golden horns who came from the sea." Several versions of the tambo refer to him as Sang Sapurba, who is also a hero in the *Sedjarah Melaju*.[6] He married the sister of Datuk Suri Diradjo, the direct descendant of Maharadja Diradja, and was acknowledged as the new king. In order to support the new king the first *balai* (council hall) was built and the first four *penghulu* (forerunners of the genealogical chiefs) were installed. From this marriage one of the future adat givers, Datuk Ketemanggungan, was born. After the king's death, his widow married a sage—in some versions he is also referred to as Tjati Bilang Pandai. They had two sons and several daughters. Together with their uncle, Datuk Ketemanggungan and his half-brothers were the rulers of Minangkabau. Datuk Ketemanggungan and one of his half-brothers, Datuk Perpatih nan Sabatang, formulated the foundation of Minangkabau adat. They transformed the large old settlements into nagari, each with its own balai; they divided the nagari into several suku,[7] and instituted the penghulu-

---

[6] Sang Sapurba was a son of Iskandar Zulkarnain. He is believed to have become the first king in Minangkabau after having killed a mythical snake that was devastating the land. See W. G. Shellabear, ed., *Sejarah Melayu*, 2d ed. (Singapore: Malaya Publishing House, 1950), pp. 18–30.

[7] *Nagari* is usually defined in the old ethnographic literature as "village republic." Settlements range from a conglomeration of small huts (*taratak*), through various types of villages, to the clearly defined political community of the *nagari* which in Minangkabau adat theory is considered to be the most developed type. On these types of settlements, see A. M. Datuk Maruhun Batuah and D. H. Bagindo Tanameh, *Hukum Adat dan Adat Minangkabau* (Djakarta: Poesaka, 1956), pp. 58–60. Nagari is par excellence a community with political and judicial powers.

Suku is neither a territorial nor a purely genealogical social unit. Its members consist of mythical blood relatives, descendants of the earliest settlers,

ship in every suku. A penghulu was a "kalipa radjo," the substitute of the king in the respective suku, whose authority derived from the consensus of the people.

Meanwhile, the arrival of Adityawarman,[8] a historic figure from the East Javanese kingdom of Madjapahit, created dissension among the adat givers. Datuk Ketemanggungan thought that the newcomer was a prince, but his half-brother, whose father was a sage, considered him only a minister. Although the brothers accepted Adityawarman as brother-in-law, their disagreement about him led to the division of the Minangkabau nagari into adherents of two political traditions: the followers of Datuk Ketemanggungan, who acknowledged Adityawarman's royal status, joined the Koto Piliang; [9] and the followers of Datuk Perpatih nan Sabatang, who refused to recognize Adityawarman as king, formed the Bodi Tjaniago tradition. The question of the proper position of the newcomer in the already established system of penghuluships led to a civil war. The followers of the Bodi Tjaniago system were defeated, but, following Datuk Perpatih nan Sabatang, they persisted in their refusal to accept the authority of the king. Before the two adat givers died, they instructed their followers to intermarry and to consider themselves as parts of a united whole. The incorporation of the institution of kingship did not change the existing political system. The king remained outside the system although he was henceforth considered an inseparable part of the Minangkabau World.

Once the heartland was acquired, it ceased to expand, but the Minangkabau people continued their geographical exploration and the establishment of new settlements. These new territories, called rantau, grew in accordance with the expansion of the Minangkabau people. Unlike the heartland, which was ruled by the penghulu, the

and also newcomers who have been admitted to the *suku*. Umar Junus, "Some Remarks on Minangkabau Social Structure," *Bijdragen tot de Taal-, Land- en Volkenkunde* (hereafter *BKI*) 120, no. 3 (1964), 293–326.

[8] Adityawarman was a fourteenth century Minangkabau king, who also belonged to the royal house of Madjapahit. See N. J. Krom, "Het Hindoe Tijdperk," in F. W. Stapel, ed., *Geschiedenis van Nederlandsch-Indië*, 1 (Amsterdam: Joost van den Vondel, 1938), 272–274. For a refutation of Krom's theory, see C. C. Berg, "De Sadeng-Oorlog en de Mythe van Groot-Madjapahit," in *Indonesië*, 5 (1951), 385–422.

[9] These two political traditions are called *lareh* or *laras*. See de Josselin de Jong, *Minangkabau*, pp. 73–84; also W. J. Leyds, "Larassen in Minangkabau," *Koloniale Studiën* (hereafter *KS*), 19 (1926), 387–416.

rantau were ruled by *radja,* representatives of the king.[10] Both the
heartland and the rantau, however, belonged to the Alam Minangkabau. The rantau served not only as a political expediency for the
royal family but also, and more important, as a gate to and from the
outside world.

As a world in itself Alam Minangkabau was a convergence of
the static luhak and the ever-expanding rantau. This world consisted of the indigenous political tradition of penghuluship and the
imported tradition of kingship. But this dichotomy in the political
system was bridged by the coexistence in the heartland of the Koto
Piliang and the Bodi Tjaniago traditions. The former recognized the
hierarchical position of the penghulu whereas the latter considered
all penghulu as equal. Alam was also a conglomeration of a number
of smaller worlds, the nagari, each with its own "independent" political community, council hall, mosque, road, and public bathing
place; a nagari also had a definite boundary and its own recognized
fringe territories.[11]

Through the tambo concept of the Minangkabau World, its
history can be seen as a continuing process of incorporation of
outside elements into the existing Alam. The main function of
outside influences, however, was to stimulate the Alam's potential.
When Sang Sapurba married a descendant of Maharadja Diradja
he infused new royal blood into his wife's family. Through this act
he elevated her family which until then had been merely equal to
the others. Datuk Ketemanggungan's attitude toward Adityawarman
was predictable because he himself was of royal blood. Datuk
Perpatih nan Sabatang's opposition to the new king was motivated
not only by his own nonroyal and nonrantau background—he was
the son of a sage—but also by his concern over the threat Adityawarman posed to the established order. The conflict was resolved not
because the rantau elements replaced the existing system, but rather
because they converged with it.

The Tambo, however, does not make Datuk Perpatih nan Saba-

[10] On the different political traditions of the radja system on the Minangkabau western coast, see C. A. Francis, "Korte beschrijving van het Nederlandsch grondgebied ter Westkust Sumatra, 1837," *TNI,* 2 no. 1 (1839),
28–45, 90–111, 203–220.

[11] Cf. Harsja Bachtiar, "Negeri Taram: A Minangkabau Community in
Minangkabau," in Koentjaraningrat, ed., *Villages in Indonesia* (Ithaca: Cornell
University Press, 1967), pp. 361–362.

tang a symbol of purely Minangkabau genius. Unlike his half-brother, who never left the Minangkabau World, he was the prototype *perantau* adventurer. The division of Minangkabau into several suku was introduced by Datuk Perpatih nan Sabatang on his return from China. Adat inheritance law was wisdom he had gained during his adventures abroad. On his return to Minangkabau a quarrel arose between him and Datuk Ketemanggungan because, without knowing it, Datuk Perpatih nan Sabatang almost married his own sister. At the time there was no law against this. Out of the quarrel, the incest regulation developed. Through continuing exploration and social conflicts, the Alam Minangkabau unfolded its own potentialities and incorporated outside elements. Incorporation means a convergence in which the original elements are still identifiable, rather than a faceless synthesis. Ideally, change was quantitative; it was thought to enrich the Alam.

The tambo conception of history clearly reflects the influence of Islamic mysticism on the adat world view. The meaning of history can be seen in the harmony of its inward and outward qualities. From universal and transcendental unity, history moves toward the attainment of a harmony of individual and society with the cosmic order. Inwardly history provides guidance for the achievement of individual salvation—in the harmony between self and the cosmic order; outwardly it moves toward the perfection of society. The gradual enlargement of the Minangkabau World, the incorporation of new elements, and the unfolding of its own potentialities have similar purposes toward the fulfillment of its historical goal. The outward meaning of history is expressed in a mundane manner by pidato adat, which sets forth the goals of adat as "a happy world [with its] good harvest [in which] the population keeps increasing, the nagari is peaceful, the inhabitants are always in agreement, [where] peace is close at hand and strife is a far away." In short, it is a world in which man is in harmony with nature and his society.

But is history an automatic development, which reaches its destination without guidance? The eschatological Islamic conception of history faces the dilemma posed by God's interference and man's independence. Minangkabau, however, is confronted with the notion of the perpetual validity of old wisdom and the idea of imperative change. Metaphorically this notion is expressed in the adat conception of two *tjupak* (measurement made of bamboo). The first is *tjupak usali,* the original tjupak, from which the artificial tjupak derives its standard. *Kato* (word), which is a source of adat wisdom, is divided into four categories: *kato usali* (original words), *kato pusako* (inherited words), *kato dahulu* (old words), and *kato kudian* (words still to be found).[12] They range from the permanent and eternal, through the changeable, to the still-to-be-found words. The latter should not be the repudiation of the former, just as "adat which is made adat" (*adaik nan diadaikkan*), the adapted adat, should not be in opposition to "adat which is truly adat" (*adaik nan sabana adaik*).[13] Deviation from established form means the crisis of the Alam. It could hinder the movement of history toward its goal, the perfection of society. In the process of change, the principle that "nature should be the teacher" must also be applied. This principle, which implies the basically repetitive character of natural laws, stresses the importance of experience and the achievements of the past.

The Minangkabau conception of history, expressed in the tambo and supported by innumerable adat sayings, is then neither unilineal nor cyclical, but rather a spiral with widening circumferences. History moves toward its goal, but the foundation of the Alam and the rhythm of its development are supposed to be permanent. This conception is not simply a basis for perceiving the past and interpreting historical events, but, more important, a message for the future.

The contradiction inherent in this historical conception, with its imperatives of change and permanent form, is a major factor in the social conflict that occurs during the process of change. The notion of imperative change can be a source of social dynamism, but concern over permanence can become the foundation of Minangkabau

---

[12] For a discussion of the role of words in Minangkabau adat, see Darwis Thaib, *Seluk Beluk Adat Minangkabau* (Djakarta: Nusantara, 1965), pp. 20–57.

[13] There are four categories of adat: "adat which is truly adat" (*adaik nan sabana adaik*), "adat which has become adat" (*adaik nan taradaik*), "adat which is made adat" (*adaik nan diadaikkan*), and "adat ceremonial" (*adaik istiadaik*). Discussions of these categories can be found in any book on Minangkabau adat.

conservatism. This contradiction inherent in the tambo makes understandable the central position which problems of change occupy in Minangkabau thought.

Problems of Change in Minangkabau Thought

One of the most influential modern adat theoreticians, Datuk Sangguno Diradjo (d. 1940's), wrote a book in 1921 focused on the question of change.[14] The book begins with the description of an imaginary adat meeting, which has undertaken to change a number of adat customs. These changes, according to the participants in the meeting, are intended for the welfare of the people. But, the author asks through one of his characters, have the premises of welfare been carefully deliberated? Have the potential consequences of the changes been carefully evaluated? The same character later expounds the long-lasting validity of the then already replaced customs for dealing with the present situation and the possible undesirable effects of the changes. Nevertheless, because these changes were introduced through the correct adat procedures, through the *mufakat* (consensus) of the members of the council, the nagari and the people have to accept them. The author uses this imaginary dilemma, between the risks of change and the legitimacy of mufakat, in order to emphasize the intrinsic dualism of adat as a permanent and ever-changing order.

According to adat, two kinds of laws govern Minangkabau; the first "descends from heaven" and the second "emerges from the earth." The former is religious law, which is based on Kitabullah (the Koran) and is under the jurisdiction of religious experts. The latter is adat law, which is partly the legacy of the two legendary adat-givers and partly the result of the consensus of successive generations of adat-functionaries. The legacies of the adat-givers —such as the matrilineal inheritance law, the central position of the penghulu, and the division of nagari into several suku—are considered permanent and unchangeable. This part of adat "neither cracks in the sun nor rots in the rain." [15] Only the other parts of

---

[14] I. Datue' Sangguno Diradjo, *Mustiko 'Adat 'Alam Minangkabau* (Djakarta: Perpustakaan Perguruan, Kementerian P. P. dan K., 1955), chaps. 1–3.
[15] In Minangkabau: "Indak lakang dipaneh, indak lapuek diudjan."

adat may be changed and must be reviewed in the light of changing circumstances—"when floods come, the bathing place moves." [16] In this aspect of adat, the principle of "what is good should be used, what is bad should be abandoned" [17] must always be applied. Not unlike the concept of the ever-expanding rantau, the legacies of the successive penghulu are also open to the incorporation of new elements. But the continuities, the incorporations, and also the replacement of the existing adat regulations are entirely dependent upon the mufakat of the nagari council, the high governing body.

Mufakat, the process and the result of deliberation, is the procedure for dealing with general problems in the nagari and reviewing the existing social regulations. The power of mufakat is based not only on the legitimacy of penghulu and other adat functionaries who participate in the process, but also on its sacral nature. The basic function of mufakat is the realization of the abstract notion of truth (*nan bana*) which is "the real king in the nagari." Regulations and precedents formulated by consensus are theoretically expressions of truth itself. The decision of consensus is binding because it is implicitly the only expression of truth for dealing with a specific problem. In expressing truth, mufakat, however, should be based on appropriateness and propriety (*alué* and *patuik*), which follow established precedent and conform to the sense of social responsibility. Appropriateness means respect for the relevant social hierarchy, "using stairs to go up, using a ladder to go down," and conventional patterns. Mufakat that ignores these requirements is, therefore, invalid.[18]

Mufakat and other human activities are guided by *akal*, reasoning. It is by using akal man searches for truth and perceives reality. In itself akal can identify the contrasting elements in reality, such as bad and good, the beginning and the end, body and soul, "yes" and "no," being and nonbeing. But the validity of akal as a faculty for guiding man's life depends not only on its ability to perceive overt phenomena and to determine what is possible and what is not, but also on its use in deliberating what is proper and what is

[16] "Sakali aie gadang, sakali tapian baralieh."
[17] "Nan elok dipakai, nan buruek dibuang."
[18] On this problem, see also Thaib, pp. 37–51.

not. A judgment of akal is considered valid if it combines in itself logical possibility (*mungkin*) and ethical propriety (patuik).[19] Without the latter, which emphasizes a sense of social responsibility, akal might even lead man astray. In order to combine these two requirements, mungkin and patuik, akal should be accompanied by *iman*, the full recognition of God. Iman not only serves to sharpen the ability of akal but also functions as the controlling agent for akal. Perfect akal is akal guided by iman with the sense of duty to oneself, society, and God. Another important requirement in the process of mufakat is *ilmu* (knowledge), which is based on the laws of nature and the understanding of past events. In its mundane form ilmu is the ability "to learn from the past, to take the victor as the model." [20]

The overwhelming power of mufakat in dealing with all matters of common interest is supported by adat assumptions concerning the superiority of council members in akal, iman, and ilmu. The adat-functionaries, particularly the penghulu, are supposed to excel also in wealth and generosity.

Within this context new elements can be introduced only if they have passed several tests. An innovation can be accepted if it is logically possible and morally proper, and if it does not deviate from the basic adat foundation. Since the disruption of social harmony in the small world of nagari is not a risk worth taking in the face of change, the advocate should also realize that "what is good [for him] should also be good for others."

The question of imperative change within this basically conservative social framework becomes more complex through the dualism in the Minangkabau conception of the individual and society.

Individual and Society

Traditional views of the individual and society can be illustrated by an episode from the most famous Minangkabau epic, the *Kaba*

[19] Examples of this reasoning are: It is possible to make a ricefield in somebody's yard, but is it proper? It is proper to make it on the top of the mountain, but is it possible? See Taufik Abdullah, "Some Notes on the *Kaba Tjindua Mato:* An Example of Minangkabau Traditional Literature," *Indonesia*, 9 (April 1970), 14–15.

[20] In Minangkabau: "Baradja ka nan sudah, maambiék tuah ka nan manang."

Tjindua Mato. Before Dang Tuanku, the King of the World (Radjo Alam), leaves for the Seventh Heaven, he says to Tjindua Mato, his viceroy, "We are two persons with one soul. . . . Physically you are the ruler. In spiritual reality it is I." Tjindua Mato in this epic is not only his own personality, but also the manifestation of Dang Tuanku's inner self. It is the latter who is sacred and the source of wisdom, but it is Tjindua Mato who manifests the wisdom. Tjindua Mato is a divine emanation but at the same time a human being in constant contact with divine power.[21] The elusive nature of these inward and outward qualities is also evident in the Minangkabau view of the relationship between individual and society.

The discussion of this problem must proceed on two levels—philosophical and structural. The first is expressed in *pepatah adat* (adat aphorisms). The second is apparent in social structure, which is regulated by adat law. In the absence of a functional hierarchical central authority, the pepatah adat in the form of philosophical sayings are the symbols of Minangkabau unity and continuity. They bridge local variations and assure continuity over time. As a source of wisdom, the pepatah are a guide for maintaining social harmony and achieving an ideal society. Thus they are used not only to support but also to challenge the existing order.

According to the pepatah, the individual and society are like "bamboo on the steep river bank," two entities that cannot be separated. The relationship of these inseparable entities is determined by the cycles of authority and obligation, in which the object and the ultimate source of authority reside in the same locus. The *kemenakan* (nephew), who symbolizes the individual, should acknowledge the authority of his *mamak* (uncle), who in turn should rely on the penghulu. The latter should base his judgment on the mufakat as the expression of society's wishes and wisdom. In this hierarchical order of authority an individual should be seen under the full control of his society. But the pepatah also emphasize that the kemenakan is not only the object but also the ultimate source of authority. Outwardly a penghulu is the king, but essentially he is the subject of his kemenakan. His power is not based on his personal charisma but on the legitimacy invested in the penghuluship by his kemena-

21 See Abdullah, "Kaba Tjindua Mato."

kan. A penghulu "is great [because] he is made great [by his kemenakan]." [22] His right is based on *sakato alam,* the consensus of his small world, his people.

The rights and obligations of the individual are determined by the particular level of social organization in which he is involved. As a member of the family he is expected to stand by this lowest level of social organization. In inter-suku relationships he must defend the interest of his suku. In inter-nagari relationships he must be a champion of his nagari. The higher the level of social organization, the fewer his rights and the heavier his responsibility. But again, the rights and obligations of the individual in this hierarchical social organization should also be seen in the context of the dependency of the higher levels on the lower. The existence of a nagari, which is a small world within the context of the Minangkabau World, is dependent on its suku, which in turn is formed by a conglomeration of matrilineal families. [23] The cycle is completed with the essential obligation of the family toward its members. With this circular concept of authority and reciprocal obligations, the pepatah emphasize the notion of a harmonious world in which all component parts, though different, are of equal importance. This concept not only affirms the wisdom of the "harmony of contradictions" but also underlines the prevailing individualism in the Minangkabau social system. [24]

Minangkabau social structure, which is regulated by adat law, is based on the matrilineal *mamak-kemenakan* (uncle-and-nephew) network. It centers on the figure of the mother, as the focus of the inherited communal house (*rumah gadang*) and inalienable land property. As the head of family, the mamak, who is usually its oldest male member, is responsible for the maintenance of inherited property (*harato pusako*) and the welfare of his sisters' children, and is the representative of the family in suku affairs. The kemenakan, in turn, must consider the mamak as the only "king" (*baradjo ka*

[22] Cf. M. Nasroen, *Dasar Falsafah Adat Minangkabau* (Djakarta: Pasaman, 1957), pp. 128–136.

[23] Nasroen, pp. 67–90; see also Chairul Anwar, *Menindjau Hukum Adat Minangkabau* (Djakarta: Segara, 1967), pp. 19–22.

[24] Cf. Roesad, "Minangkabausche Toestanden," *Orgaan van den Nederlandsch-Indischen Politiek-Economischen Bond* (hereafter *PEB*), 4 (1923), 587–590.

mamak) whom he must "ask for permission whenever he leaves, inform whenever he returns." [25]

The concept of this network is also applied in characterizing adat social classes. As a class term mamak denotes the family of the original settler (*urang usali*) of the nagari, which has recognized the newcomer (*urang datang*) as its kemenakan. The latter is accepted into the former's suku and lives under the same penghulu's jurisdiction. The original family belongs to the so-called adat aristocracy, or *urang babangso*, from whose ranks the penghulu and other adat functionaries are usually elected. In this respect mamak-kemenakan can be divided into two categories of social classes. The first is "kemenakan as recognized by adat," in which the kemenakan family is originally the "guest" of its "host" mamak. After paying adat dues to the nagari and fulfilling other adat requirements to its host, the kemenakan receives a piece of land from the latter. The kemenakan is henceforth recognized as a scion of the original mamak family. The rights and obligations of such mamak-kemenakan families reflect those which are based on kinship.[26] The second type of class category is the "kemenakan under the knees" (*kemenakan dibawah lutuik*), in which the kemenakan is the "client" of his "patron" mamak. Originally, the kemenakan was a semi-serf of his mamak family, which had given him land to till while retaining the ownership of that land. Generally this type of kemenakan developed from prisoners of war or debtors. In the early 1860's the Dutch government abolished this lowest adat class which had expanded considerably in the early nineteenth century during the Padri War. The newly freed "kemenakan under the knees" were officially elevated to the second class, although on adat occasions such as weddings, their original status still comes to the surface.[27]

[25] A full description of the duties and obligations of both *mamak* and *kemenakan* is given in *Adatrechtbundels*, 9 (1915), 115–129.

[26] A. M. Datuk Maruhun Batuah and D. H. Bagindo Tanameh, *Hukum Adat dan Adat Minangkabau*, p. 17.

[27] The institution of "kemenakan under the knees" is more prevalent in some nagari than in others. A discussion of this institution in the nineteenth century is given in A. W. Verkerk Pistorius, "Iets over de slaven in de Padangsche Bovenlanden," *TNI*, 3d series, 2, part 1 (1868), 434–443. The author describes the situation in Silungkang. On Silungkang in the twentieth century, see Junus. It is worth noting that the so-called Communist rebellion in January 1927 also broke out in Silungkang.

In itself the mamak-kemenakan network does not facilitate social mobility. The nephew remains in his position until it is his turn to become mamak. A penghulu, in principle, cannot be chosen from the families of the two lower classes. Upward mobility in adat social organization is determined by criteria outside the mamak-kemenakan network. A new penghuluship can be established if the original family has become too large and the family is willing to fulfill the requisite adat regulations. In some parts of Minangkabau, rich and large families of "kemenakan by adat" may also have their own penghuluship [28] whose creation depends entirely upon the consent of the nagari. Mobility and status, in other words, are matters of social concern rather than personal right.

Side by side with this matrilineal network the Minangkabau social system also recognizes a father-son network. It is characterized by its inter-suku relationship. The father is the *sumando*, the "inmarried" male in his son's matrilineal family, and the son is the *anak pisang*, the child of a male kinsman of the father's lineage. Although this affinal relationship is not an elaborate system, the marriage which preceded it is, in fact, a "battle of honor" of the respective suku.[29] Understandably then, whereas social status is based on the uncle-nephew network, behavior is judged on the basis of the father-son network. The son of a religious leader is expected at least to lead a devout life. The mamak is responsible for the material welfare of his kemenakan, but it is the father who is expected to see to the spiritual growth of his children. An individual, who is father to his children and mamak to his sisters' children, is expected to fulfill both sets of responsibilities. In the conflict between son and nephew, naturally a very common phenomenon, considerable tact is necessary; it is like "drawing a hair out of flour, so that the hair does not break and the flour is not scattered." [30]

These overlapping social networks are integrative factors in the

---

[28] See *Adatrechtbundels*, 11 (1915), 93–114.

[29] Taufik Abdullah, "Adat and Islam: An Examination of Conflict in Minangkabau," *Indonesia*, 2 (Oct. 1966), 7–8.

[30] In Minangkabau: "Sarupo maelo rambuik dari tapueng, rambuik djan putuih, tapueng djan taserak." On the conflict of these two responsibilities, see, for example, Muhammad Radjab, *Sistem Kekerabatan di Minangkabau* (Padang: Center for Minangkabau Studies Press, 1969), pp. 57–62.

Minangkabau nagari. Virtually all inhabitants of a nagari can become related through these two networks and the prevailing intermarriage system. This social system is a factor in the continuing pluralism and confusion in the Minangkabau legal system,[31] as well as a source of social conservatism. Theoretically an individual can change his position according to his advantage; a son in a particular case can claim to be a nephew in another. Despite the growing influence of Islamic law and the effects of the money economy, for example, adat matrilineal inheritance law is still a major source of legal and social problems.

The Minangkabau have always been fascinated by adat ideals, as expressed in the pepatah, illustrated in tambo and other traditional literature, and repeated on all adat occasions. Their lives are dominated by the elaborate adat social networks and the complex adat regulations. It is the balai (council hall) and its adat functionaries who are the guardians of social norms and regulate social reality. The concentration of power in the hands of the balai and the adat functionaries creates internal tensions. In this context *marantau,* or going outside the nagari, can be seen not only as an educational venture for unmarried youths and an economic necessity for adults, but also as a means for easing these tensions.

In the nagari itself the Minangkabau social system recognizes its own "internal rantau," in which peripheral and even deviant sets of values can be expressed. Typical of an internal rantau in traditional Minangkabau is the *lapau,* the village coffee house which is sometimes labeled *balai randah* (the lower council). As its nickname indicates, it is a place for social criticism of members of the balai and the ideas they represent. At its best the coffee house, which is also frequented by people from other nagari, can be a source of change in the nagari. At its worst it is a playground for the Minangkabau tradition of sarcasm. The lapau is a place where cynics and advocates of change might find their common "internal rantau."

Tambo and pidato adat emphasize the dynamic character of the Alam Minangkabau, which must constantly unfold its potentialities in order to achieve the perfect society. The rantau element can be

[31] Nancy Tanner, "Disputing and Dispute Settlements among the Minangkabau of Indonesia," *Indonesia,* 8 (April 1969), 21–68.

incorporated after its possible place and proper function in the existing order have been determined through the mufakat of the penghulu. But this must be done without endangering the permanent
basis of the Alam and the eternal rhythm of its history. The inherent contradiction in the foundation of the Alam Minangkabau
frequently transforms the internal rantau into an active counter-
institution which challenges the entire system. This internal rantau
can take the form of a new *madrasah* (religious school) in the case
of a religious movement or, in modern Minangkabau, of a voluntary
association. The latter, in which adat assumptions and status might
be irrelevant, offers an alternative institution for advancing individual ideas and wishes. Here membership is not dependent upon
adat status but is the result of personal choice. Minangkabau modern history demonstrates that voluntary associations not only undermine the adat council's power but also very often capture the
initiative from it.

ISLAM AND THE RELIGIOUS SCHOOLS

According to tradition, the Alam Minangkabau is a harmonious
world of Islam and adat. This harmony was expressed in the traditional concept of three kings: the King of Adat (Radjo Adat), the
King of Religion (Radjo Ibadat), and the King of the World (Radjo
Alam). In religious matters the Radjo Ibadat was the highest authority, adat was under the jurisdiction of the Radjo Adat, and the
ultimate authority on both adat and religion was the King of the
World. On the nagari level religious functionaries were included in
the adat hierarchy. In the nagari of the Koto Piliang tradition, adat
functionaries included penghulu, *manti* (adat clerks), *dubalang*
("police"), and *malim* (religious officials). Together they were
called the *urang ampek djinih* (the four functionaries). Like other
adat personnel, the malim had to be elected from a family holding
the office by ascription. In the Bodi Tjaniago tradition the society
was politically divided into three classes: penghulu, *imam-chatib*
(religious functionaries) and *urang banjak* (the masses). In the
Minangkabau tradition of aphorism this harmony was defined as
"adat is based on *sjarak* (religious law), sjarak is based on adat."
Adat was supposed to maintain the harmony of society, whereas

sjarak was intended to achieve harmony between the self and the cosmic order.[32] The unity of the nagari was symbolized by the existence of one balai and one mosque.

This notion of a harmonious world was attacked in the early nineteenth century by the Padri movement.[33] This movement, started by three Minangkabau *hadji* (pilgrims returned from Mecca) who had been influenced by Wahabism, rejected the whole notion of balance between adat and religion and of harmony between the self and the cosmic order.[34] The Padri stressed the outward manifestations of religiously correct behavior rather than simply "purity of heart." In several nagari conquered during the Padri war traditional political institutions were abolished, and the nagari were ruled jointly by an imam as the political chief and a *kadhi* (judge) in charge of religious matters. The establishment of Padri power in a nagari gradually attracted into the new system the former office holders, the penghulu and other members of the balai. By the end of the second decade of the nineteenth century the character of the movement had changed considerably. In its first stage of development the Padri movement was one of religious teachers and their supporters, whose loyalty was commanded by a fundamentalist ideology; in this stage splits between opponents and adherents of the Padri disrupted the unity of several nagari. In the second stage, traditional loyalty to the nagari again superseded loyalty to ideology. In other words, social polarization within each nagari came to an end, and the conflict changed into inter-nagari warfare. Although the Padri leaders continued to be important, particularly in times of war, in daily life the traditional political structure was either revived or remained intact.[35]

The increase in the Padri's following meant not only the de-

[32] Abdullah, "Adat and Islam," pp. 1–14.

[33] The standard work on the Padri War is H. J. J. L. Ridder de Stuers, *De Vestiging en Uitbreiding van Nederlanders ter Westkust van Sumatra*, 2 vols. (Amsterdam: van Kampen, 1849–1850); see also M. Radjab, *Perang Paderi di Sumatera Barat, 1803–1838* (Djakarta: Balai Pustaka, 1954).

[34] H. A. Steijn Parvé, "De Secte der Padaries (Padries) in de bovenlanden van Sumatra," *Tijdschrift voor Indische Taal-, Land- en Volkenkunde* (hereafter *TBG*), 3 (1855), 249–278.

[35] Cf. Lady Raffles, ed., *Memoir of the Life and Public Services of Sir Thomas Stamford Raffles* (London: J. Murray, 1830), pp. 347–350.

crease of its former élan but also the beginning of the accommodation process.[36] This process was intensified in 1821 by Dutch intervention in the war. The outside stimulus, from the Wahabists in
Arabia, now in retreat, began to weaken. When the war ended in
1837, it was obvious that the Padri leaders had not substantially
changed Minangkabau political and social structure. They did not
completely reform the heterodoxy of the Minangkabau religious
system. They did, however, strengthen the social force of religion
and enlarge its scope throughout the social system.[37] A new adat
formulation was introduced; the contrast between *adat djahiliah*
(syncretic and unenlightened adat) and *adat Islamiah,* which was
in accord with religious law, was emphasized. The highest adat
category, "adat which is truly *adat,*" was now taken to be the
Koran and *hadith* (the traditions of the Prophet). A new aphorism
on the relation between adat and religion was also introduced:
"*Adat* is based on sjarak, sjarak is based on Kitabullah [the Book
of God]." The subordination of adat to religious law was expressed
in a saying that "sjarak designs, adat applies." Ideally then, adat
was the correct manifestation of religious law.[38]

More important than this formulation, which was still to be contested, were the strengthened position of religious teachers and the
expanded web of religious schools which also resulted from the Padri
movement. For lack of other social institutions that could maintain and articulate scriptural knowledge for the general populace,
Islam had to rely on its religious schools. Traditionally there were
two kinds of religious schools. The first was the *surau mangadji*
(Koranic recital school), one of which was usually located in every
subdivision of a nagari (kampuang). There children were taught
elementary religious doctrines and practices. The second was the
madrasah, where scriptural knowledge was taught.[39]

[36] Ph. S. van Ronkel, "Inlandsche getuigenissen aangaande den Padri-
oorlog," *De Indische Gids* (hereafter *IG*), 37, no. 2 (1915), 1099–1119.

[37] On the concepts of force and scope, see Clifford Geertz, *Islam Observed* (New Haven: Yale University Press, 1968).

[38] Abdullah, "Adat and Islam," pp. 14–18.

[39] *Surau* has been defined as "a building where education in reading and
understanding the Koran and other Islamic texts is conducted. It is established by either an individual or members of families or the population of
the whole suku. "Een Malaijer in het Hollandsch beschreven" and
"De masdjid's en inlandsche godsdienstscholen in de Padangsche Bovenlan-

The tradition of madrasah began in the seventeenth century in the coastal town of Ulakan. This was the first Islamic center in Minangkabau, where the early religious teachers received their training. According to tradition, these men excelled in one or two branches of the religious sciences. As a result, the old Minangkabau madrasah was also highly specialized. Ulakan was the center for mystic teachings, Padang Gantiang was the center for jurisprudence, and Lubuk Agam was the best madrasah for Koranic exegesis. According to early madrasah tradition, Alam Minangkabau itself represented the unity of the pillars of the religious sciences—*fikh* (law), *tauhid* (theology), and *tasauf* (mysticism).[40]

The specialized character of the madrasah forced a religious student, or a *murid* (pupil), to attend several in order to complete his training. In the process, the murid acted as a link between the scattered madrasah. The development of the Padri movement, for example, cannot be understood without taking account of the integrative role of the pupil, whose loyalty to his *guru* (teacher) was lasting.[41] Outside the school the pupil was known as an *urang siak* (a pursuer of religious knowledge).[42] He was a traveler who usually commuted between the madrasah and the surrounding nagari. Bound to the community at large by mutual needs and obligations, he was a distributor of elementary religious knowledge as well as an executor of religious rites. As a link between the secluded madrasah and the community, the urang siak can be considered

---

den," *IG*, 10, 1 (1888), 312–333. The distinction between *surau* and *madrasah* in this essay is used only for the sake of convenience. All traditional religious schools, including those of the mystical religious brotherhoods (*tarékat*), are called surau. They are named after either their founding teachers or their location.

[40] Ph. S. van Ronkel, "Het Heiligdom te Oelakan," *TBG*, 56 (1914), 281–316; see also Datuk Mangkuto Alam, "Agama Islam di Minangkabau," *Pandji Islam*, June 2, 1941.

[41] See a memoir of a moderate religious reformer during the Padri War, Sjech Djilal-Eddin, in J. J. de Hollander, ed., *Verhaal van den aanvang der Padri-onlusten op Sumatra* (Leiden: Brill, 1857).

[42] The *urang siak* is also called *fakir*. In the middle of the nineteenth century, according to "an incomplete list" of a Dutch official, there were at least fifteen big madrasah—with an enrolment ranging from one hundred to a thousand—in the Minangkabau heartland (*Bovenlanden*). See A. W. P Verkerk Pistorius, "De Priester en zijn invloed op de samenleving in de Padangsche Bovenlanden," *TNI*, 3, no. 2 (1869), 423–455.

a cultural broker who also served as a channel for inter-nagari communication. The community generally supported the urang siak by providing food and other necessities. Religiously it was meritorious to support an urang siak; according to adat it was a social obligation.

Generally, the guru of a large madrasah belonged to the original settlers of the nagari. His madrasah was located either on his own matrilineal land or on the *tanah ulajat* (the communal reserved land) furnished by his nagari. Usually he was also a hadji who after living as a traveling urang siak had continued his studies in Mecca. The guru was a personification of the madrasah itself. It was his blessing that could open "the mind and the heart" of the murid, a development vital for the pursuit of difficult scriptural knowledge. These characteristics of the teachers formed the basis of their students' loyalty. The guru-murid network extended beyond a particular madrasah. When a murid himself became a guru with his own madrasah, he nevertheless remained the spiritual murid of his former teacher. His obligation to the teacher was also extended to the latter's successor.

The guru-murid network as a basis of social relationships was more pronounced in a madrasah that was also a center of tarékat (mystic) teaching. The guru was not only the teacher but also the spiritual leader of those who wanted to intensify their religious devotion. He was an expert in the esoteric and sacred sciences and the intermediary between the devotee and God. Complete obedience to him was the essential path toward the attainment of the highest knowledge.[43]

Although the position of the religious teacher was not included in the official adat hierarchy, his influence went beyond that prescribed by adat for a penghulu. In his own nagari a religious teacher could often command the loyalty of the people outside his own suku. In the supra-nagari sphere he stood outside the nagari adat communities. In other words, unlike the jurisdiction of the penghulu, which was defined by adat, the influence of the guru-murid network transcended the adat boundaries.[44] The crucial position of

[43] H. Aboebakar Atjeh, *Pengantar Ilmu Tarékat* (*Uraian Tentang Mystik*) (Bandung: Tjerdas, 1964), pp. 65–76.

[44] Verkerk Pistorius, "De Priester," pp. 423–431; cf. Deliar Noer, "The Rise

the religious teacher was also based on his acknowledged authority on religious law. His judgment on religious issues was theoretically binding. The adat religious functionaries, imam, chatib, or malim, were only the executors of law. They were in charge of the mosque and religious rites, such as marriages, funerals, and religious celebrations. The official *sidang Djumat* (Friday council), which was held after the Friday prayer in the mosque, could only discuss and give judgment on general religious matters.[45] On special and particular issues the Friday council had to ask the religious expert (ulama) for *fatwa*, or opinions.

In the absence of a religious head or council that could give final word in religious matters, religious disputes always directly affected the general populace. Doctrinal conflicts which in the past frequently occurred among the guru could not be confined to their respective madrasah. In the pre-Padri period, intra-nagari war might take place as a consequence of doctrinal conflict.[46] Because of the crucial position of the religious teacher and his madrasah, any religious movement usually directed its first attack against the existing madrasah, as the representative of the religious establishment, rather than against an adat institution. The first attempt of the early Padri leaders was to influence the most powerful religious teacher. Failing this, they allied themselves with other religious teachers and jointly attacked the former potential ally.[47] In the second half of the nineteenth century the Naqsjabandijah tarékat school began to extend its influence by attacking other schools, particularly the Sjatariah, which was at that time very powerful.[48] In the 1890's, when Achmad Chatib launched his orthodox movement from Mecca, he denounced the Naqsjabandijah as well as

---

and Development of the Modernist Muslim Movement in Indonesia during the Dutch Colonial Period (1900–1942)" (Ph.D. thesis Cornell University, 1963), pp. 357–358.

[45] On the *sidang Djumat*, see "Godsdienstige Rechtspraak ter Sumatra's Westkust," *Adatrechtbundels*, 39 (1937), 212–217.

[46] De Hollander, p. 47   [47] Steijn Parvé, p. 268.

[48] On the numerous tarékat schools in Minangkabau, see Ph. S. van Ronkel, *Rapport: Betreffende de godsdienstige verschijnselen ter Sumatra's Westkust* (Batavia: Landsdrukkerij, 1916), pp. 9–15. On the early development of the Naqsjabandijah school, K. F. Holle, "Mededeelingen over de devotie der Naqshabandijah in den Ned.- Indischen archipel," *TBG*, 30 (1886) 67–81.

adat inheritance law as deviations from the true teachings of Islam.[49]

As there was no adat machinery to enforce religious conformity, these series of religious movements, each characterized by the emergence of new madrasah, often led to social polarization. The traditionalist religious teachers were forced to debate openly with the reformers. In these debates the layman could follow the appeals of those religious teachers to whom he was most attracted. Under these circumstances religious reformers could always gain a following. The spread of these movements was facilitated by the independent character of the Minangkabau nagari, which was due to the absence of any functioning supra-nagari adat organization that could enforce or obstruct changes introduced within one nagari.

The so-called conflict between adat and religion, always a dominant theme in Minangkabau history, should be seen as a direct result of religious controversy among religious teachers. The attack on a religious order that had already been incorporated into the adat system was a direct challenge to adat authorities. In the face of religious reformation, adat authorities, ideologically committed to the notion of balance between adat and religion and the maintenance of social harmony, allied themselves with traditionalist religious teachers. The desertion of their people to the new religious orientation represented not only an encroachment on their power but also a threat to the unity of the nagari. The militant Padri had precipitated the most dramatic civil war in Minangkabau, which resulted in the destruction of the monarchy; later religious movements

[49] Sjech Achmad Chatib (1860–1916) came from Kota Gedang, near Bukittinggi. He went to Mecca at the age of fifteen and never returned to Minangkabau. An imam of the Shafiite school in the Mosque of Haram in Mecca, he was one of the most important teachers of the Minangkabau reformists. His former students scattered throughout the archipelago. See Hamka, *Ajahku: Riwajat Hidup Dr. H. Abdul Karim Amrullah dan perdjuangan kaum agama di Sumatera* (Djakarta: Widjaya, 1958), pp. 220–232. Achmad Chatib wrote many books on religious matters, most of them printed either in Cairo or Mecca. For a discussion of some of his works, particularly those containing his attacks on Minangkabau inheritance law, see E. Gobée and C. Adriaanse, eds., *Ambtelijke Adviezen van C. Snouck Hurgronje*, 3 (The Hague: Nijhoff, 1965), 1845–1851. His attack on the Naqsjabandijah school was based on the crucial role of the teacher as intermediary (*rabithah*) between devotee and God. See Al 'Allamah Sjech Achmad Chatib, *Fatwa tentang Tarekat Naqasjabandijah* (trans. and ed. by A. Mn. Arief) (Medan: Islamijah, 1965).

similarly disrupted nagari unity. Religious conflict often became purely an adat issue, when the followers of new religious views tried to establish their own mosque.[50] Such action was a direct assault upon adat, because one mosque and one balai were the preeminent symbols of nagari unity.

Another factor that transformed religious controversies into adat and religious conflict was the fundamentalist tendency of the new religious orientations. With their totalistic approaches, these religious reform movements—particularly the Padri and the early twentieth-century orthodox movement—denounced the relativistic way of Minangkabau reasoning and challenged adat conceptions of power. Since ultimate power resided in God's hand, the law of God should prevail in social life, and the experts of this law should occupy a position superior to that of the executors of the law made by man.

The continuing process of Islamization, which was always reinforced by new ideas from the center of the Islamic world, was characterized by heated controversies between the old and the new orientations, and by conflicts between adat authorities and the religious reformers. The existing madrasah, with their guru and murid, gave spiritual backing to adat authorities in their attempt to maintain social harmony and the ideal of consensus. Unlike the balai or mosque, the madrasah was not an adat symbol of nagari unity which could not tolerate challenge. Since a new madrasah could always emerge with the appearance of a new qualified teacher, the madrasah was a continuing source of dynamism in the nagari. It opened the possibility for reviewing its own alam—religious doctrine as well as adat assumptions. The dynamism of the madrasah was obvious when Minangkabau itself was under the domination of an infidel government, whose power was not based on the consensus of the people. Accordingly, during the colonial period the madrasah became a nerve center of resistance.

THE COLONIAL IMPACT

By 1833, twelve years after the Dutch first intervened in the Padri war, the Padri leaders, the remnants of the Minangkabau royal family, and their respective supporters had found a common cause in the

---

[50] Ph. S. van Ronkel, "De Twee Moskeeën en de Adat," *Koloniaal Tijdschrift* (hereafter *KT*), 6, no. 2 (1917), 1589–1599.

idea of independence.[51] In order to counteract this new trend the Dutch High Commissioners in 1833 issued the so-called *Plakat Pandjang* (Long Declaration), in which they declared that the sole Dutch objective was the maintenance of order. In that declaration, Dutch high officials promised, among other things, that the Minangkabau would remain under their own chiefs, and that no taxation would ever be levied. In return for the service of keeping order, the Dutch asked only that coffee and pepper cultivation be expanded.[52] When the Minangkabau heartland was finally conquered in 1837 with the fall of the last important Padri fortress in Bondjol, the basic ideas of the Plakat Pandjang were still upheld. But in consolidating their power, the Dutch found that there was no formal supra-nagari organization that could be used as a link in the administrative hierarchy. The political traditions of the various nagari had no uniformity. Traditional chiefs differed not only in their titles but also in their legal positions. The Dutch also found that the so-called independent spiritual leaders, or the religious teachers, were very influential in the supra-nagari sphere.

The basic plan of the Dutch was to achieve a working harmony between the existing political traditions and the new administrative system.[53] It was expected to be economically profitable and at the same time weaken the position of religious teachers. For these purposes, the establishment of a viable link between the nagari and the Dutch administration was of utmost importance. Until 1860 the Dutch continued to use the regent system, which they had introduced during the Padri war. In this system, patterned on Javanese practice, the regent ruled as the Dutch representative over several nagari. In 1860, another system, thought to be more suited to Minangkabau social structure, was introduced. The office of *tuanku laras* as head of a nagari federation (laras) was instituted. The laras was expected to become a functional supra-nagari organization

---

[51] Cf. de Stuers, 1: 188, 193–195.

[52] The complete text of the *Plakat Pandjang* is in de Stuers, 11: 87–89.

[53] The best account of the historical development of Dutch administrative policies in dealing with Minangkabau *nagari* is B. Schrieke, "Het Probleem der Bestuursorganisatie ter Sumatra's Westkust," KS, 11, no. 1 (1927), 57–106. Unless otherwise cited my analysis is based on Schrieke's article and C. Westenenk, "De Inlandsche Bestuurshoofden ter Sumatra's Westkust," KT, 2 (1913), 673–693, 828–846.

and the tuanku laras, the link between the administration and the traditional chiefs (penghulu). He was appointed by the Dutch government and expected to become a kind of hereditary native bureaucratic aristocrat. Even though the office of tuanku laras was outside the adat hierarchy, which did not recognize a supra-nagari head, the Dutch government made the tuanku laras the highest authority in adat matters. Instead of the balai, it was now the tuanku laras who made the binding decisions in adat and other administrative matters in the nagari. The most obvious consequence of this change was, naturally, the erosion of the balai as a governing institution. This process was further intensified by the introduction in the early 1870's of Western criminal law whereby the government deprived the balai of its punitive sanctions.[54] Reportedly, by the end of the nineteenth century, in many parts of Minangkabau the balai had all but lost its power. The erosion of the balai was accompanied by the decline of the penghulu's prestige as the result of the unprecedented duties imposed on them as "the carriers of *rodi kompeni* (government corvée)." Under the supervision of tuanku laras, the nagari chiefs and penghulu were held responsible for coffee cultivation, over which the government had the monopoly, and the performance of corvée. From the people's point of view the penghulu with these new duties had become tools of the government instead of leaders of the people.

Although the government did try to keep the traditional prestige of the penghulu, in doing so, it only accelerated the process of erosion. In order to enhance the penghulu's position, a regulation was issued exempting a penghulu's family from corvée. Since Minangkabau adat contained provisions for the institution of new penghulu or the division of existing penghuluships, this regulation became a most important stimulus for the proliferation of new penghulu. Rich and large families, by fulfilling adat requirements, could institute their own penghulu. The consequence was a further dispersion of prestige at a time when the position of the penghulu was already deteriorating. In order to halt this decline the govern-

[54] Ph. S. van Ronkel, "De invoering van ons strafwetboek ter Sumatra's Westkust naar Aantekeningen in een Maleisch handschrift," *Tijdschrift voor Binnenlandsch Bestuur* (hereafter *TBB*), 46 (1914), 249–255. See also Batuah and Madjo Indo, pp. 112–117.

ment attempted to control the institution of penghuluships. In 1887 a regulation was issued requiring registration of all existing penghuluships. It was also stipulated that a new penghuluship could be created only with the approval of the local administration. But again, this meant that penghuluship too had become an administrative matter.

Dutch concern over the prestige of the penghulu was also motivated by the desire to exclude religious teachers from political influence. From the early 1870's the Dutch government barred religious teachers and hadji from appointment as tuanku laras or nagari chiefs.[55] It even tried to prevent the election of hadji to penghuluships. This anti-Islamic administrative policy was based on the assumption that penghulu and religious teacher were two competing roles in Minangkabau. The penghulu was thought to be not simply traditional chief and guardian of adat but also the personification of adat itself. Religious teachers and hadji were treated not as parts of the adat community but rather as outside forces that would undermine adat. This assumption led the government to move rapidly against any religious reform movement. When Sjech Achmad Chatib launched his orthodox movement in the 1890's, the government quickly reacted with a plan to codify adat law, in order to secure the power of the penghulu and to protect adat against the corrupting influence of Islam.[56] This artificial "containment" policy only intensified the conflict between penghulu and religious teacher, and tended to ossify adat. The penghulu, whose power had been greatly undermined by the government, became more sensitive toward the possibility of the further erosion of his prestige.

The conquest of the Minangkabau heartland weakened the traditional political system and led to a serious crisis in Minang-

[55] In November 1873, a hadji was appointed as a tuanku laras. Within a month, the Governor of the West Coast of Sumatra issued a statement that it was unwise to choose a hadji for any governmental office. Van Hasselt, who journeyed throughout the interior of central and western Sumatra in the late 1870's, reported that there was not a single hadji in government service. A. L. van Hasselt, *Volksbeschrijving van Midden Sumatra* (Leiden: Brill, 1882), pp. 60–61.

[56] On the advice of C. Snouck Hurgronje the proposal was rejected. Snouck's argument is a classic of its kind; see his "Advies" in *Adatrechtbundels*, 1 (1911), 21–44.

kabau self-confidence. The erosion of the penghuluship and its dependence on the government were seen not simply as signs of weakening social ties but also as deviations from the Minangkabau paradigm, its Alam. The coffee monopoly and corvée were perceived as symbols of an intolerable situation. Contemporary Minangkabau referred to the times as a period in which *rodi,* not adat, prevailed.[57] It was a time when "adat is only in the pepatah, and religion is only in the Book." These aphorisms expressed not only the growing discrepancy between ideal and reality but, more important, a feeling of despair at the inability to bridge the gap. Religion, another pillar of the Minangkabau World, was also in crisis. At the turn of the century, the Naqsjabandijah tarékat school, which denounced other mystic schools as heretical, was itself under fire. The orthodox movement rejected the Naqsjabandijah doctrine of the intermediary role of the teacher as heresy (*bid'ah*).

In this situation, when the feeling of disruption of the old order was prevalent, the government initiated another change. In 1908, as a direct response to the continuing decrease of coffee production, which had begun in the last quarter of the nineteenth century, the government abolished the coffee monopoly and introduced money taxation. From a purely economic point of view the new policy was advantageous to the people since they could sell their coffee at considerably higher prices. The timing of its introduction, however, was not determined by the existing social conditions, but by the government's overall new aggressive policy in the so-called Outer Possessions. The government in the first place did not consult the tuanku laras, the nagari chiefs, and the penghulu, whose authority it officially recognized. By ignoring the still highly esteemed mufakat, the government intensified the resentment of the penghulu and also made the position of the tuanku laras and particularly that of the nagari chiefs more difficult. Secondly, the Dutch government now bluntly proclaimed itself ruler, instead of the "protector" or "friend" who had issued the Plakat Pandjang. The introduction of taxation was felt as an intolerable humiliation by the Minangkabau, who had never considered themselves as "nephews of the Company."

[57] The earliest published reference to this is given in A. M. B. M., "Pada menjatakan pengadjaran orang boemipoetera di Padang Darat (Padangsche Bovenlanden)," *TBB*, 9 (1894), 411–417.

The silent opposition, which ignored the new regulation, soon developed into rural uprisings. When the government tried to enforce
tax-collection, the penghulu whose power had been encroached
upon emerged as the defenders of the people and became the leaders of the rebellion. The tarékat leaders, particularly those of the
Sjatariah school, whose religious doctrines had also been under
fire, became its spiritual leaders. They provided a religious foundation for the scattered uprisings. In the eyes of the people, the authorities were illegitimate, not deriving their power from popular
consent, and *kafir*, unbelievers, who humiliated true religion.[58]

These antitax rebellions of 1908 were basically defensive in
character, aiming at the prevention of further decline of the old
order. The eruptions were the direct consequence of accumulated
resentment and bitterness against the steady encroachment upon
the traditional order. The old conception of Alam Minangkabau
appeared to be on the verge of disintegration. In this period of uncertainty, the rebellions reflected the transitional state of the society. They were directed against the unintelligible outside forces
that increasingly dominated people's lives. Dutch guns and military
campaigns easily defeated these attempts to restore the old order.
The nostalgic struggle which was reinforced by a belief in invulnerability in the face of the kafir rulers ended in despair. "With strong
repressive measures" [59] the scattered uprisings were suppressed and
taxation was finally enforced.

The tragic events of 1908, however, began a new era in
Minangkabau. They marked the beginning of economic change
and the increasing predominance of urban influence in the nagari.
The period of rapid penetration of the money economy into the
nagari began, and the traditional notion of the nagari as a largely
self-sufficient community broke down. Following the introduction

[58] See W. J. Kroon, "De invoering van belastingen op Sumatra's Westkust," *TBB*, 51 (1916), 342–351, 503–509; 52 (1917), 170–179; and
G. A. N. Scheltema de Heere, "De belastinginvoering op Sumatra's Westkust," *IG*, 14 (1923), 122–156.

[59] F. Heckler, "Memorie van overgave betreffende de toestand van het
Gouvernement van Sumatra's Westkust" (1905–1910), State Archives, The
Hague (hereafter SA), *Mailrapport* (copies of letters, reports, decisions of
colonial authorities sent to the Minister of Colonies; filed by year and
number) 387/1910—*Verbaal* (minutes; filed by date and number), April
21, 1911, no. 8, p. 7.

of the money tax system, the government removed some obstacles to economic growth. The ban on rice export and controls over rice production were abolished. The traditional eastern outlet through the Straits of Malacca was reopened.[60] In 1911, the government introduced the People's Credit system, which was put under the jurisdiction of adat authorities. By 1916, this network of village banks had spread throughout the greater part of Minangkabau.[61] The positive response of the Minangkabau to these new economic opportunities was encouraged by the existence of the rotating market system. Since the end of the nineteenth century in every subdistrict certain nagari once or twice a week held their own market days. On its market day, the nagari became the economic center for its neighboring nagari. This rotating market system was repeated on the district level. Each district administrative center once a week became the focal point where people from several districts conducted their business.[62]

Unlike the nagari, which generally grew out of old settlements, the towns in the interior were usually built for specific purposes. Originally Dutch military fortresses during the Padri war and later adapted to coffee storage, the towns became the administrative-economic centers of the district. In some ways the towns in the interior could be considered as the rantau of the heartland to which people from surrounding nagari were attracted. Those town dwellers who did not come from the town itself were placed under a *penghulu dagang* (literally, penghulu for travelers) who was the temporary adat head in the quasi-adat community. They were perantau from their home nagari who could now settle in the heartland, in the new rantau, and establish their own households, which they could not have done in the past. Despite the powerful hold of the matrilineal family, which centered in the inherited communal house and landed property, a trend toward the growing importance of nuclear families developed in these separate urban households.

---

[60] B. Schrieke, "The Causes and Effects of Communism on the Westcoast of Sumatra," in his *Indonesian Sociological Studies*, 1 (The Hague and Bandung: van Hoeve, 1955), 95–106.

[61] J. Ballot, "Memorie van Overgave" (1915), *Mailrapport* 14/1916— *Verbaal*, April 5, 1916, no. 15, pp. 83–87.

[62] *Ibid.*, pp. 98–100. On the history of the market, see H. W. Stap, "De Nagari Ordonnantie ter Sumatra's Westkust," *TBB*, 53 (1917), 699–765.

This process, which tended to weaken the mamak-kemenakan relationship, was an important aspect of Minangkabau social development. In the rantau nuclear family, the father gradually began to assume also the role of mamak within his own family.[63]

It was also in these towns that the slow progress of accommodation to the new situation began. During the second part of the nineteenth century, the Dutch government had introduced a new school system which was designed primarily for the training of lower government officials and for combatting illiteracy. In the district capital the government established five-year vernacular schools. In Padang and Bukittinggi, the two largest towns, "European schools" were founded. In the mid-1850's, a *Kweekschool* for training teachers was set up. By the end of the century, this school, which was popularly referred to as the *Sekolah Radja* ("School for Rulers"), had become the most important educational institution. From it many early Minangkabau modernizers graduated.[64] Throughout the later part of the nineteenth century and the first decade of the present century, the development of the government school system in the rural areas was very slow. Popular suspicion of the intentions of the kafir government and the fact that establishment of schools was entirely dependent on the initiative of nagari chiefs or the tuanku laras, were two of the factors that obstructed their development. But in the early 1910's with the introduction of the so-called *volkschool*, the three-year school, which was directly under government control though financed by the respective nagari communities, the school system began to expand rapidly. In 1913, for example, in addition to the existing 203 private and subsidized elementary schools, the government initiated the establishment of 111 new volkscholen. By 1915 the number of these schools had increased to 358.[65] Some nagari, particularly Kota

---

[63] This is a somewhat exaggerated statement. In spite of the stronger authority of the father over his own children, the mamak is still highly respected today. Even among educated Minangkabau perantau families the mamak remains a person to be consulted. I agree with Junus' criticism, in his "Some Remarks," of Maretin's models of the Minangkabau family system. See J. V. Maretin, "Disappearance of Matriclan Survivals in Minangkabau Family and Marriage Relations," *BKI*, 117 (1961), 168–195.

[64] *Gedenkboek Samengesteld bij Gelegenheid van het 35 jarig bestaan der Kweekschool voor Inlandsche Onderwijzers te Fort de Kock (1873–1908)* (Arnheim: Shreme, 1908).

[65] Ballot, pp. 81–82.

Gedang (near Bukittinggi), produced many schoolteachers and government officials. In 1911 Kota Gedang through its Study Fund managed to send two students to Holland. In 1914 the nagari had its own Dutch-Native School (HIS).[66]

These economic and social developments were accompanied by intellectual and religious conflict. In the first quarter of the century, Minangkabau experienced numerous rural uprisings, decline of the traditional political system, and intense examination of the assumptions of its world, Alam Minangkabau. The traditional concept of the Minangkabau World was put to the test in facing unprecedented influence from the outside world.

DATUK SUTAN MAHARADJA AND THE PERIOD OF CULTURAL TRANSITION

In 1911 a writer in *Pewarta Deli*, a newspaper published in Medan (East Sumatra), reported that the situation on the West Coast of Sumatra had markedly changed since his last visit ten years earlier.[67] In 1916 van Ronkel, in his report on religious movements in Minangkabau was also impressed by the rapid change that had taken place in Minangkabau. He wrote: "About ten years ago, people still thought that sending their children to government schools would only make them kafir." But by 1916, according to him there were many complaints concerning inadequate school facilities. The number of Minangkabau youths who went to Java to continue their studies was also growing.[68]

Increasing participation in the money economy and the opening of new rantau not only provided more outlets for individualist inclinations in an adat-dominated society, but also contributed much to a more positive attitude toward the new influences. This development was further intensified by an upsurge of Islamic modernism, which began as a fundamentalist movement.

[66] K. A. James, "De Nagari Kota Gedang," *TBB*, 49 (1915), 185–195.
[67] Reprinted in *Oetoesan Melajoe* (hereafter *OM*), April 22, 1914.
[68] Van Ronkel, *Rapport*, p. 34. In the 1850's, two Minangkabau were among the first graduates of the so-called Dokter Djawa School for training vaccinators. In 1918, according to Resident LeFebvre, seventy of the two hundred students of the STOVIA, the "native" medical school in Batavia, came from the West Coast of Sumatra. Minangkabau students also attended other secondary schools in Java. J. D. L. LeFebvre, "Memorie van Overgave" (1919), *Mailrapport* 2904/1919, pp. 56, 73.

The mood in this period of transition is best expressed in the writings of Datuk Sutan Maharadja who emerged in the 1900's as a leader of the so-called Young Malay Party. An early advocate of modernization in Minangkabau, Dt. St. Maharadja, who was known as the father of Malay journalism, ended up as a disillusioned adat ideologue. From the early 1890's until his death in 1921, he was constantly in the center of Minangkabau intellectual, social, and political movements. Either an initiator, a supporter, or an opponent of these numerous movements, he was never an idle observer. His life and his struggles in a way symbolize the Minangkabau encounter with the outside world and the attempt to rediscover Minangkabau's own genius.

The Father of Malay Journalism

Datuk Sutan Maharadja was his title as penghulu in his nagari, a position he inherited from his mamak. His personal name was Mahjuddin, but adat required that a penghulu be always referred to by his title. His father and paternal grandfather were both also penghulu in their respective suku. Dt. St. Maharadja was born in November 1860 [69] in Sulit Air. Aside from acquiring expertise in adat from his father, a famous adat theoretician, he also imbibed a strong hostility toward the Padri and their alleged followers. His paternal great-grandfather had been killed in the Padri war and his grandfather was a leader of the anti-Padri faction in Sulit Air. After Sulit Air was conquered by the Dutch in the mid-1820's, this grandfather became commander of the Sulit Air contingent against the Padri nagari. In 1860 the Dutch appointed him the first tuanku laras of Sulit Air. His son, Dt. St. Maharadja's father, succeeded him as the second tuanku laras.

Because of his early association with the Dutch, Dt. St. Maharadja belonged to the first generation of "Western-educated" Minangkabau. His father, Datuk Bandharo, was for some time a student

[69] This biographical sketch is based on Dt. St. Maharadja's scattered writings, particularly his unfinished autobiography in *Soenting Melajoe*, Sept. 17–Nov. 22, 1920; [Editor], "Kaoem Moeda di Minangkabau III," in *Pandji Islam*, Feb. 17, 1941; Datuk Mangkuto Alam, "Datoek Soetan Maharadja," *Pandji Islam*, May 5, 1941. Also relevant are the writings of his opponents in *Pertja Barat* (1911–1913) and *Warta Hindia* (1912, 1921). His government position can be checked in *Regeerings Almanak*, 1888.

of the Sekolah Radja in Bukittinggi. In 1873, through his father's friendship with a Dutch official Dt. St. Maharadja and two other boys from his nagari were admitted to the European elementary school in Padang. But after some months all were expelled because one of them had been involved in a fight with a Dutch boy. By his own account, Dt. St. Maharadja might still have had a chance to continue his studies since he was a son of a loyal tuanku laras, but in 1875 Dt. Bandharo resigned in protest against the government's plan to impose a regulation stipulating government ownership of all unoccupied land. In 1876, on the advice of a Dutch governor, a close acquaintance of Datuk Bandharo, Dt. St. Maharadja became an apprentice to an influential public prosecutor in Padang. During this period he was the constant companion of a retired schoolteacher who was (at that time) studying law with a Dutch lawyer. In this way Dt. St. Maharadja began his training in law. When the schoolteacher was appointed as an unsalaried attorney, Dt. St. Maharadja was asked by his master to assist a retired Dutch resident in compiling a Nias-Malay-Dutch dictionary. In 1879, Dt. St. Maharadja was appointed a salaried clerk in the office of the public prosecutor. In 1882, he was promoted to deputy public prosecutor of Indrapura. In this coastal town of Southern Minangkabau, he began to get acquainted with mystic teachings, such as Samaniah, Sjatariah, and particularly a certain tarékat Mim.[70] In 1883, he was again promoted and transferred to Padang and later to Pariaman, a northern coastal town. He believed that his success was due to his ability to apply adat moral teachings in practice. In 1891, however, Dt. St. Maharadja resigned from his job because he failed to get a promotion.

For some years after his resignation, Dt. St. Maharadja worked as a part-time detective in government employ. His main occupation, however, was the editing of the *Palita Ketjil* (Little Light), the oldest Malay newspaper in Sumatra, first published in the 1880's. Like most of the old newspapers, the *Palita Ketjil* dealt mostly with commercial news and advertisements. But, after Dt. St. Maharadja joined the newspaper in March 1891, *Palita Ketjil* became the first forum for the limited number of educated individuals,

---

[70] For a brief discussion of these mystic teachings, see van Ronkel, *Rapport*, pp. 9-15.

mostly schoolteachers and government officials. His work as editor not only established his position as "father of Malay journalism" but also his role as a prominent defender of adat. In 1893, Achmad Chatib denounced adat matrilineal inheritance law. Like other fundamentalist reformers, such as the Padri propagators, Achmad Chatib did not hesitate to conclude that the Minangkabau had been living in a forbidden (*haram*) social system. The exposure of the religiously unlawful foundation of Minangkabau society also meant the rejection of the notion that religion and adat could exist in harmony. In refuting Achmad Chatib's attacks, Dt. St. Maharadja soon emerged as the leader of the opposition. He saw these attacks as a sign of the reemergence of the Padri movement. He warned against this supposed trend, which in the past had created a deep crisis in Minangkabau. He organized a Kongsi Adat (Adat Association) to defend Alam Minangkabau against the encroachment of the "Mecca people," whom he called the Kongsi Padri.[71] In 1895 Dt. St. Maharadja resigned from *Palita Ketjil* and became an editor of *Warta Berita* (News Report), which was published by Padang aristocrats. In 1904 he joined *Tjaja Soematera* (Light of Sumatra), owned by a Dutch publisher. During his tenure he began what he conceived of as the "adat democratic revolution" against the coastal aristocratic cliques.

In basing his "revolution" on original Minangkabau adat, Dt. St. Maharadja was also influenced by events in Japan and Turkey. He started the "adat democratic revolution" in 1906, while engaged in a debate with a Chinese-Malay newspaper on the effects of Japan's victory over Russia in 1905. This historic event prompted a Chinese-Malay newspaper to introduce the slogan "Asia for the Asians" and to proclaim Japan as the strongest power in Asia. Dt. St. Maharadja, with his loyalty to the Dutch and his strong belief in "Malay-ism," interpreted these ideas as nothing less than the threat of "yellow peril." In the face of this threat, according to him, "ruler and ruled should be united." [72] In Padang, the "native" ruler was the regent, who was supported by various aristocratic cliques. In his struggle

[71] See B. Schrieke, "Bijdrage tot de Bibliografie van de huidige godsdienstige beweging ter Sumatra's Westkust," *TBG*, 59 (1919–1921), 249–322.

[72] *OM*, Dec. 22, 1917.

against the regent, Dt. St. Maharadja referred to his followers, mostly highlanders, as "Kaum Muda" (Group of the Young) after the model of the Young Turks. The regent and his assistants were likened to the corrupt Sultan Abdul Hamid and his ministers. *Tjaja Soematera* became the organ of the Kaum Muda in advocating the restoration of the genuine Minangkabau adat and in exhorting people to take the path of *kemadjuan* (progress).

In late 1910, Dt. St. Maharadja left *Tjaja Soematera* and published his own newspaper *Oetoesan Melajoe* (Malay Messenger). Through this new enterprise he began to accumulate capital for the establishment of a Minangkabau-owned printing house. Despite the charge of his enemies, notably the Padang aristocrats, that he was no more than "a beggar," [73] "The Printing House of the People of the Minangkabau World" was finally set up with the support of traders in Padang. After January 1912, *Oetoesan Melajoe* was no longer produced by a Chinese printer. It was also in this new printing house that *Al-Moenir* (The Enlightenment), the first journal of the Islamic modernists, was printed. The director of this journal was Dt. St. Maharadja's son-in-law, a close assistant of Hadji Abdullah Ahmad (1878–1933),[74] leader of the Islamic modernists. At this time Dt. St. Maharadja developed a very close relationship with this group whom he also called the Kaum Muda, a religious counterpart of his secular adat movement.

The objective of *Oetoesan Melajoe* was the attainment of kemadjuan in "skills, manufacture, knowledge, agriculture, and commerce." In order to pursue his many-sided interests, Dt. St. Maharadja also published and participated in several journals. In 1912 under the editorship of his daughter Zubaidah Ratna Djuita and Rohana,[75] the first woman educator in Minangkabau, Dt. St. Maharadja published *Soenting Melajoe* (Malay Ornament), the first feminist magazine in Sumatra. This publication opened the initial phase of the feminist movement in Minangkabau. In 1913, Dt. St. Maharadja

[73] *Pertja Barat*, Feb. 18, 1911.

[74] On the role of Hadji Abdullah Ahmad in the modernist Islamic movement in Minangkabau, see Almasip, "Hadji Abdullah Ahmad," *Pandji Islam* (Jan. 1939), pp. 3064–3065, 3087–3088, 4006–4007; Hamka, *Ajahku, passim*.

[75] Rohana (b. 1884–   ) was a sister of the famous Indonesian nationalist leader Sutan Sjahrir. On her life, see "Kartini Ketjil dari Minangkabau: Sitti Rohana," *Pandji Islam*, May 12 and 19, 1941.

broke with his son-in-law over the management of the printing house, and his relationship with the Islamic modernist groups rapidly deteriorated. To challenge *Al-Moenir*, he then published *Soeloeh Melajoe* (Malay Torch).[76] In 1914, Dt. St. Maharadja through his newspaper also took a leading part in the current anti-Arab and anti-Chinese campaigns, which were largely based on economic competition and the alleged arrogance of the Chinese and Arabs toward the "Malay" people.

Dt. St. Maharadja was undoubtedly one of the most versatile writers of his time. His newspapers not only conveyed his ideas and his wide-ranging interests, but also promoted his social and political activities. The main function of his newspapers, and also of other Malay newspapers, was educational rather than informative. Because almost all early Minangkabau editors and writers participated directly in the events they reported, the tone of their newspapers was very argumentative. It was typical of these early publications to take strong views on all issues. The moods of Minangkabau in its attempt to elevate itself are clearly reflected in its early journalism. Through Dt. St. Maharadja's biography certain characteristics of Minangkabau intellectual and social change can easily be traced.

The Kaum Muda Phase

In 1901 Dt. St. Maharadja was one of the correspondents of the newly published *Insulinde* (1901–1904), a journal of government schoolteachers and educated people "who want to pursue knowledge." This journal, published in Padang, had correspondents scattered throughout Java and Sumatra. *Insulinde* consistently promoted the idea of kemadjuan. Every issue was filled with an appeal to the "Indies" to "become progressive" (*mendjadi madju*). It urged the schoolteachers to become the leaders as well as the educators of the people. In this period, when the world was changing rapidly, the editor of the journal argued, schoolteachers had a

[76] The objectives of *Soeloeh Melajoe* according to its motto were "to explain knowledge, to enlighten *akal* and [to encourage] *kemadjuan* in the fields of manufacture, skills, commerce and agriculture." *Soeloeh Melajoe* was to guard *adat* and maintain religion "so that our religion and our belief [*iman*] are not insulted by the new people [the religious Kaum Muda]," *Soeloeh Melajoe*, April 15, 1913.

crucial role to fill. They had been exposed to some aspects of the dunia madju (modern world) and were able to circulate and distribute new ideas. "If we remain in a state of complacency," the editor asked, "what will happen to our people?" [77]

It was not by chance that the urgency to enter the dunia madju was so pronounced in Padang. Padang was the biggest coastal town, the capital of the West Coast of Sumatra, where most of the Dutch officials resided, and where the "Eastern Orientals," Chinese and Arabs, made their living. It was also the place where Minangkabau interior and rantau political traditions overlapped. Unlike other rantau territories, which were ruled by a radja as representative of the king in the interior, Padang had originally continued the penghulu tradition brought by the early settlers from the heartland,[78] but since the early seventeenth century, when Atjehnese chiefs gained political dominance in Padang, a new hereditary aristocratic class had begun to develop. After the Atjehnese chiefs were conquered by the Dutch trading company, this development was reinforced by the cooperation of the Dutch with the Minangkabau king.[79] While maintaining its penghulu tradition, based on the uncle-nephew network, Padang also developed a "bureaucratic aristocratic" class based on father-son relationships. Adat was dominated by the penghulu, whose authority and jurisdiction rested on genealogical principles, while territorial administration was under the jurisdiction of the aristocracy. These overlapping political traditions became vulnerable after the Padri War with the growing influx of people from the Minangkabau heartland. These newcomers, who soon formed the largest section of Padang's social and economic middle class, with their ideals of the wisdom of mufakat or consensus, were never at ease with Padang's aristocratic cliques. In the nineteenth century, Padang was in many ways a typical "Indies town," [80] with pronounced social stratification

[77] "Sumatra," *Insulinde*, 1, no. 1 (1901), 22.

[78] "Panghoeloe's in het district Padang," *Adatrechtbundels*, 39 (1937), 218–228.

[79] On the historical event, see H. Kroeskamp, "De Westkust en Minangkabau" (dissertation, State University of Leiden, 1931).

[80] On the concept of "Indies town," see W. F. Wertheim, *Indonesian Society in Transition* (The Hague and Bandung: van Hoeve, 1958), pp. 168–173. A description of Padang in the 1880's can be found in M. Buys, *Twee jaren in Sumatra's Westkust* (Amsterdam: Ketinga, 1886), *passim*.

and different cultural orientations. By the end of the century, however, with the expansion of the Western school system, the cultural barriers began to break down. Among the young educated coastal aristocrats and the native officials from the interior, a new style of life began to develop. It was among this group, whose interests were characterized by club and newspaper activities, that the idea of kemadjuan first developed.

This idea grew from a desire to enter the dunia madju represented by the Europeans. "Even though we might not be able to match the level of the Europeans," according to a writer of *Insulinde*, "it is sufficient to bring ourselves closer to them." [81] This fascination with the dunia madju was accompanied by an optimistic conviction that entrance into it would indeed be possible. The example of Japan strongly supported this optimism. Japanese success in entering the modern world was believed to be due not to outside help or pressure but to "the motivation which originated in and was developed by the people themselves . . . , and the leaders and chiefs who also endeavored to develop . . . the country and to educate the people." [82] In 1904, Abdul Rivai (1871–1937), a Minangkabau medical student, at that time an editor of *Bintang Hindia* (Star of the Indies) in Holland, introduced "national pride" as another aspect of kemadjuan. He developed the idea of national pride into a justification of kemadjuan, as well as a driving force for its attainment. According to Rivai, kemadjuan should not mean the elimination of national identity, because the world of kemadjuan itself required incessant competition between nations; therefore "the Indies should remain the Indies no matter how developed and how high their status might be." [83] Rivai's appeal may have been politically rather than culturally motivated, but it focused on an important issue. Concern over kemadjuan became intertwined with

[81] *Insulinde*, 1, no. 1 (1901), 22–23.

[82] *Insulinde*, 2, no. 13 (1902), 518–519.

[83] *Bintang Hindia*, 4, no. 3 (1904), 38. Abdul Rivai was culturally one of the most "Westernized" Minangkabau intellectuals. He was also one of the sharpest critics of the Dutch colonial regime. On the intellectual aspect of his life, see M. Amir, "Psychologie Dr. Abdul Rivai," *Pedoman Masjarakat*, 5, no. 8 (Feb. 23, 1939), 141–148. Some of the best of Rivai's anticolonial writings are collected in Parada Harahap, *Riwajat Dr. A. Rivai* (Medan: Indische Drukkerij, 1939).

the idea of cultural identity. The early protagonists of kemadjuan saw the issue as simply involving an urgently needed abandonment of "backward tradition" and an entrance into the new world by imitating the Dutch model. But the victory of Japan in 1905 confirmed Rivai's prognosis that kemadjuan could also mean competition between nations. This historic event forced the protagonists of kemadjuan to look inward to their own cultural heritage.

At this juncture Dt. St. Maharadja began to formulate an ideological and political foundation for his role as a champion of Minangkabau kemadjuan. He emerged as leader of a group referred to by Dutch journalists as the "Young Malay Party." He called himself the leader of the Kaum Muda in the struggle against the Regent and the coastal aristocracy.[84] He also claimed to be the spokesman of "the Malays" in their competition with the Chinese, whom he regarded as the personification of the "yellow peril." Through these multiple roles Dt. St. Maharadja not only tried to promote kemadjuan, but also attempted to find a niche for himself in the social hierarchy of Padang. Even though a penghulu in his nagari, he could not aspire to the elite in Padang. By both adat genealogical and aristocratic criteria his social position—much like that of other Minangkabau newcomers from the interior—was below that of the long-settled Minangkabau population of Padang, but above that of the "native" non-Minangkabau sectors of the society. By taking the office of Regent, which he saw as a holdover of Atjehnese influence on Padang's social system, as the target of his "democratic adat revolution" in 1906, Datuk Sutan Maharadja, along with his group, challenged the whole social structure of Padang. The Regent was the native administrative head as well as the higest authority on adat. He was also the chairman of the Padang religious council (*kerapatan agama*, or *raad agama*), which was the only adat institution of its kind that was supported by political power. Dt. St. Maharadja expected that the breakdown of the Padang political structure would demonstrate the illegitimacy

---

[84] A lengthy discussion of the "adat democratic revolution" is given in G. de Waal van Anckeveen, "Maleische democratie en Padangsche toestanden," *Sumatra Bode*, March 27, 28, 1907; reprinted in *Adatrechtbundels*, 1 (1911), 114–128; see also Schrieke, "Bijdrage tot de Bibliografie," pp. 278–281.

of the coastal aristocracy according to adat, and would lead eventually to the reestablishment of an adat class structure.

Thus Dt. St. Maharadja's movement intensified the conflict between the rantau-aristocracy, who tended to look down on the newcomers from the interior, and the penghulu-oriented highlanders. This "revolution," with which Dt. St. Maharadja set out to lead Padang back into the fold of the Minangkabau World, provided him with a rationalization for his paradoxical role—a penghulu of Sulit Air acting as champion of kemadjuan in Padang. Moreover, by using adat as the basis for kemadjuan, he not only made progress an adat imperative, but also responded to his personal need for social recognition.

According to Dt. St. Maharadja's reminiscences of his adat movement, an essential part of kemadjuan was "democracy." This idea was also the raison d'être of the Kaum Muda, who, like the "Young Turks," wanted to abolish the "cleavage between ruler and ruled." Since the essence of Minangkabau adat, with its mufakat, was also democracy, the "adat revolution" against the Regent and his aristocratic clique should not be seen as a step backward, but rather as a necessary step toward kemadjuan.[85] Kemadjuan should not be understood as an imitation of the outside world, but rather as the unfolding of ideals inherent in Minangkabau adat. The meaning of kemadjuan was not the transformation of society but the "glorification of Mount Merapi," the nexus of the Minangkabau World. Kemadjuan was imperative, according to Dt. St. Maharadja, because it was the duty of the Minangkabau to realize their adat ideals.

The conception of adat as the basis of kemadjuan was best demonstrated in his program to promote women's education. He took a leading part in establishing schools for girls and making women's education more than ever before a public issue.[86] He pointed to the discrepancy between adat ideals and social reality—the high status of women in the matrilineal society and their ambiguous social position. This discrepancy could only be bridged by the promotion of women's education, enabling them to enhance their welfare and

[85] *OM*, March 22, 1917.
[86] Problems of women's education also appeared in several issues of *Insulinde* in 1901 and 1902.

preparing them for an eventual role as the educators of their children.[87] In 1907, when Dt. St. Maharadja was still director of his own school for boys, which he had established in 1902, he began to engage himself in the development of weaving schools for girls through a newly founded organization, the Keradjinan Minangkabau, Laras Nan Dua (Endeavor of Minangkabau, the Two Laras). In 1908 he initiated the first Malay trade fair, where he promoted weaving activities in Padang. The Trade Fair, supported by the increasing number of Minangkabau trading groups, was so successful that it became an annual event. As one direct outcome of this fair, three Minangkabau girls were sent by the government to Belgium for an exhibition of their weaving craft.[88] In 1909, Dt. St. Maharadja set up the first weaving school for girls, the Padangsche Weefschool. Five experienced women weavers from his nagari, Sulit Air, were invited to be teachers there. With the financial support of Padang traders, the school modernized traditional weaving techniques. In 1912, instead of sending teachers, Sulit Air sent several students to study at the school. In three years Dt. St. Maharadja had not only succeeded in "reviving the old legacy of Minangkabau ancestors" but in updating it as well.[89] Despite the attacks of some coastal aristocrats, who accused him of enslaving young girls, he made his school into a model for several new weaving schools in Padang.[90] The culmination of these efforts came in January 1914 with the organization of the Sarekat Sekolah Tenun (Association of Weaving Schools) to which Dt. St. Maharadja was elected advisor. His activities were not confined to Padang alone; his writings in *Oetoesan Melajoe* and *Soenting Melajoe* spread his ideas among the local notables and the still small number of educated Minangkabau women. Not infrequently he visited localities which had favorably responded to his pleas. To some degree he was also responsible for the establishment of women's educational organizations in several nagari and towns such as Sulit Air (1912), Kota Gedang (1912), Padang Pandjang (1915), Lintau (1916), Matur (1916), and others.

The situation in the second decade of this century indeed differed from that of the late nineteenth century, when the government had closed two girls' schools for lack of pupils. By 1914, how-

[87] *OM*, Feb. 12, 1912.
[89] *OM*, March 9 and 25, 1914.
[88] *Sumatra Bode*, Oct. 17, 1908.
[90] *Tjaja Soematra*, June 15, 1914.

ever, it could no longer provide enough seats—Minangkabau had become the Islamic region with the highest percentage of girls in schools.[91] There were already several Minangkabau girls in the prestigious Sekolah Radja. Nevertheless, with different emphases, women's education remained a major issue of public debate. The debate gained momentum in 1914 when "a sixty year old man" who called himself "Uilenspiegel" wrote an anti-women's-education article in *Oetoesan Melajoe*. "Our mothers never went to school, yet they led prosperous lives," he said. "We should not change the legacy of our grandmother who was called Eve," because, it seemed to the writer, "all women who have been to school always want to seek their own fame and glory. People look at them as individuals who have been uprooted from our Islamic people. They only want fame and compliments."[92] Dt. St. Maharadja, the editor of the newspaper, was the first to attack Uilenspiegel. Why should out-dated customs not be changed, "while nature is destined by God to be changeable?" Uilenspiegel's article provoked reactions from several parts of Minangkabau and also from Batavia. Responses came especially from Western-educated women, most of them teachers in government schools. For more than three months pro-tests against this article dominated the Padang newspapers. Some women writers even proclaimed that they did not want to depend on men, because dependence meant slavery. "We, the women of today, do not want to be fooled by men (as happened in the period of Uilenspiegel's mother)."[93] Only after a strong appeal against this emotional outburst had come from a respected teacher, who urged educated women to ignore the outdated Uilenspiegel, did the reac-tion begin to abate. Women's education can indeed be considered a major issue in the discussion of kemadjuan. Women's central position in Minangkabau matrilineal society—as a symbol of family continuity as well as the personification of the adat communal house—and the accepted religious ethic, with its puritanical ten-dencies, made the issue a real test case in the attempt to achieve kemadjuan.

The urgent need for a further unfolding of adat ideals, accord-

[91] C. Lekkerkerker, "Meisjesonderwijs, coëducatie en meisjesscholen voor de Inlandsche bevolking in Nederlandsch-Indië," *KT*, 3 (1914), 865–884.
[92] *OM*, Jan. 3, 1914.   [93] *OM*, Jan. 7, 1914.

ing to Dt. St. Maharadja, was a result of outside pressure. "The glory of Mt. Merapi" had long been in decline, and the Minangkabau people had been looked down upon by other nations. The Minangkabau seemed to have lost their confidence in meeting the outside world. Because of this it was the duty of the Kaum Muda to revive the traditional Minangkabau spirit of confidence and independence.[94] It was the duty of the Kaum Muda to make the people progressive and to oppose the Kaum Kuno, "who are only interested in promoting their own interest." [95]

As leader of the secular Kaum Muda of 1906, Dt. St. Maharadja had numerous enemies. Many advocates of progress disapproved his conception of adat as the basis for kemadjuan. The coastal aristocrats looked on him as an enemy who questioned the legitimacy of their social status. In the interior many educated penghulu resented his erratic behavior, particularly his "I-know-better" attitude. But his ideas and his activities, either in publication or in establishing organizations and schools, were supported by many active officials and trading groups. He, more than anyone else at that time, gave a satisfactory solution to the problem of kemadjuan. His strong emphasis on activism and individual independence was also in accord with the appeals of the Islamic modernist movement.

In the beginning of the 1900's, several former students of Sjech Achmad Chatib launched an orthodox reform movement, which had been sparked by their teacher. They particularly attacked the heterodoxy of the tarékat schools and unlawful innovations (bid'ah) in religious practices. In their purification movement, the young reformers, who were known as the religious Kaum Muda, were also influenced by the great Egyptian reformist, Sjech Muhammad Abduh (1849?–1905). By the second decade of the century these young religious scholars, ulama, began to denounce traditional religious experts for relying in their judgments solely on *naql*, the established religious authorities. They argued that belief (iman) based on *taqlid* (unquestioning acceptance of religious teachers) was not valid, because the real sources of law were the Koran and hadith, the Prophetic Tradition. With this appeal to return to the original sources, the young reformers propagated *idjtihad*, the striv-

94 *OM*, March 14, 1914.   95 *OM*, March 11, 1914.

ing to attain truth, by using akal (reasoning). "The man who does not use akal is an inferior human being . . . he can be considered as one whose objective in life is only motivated by his desire to satisfy his appetite." [96]

Appeals for a rational attitude toward religion and for a return to the orthodoxy of Islam not only aimed at the liberation of the Islamic community (*ummat*) from inhibiting traditions but also at recalling for it Islam's inherent greatness. The denunciation of tarékat schools by the Kaum Muda ulama was also focused on the former's escapist attitudes. They refuted the notion, still prevailing in traditional religious circles, that religious knowledge was the only thing of importance in this world. "Islam," according to one of their spokesmen, "is not only a religion for the world hereafter, but, more important, a guide for life in this world." [97] Their view was expressed in the attempts of the older generation to prevent youngsters from pursuing those sciences based on reasoning (*akaliah*). "In the past our people were trapped in the valley of suffering and destruction, because of the corrupt teachers and traders of religion, who persuaded and tied our people to the religion of ignorance." [98]

The purification of religion from deviations and the rejection of taqlid were seen as the first steps toward the rediscovery of the real ethics of religion which in the past had brought Islam to the peak of its civilization and temporal power. These appeals were not motivated by the desire to transform the Islamic theological foundation, but rather to prepare the ground for social change, in order to create a religiously based rational society. Kemadjuan, therefore, should be seen as the renaissance of Islam, rather than as a transformation of its religious foundation.

Adat and Religion

In order to reactivate the traditional function of the nagari council, the government in 1914 abolished the office of tuanku laras, who was the administrative as well as adat head of a nagari

[96] Hadji Abdullah Ahmad, *Pemboeka Pintoe Sjorga* (Padang: Al-Moenir, 1914), p. 47.

[97] *Ibid.*

[98] Hadji Abdullah Ahmad, *Ilmoe Sedjati*, 2 (Padang: Sjarekat Ilmoe, n.d.), 75.

federation, and replaced it with that of *demang* (district-chief) with a purely administrative jurisdiction. The government also issued a Nagari Ordinance, which made the nagari council into a link between the administration and the people. But the ordinance stipulated that the members of the council should be limited to the so-called core-penghulu, whose legitimacy was recognized by the government. The nagari-chief could be elected only from among the core-penghulu.[99] This measure both repudiated the right of all penghulu to sit in the council and created an artificial division between the traditional leaders. According to the Minangkabau conception of authority, which was upheld by Dt. St. Maharadja and other adat guardians, this ordinance was clearly a major deviation from adat, since "the penghulu no longer have the same jurisdiction" (*penghulu indak saandiko*).

At the same time the government abolished in Padang the office of Regent, as the native head of administration, adat, and the religious council. This act deprived the Padang aristocratic establishment of its symbol of unity and removed the adat religious council's political backing. Adat religious functionaries and traditionalist religious teachers, known as the Kaum Tua (Old Group) ulama, could no longer use the once Regent-dominated religious council in their disputes with the modern-oriented religious teachers. In 1914, anticipating the social consequences of this administrative change, the Dutch administration appointed Hadji Abdullah Ahmad and two of his Kaum Muda colleagues as counterparts to the Kaum Tua ulama in a new religious council. It was expected that religious controversies could be settled in the council rather than be disputed in public. The appointment, however, only gave the Kaum Muda ulama more prestige and enabled them to conduct their reform movement more effectively. They began by attacking several moot points in religious practice (*chilafiah*), such as the way to celebrate the Prophet's birthday, and the dates of the

[99] Criticisms of the *Nagari Ordonnantie* (*Staatsblad* [hereafter *Stbl*], 1914–774) were also voiced by Dutch district officials (*Verbaal,* March 4, 1919, no. 23). In 1918 an amendment was enacted (*Stbl,* 1918–677) in which the opportunity to become a member of the nagari council was given to non-*penghulu urang patuik,* the unofficial village elite, such as religious experts (*alim ulama*) and "intellectuals" (*tjadiek pandai*).

beginning and the end of the fasting month.[100] By denouncing prevailing practices in these matters as deviations from the correct path of Islam, the religious Kaum Muda exposed the dogmatic mentality of their Kaum Tua opponents and undermined the position of adat religious functionaries. These seemingly trivial religious issues therefore had far reaching consequences. The Kaum Muda ulama tried to "liberate" people by testing traditionally accepted practices against the original sources of religion. The "liberation" movement directly challenged the right of adat religious functionaries to act as officiants in religious rites which had been incorporated into adat.

A consequence of exposing these issues in public was a rather poignant social polarization. The central mosque of Padang, which was under adat jurisdiction, now had two Imam, representing the Kaum Tua and Kaum Muda respectively, with their opposing followers. The end of the fasting month (Idulfitri), which is a time for forgetting and forgiving past mistakes, was celebrated separately by the two groups. In some parts of the Minangkabau interior, where adat authorities were still powerful, religious conflict was even more intense than in Padang. Religious issues often estranged father and son and husband and wife. The reformers thought that it was worth risking social polarization for the sake of aqidah, religious doctrine. From the point of view of adat guardians, to whom the need for social harmony remained paramount, social crisis had now reached its climax. Not only had the penghulu been artificially divided but now "the malim [religious experts] also no longer have the same Book."[101] Religious laws were no longer to be unquestioningly accepted but had to be subjected to scrutiny by the use of akal.

The anxiety of Dt. St. Maharadja and other adat-oriented leaders grew when in March 1916 a branch of the Sarekat Islam (Islamic League) was established in Padang.[102] The Sarekat Islam, which was founded by two influential Kaum Tua religious teachers,

---

[100] Schrieke, "Bijdrage tot de Bibliografie," pp. 279–325; Hamka, pp. 90–105.

[101] OM, Nov. 17, 1916.

[102] The Sarekat Islam originated from the Sarekat Dagang Islam (Islamic Merchants' Association), which was established in 1912, in Surakarta (Central Java). On the early growth of this first mass-party in Indonesia, see Robert

seemed at that time to emerge as a third force in the religious and social conflict.[103] Although the majority of its members were followers of the founders, and were generally peddlers and farmers in the neighborhood of Padang, most of its leaders belonged to the religious Kaum Muda. Concern over the growth of Sarekat Islam was due to its reputation as a rebellious party in Djambi and to the possibility that it might become a channel for spreading political ideas that originated in Java. Even though five months after its establishment the party split into two opposing groups, the Kaum Muda and the Kaum Tua respectively, it remained highly suspect. The Kaum Tua faction of Sarekat Islam, which had rapidly gained influence among the rural religious teachers in the interior, was regarded as a nuisance by the local administration and as competition by the adat authorities. Its Kaum Muda faction, under the leadership of Western-educated persons, was suspected of accelerating the reformists' attacks on traditional religious views. In the middle of 1916, through the influence of a Minangkabau perantau schoolteacher, several groups of the first Indonesian nationalist party, Insulinde, were also established.

Profound concern over all these developments—the division of the penghulu, the intensification of religious conflicts, and the emergence of the Java-based political parties—led Dt. St. Maharadja, the representative of the interior penghulu, to cooperate with his former enemies, the aristocrats of Padang. In September 1916 they established the first Minangkabau adat party, the Sarekat Adat Alam Minangkabau (SAAM—Adat Association of the Minangkabau World). Dt. St. Maharadja was elected as first president of the central board, which consisted of eleven adat functionaries from both the interior and the rantau regions. Several branches of this adat party were soon organized in the heartland. The members and leaders of the party in Padang were generally the coastal aristocrats. In the interior the leadership of the SAAM was composed of native officials, nagari chiefs, and traditionalist adat religious functionaries who belonged to the Kaum Tua group. Most of its members were local penghulu and their respective adat staff. The main objective of

---

Van Niel, *The Emergence of the Modern Indonesian Elite* (The Hague and Bandung: van Hoeve, 1960), pp. 85–100.

[103] *Warta Hindia*, April 20, 1917, and *OM*, April 22, 1917.

the SAAM was to elevate the Minangkabau people in accordance with inherited values and to guard Alam Minangkabau against the infiltration of any detrimental movement. Based on adat social philosophy, the organization sought to revive harmony in social relationships.[104] In this endeavor, the SAAM stressed the importance of close cooperation between the adat group and the Dutch government. It wanted to make adat institutions, such as the balai, an inseparable part of the administrative system. The adat party (SAAM) was expected to become the medium for the penghulu's cooperation in the face of challenges to adat institutions and the traditional authority of the penghulu.

Besides establishing the adat party in his efforts to block the spread of the Islamic modernist movement, Dt. St. Maharadja also began to formulate his conceptions of adat and religion. In so doing he not only conformed to the general tendency of all religious reformers in Minangkabau to reformulate adat but also defended his conception of Alam Minangkabau with its two pillars—religion and adat. Not an active penghulu himself, he tried to make adat into a certain kind of ideology with its own basic assumptions and apologetics. This attempt is clearly reflected in his scattered writings from 1914 until his death in 1921.

In the period when the religious Kaum Muda emphasized the importance of the application of correct religious regulations in personal behavior as well as in social conduct, Dt. St. Maharadja stressed the significance of the search for the essence of religion. In spite of his earlier attacks on tarékat schools, his views now approximated the argument of the Islamic heterodox mystics that religious law or sjarak (shariah) was only the lowest step in man's approach to God. It was merely concerned with man's outward behavior, which might not be related to his inward qualities. Sjarak, therefore, should not be identified with religion itself. It was through tarékat, which literally means the path, that man could begin to approach God properly. Once man entered the realm of tasauf or mysticism, the outward quality of sjarak lost its significance. By practicing tasauf, religious devotion was intensified and, at the same time, a man was prepared for the attainment of the highest knowledge, makrifattullah, which was the essence of

104 OM, Oct. 3, 1916.

religion. It was through tasauf that a man could understand the nature of the spiritual world and realize that the natural and the spiritual worlds (*alam arwah*) were bridged by the ephemeral world (*alam mitzah*).[105] The mystic concept *makrifat*, "the subjection of self to ilmu [knowledge]," was also one of the "Nine Principal Laws" (Undang Nan Sambilan Putjuak) of Minangkabau.[106] It was "the knowledge of the depth of the deepest sea and the largeness of the largest country, and . . . the knowledge of the infinite." [107]

Indeed, tasauf could not be separated from adat, because they derived their basic ideas from the same principle. The adat conception of the creation of the universe was identical with that of tasauf. According to pidato adat:

> When nothing was existent, the universe did not exist,
> Neither earth nor sky existed,
> Adat already existed.

This was "adat which is truly adat." "It is the adat of fire to burn, . . . the adat of water to wet." Adat then, which was identical with natural law, was the principle which existed before all else. Dt. St. Maharadja equated this original adat with the Nur Muhammad, through which God created the universe, as described in the tasauf teachings. When God said to Nur Muhammad "Kun" ("Be it"), "the earth and the sky" were formed.[108]

The incorporation of the mystic idea of Nur Muhammad into Minangkabau cosmogony was not at all new. Its origin can perhaps be traced to the early stage of Islamization of Minangkabau, but it was Dt. St. Maharadja who was the first to identify Nur Muhammad with the original adat. Since these two conceptions were in fact one entity, Dt. St. Maharadja reasoned, Alam Minangkabau should be seen as the unfolding of the potentialities inherent in the adat world-view and that of religion as represented by tasauf teaching. The religious Kaum Muda and their followers, who denounced the tarékat schools, had therefore proved themselves to be "persons

---

[105] *OM*, July 15, 1914; *OM*, Sept. 17, 1918.
[106] On the Nine Principal Laws, see "Artikelen van Datoek St. Maharadja in de *Oetoesan Melajoe* 1911–1913," *Adatrechtbundels*, 27 (1928), 291ff. Another version of the Nine Principal Laws is given in Batuah and Madjo Indo, *Tambo Minangkabau*, p. 100.
[107] *OM*, Sept. 17, 1918.   [108] *OM*, June 11, 1917.

who do not love their nation and their country. They are not to be expected to enhance the glory of Mt. Merapi."[109] In his identification of original adat with religious mysticism, he rejected the notion that adat law should be directly based on sjarak. In defiance of the generally accepted formula that adat as a social regulation should be the application of religious law or sjarak, Dt. St. Maharadja regarded adat and sjarak as two different sets of laws. Adat could not be based on sjarak because it had already existed before sjarak was introduced to Minangkabau. He agreed that "Sjarak is based on Kitabullah," but, he emphasized, adat was based on "propriety and appropriateness,"[110] which stem from truth. It was the notion of truth, not sjarak, that was the ultimate basis of adat. Truth was "the king in the nagari," "who stands by himself." Since truth is a mystical conception, the logical consequence of Dt. St. Maharadja's reasoning is clear: in the last analysis adat and religious law originated from the same principle and both were of equal significance in Minangkabau life. In social life it was adat law that should prevail; religion was primarily an individual search for God.[111] Religion therefore should not be under the control of society but should be left entirely to the individual.[112]

With this argument he pointed out that the Kaum Muda ulama, who insisted on the predominance of sjarak in social life, had in the first place undermined the legitimate power of adat and, secondly, repudiated the religious principle of individual right. By drawing a sharp contrast between religion as a world-view, which was identical with adat, and religion as a set of laws different from adat law, Dt. St. Maharadja, while finding a solution for the crucial problem of adat and religion, at the same time challenged the orthodox idea of the complete unity of Islamic doctrine.

His solution to the question of adat and religion was typical of Minangkabau relativistic thinking in avoiding a direct confrontation with the totalistic sjarak. His solution suggests the profound concern over the eventual breakdown of the very foundation of Alam Minangkabau in the face of the challenge of Islamic orthodoxy. Nevertheless, Dt. St. Maharadja's kemadjuan-oriented solution iso-

[109] OM, Oct. 8, 1919.   [110] OM, Jan. 6, 1919.
[111] OM, July 29, 1914; OM, July 13, 1918.   [112] OM, Sept. 13, 1916.

lated him from the tarékat leaders, while his attempt to restore the pre-Padri formulation of religion and adat put him at variance with contemporary adat theoreticians. Some tarékat leaders whose doctrines he tried to defend shunned his religious writings as "pieces without substance." [113]

While theorizing about sufism and stressing the importance of "the state of men's hearts," Dt. St. Maharadja was also concerned with the question of competition for secular advancement and proper outward behavior. Instead of emphasizing the ethic of humility—an important requirement in mystic practices—he promoted the idea of adat glory. Unlike the mystic practitioners who considered natural desire or *nafsu* as destructive for the attainment of the highest knowledge (makrifat), he, following the Islamic-modernist and the secular-kemadjuan protagonists, stressed its positive aspect. Nafsu under the control of reason, according to him, was not only important for the achievement of kemadjuan but also essential for life itself.[114] Significantly, Dt. St. Maharadja also claimed to be a follower of theosophy, which, with its idea of universal humanism, was quite popular among Western-educated Indonesians at that time.[115]

Not since the early nineteenth century, when the Minangkabau World was attacked by the Wahabist-oriented Padri, had the need for a reformulation of adat been more intense than in this period of economic and political change and religious conflict. The advance of the religious Kaum Muda with its fundamentalist tendencies, the penetration of the money economy, which had further weakened adat institutions, and the decline of penghulu prestige, forced adat theoreticians to review adat, which "neither rots in the rain nor cracks in the sun." Unlike Dt. St. Maharadja, other prominent contemporary adat theoreticians based their reexamination on the

113 Van Ronkel, *Rapport*, p. 23.

114 On this question he was very much influenced by A. Karim (or La Piete), a retired native school superintendent (*OM*, July 14, 1917).

115 From 1917 until 1920 every week, if not every day, articles or series of articles on theosophy were published in *Oetoesan Melajoe*. Most of them were written by Minangkabau schoolteachers, who were graduates of the Kweekschool in Bukittinggi. At the beginning of the century this school was the center of the Theosophical Society in Minangkabau. Most of the popular Dutch teachers in the school were theosophists. Interview with the well-known painter Wakidi (Bukittinggi, July 1968).

relationship between adat as local custom and sjarak. Their discussion aimed at a meaningful interpretation of the generally accepted adat aphorism that "adat is based on sjarak; sjarak is based on the Book." Most of the adat theoreticians asserted that this problem should be seen from the two aspects of adat in its relation with sjarak. In its first aspect, adat, with its principle of consensus and its matrilineal social system, was the sole legitimate order to be respected by sjarak. The second aspect of adat was its function in applying sjarak regulations in social life, as illustrated by the adat formula, "sjarak designs, adat applies" (*sjarak mangato, adat mamakai*). Adat law, then, was the social order itself, as well as the social manifestation of sjarak.[116]

This new formulation was hardly a satisfactory solution for the Kaum Muda ulama. In their opinion the new formulation completely ignored the validity of sjarak as the total basis of the social order, and, furthermore, opened up the way for conflicting interpretations of the boundary between these two aspects of adat. The solution offered by the adat theoreticians also contained some rational fallacies in its compromising of the Eternal and Sacred Law with the ever-changing and mundane adat.[117]

The Kaum Kuno Phase

The first two decades of the present century were characterized by conflict between ideologies and generations in which social

[116] In May 1916 a reader of *Oetoesan Melajoe* wrote to its editor on several crucial questions pertaining to the relationship of adat and religion. Dt. St. Maharadja invited some well-known adat theoreticians to participate in answering these questions. Four prominent adat theoreticians from Batu Sangkar, Bukittinggi, and Pajakumbuh joined the effort. The participant from Pajakumbuh was Datuk Paduko Alam, the author of the beautiful Minangkabau *Kaba Rantjak Dilabuah*, which has been translated into English by A. H. Johns, Southeast Asia Program no. 32 (Ithaca: Cornell University, 1958). On the symposium, see *OM*, May 11 and June 25, 1916.

[117] The best known example of the confrontation between Kaum Muda ulama and adat theoreticians was the debate between Sjech Abdul Karim Amrullah, also known as Hadji Rasul (1879–1945), and Datuk Sangguno Diradjo. For this debate, see Datuk Sangguno Diradjo, *Kitab Tjoerai Paparan Adat Alam Minangkabau* (Fort de Kock: Geb. Lie, 1919); *Kitab Pertjatoeran Adat Lembaga Alam Minangkabau* (Fort de Kock: Geb. Lie, 1923); Abdulkarim Amrullah Aldanawwi, *Kitab Pertjatoeran Adat Lembaga Orang Alam Minangkabau* (Padang Pandjang: Soematra Thawalib, 1921). See also Hamka, pp. 119–122.

status and position in adat hierarchy played a role. When Dt. St. Maharadja emerged as leader of the Kaum Muda in 1906, he fought not only against the aristocratic group in the rantau-town, Padang, but also against the penghulu in the interior, who, he thought, had forgotten their original adat functions. He allied himself temporarily with the former students of his foe, Sjech Achmad Chatib, when the latter started to support his drive toward kemadjuan. The notion that a definite ideology should be the only basis of the existence of the Kaum Muda was stressed by Dt. St. Maharadja after his split with the religious Kaum Muda. The Kaum Muda, according to him in 1915, was "a group of people who are opposed to the ancient tradition," that is, "the autocratic power of the ruler." The Kaum Muda were "the liberal democrats," who believed in equality and the wisdom of mufakat, "whose main concern is the welfare of society." With the abolition in 1914 of the "autocratic ruler," the Regent in Padang, the very existence of the Kaum Muda therefore became a contradiction.[118] The persons who called themselves "Kaum Muda," according to Dt. St. Maharadja, were "illusory human beings," who neither understood what they were doing nor had a clear perception of themselves. If they thought that they were fighting against "autocracy," they should realize that autocracy was not recognized by adat either. But if they were fighting against adat, as Dt. St. Maharadja thought they were, they were in fact staunch conservatives, who repudiated "democratic *adat*." [119]

By this time Dt. St. Maharadja had joined the traditionalist ulama in their fight against the religious reformers, who had in the meantime secured the cooperation of Western-educated persons. In 1914, the Islamic modernist group and some Western-educated intellectuals, with the support of trading groups in Padang, established two educational organizations, the Sarekat Usaha (Association of Endeavor), and Sarekat Ilmu (Association for Knowledge). The first was particularly active in establishing Western schools which provided religious education as well; the latter was preoccupied with publishing modernist-oriented religious texts. In 1915, the Kaum Muda ulama also began to reform religious schools, transforming the old surau or madrasah into a graded school system. With these programs, the Kaum Muda ulama laid a foundation for

[118] *OM*, Nov. 3 and Dec. 22, 1915.   [119] *OM*, Dec. 23, 1915.

insuring the continuity of their views in religious circles and also
began to bridge the gap between the Western- and the Islamic-
educated younger generations. Hadji Abdullah Ahmad, the prime
spokesman of the Kaum Muda ulama, planted the seed of religious
modernism in the younger generation through his writings and his
special class for MULO (a type of Dutch secondary school) students in Padang.

A significant effect of spreading Kaum Muda influence was the
increasing isolation of Datuk Sutan Maharadja and his adat-oriented
kemadjuan group from the new generation. They and the adat-
party, the SAAM, found themselves closer to the Kaum Tua ulama.
They now called themselves the Kaum Kuno ("Conservative
Group"), and thus emerged as opponents of the religious and
secular Kaum Muda. Aside from the religious dispute, which has
been discussed, the main issues were political orientations and the
meaning and direction of kemadjuan. On the latter aspect particularly, the Kaum Kuno engaged in public debate with the young
Western-educated intellectuals, who seriously challenged the ade-
quacy of adat as the basis for progress.

In 1918 the Kaum Kuno had to observe several activities of the
secular and the religious Kaum Muda. In January, branches of
the Jong Sumatranen Bond (Young Sumatran Union—JSB) were
organized in Padang and Bukittinggi. The goal of this youth organization, which had been founded on December 17, 1917, in
Batavia by Sumatran students of the STOVIA medical school, was to
unite all Sumatran students in preparation for their future roles as
"leaders of the people." In February, the students of the Kaum
Muda religious school in Padang Pandjang established their own
organization, the Sumatra Thawalib (Students of Sumatra), which
was to become the intellectual center of a Minangkabau radical
political movement. In June, about thirty local organizations joined
to form an all-Sumatran party, Sarekat Sumatra (Sumatran
League). This party soon transferred its headquarters from Bukittinggi to Batavia.[120] Basing its program on the application of
indigenous democracy to modern government, the Sarekat Sumatra

---

[120] On the transfer, see Taufik Abdullah, "Minangkabau, 1900–1927: Preliminary Studies in Social Development" (M.A. thesis, Cornell University,
1967).

focused its political campaigns on demands for wider participation of Indonesians in local and central councils.

The promotion of Sumatra rather than Minangkabau alone as a basis for identity and the growing importance in Minangkabau affairs of the perantau intellectuals in Java did not necessarily trouble Dt. St. Maharadja and his adat party. In 1916, in elaborating the ideological basis of the SAAM, he pointed out that residence and blood were not the crucial elements of Minangkabau identity. A man could be considered a Minangkabau if he belonged to the Minangkabau social system and followed the Minangkabau way of life. In emphasizing the open character of Alam Minangkabau, to which outsiders could be admitted, he also stressed the important position of the perantau as prescribed by adat.[121] This concept of an ever-enlarging alam explains his first reaction to the Jong Sumatranen Bond and the plan to establish the Sarekat Sumatra. His belief that the Western-educated younger generation was realizing its function as perantau led Datuk Sutan Maharadja to become one of the first contributors to the new organization.[122] With similar optimism, he welcomed the proposed plan for establishing the all-Sumatran organization. He urged the organizers, most of whom were government schoolteachers and other Western-educated Minangkabau, to look beyond Sumatra, toward the future unity of the whole Malay race. He reminded them that one of the objectives of the Minangkabausche Bond (Minangkabau Union) in 1910 had been the re-unification of Minangkabau with its rantau territories, such as Negeri Sembilan (Malaya) and the western coast of South Atjeh. Therefore, he suggested, the proposed all-Sumatran organization should aim at "the exaltation of the glory of Mount Merapi."[123] The idea of the unity of Sumatra or even of the Malay race should be understood as the extension of Minangkabau rather than its submergence within a larger unity.

This Minangkabau-centered ideal of unity was, however, anathema to the promoters of Sumatran nationalism, who realized that the main requirement for unity was the gradual minimization of ethnic differences. They proclaimed that the kemadjuan of Sumatra

[121] *OM,* Oct. 23, 1916.
[122] *OM,* Dec. 22, 1917; *Jong Soematra,* 1, no. 1 (Jan. 1918), 1.
[123] *OM,* June 5, 1918.

could be achieved only through this kind of unity. The Sarekat Sumatra, furthermore, was dominated by Dt. St. Maharadja's enemies, Abdul Muis and Abdul Rivai, both perantau intellectuals who had been politically active in Java. After his visit to Minangkabau in late 1918, Abdul Muis, the vice-president of the Sarekat Islam, became the most prominent perantau leader in the political activities of the Kaum Muda. He and other Western-educated leaders, by instigating rural rebellions and establishing urban political parties, laid new foundations for Minangkabau opposition to the Dutch. But with their strong sense of "Minangkabau-ism" the Kaum Kuno, particularly the adat party, viewed this development as an extension into their region of Java's grievances, which might complicate their cooperation with the Dutch. As spokesman of the SAAM, Dt. St. Maharadja denounced the politically-oriented Kaum Muda for their ingratitude to the Dutch, who since the seventeenth century had been the loyal "protectors" and "friends" of the Minangkabau people.[124] Some leaders of the SAAM went so far as to advise the government to conduct an inquiry into the political activities of the Kaum Muda, whom they accused of plotting the overthrow of the government. To Dt. St. Maharadja and his colleagues, the Kaum Muda group were either "Wahabists" or "Bolshevists," under the yoke of "Prince Abdul Muis." [125]

The bitterest disappointment for Dt. St. Maharadja was his rejection by the young Western-educated perantau intellectuals in whom he once had placed his hopes. These men had grown up in the period of kemadjuan and while at school in their hometowns they had witnessed the growing intensity of religious and intellectual conflict. Coming from the upper class of Minangkabau colonial society, they were generally children of urban families, among whom the power of the mamak had been declining. In Java they became acquainted with students from other parts of the archipelago and quickly came under the influence of "Westernized Batavian" society. This background played an important role in their efforts to define their goals and future roles. Only several months after the establishment of the JSB, one of its leaders, Bahder

---

[124] On the pro-Dutch activities of the SAAM, see for example Hendrik Bouman, *Eenige Beschouwingen over de ontwikkeling van het Indonesisch nationalisme op Sumatra's Westkust* (Groningen and Batavia: Wolters, 1949), pp. 34–35.

[125] *OM*, Aug. 9, 12, 18, 1919.

Djohan (b. 1902), a STOVIA student, wrote that his group, the Kaum Muda, "by uniting Sumatra are struggling to achieve an ideal Sumatra, that is a Sumatra whose population highly respects adat and custom but [which is based on] Western civilization and knowledge." The Kaum Kuno, on the other hand, "want to develop Sumatra by strengthening adat so that the inhabitants of Sumatra can live in peace and order." [126] In addition to defining the distinction between the Kaum Muda and the Kaum Kuno, this statement clearly offered a new concept of kemadjuan. Instead of adat, the young leader boldly took "Western civilization" as the basis of kemadjuan; adat was simply to be respected. It was on these two issues, the basis of kemadjuan and the reasoning of adat, that the younger generation of the Kaum Muda and the Kaum Kuno focused their debates.

The two generations based their arguments on the acknowledged need for kemadjuan and "the law of evolution" that moved toward "the perfection of morality and intelligence." But what was to be the character of this evolution? A moderate Western-educated Kaum Kuno intellectual, who called himself "Fauna," emphasized that every nation with its own system of values, no matter how simple its life, always experiences change. A nation's drive toward kemadjuan, as the manifestation of the "law of evolution," should therefore be based on its own system of values. Kemadjuan was worthless if it was simply an imitation. The author advised the Kaum Muda that in the pursuit of kemadjuan the experience of Japan should be taken as an example. "Only science and knowledge should be learned from the white people," but the basis should remain "our adat and morality." [127] Dt. St. Maharadja took a more extreme position in reaffirming his early concept of kemadjuan as the unfolding of adat ideals. In his writings from 1918 till 1921, he tried to "reconstruct" Minangkabau history in order to prove the inherent greatness of adat and the noble origin of the Minangkabau people. In this context, the repudiation of adat as the basis of kemadjuan meant blindness toward the intrinsic greatness of Alam Minangkabau. The imitation of other nations was nothing but self-humiliation.

Refuting the arguments of the Kaum Kuno, Amir (1900–1952),

126 *Jong Soematra*, 1, nos. 6, 7, 8 (June, July, Aug., 1918), 120–121.
127 *Jong Soematra*, 1, no. 11 (Nov. 1918), 221–224.

a STOVIA student who was the most able spokesman of his group, pointed out that kemadjuan should be understood not simply as material development but, more significantly, as "the progress of mind." It not only required a new attitude toward adat but also needed "Western mind," which, instead of replacing adat, would "even strengthen our feeling of nationality." [128] By taking this position, the Kaum Muda ignored the dual nature of adat as inherited custom, on the one hand, and as the Minangkabau world-view, on the other. By proposing the incorporation of "Western mind" into adat, the young perantau questioned the traditional conception of the adat world-view as the Alam's permanent basis. This intellectual boldness was largely motivated by their own image of themselves. They had begun to see themselves as future leaders and modernizers, as well as "builders of a new nation." Within the context of their self-defined roles, the Western-educated Kaum Muda refused to take "the past glory" as the basis of kemadjuan. Their "new nation" should be founded on the awareness of "the future, the beautiful, golden, bright future, where there shall be no sorrow and ignorance." [129] The slogan "kemadjuan" therefore lost its significance without an accompanying intense "love of fatherland," the country and the nation which should be transformed.

Within this enlarged program, the young Kaum Muda launched the second phase of the feminist movement. Dt. St. Maharadja, with his *Soenting Melajoe,* girls' weaving schools, and women's organizations, had started the first phase of the movement; he had pressed for the encouragement of women's education. But now, with the slogan "vrijheid" ("freedom"), the Kaum Muda insisted on the abolition of all limitations on women's education. In 1918, with the support of some adult Kaum Muda leaders in Padang, Saadah (1898–1968), a graduate of the Teachers' Training School, published *Soeara Perempoean* (Women's Voice), "to encourage Sumatran girls to catch up with our more educated sisters from Java, Menado and Sunda." [130] Not unlike *Soenting Melajoe,* the Kaum Muda with their *Soeara Perempoean* began their argument by ex-

---

[128] *Soeara Perempoean,* 1, no. 5 (Sept. 1918), 114.

[129] M. Amir, "De dienst aan het Vaderland," *Jong Soematra,* 4, no. 6 (June 1921).

[130] *Soeara Perempoean,* 1, no. 5 (Sept. 1918), 64.

posing the discrepancies between adat ideals and social reality. "It is true," according to one writer, "that in adat women have high status, but in fact their freedom is meaningless. They live like birds in a cage. Is this equality?" [131] Unlike *Soenting Melajoe,* which persisted in taking adat as the basis for women's progress, *Soeara Perempoean* tended to idealize "Western adat." To Dt. St. Maharadja and his Kaum Kuno group, "vrijheid" meant not simply freedom for women to pursue higher education but, in effect, the breakdown of the Minangkabau family system. Echoing the concern of the opponents of women's education at the beginning of the century, *Soenting Melajoe* now warned against "over-educated" women who eventually might abandon their essential role as the guardians of the matrilineal family. The end result of vrijheid therefore would be the elimination of Alam Minangkabau itself. In practice, the notion of vrijheid was therefore seen as both morally destructive and religiously unlawful.

These conflicts of ideology and generation were indirectly intensified by the open support given by the older generation Kaum Muda to the young Western-educated perantau. The modernist ulama either ignored the debates, which were sometimes conducted in Dutch, or continued their program for influencing the younger generation. Hadji Abdullah Ahmad, a religious teacher at a MULO school, from which a large number of younger generation adherents of the Kaum Muda had graduated, became also one of the advisers of the Young Sumatran Union.

The debate was aggravated by mutual public abuse by the contending groups. "The present day Kaum Muda," according to a Kaum Kuno intellectual who had been a prominent figure in the Kaum Muda of 1906, "is only a bunch of younger people wearing *modern* clothes and given modern knowledge. Now they not only ignore . . . adat, . . . but even say that 'adat is backward.'" [132] Indeed, as another Kaum Kuno leader suggested, while everyone now wanted to pursue kemadjuan and "to be progressive," their "kemadjuan is a fraud because their aim is to replace adat by 'Western adat'"; as a result, they had become persons "who are neither Dutch nor *'inlander* [native]'"; instead of Kaum Muda, they should

131 *Soeara Perempoean,* 1, no. 6 (Oct. 1918), 136.
132 *OM,* Oct. 28, 1918.

be called Kaum Sesat, the Straying Group, who were "useless for the kemadjuan of the nation." [133] On the other hand, the Kaum Muda, who claimed to be the ones "who want to elevate the still low status of their nation" [134] viewed the Kaum Kuno as a "sphinx" and as "adat-intoxicated" conservatives.[135] The Kaum Kuno in their opinion had become complacent, fascinated with the illusory glory of the past, and had forgotten that the future did not belong to them.

The confrontation was extremely painful to the early protagonists of kemadjuan. They now realized that the very ideas they had propagated had become disruptive for their conception of Alam Minangkabau. Their response to the inherent dynamic of adat for the achievement of a perfect and harmonious society had become a cause for conflict between generations. "If this situation can be called kemadjuan," lamented a follower of Datuk Sutan Maharadja, "it is truly a cursed kemadjuan." [136]

In the rather abusive debate between the two groups, their respective spokesmen, Dt. St. Maharadja and some leaders of the Young Sumatran Union, came under attack. A perantau intellectual accused Dt. St. Maharadja and his group of hindering and obstructing "the development of their own children and nephews"—they only wanted "to kill the seeds they had planted." [137] However, some leaders of the Young Sumatran Union were criticized by their followers, who began to argue against the continuing attacks on Dt. St. Maharadja. For, had not the leader of the Kaum Kuno in his time been a pioneer of kemadjuan, and, furthermore, did not the Kaum Kuno ideas he tried to propagate still reflect the thought of the majority of the people? By attacking him, the Union only undermined the role it wanted to play, as the "builder of the new nation." [138] When preparing for its first congress in 1919, the Union's leadership began to adopt a conciliatory attitude. It urged the unity of the Kaum Muda and the Kaum Kuno for the sake of the country. But by that time, the Kaum Kuno realized that they had in fact lost out to the younger generation.

While acknowledging their failure, the Kaum Kuno believed

[133] Jong Soematra, 1, no. 11 (Nov. 1918), 222.
[134] Soeara Perempoean, 1, no. 5 (Sept. 1918), 110–111.
[135] Jong Soematra, 1, 6, 7, 8 (June, July, Aug., 1918), 124.
[136] OM, Oct. 12, 1918.   [137] Neratja, Aug. 26, 1918.
[138] Jong Soematra, 1, 11 (Nov. 1918), 212; OM, Dec. 14, 1918.

nevertheless that progress was still a necessity and they were determined to start anew the struggle for kemadjuan. In January 1921, Dt. St. Maharadja made his eleven-year old daughter an apprentice editor of *Soenting Melajoe* in the hope that she would become a woman leader, "the Sumatran counterpart of Kartini in Java." [139] He had to begin all over again because his older "Kartini," the first editor of *Soenting Melajoe*, had deserted him and joined her Kaum Muda husband. In order to secure the future course of kemadjuan, a solid foundation had to be laid. A close associate of Dt. St. Maharadja proposed that children henceforth be taught elementary mysticism and adat moral teachings. It was hoped that with this spiritual and moral foundation secured, deviations from the "correct course" of kemadjuan could be avoided.[140] After 1920, Dt. St. Maharadja wrote numerous and repetitious articles on his view of the position of Minangkabau vis-à-vis the outside world and on the position of Sufi doctrine in Minangkabau belief.

But his time was running out. In February 1921 the workers of the first Minangkabau printing house went on strike. They were offended by Dt. St. Maharadja's constant interference in their work. He had to be temporarily suspended as the editor-in-chief of *Oetoesan Melajoe*.[141] Meanwhile he also had to face trial for slander. The leader of the Kaum Muda faction of the Padang aristocrats accused Dt. St. Maharadja of insulting him publicly. For the first time in his long career the former public prosecutor lost a case in court. He was granted two weeks to appeal the decision, but only a week after the trial, on June 28, 1921, Datuk Sutan Maharadja died. He had failed to realize his plan to write a complete autobiography and a comprehensive study of Minangkabau adat. He did not witness the split which soon occurred between the older Kaum Muda and their junior Western-educated counterparts, and the mounting attacks by the perantau intellectuals on numerous aspects of adat. Nor did he observe the emergence of competing adat parties and the growing influence of the Islamic modernists on Minangkabau political and educational development.

[139] *OM,* Jan. 18, 1921; *Sumatra Post,* April 22, 1921.
[140] *OM,* Sept. 14, 1918.
[141] *OM,* Feb. 19, 1921, *Warta Hindia,* nos. 19 and 23, Feb. 1921.

CONCLUSION

The first decades of this century were a period of profound examination of the Minangkabau World and search for a new meaning of the concept of Alam. The presence of Dutch colonial power, while weakening the traditional system, had also stimulated its potentialities. Encroaching upon adat and undermining Minangkabau conceptions of the "glory of Mount Merapi," the Dutch nevertheless opened up a new rantau and offered different models for an expanding world. Thus, on the one hand, they created frustration and despair, and, on the other, they opened new and promising avenues for exploration. In the face of this twofold effect, the Minangkabau were forced to review their conceptions of their own world and to rationalize their attitudes to the new situation. A crucial question was how accommodation to the new environment could be achieved without damage to the Alam and without injury to traditional pride. In this process of examination, Minangkabau experienced several phases of ideological and generational conflict. Every stage of development created new problems and new issues, and every social group tried to offer its own formulation of Alam Minangkabau and its "pillars."

The career and activities of Dt. St. Maharadja reflect his attempts to give reality to traditional ideas as expressed in the tambo and in adat aphorisms. Perceiving himself as an instrument for manifesting adat ideals, he first emerged as a leader of the Kaum Muda who advocated kemadjuan. In striving toward the utopian society of adat, he and other kemadjuan protagonists, in accord with the tambo, did not hesitate to incorporate outside elements into the existing Alam. The point at which Dt. St. Maharadja turned into a prominent leader of the Kaum Kuno was when he realized that the kemadjuan he had been promoting had developed into a threat to the very foundation of the Minangkabau World. He also played a leading role in challenging Islamic modernists, who, in his opinion, tried to transform Minangkabau into a thoroughly "Arabized" society.

The history of the quest for harmony between the two pillars of Alam Minangkabau—adat and Islam—shows that every attempted solution eventually became the target of a new religious movement.

The continuing flow of ideas from the centers of the Islamic world constantly rejuvenated religion, but also forced continuing reformulation of adat. Claiming universal validity for its religious law, Islam effected qualitative change in adat and at the same time became a basis for Minangkabau modernization. The Islamic modernists, with their emphasis on iman and akal and their ethic of individual independence, by the middle of the 1920's formed a powerful social group in Minangkabau. Their network of schools not only met the need for education in the drive toward kemadjuan, but also produced a new generation of Islamic-educated persons who were soon to dominate Minangkabau political and social life.

The attempts to overcome the dualisms in the Minangkabau world-view and social system were reflected in the insistence of the Padri and of the orthodox Islamic modernists upon the subjection of adat to sjarak. They were similarly manifested in the desire of the perantau intellectuals to incorporate "Western mind" into the adat world-view. The tambo tradition, with its imperatives of change as well as preservation of the foundation of Alam Minangkabau, while offering an invitation for the incorporation of rantau elements into the existing order, was also a bastion against the potentially corrupting impact of such elements. Thus the Minangkabau experience in the early twentieth century was neither a traumatized surrender to the outside world nor a retreat into an idealized past, but rather an increasing effort to project the very essence of Alam Minangkabau, with its spiralling rhythm of history.

Judicial Institutions and Legal Culture in Indonesia[*]

✧✧✧✧✧✧✧✧✧

Daniel S. Lev

INTRODUCTION

This essay will examine patterns of change in Indonesia's legal system since the Revolution, in order to try to make clear why and how functions of law in the colony have come to be served by institutions other than the law in the independent state. It will also explore how judicial institutions relate generally to political and economic processes and to cultural values. The end result should be the beginning of an assessment of the place of legal institutions in Indonesian state and society. If the approach followed here is a valid one, it may lead to useful generalizations about legal processes elsewhere, at least in new states, and a few comments will be made on this score in a brief conclusion.

The essay is developed around two concepts which require some definition. One is "legal system," the other "legal culture."

The burden of the concept of legal system, as it is used here, is *procedure*. What we want to understand, essentially, is how men get things done in society, how they manage their conflicts, what kinds of roles they rely upon for assistance, how these roles are related systemically, and what resources of authority they have. It is in the context of these questions that the functions of legal systems, which everywhere and always share their functions with

* I am particularly grateful to Benedict Anderson and Clifford Geertz for their detailed criticisms of this paper. I also want to thank, for their criticisms, suggestions, and other kinds of help, Harry Benda, Lawrence Friedman, Claire Holt, George Kahin, Arlene Lev, G. J. Resink, Philip Selznick, and Nusjirwan Tirtaamidjaja.

other kinds of institutions, have to be analyzed. A legal system consists of formal processes, which constitute formal institutions, together with the informal processes surrounding them. In modern states the central institutions of legal systems are bureaucracies, including the courts upon which our discussion will concentrate. A legal system's primary source of authority is the political system, whose legitimacy (or lack of it) extends to the substantive rules which legal systems apply and whose organization, traditions, and style determine, indeed, how far specifically legal processes are (or can be) used for social management and the pursuit of common goals.[1]

Legal culture is a relatively new concept.[2] It has the advantage of calling attention to *values* relating to law and legal processes but which may be distinguished analytically from them and considered independently. As the concept of legal culture is used in our discussion, it is made up of two related components—procedural legal values and substantive legal values. Procedural legal values have to do with the means of social regulation and conflict management. These values are the cultural basis of the legal system, and they help to determine, most importantly, the "system space" allotted to distinctly legal, political, religious, or other institutions at any time in a society's history.

The second, substantive, component of legal culture consists of fundamental assumptions about the distribution and uses of resources in society, social right and wrong, and so on. Because these assumptions change over time, as societies themselves change, the concept of substantive legal culture requires a dynamic element. This is provided by a notion of ideological themes of economic, social, and political ideas which, as they evolve more or less quickly, are reflected in substantive legal behavior. These ideological themes may or may not be culturally specific. They can be expressed either in terms of polar opposites—personal freedom and authority,

1 The work of J. P. Nettl, *Political Mobilization* (New York: Basic Books, 1967) on constitutional and elitist "political cultures" provides useful analytical insights into the relationships between social-political structure and legal processes.

2 The most recent and useful statement so far on legal culture is by Lawrence M. Friedman, "Legal Culture and Social Development," *Law and Society Review* (hereafter *LSR*), 4, no. 1 (1969) 29–44.

private ownership and public ownership, decentralization and centralization, punishment and therapy—which compete for dominance, or in terms of unidirectional change—emancipation of women, corporate organization, and so forth.[3]

In this essay, following a historical introduction, the first part of our discussion will deal with judicial roles and change in the legal system. Aspects of legal culture are touched on throughout, but become prominent in the discussion of "process" and dominate the concluding part of the essay on "substance." The organization of the essay into sections on institutions, process, and substance is not very satisfactory, and much of the treatment of substance really belongs under process. It has been done this way, however, in order to emphasize the relationships between legal system and legal culture. Finally, the essay concentrates on national law rather than local law, and the issues selected for discussion are related to the evolution of national political and legal systems. No attempt is made to deal with all major aspects of Indonesian law, and, as a nonlawyer, I have taken liberties in relegating formal matters to footnotes or ignoring them.

THE EVOLUTION OF A NATIONAL LEGAL ORDER

A national legal system did not exist in Indonesia until Dutch colonialism produced an archipelago-wide state. Before then many different legal orders existed independently within a wide variety of social and political systems. These ranged from the Hinduized, hierarchical, territorially organized states of Java, founded on highly regulated irrigation systems, to the clan-based societies of Sumatra and elsewhere, with other types in between. In some cases, as among the patrilineal Batak and matrilineal Minangkabau of Sumatra, legal and judicial forms developed out of prevailing family systems. A basic "law-job" in these societies was to maintain the integrity of kinship groups and to uphold the consequences of their organization and supporting beliefs. In Java and other aristocratic societies the purpose of law was not different but more complex,

---

[3] Renner's analysis of how European private law concepts, while apparently remaining the same over time, were turned to use by a rising capitalist middle class, is in these terms a study in substantive legal culture (Karl Renner, *The Institutions of Private Law and Their Social Functions* [London: Rutledge and Kegan Paul, 1949], introd. and nn. by O. Kahn-Freund).

and the organization of royal government independent of kin associations in a bilateral society gave rise to more specific functions of law enforcement and adjudication. Written law was more characteristic historically of the latter kind of society than the former, and possibly more necessary, in that family organization provided less thorough social control. But even where, as in old Java, there were written laws and enforcement officials, relatively few matters were brought within the purview of formal government.[4] Administrative resources were inadequate to anything like full control of the population. Most issues of conflict were therefore left to the village or family, and the usual mode of settlement was probably compromise.

Nowhere in traditional Indonesia was written law important to social cohesion. This depended, rather, primarily on either kin organization or on highly developed status concepts supporting aristocratic elites. In both cases authority was ascriptive, suffused with family and religious significance, and concepts of law were bound to eternal orders of family, locality, religion, and status, changeable in fact but not in theory. It was not a distinct idea of law, but rather these notions—family, locality, religion, status—that gave meaning to society. Even in the kingly polities there was less a concept of the law than of discrete laws (in Java, the _angger_) which emanated sporadically from the palace as edicts of the reigning prince, each standing independently with a name of its own and more or less specific subject matter.[5] In societies where only the elites were literate, as in early medieval Europe as well, such laws were far less compelling than the power of the palace and the authority of the aristocracy.

Islam introduced a new legal tradition into the archipelago. Islamic law has never been adopted fully anywhere in the world, a frustrating reality which has produced some tension in Islamic political thought. In Indonesia those parts of the law other than the ritual obligations to God (_ibadah_[6]) which were accepted, particularly rules of matrimony and (less so) inheritance, were often

[4] Soemarsaid Moertono, _State and Statecraft in Old Java_, Cornell Modern Indonesia Project Monograph Series (Ithaca: Cornell University, 1968).

[5] See Soeripto, "Ontwikkelingsgang der Vorstenlandsche Wetboeken" (dissertation, State University of Leiden, 1929).

[6] The most common Indonesian transcriptions are used for all Arabic terms.

revised to suit local values. In itself this created little difficulty, for Islamic legal doctrine recognizes the place of custom, except where (as in Minangkabau) the kinship system utterly contradicted the assumptions made by early Arabian Islamic jurists and by the Prophet Himself. Even when they were amended, the rules once accepted were still regarded as Islamic law, deriving their validity from the religion and the authority of the *ulama* (Islamic religious teachers). In the Indonesian context Islam offered new and more egalitarian principles of social behavior for which men could opt against the compulsions of older traditions,[7] in the same way that Christianity would later offer a partial way out of traditional Indonesia. In each case the law—first the Islamic law and then the colonial European law—performed a defining and symbolic function, providing new kinds of legitimate rights guaranteed by a community which those rights helped to identify.

Along with the specific legal categories that it brought to Indonesia, Islam also contributed a novel conception of law itself. Sunni Islam is divided among four different doctrines of law (*madhab*)—the school of Sjafi'i was eventually adopted in Indonesia—but the idea of law in Islam is divorced from the particular interests of local communities and generalized to the entire *ummat* (community of Islamic believers), conceived originally in universal terms including all Moslems. Through the medium of Islam a supralocal level of social and political conception became possible even before the Dutch began to link the country together administratively. This is evident in the influence of Arabic on Malay, which was commonly used in contacts among Indonesian groups and eventually became the national language. Just as no single total language could exclusively prevail in all of Indonesia, neither could the law concepts of any one group suit all the others. Islam with the help of Malay began to fill the void. In Indonesian the most basic notions of law itself (*hukum*), justice (ke*adila*n), custom (*adat*), right (*hak*), judge (*hakim*), are borrowed from Arabic. In some places the word hukum used alone still means Islamic law, and elsewhere it often also means national law as opposed to local custom. In both cases it is clearly supralocal.

---

[7] J. Prins, *Adat en Islamietische Plichtenleer in Indonesië* (The Hague and Bandung: van Hoeve, 1954), *passim*.

Yet Islam did not produce a national legal culture in Indonesia anymore than it did or could produce a unified state. It failed fully to supplant existing religions that were hostile to it, but instead often became entangled with them. Nor could Islam completely overcome essential differences between the major societies of the archipelago; rather it gradually fell prey to those differences. The religion contributed to the incipient formation of what H. Geertz has called a metropolitan superculture along the commercially active coastal (*pasisir*) areas, but before the Dutch arrived no great cities had emerged there for long enough to exercise a persistent political and economic domination over the entire country.[8] And of course there was no central governing power to develop lines of economic and administrative control out of which a nationwide bureaucracy would have evolved. Dutch colonial authority in time contributed this, establishing new nationally relevant administrative and legal functions as Islam had earlier provided new nationally applicable law concepts.

The colony, eventually encompassing all of modern Indonesia, created the framework of the state. Local change aside, Indonesians had little more control over the process than they had over the devastating economic effects of the "culture system" in nineteenth-century Java.[9] New institutions, new skilled roles, and new social and political symbols were imposed from another tradition, which in part became that of Indonesians who gradually entered the world of colonial law. With independence these institutions, roles, and symbols would be challenged, bent to new shapes, and rearranged, but they could not be rejected altogether without threatening the very idea of a national state. There was little else to fall back on that was not inherently divisive.

What was the character, then, of the colonial legal order which Indonesia inherited? Only the briefest introduction is possible, but it is necessary.[10]

[8] H. Geertz, "Indonesian Cultures and Communities," in Ruth T. McVey, ed., *Indonesia* (New Haven: HRAF Press, 1963) pp. 35ff.

[9] See C. Geertz, *Agricultural Involution* (Berkeley and Los Angeles: University of California Press, 1963).

[10] See generally Johannes H. Carpentier-Alting, *Grondslagen der Rechtsbedeeling in Nederlandsch-Indië*, 2d ed. (The Hague: Nijhoff, 1926); Supomo, *Sistim Hukum di Indonesia, sebelum Perang Dunia II* (The Legal System

In the first place the colonial legal order, like the social order, was a plural one, based implicitly on an assumption of racial inequality. This was true in varying degree of all colonies in the age of imperialism. The striking characteristic of the Netherlands-Indies legal system was its remarkable adherence to the internal logic of colonial society and purposes, not complete but more so than in most colonies. What other colonial governments were usually satisfied to achieve through stratificatory pressures, the Dutch tended to ensure with a statute. Each major social group had its own law, applied differentially by two distinct judicial hierarchies —three, actually, including the Islamic family law courts, which the colonial government did not establish but did regulate. European law was not restricted to Europeans, however. Indirect rule and the political alliance between the Dutch and Javanese nobility required privileges for the latter. The uppermost reaches of the aristocracy (*prijaji*) were thus accorded a special forum for their legal disputes and the right to register births and deaths in the civil registry (*burgerlijke stand*). This last privilege was also extended, for the same reasons, to high-level civil servants and commissioned military officers. The only other Indonesians served by the burgerlijke stand were those who in some way had opted for European status, either by formally submitting to European law or by converting to Christianity.[11] But among non-Europeans the highest prijaji alone enjoyed the guarantees of European criminal procedure. All others were subject to the procedural code for Indonesians (the Inlandsch Reglement, Native Regulation, later revised as the Herziene Inlandsch (Indonesisch) Reglement, HIR) which was simpler, less demanding of authorities, and therefore less protective of individual rights.

The racial criterion of colonial law was similarly qualified by other special functions of particular groups. Economic position

---

in Indonesia before World War II), 3d ed. (Djakarta: Noordhoff-Kolff, 1957). In English, see the introduction by E. Adamson Hoebel and A. Arthur Schiller to the translation of Barend ter Haar, *Adat Law in Indonesia* (New York: Institute of Pacific Relations, 1948).

[11] Although it was possible, very few Indonesians from any class did in fact assimilate voluntarily to European law status. Alexander C. Tobi, *De Vrijwillige Onderwerping aan het Europeesch Privaatrecht* (Leiden: van Doesburgh, 1927; Batavia: G. Kolff, 1927).

was a compelling determinant of legal parity. As commercial efficiency has everywhere demanded common norms of transactions, it was probably inevitable that Dutch commercial power would insist on applying its law to a group as economically significant as the Chinese.[12] In addition, Indonesians who engaged in certain kinds of urban business or specific transactions were presumed by a useful fiction to have acquiesced in the relevant rules of Dutch commercial law—e.g., contracts, notes, checks, and the like. This was a matter of convenience. Otherwise Indonesians were assumed —and the assumption helped to ensure the reality—to live an autonomous legal life little concerned with "modern" commerce. They were governed in theory by their own customary (adat) law, applied either by traditional courts or by the government courts (*landraden*) for Indonesians. Relations between the several law groups in the colony, when not dominated by European law, were governed by a highly developed body of conflicts rules.[13]

Whatever the inconveniences caused by legal pluralism, they were outweighed by the disadvantages of weakening the myths of Indonesian economic and political incapacity. By the twentieth century, when the great debate took place over unification of the law for all groups—a debate which the unifiers lost during the colonial period but won after independence—the fear that Indonesians might compete economically with the Dutch and Chinese was probably minor. But too many fundamental assumptions of colonial authority depended upon a functional separation of population groups to permit even symbolic unification. Van Vollenhoven and ter Haar, the learned adat law scholars who successfully opposed unification, were in no way disingenuous in their arguments; both men were sympathetic toward Indonesian cultures and no doubt feared the consequences of, and probably saw injustice in, an abrupt imposition of unified codes derived largely from

[12] The commercial law was also applied to other "foreign orientals," mainly Arabs and Indians. As a result of growing pressure from Chinese nationalism overseas, in 1917 the Chinese were brought under the regulation of the European civil code personal law except for rules of adoption. They had been subject to the commercial code since the nineteenth century.

[13] See Roeland D. Kollewijn, *Intergentiel Recht* (The Hague and Bandung: van Hoeve, 1955); Gouw Giok Siong, *Himpunan Keputusan2 Hukum Antargolongan* (Djakarta: Penerbitan Universitas, 1959).

European models. But although the scholars' motives were different from those of the colonial authorities, these views were consistent with colonial conservatism. During the nineteenth century, the seedtime of colonial administrative and legal development, the priority given commercial agriculture required the maintenance of an exploitable mass agrarian base, which the notion of "different people, different needs" helped to achieve. Later, however insignificant an explicit policy of differentiation was for economic purposes, it was imbedded in the supporting myths of the colonial state.

During most of the nineteenth century the Dutch believed that Indonesian customary law was based largely on Islamic law, and the jurisdiction of Islamic courts was accordingly recognized over a wide range of family law matters. This may have been a boon for Islam in areas like Central and East Java where antagonism toward the religion was powerful enough to stem its expansion. The Dutch were drawn into this historical religious conflict between the forces of Islam and pre-Islam in Java, Sumatra, and elsewhere. Along with European prejudice against Islam, a growing sophistication about Indonesian society gradually enabled the Dutch to revise their earlier views of Islamic influence. When the adat law scholars of Leiden emerged in the twentieth century, the additional factor of tendencies peculiar to ethnologists (and also to the continental school of historical jurisprudence) placed them on the side of "tradition" against the claims of Islam. Thereafter Islam was no longer regarded *a priori* as a fundamental source of Indonesian law, but had to prove the fragmentary reception of its legal norms into adat law. This was a significant turning point in colonial policy, one in which the adat law scholars won out over the more complex vision of the famous Islamicist, C. Snouck Hurgronje, who had favored accommodation with Islam and a general political and social (and legal) modernization.[14] Islamic leaders today still regard van Vollenhoven, ter Haar, and the new adat law policy with as much resentment as their opponents re-

[14] The most enlightening discussion of the differences between the views of Snouck and those of the Leiden adat law scholars is in Harry J. Benda, *The Crescent and the Rising Sun, Indonesian Islam under the Japanese Occupation, 1942–1945* (The Hague and Bandung: van Hoeve, 1958), esp. pp. 61–99.

gard them with favor. In the 1930's, as one consequence of the new outlook, the colonial government transferred jurisdiction over inheritance disputes from Islamic courts to the landraden; Islamic groups have tried to get it back ever since. The conflict between adat and Islam, which basically involves the limits of Islamic expansion, remains an essential theme of political and therefore legal culture in Indonesia.

Although no extended discussion of adat law itself can be undertaken here,[15] two general points about colonial adat law policy deserve attention. One is that, here more than in any other European colony the Dutch built an appreciation for customary law into the legal order through legal structure, education, and ideology. This appreciation, however, was probably more Dutch than Indonesian. The views of Indonesian leaders toward adat law were (and are) ambivalent. For although adat was distinctly Indonesian and symbolically attractive, the European codes smacked of social prestige, political superiority, and modernity; adat law acquired overtones of backwardness.

Second, despite Dutch emphasis on the place of adat law, its future was inevitably jeopardized by the emergence of a national level of politics and administration. In the Netherlands Indies, as in other colonies, the several ethnic groups could not represent much more to the government than units of population whose sensitivities should be respected if only to keep the peace. The relationship between colonial elite and subject peoples obviously did not constitute an integrated political community, and therefore was most easily treated as an administrative one. As a result, the law of colonial Indonesia looked vaguely like that of medieval France, except that customary differences between provinces in Indonesia grew from incomparably greater variations of social structure, religion, and culture. But after independence, though the process had already begun with the expansion of Dutch authority, as in old France, in Indonesia too a more intense effort was made to extend the *Pays du Droit Ecrit* at the expense of the *Pays du Droit Coûtumier*. When an Indonesian elite assumed national power, a prolonged and painful attempt was begun to transform the colonial

15 The literature on Indonesian adat law is enormous. A partial bibliography is provided in ter Haar, pp. 234–248.

administrative state into a national political community, and local adat law felt the impact early.

The development of a national Indonesian "law community"—meaning here all related legal roles within the legal system—was more closely connected with *droit écrit* than *droit coûtumier*. Under indirect rule traditional Indonesian legal officials were not all eliminated, but a higher Dutch authority was imposed upon them, circumscribing their functions even as their positions were maintained. The plural legal system gave rise to informal linkages between the traditional and colonial legal orders, mainly in the form of special Indonesian roles concerned with understanding and manipulating unfamiliar Dutch legal machinery. One such link between the two legal universes was the *pokrol bambu*, an untrained but often knowledgeable "bush lawyer" about whom more will be said in our discussion of procedure. But it was in the major cities, in the colonial administrative service, in the government courts, and in the law schools of Holland and Batavia that a new group of professional lawyers [16] began to emerge from within the colonial legal order. As legal studies became an evident route to success in the colony, a full term law faculty was finally opened in Batavia in 1924, though Indonesian students had gone to the Netherlands for advanced training before then. Most early Indonesian law students were high born Javanese who, from their knowledge of the Dutch language, were already familiar with the national level of colonial authority. Upon graduation most joined the Indonesian part of the judicial service. None was appointed to higher European jurisdictions before the Japanese occupation, and only one or two were given posts at higher levels of the European procuracy. A handful became private advocates. A few became highly respected legal scholars, primarily under the adat law research program of the Department of Justice; one of these, R. Supomo, became a law professor.

The legal traditions and symbols to which these men and many other professionals became committed could not easily be defended in the independent state, not basically because trained lawyers were so few but because the political and social order changed so

---

[16] The term "lawyer" will be used throughout our discussion in the Indonesian sense to mean anyone with advanced law training, regardless of profession.

radically. Colonial government was in fact based on the rule of law
—a term used here in the Weberian sense of an essentially "rational-
legal" organization of the state. That violent force implicitly un-
derlay the colonial system as it applied to most Indonesians is
irrelevant, for the primary clientele of the Netherlands-Indies government was not Indonesian but European. The immediate and
central audience of the courts, procuracy, advocacy, notariat, and
higher bureaucracy, was one that lived by a larger measure of
contract than status, to use Maine's terms. These institutions of the
law were nearly as powerful as in the Netherlands itself, and the
law community was substantial, an integral part of a specialized
government apparatus serving well-defined private interests. Law
officials were themselves symbols of the law, and the law represented the consensus of the Dutch colonial community and its interests. In the independent state, this would disappear. The governmental structures inherited by the new state were explicitly based
on contract conceptions, ideas related to the rule of law, but politics
was much more a matter of status.

INSTITUTIONS

Independence: Pervasive Politics and the Decline of Law

The colonial legal system began to crumble during the Japanese
occupation. There was a change in the spirit of the law as it was
applied by military government, and the first major steps toward
unification were taken at that time, between 1942 and 1945. The
dual government judicial structure was replaced by a single three
instance hierarchy of courts using the procedural code for Indonesians, which has remained since. Indonesian officials now filled
the bureaucracy, courts, prosecution, and other offices. Most important, of course, Dutch authority was broken, a condition which
the Revolution that followed made permanent. Yet for all the
bitterness Indonesian leaders felt against Dutch colonialism, the
Revolution did not bring an impulsive abolition of colonial law.
Retaining old legal forms, which were familiar, permitted procedural continuity until something new and secure could be worked
out. As the Revolution was one of limited purposes, to gain independence, there were few new programs of social, economic, and
legal change.

But long before many lawyers realized it, the bases of the old legal order were obliterated by the Revolution and the political struggle which then ensued. The weakness of the old law—"law" here being short for formal law community, procedures, and related norms—did not become absolutely clear until the period of Guided Democracy, particularly in the early 1960's. Evidence of its deterioration existed before then, but an ideological lag allowed men to assume that the independent state was a *negara hukum*, a *rechtsstaat*.[17] A true counter-symbol—*hukum revolusi*, revolutionary law—arose under Guided Democracy, when President Sukarno no longer hesitated to challenge other symbols which lawyers believed imperative.

The decline of formal law followed upon an explosive expansion of political activity. An ideologically based party system emerged, incorporating both the historical conflicts centering on Islam and a more recent class struggle. Nearly everyone was automatically classified in one *aliran* (literally, "current") of national politics or another. Little room was left for consensus, even on the form of the state. Contending claims to legitimacy turned the government itself into a weapon in the great issues of politics. Consequently the bureaucracy—both the central administration and the *pamong pradja*, the regional administrative arm of the central government— began to break down as standards of meritorious conduct became confused. Ideals of businesslike and impersonal behavior inculcated by the colonial administration now competed with symbols of political and ideological loyalty. Government administration, moreover, became an area not only for ideological contention but also for claims to status in the new state. For bureaucrats too the Revolution had promised improvement of social and economic positions. Civil servants, therefore, like the rest of society, organized by ministry and function either to press claims for advancement or to defend themselves against the claims of possible competitors; among others, judges, prosecutors, and police began to quarrel before the Revolution had ended. Whatever justification of the status

[17] *Negara hukum* can be translated as "rule of law," but the conception of it among Indonesian lawyers and intellectuals is closer to the Continental administrative than the Anglo-American judicial notion. See Otto Kirchheimer, "The *Rechtsstaat* as Magic Wall," in Kurt H. Wolff and Barrington Moore, Jr., eds., *The Critical Spirit: Essays in Honor of Herbert Marcuse* (Boston: Beacon Press, 1967).

quo existed was either rooted in the colonial past or was, like economic development, too abstract to be relevant.

The impact of this turmoil of conflict on the formal legal system was devastating. All available resources had to be mobilized by the contending camps. The stakes were too great for political leaders to agree on areas of no contention. As the sphere of legitimately "nonpolitical" activity was reduced, the likelihood that legal processes would or could be used to accomplish anything declined. Political norms took precedence, assuming naturally a primarily partisan character inappropriate to such problems of institutional control as the maintenance of bureaucratic norms.

With the expansion of political conflict, the economic rationale behind the inherited legal system began to dissipate, and the economic functions of formal law officials either faded or changed. Commerce—largely in the hands of Chinese and, until 1957, Dutch businessmen—lost its preeminence to politics and so became dependent upon political influence and corruption. Legal processes, and therefore especially courts and advocates, became more and more irrelevant to the private economy. The living law of commerce fled underground, creating more productive and informal procedures as it went. Thereafter the skills required had little to do with written law, except in some formal matters that still demanded the limited services of notaries and occasionally advocates, but a great deal to do with personal contacts, influence peddling, and bureaucratic *savoir faire*. Here the fixer, the arranger of deals, was in his element.

Wertheim has pointed to several sources of corruption in Indonesia: the demoralization caused by occupation and revolution, inadequate salaries for government servants, the example of the urban *haut monde*, political party demands, and uncontrolled army officers. He also calls attention to the influence of traditional patrimonial-bureaucratic norms and personal status loyalties of great binding power in a society where identification with the state is less persuasive than what Geertz has called primordial attachment to family, clan, religious group, and so on.[18] The character of

18 W. F. Wertheim, "Sociological Aspects of Corruption in Southeast Asia," in Wertheim, *East-West Parallels, Sociological Approaches to Modern Asia* (The Hague: van Hoeve, 1964); C. Geertz, "The Integrative Revolu-

political and ideological conflict in postwar Indonesia made it that much harder for men to relinquish their ties to these lesser and safer social units; the rewards of loyalty to the latter were socially and psychologically as great or greater than the financial and status rewards offered by government service.

In effect, then, not only the economic but also the social and cultural rationale behind the old legal order began to disappear.

The position of lawyers, like that of most skilled groups in any society, depends on the extent to which their professional values are generally accepted by other institutional subsystems. Where social values tend to support a mixture of traditional and charismatic authority, in Weber's terms, professional lawyers will probably be weak. Their procedures are adhered to only with obvious strain. The temptations to deviate from them are enormous. But the crux of the matter is that those procedures appear to lose meaning. The myths behind formal legal processes are tested too often and found to be exactly that, myths, which therefore can no longer serve a legitimating function. An upright judge, acting according to the "rational-legal" norms of his profession, is suspected anyway of corruption and bias, not only because there are in fact corrupt and biased judges, but more importantly because politics and administration generally are known to be filled with corruption. The common picture of the political game is that it is played not more or less according to legal rules, but according to rules of influence, money, family, social status, and military power.

As new political symbols gained currency and old law myths faded during the years of Guided Democracy, the formal law community came under brutal attack. Sukarno played on the only apparently contradictory themes of traditional cultural identity and revolutionary movement. Until these ideas caught on, lawyers may have been growing lean, but they were still respected. Now they were challenged as a conservative, even reactionary, element that must be forced to submit to a new order, defined by men of political skills—Feith's "solidarity makers" in contrast with "administrators," of whom lawyers as a group were the epitome.

tion," in C. Geertz, ed., Old Societies and New States, The Quest for Modernity in Asia and Africa (New York: Free Press, 1963).

The professional civil service and the formal law community both represented a close link with the colonial past. Professional lawyers particularly grew directly out of the colonial experience, and they suffered the additional disadvantage that their skills were less familiar historically than those of political leaders. Moreover they were attached to the written law, thus colonial law, which in the independent state came under constant attack, though new "national" law could not be produced.

But there was more to it than that. Political leaders required freedom of movement to develop the bases of their authority in traditionally persuasive rather than "rational-legal" terms. Procedural controls were rejected when flexibility was at a premium. Sukarno's hukum revolusi was precisely a symbol of flexibility and freedom from constraint, a political symbol *par excellence*, moreover, with a millennial resonance to it in a society, perhaps mainly Java, that sought historical fulfillment in the new state. Compared with this, the negara hukum was drab and restraining; and besides, the rule of what law?

Sukarno pointed Liebknecht's finger at the lawyers at their own conference in 1961: "You cannot make a revolution with lawyers." [19] They must adjust or be left behind. But as he explained what the Revolution meant, Sukarno made it clear how hopeless the lawyers' position was. "We cannot run a revolution according to theory . . . a revolution is unpredictable . . . a revolution rejects yesterday." Consistency, predictability, and reliance on the past—all are fundamental to lawyers' law. The orientations of the political leader and the lawyer, as modal types, were completely at odds. That side would win which served the larger clientele; there was no question at all about the outcome.

The Formal Judicial System: Quest for Status and Internal Relationships

In this and the next two parts of the essay I want to deal with problems of institutional change as they affected the formal law

[19] *Hukum dan Masjarakat* (the national law journal) Nomor Kongres I (Djakarta: Djambatan, 1962).

community.[20] The discussion here will concern internal adaptations of the judicial system.

The strength of formal law depends partly (only partly) on the size and quality of the law professions. Quality here means the level of training of lawyers, whatever their function, and the extent to which they are imbued with common legal values. Sharing those values, lawyers may still compete with one another depending on the roles which they occupy, but they will all have an interest in maintaining legal institutions and the procedures which are lawyers' magic. Independent Indonesia started with few lawyers, and the disparate origins of those who filled the formal law roles made the network of judicial organizational relationships more brittle than it might have been.

To begin with, only a few Indonesian advocates established themselves during the late colonial period, not more than two or three dozen. It took an extraordinarily independent man, often from the pasisir areas of Java if not from Sumatra or Sulawesi, to reject his family's bias in favor of government service and take his chances in private practice.[21] The odds were against success,

[20] The *pokrol bambu* and Islamic judge are slighted here not because they are insignificant, but because the formal secular roles dealt with in this section illustrate problems of change better, and the pokrol bambu especially is more interesting to deal with in a discussion of process. The formal structure of the judiciary should be introduced here. There is a first instance court (pengadilan negeri) in every *kabupatèn* (a large district). Trials here are usually heard by a single judge, though a panel is now required in certain categories of cases; shortage of personnel makes collegial courts impossible for all cases. At the second instance twelve appeals courts (*pengadilan tinggi*) have been established in major cities, though not all of those more recently created have full staffs yet. The Supreme Court in Djakarta is a court of cassation with power of review in questions of law, not of fact. The Department of Justice has administrative and financial responsibility for all pengadilan negeri and pengadilan tinggi. Otherwise the courts are responsible in their judicial functions to the Supreme Court. See further R. Tresna, *Peradilan di Indonesia dari Abad ke Abad* (Amsterdam and Djakarta: Versluys, 1957). Land reform courts were created in the early 1960's, but they have been inactive since the coup of 1965 and appear not to have been very effective before then for a number of political and economic reasons.

[21] As one of Indonesia's most famous early advocates, Besar Martokusumo, tells it: "When I graduated from Leiden . . . I let my family know that I intended to become an advocate. . . . They were very much against this. They couldn't understand or approve of such an occupation for a man with my [social and educational] background. It was sinking to a very low level.

both because of the exclusivism of Dutch lawyers and because the latter enjoyed natural links into the world of commerce which they served. Once having won recognition, however, the Indonesian advocate usually moved easily in the European sphere of legal society. His practice brought him into contact with the higher levels of the colonial bureaucracy and the strictly run Dutch courts. He was engrossed in the money economy and frequently high finance.[22] By and large he was more likely than the Indonesian judge, for example, to have become a national urbanite with contacts nearly everywhere in the archipelago. In general Indonesian advocates tended to be both strongly nationalistic and deeply committed to the formal law as a way of ordering national life; few of them made good ideologues in the independent state, whatever their political affiliation.

Most young Javanese prijaji who took law degrees—and later, though to a lesser extent, others from outside of Java [23]—sought positions in government. Aside from the status attaching to government service in the bureaucratic traditions of Java, one was also more likely to succeed as a judge than in the private professions. As landraden were opened up to Indonesians early in this century, graduate lawyers often went directly into the judicial service; there they served as clerks for a time before moving up to the bench and eventually, in some cases, to the chairmanship

---

Government was proper—the pamong pradja—but certainly not private law practice. I went ahead anyway, despite family pressure, and opened up my own law office. Eventually the family came to accept this, though grudgingly at first."

[22] See for example the personal financial reports of Iskaq Tjokrohadisurjo, a long time advocate and PNI (Nationalist Party) leader accused of malfeasance while Minister of Economic Affairs; in his published defense, *Rasa Keadilan Berbitjara* (Djakarta: Departemen Penerangan/Propaganda, Dewan Partai, PNI, 1960), pp. 66–69.

[23] Javanese and Sundanese dominated the law professions, particularly when these were first opened up to Indonesians, mainly because Java was the center of the colony, longer in close contact with the Dutch than most other islands, and better prepared in effect to take advantage of colonial offerings. The police remained the most Javanized; few men from other areas chose to join the police, and it may also be that the Dutch preferred Javanese to others. Conceivably Java, with its own traditions of written law and highly organized bureaucratic forms, was in general more receptive to new law professions than were other ethnic areas.

of a court. Seldom did they have experience elsewhere either in or out of the government. Of the fourteen judges who served on the Indonesian Supreme Court between 1945 and 1968, excluding the most recent appointments of February 1968, only one to my knowledge had worked briefly as a private advocate during the colonial period.

Judges and advocates together formed the core of the trained Indonesian law community. Their total number was quite small. During the occupation, Supomo compiled a list of Indonesian (excluding Chinese) lawyers for the military administration. There were 274.[24] This list was probably short a few, but the maximum number by 1950, including those who completed degrees during the Revolution, was approximately 300 in a population at that time of about 90 million.

The prosecution presents a different picture from the judiciary and advocacy. In the colony the prosecution was bifurcated. For the European community there were legally trained *officieren van justitie,* organized in a highly prestigious *parquet,* who were on equal terms with judges and advocates. But the Indonesian *djaksa* (prosecutor) was a lowly official, with some knowledge of the criminal code and procedure for Indonesians, but subject to orders from the European Resident, and in the landraad generally regarded with contempt by judges and the advocates who might have cases there. It was these djaksa, along with many members of the regional pamong pradja, who for the most part succeeded to the Indonesian public prosecution. Their role memories incorporated both the prestige of the officier van justitie and the status hunger of the colonial djaksa.

The police were another matter. An excellently organized and well trained police force existed in the colony, and by the time of the occupation many Javanese had risen to high positions in it. Early in the Revolution Prime Minister Sjahrir extracted the national police from the Ministry of the Interior, placing them directly under his own office. Whatever the reasons for this move,

[24] There were not at first many Chinese lawyers; Indonesian Chinese began to enter the legal professions rather late. The list also excludes the *rechtskundigen,* those who received their law training in the abbreviated law course (*rechtsschool*) offered in the colony before the fully accredited law faculty opened in 1924.

one result of it was to emphasize the importance of the police force to police leaders themselves, by and large a highly professional group with long experience. Soon they began to make demands that would consolidate their rising status within both the judicial and political systems.

With independence the succession of these judges, prosecutors, and police to positions vacated by Dutch officials was made easier by several varieties of legal change: unification of the court system during the occupation, replacement of the European procedural codes (*rechtsvordering* and *strafvordering*) by the now commonly applicable HIR, and of a different order, the unavoidable general lowering of standards of recruitment into the law professions. But the glue of authority which had once made the relationship between formal law roles meaningful had disintegrated. They began to rearrange themselves through a process of bitter conflict within the judicial system, on the one hand between prosecutors and judges and, on the other, between police and prosecutors.[25] In both struggles the outcome was determined largely by political factors.

In the first case the djaksa demanded equalization of salary and rank with judges. The latter reacted with a sensitivity bred of fear, based on good evidence, that their inherited status was profoundly imperiled. While prosecutors argued essentially from an egalitarian position, judges responded with a defense of existing law and the fundamental importance of the judicial function. Since the Revolution, however, the judges' kind of argument had become less impressive. At length, in 1956, after several years of debate, a Minister of Justice whose political party had won support among prosecutors gave them the new rank and salary regulation which they sought. Judges replied with a work stoppage, which failed to achieve anything. All these events occurred during the years of the parliamentary system; no government took the issue seriously, although a few individual ministers and members of parliament, particularly those who had been advocates, did. Rivalry between judges and djaksa has been evident in a myriad major and petty issues ever since.

[25] Daniel S. Lev, "The Politics of Judicial Development in Indonesia," *Comparative Studies in Society and History,* 7, no. 2 (1965), 173–199.

The second conflict, between djaksa and police, was over a procedural issue—control of preliminary investigations, which authority the prosecution had by law and the police wanted. Essentially the critical problem was again one of status. While prosecutors now stood on the conservative argument that they had succeeded to the functions of the colonial officieren van justitie, the police insisted that their obvious investigatory expertise *and* changed conditions wrought by the Revolution called for a redefinition of functions. The prosecution was threatened with becoming a mere intermediary between the police and the courts. Eventually, in 1961, the police came out on top, as new basic statutes on the police and prosecution gave the former control over preliminary investigations. The law was made just ambiguous enough, however, in an effort at compromise, to permit a gentlemen's agreement (as police and prosecutors themselves call it) on a suitable division of labor which does not in fact exclude the prosecution from investigation of crimes. But the issue remains a serious bone of contention between police and public prosecution, one which the statutory ambiguity has kept alive.

Although there were other contributing factors, the victory of the police in this conflict was essentially political. The size of the national police organization—something over 100,000 by the late 1950's—their evident coercive power, and their status as part of the armed forces, all lent them leverage which prosecutors could not consistently match, even with President Sukarno's support. In 1959, the heart of the matter was bared when a new Chief Prosecutor demanded and received special authorization from the cabinet (led by Sukarno himself after the restoration of the 1945 Constitution) to command police officials, including military police, in criminal investigations. The authorization was legally redundant, indicating that the efficacy of the original rule of procedure had become questionable. In any event, the first time a local prosecutor tried to invoke the regulation, the police ignored him, the new regulation, and the old law altogether. As the police had support from the army on this issue, neither the Chief Prosecutor nor the cabinet could do anything about it. In other words, whenever the interests of the police were at stake, the government could not automatically avail itself of its own law enforcement agencies. There is no better illustration of institutional fragmentation, in which the authority binding specialized organizations together simply dissipates. During the course of their dispute, first the police and then the prosecution succeeded in establishing their own ministries, acquiring an important measure of autonomy which they guarded ferociously until after the coup of October 1965, when the structure of Guided Democracy broke apart.

Throughout these judicial wars pursuit of status in the new state was crucial. Legal symbols were largely reduced to elementary weapons in a political struggle for high stakes. What counted were obvious power and utility, and they produced institutional status arrangements different from those that such criteria as, say, social stability and commercial security had produced. In the colony, where the latter concerns were predominant, the hierarchy of judicial organization had the courts on top, followed by prosecution and police. But in the independent state the police edged out the prosecution, and the courts were at the bottom. The dynamics of this transformation—a sort common to other institutions after independence—may become clearer if the judicial and political systems are conceived as analytically distinct, linked and overlapping of course, but representing separate spheres of activity, with their own internal roles and functions. The apex of the judicial system is the court, a highly specialized institution which therefore is not highly adaptable. But police and prosecutors explicitly bridge the judicial and political systems (whereas courts normally do so only implicitly), serving important and apparent functions in both. In an intensely politicized society, the political system is like a magnet; there is a tendency for anyone capable of performing a political service to do so. For the police and prosecution in Indonesia, particularly under Guided Democracy, it was simply a matter of emphasizing the political functions—inherently repressive—that they already possessed. Their terms of reference, and indeed their reference groups, thereafter became almost entirely political. Courts were left out in the cold. A major indication of this rearrangement of status positions is that law students lost interest in becoming judges in favor of joining the prosecution, where they were more likely to become both moderately rich and politically significant. By 1968 there were more than twice as many graduate lawyers in the public prosecution as in the judiciary.[26]

Although some judges did take up the banner of hukum revolusi and did seek a place in the sun of Guided Democracy, by and large they were reluctant to relinquish the older symbols of their profession. But the judiciary was nevertheless pressed into political service during those years. Explicitly rejecting the *trias politica* (separation of powers) for Indonesia, Sukarno ostentatiously appointed the Chairman of the Supreme Court to the cabinet, to the dismay of many judges who perceived in the trias politica symbol some guarantee of judicial autonomy and dignity.[27] Sukarno later went further to demand the right, in a new statute on judicial organization, to interfere at any stage in the judicial process "for the pressing interests of the Revolution, the dignity of the State and People, or the interests of society." [28] This right was in fact used, both before and after passage of the law in 1964.

What this achieved was something close to traditional perceptions of government organization, in which whatever differentiation of function existed was less important than the unique source of all authority, e.g., the king. The kind of monolithic system which Sukarno sought, different parts with an undifferentiated and perfectly united purpose, was culturally comprehensible and real. It was unacceptable in the main only to intellectuals, and particularly to law professionals, whose values and interests were imbedded in nontraditional institutional conceptions.

[26] In addition many women law graduates have entered the judicial corps in recent years, an indication that few qualified men are competing for positions on the understaffed courts.

[27] Until 1959 the trias politica argument was used fairly successfully by Chief Prosecutor Suprapto to prevent political interference with the prosecution. He obscured it for his own ends, however, by insisting that as the prosecution was both an executive and a judicial institution, the cabinet therefore had no right to supervise its activities. Suprapto was a strong and honest enough man to be able to make the argument stick. After Suprapto was dismissed the Chief Prosecution moved steadily toward submission to the Palace. By 1961, under Chief Prosecutor Gunawan, it acquired a reputation for corruption remarkable even in Djakarta.

[28] Law 19/1964, art. 19.

The Advocacy and the Judicial System

Advocates played almost no part in the wars of the judicial system. Their decline after independence was even more precipitous than that of judges, and their place within the judicial system itself became exceedingly difficult. The reasons why this was so help to illustrate the character of judicial structure and process in Indonesia.

Some causes behind the weakness of the advocacy have already been mentioned: the small number of advocates, many of whom left private practice to take up positions in government after 1945 or 1950; politicization of the economy and consequent need for nonlegal skills; and the general turn away from formal processes in favor of informal ones. In the colony, as in Europe and other commercially active societies, advocates served as a crucial link between private social activity and the judicial system; with independence the decline of both formal process and commerce made this linkage less important.[29] In addition the lowering of judicial standards affected advocates. The adoption of the HIR procedural code, for example, rather than the stricter European codes, not only reduced the premium on legal skills but also made it possible to avoid using advocates at all.

What advocates could do for themselves as a professional group was limited by unfavorable economic conditions and by their lack of institutional support. The major potential source of such support—the courts, which are a natural focus of advocates' services —was all but cut off after independence.

In essence, advocates have increasingly been rejected as legitimate

[29] The relationship between economic development and the existence of a strong advocacy needs to be emphasized. As in Europe, according to Weber, the "increased need for specialized legal knowledge created the professional lawyer. This growing demand for experience and specialized knowledge and the consequent stimulus for increasing rationalization of the law have almost always come from increasing significance of commerce and those participating in it" (Max Rheinstein, ed., *Max Weber on Law in Economy and Society* [Cambridge: Harvard University Press, 1954] p. 96). On the functions of the private lawyer in judicial systems, cf. T. Parsons, *Structure and Process in Modern Societies* (New York: Free Press, 1960), p. 191.

participants in the judicial process.[30] They have not disappeared from trials, of course, but their presence has come to be regarded antagonistically by judges as well as prosecutors, in a way that goes beyond the normal conflict inherent in their relationships. One reason is that advocates represent an unwanted control. They are a threat not only to corrupt prosecutors and judges, but also to those judges who do not know the law well—which is often true of young and inexperienced judges—or do not have time to examine legal problems carefully.

Another and perhaps more fundamental reason for the hostility of judges (with exceptions of course) to advocates is that status does not inhere in the advocate's role as it does in the roles of the judge, the prosecutor, or even the police official. For judges, who are as sensitive to status norms as to functional norms, an advocate is as private and unofficial as his client; and status derives largely from public position.[31] In this context advocates cannot share in the fellowship of officialdom between prosecutors and judges, which to some extent—though in a delicate balance that varies from court to court—transcends the rivalry between these officials. Under Guided Democracy, moreover, the extraordinary power of the prosecution reinforced the judge-djaksa relationship; apart from being reluctant to incur displeasure for light sentences in cases which interested the government, many judges tended to identify "upwards" with the more influential prosecutors. There has been a readjustment in this respect since 1965, following the coup, and judges are now rather more aggressive toward prosecutors. But this has not basically altered the condition of advocates.

[30] It should be borne in mind that the civil law advocate does not have the dominating role that English and American lawyers do in the courtroom, the continental-type judge being more active in trial procedure. But the advocate is nevertheless an important trial figure.

[31] In criminal sessions differences between prosecutor and advocate are built into the setting of the trial. On the bench the prosecutor sits immediately to the right of the single judge—which probably follows prewar practice on the landraad. When both wore the toga, or in more recent years a khaki uniform, they became almost indistinguishable to inexperienced accused persons. The advocate, however, sits before the bench and to one side. In the past some judges were uncomfortable with this arrangement but reluctant to ask their fellow officials to leave the bench. During the last three years, however, in a few courts djaksa have been compelled to take seats on a level with advocates; in a few other courts they have refused to do so.

To the extent that the operation of judicial roles forms a recognizable and regular system, then, it tends to emphasize the connection between judges and prosecutors to the exclusion of advocates. In criminal cases this has stacked the cards against the accused, but probably not much more so than if advocates were more acceptable and active. Accused persons are usually at a disadvantage everywhere, depending on their social class and income. Even where the advocacy is a powerful institution, private attorneys often have as much interest in cultivating their relationship with prosecutors and judges as in defending their clients.[32] Indonesian advocates have generally been denied even this possibility, though it does not redound to the advantage of their clients. To give just one example, negotiation over severity of sentence usually takes place between prosecutor and judge, not prosecutor and advocate.

Equally important, in many institutional ways, antagonism between judges and advocates has helped to isolate from one another two major potential allies and components of a significant law community.

Political Change and the Formal Law Community

Following the coup of October 1965—which ultimately resulted in the destruction of the Communist Party, the fall of Sukarno, and the accession of the army to power—formal law and legal officials seemed to take on new importance. There is reason to be skeptical about the character and persistence of this apparent transformation. Too many observers have tried to explain it in simple political terms—the fall of Sukarno and the PKI (Partai Komunis Indonesia) and the rise of right thinking men. But there are also sound sociological reasons why modest elements of such a transformation have in fact appeared, and they are likely to have some bearing on the future development of Indonesia's legal order.

A partial explanation lies in the structural and ideological characteristics of the New Order which supplanted Guided Democracy following the coup. The postcoup regime based on the army is in some ways the most unified Indonesia has had since in-

---

[32] See Abraham S. Blumberg, "The Practice of Law as a Confidence Game: Organizational Cooptation of a Profession," *LSR* 1, no. 2 (1967), 15–39, dealing with the American case.

pendence. There is now little question who is in power for the
indefinite future. The army is itself by no means united, and it is
under challenge by political parties and youth groups, but it is
not likely to be thrown out. Its political centrality is supported by
the ubiquity of army organization in Indonesia, a condition not
only of the army's size and strength but of the weakness of political parties and the decay of the government apparatus, which
military personnel have increasingly infiltrated. Having assumed
power, army leaders are now interested in consolidating their authority, in part by institutionalizing it. Given a measure of dif-
fidence about their political legitimacy, there is also a tendency
among them to resort to symbols of formal law and justice. In addition, unlike political parties or Sukarno's past support, the army
is itself a huge administrative structure; its organizational impulses toward hierarchy and order, though qualified by politicization of the officer corps, reinforce political and economic urges to
stability with an administrative political style pointing in the same
direction.[33]

The complex of political symbols which emerged during the
reaction against Guided Democracy after the coup also seemed to
favor stronger formal law. Some of these symbols were inherent in
past conflict; they were the opposites of those to which Sukarno
had given currency. Political stability and economic development,
for example, returned from the periphery to which they had been
pushed by mobilization for unity. Corruption and repression during the past several years, dramatized after the coup by sensational
revelations about former government ministers and leaders, gave
rise to demands for correction, reform, integrity, and personal freedom. Almost overnight hukum revolusi disappeared, and negara
hukum, seldom mentioned by anyone in the late years of Guided
Democracy, was again espoused. The negara hukum was given

[33] This point should not be pushed too far, for in the exercise of power
army leaders have also tended to fall back on political practices characteristic
of earlier regimes. Moreover, despite the desire of some army leaders to
establish more permanent governing institutions, the institutional picture—
especially at the decision-making level—remains one of impermanence and
lack of functional definition. Given surface ambivalence about what kind of
political role the army should play in the future, it may be difficult to develop such institutions. Finally, the administrative character of the army tends
to be conditioned by political and other interests.

more concrete meaning than ever before by reference to the mal-
feasances of Guided Democracy. For a time, at least, Guided Democracy has itself served as an occasionally effective negative
symbol against the revival of earlier practices.

None of this means that corruption, repression, and violation
of justice suddenly stopped after 1965, though they did receive
more public attention. Some groups were excluded from the purview of formal justice: tens of thousands accused of Communist
sympathies who were interned in camps, for example, and the
many Chinese who were persecuted in East Java, North Sumatra,
Kalimantan, and elsewhere. Corruption certainly continued, and,
as high-ranking military officers were deeply involved, little could
be done about it without threatening the regime. Nevertheless, the
new conditions and symbols of politics from early 1966 on made it
possible to raise issues of law and justice whose priority had previously been very low. The relief felt by the urban elite when the
Communist Party was destroyed provided a receptive atmosphere.

These issues were first raised largely by law professionals, generally of a younger, post-independence generation. The age factor
is significant. Among judges, for example, older men tended to
eschew politics and many had avoided the Revolution against
Dutch colonialism. Younger judges were more likely to be politically
conscious and involved. In the events following the October 1965
coup they acted as one part of an increasingly outspoken and somewhat influential group of nationally oriented professionals and
intellectuals.

Judges used the novel leverage provided by this activity and by
the new political atmosphere to pursue reform of the judicial system.
They forced the resignation of the Supreme Court Chairman, who
symbolized the earlier weakness and subordination of the Court
under Guided Democracy; after his successor had also resigned in
conflict with younger judges, an older Supreme Court judge who
was acceptable to leaders of the Judges' Association assumed the
Chairmanship of the Court.[34] At the same time, along with their

---

[34] Six new judges were appointed to the Supreme Court in early 1968,
after a long period of neglect during which the Court was reduced to four
members. There are now eight judges, of whom three are in their late
thirties or forties: Chairman Subekti and Abdurrachman, longtime mem-

demand for rescission of Law 19/1964, which had made presidential interference in judicial processes legal, judges also renewed an older claim for full judicial autonomy under the Supreme Court, free of administrative control by the Ministry of Justice, a program which the Ministry has so far successfully opposed. The motivation behind this campaign was in part a self-protective exclusivism, a search for independence, power, and dignity within the political system.[35] Similarly, judges resuscitated a much less attainable demand for powers of judicial review.[36] In the mid-1950's, after losing their battle with the prosecutors, judges had introduced a proposal for constitutional review in the Constituent Assembly, which, however, was permanently suspended in July 1959. This ambitious proposal reflected in part the influence of the American example, which judges and advocates regarded with growing fascination as Indonesian courts went into decline.[37] Judicial review would make the authority of law concrete, many judges feel, and of course it

bers, Asikin Kusumaatmadja, son of the first Chairman of the Court, Mrs. Sri Widojati Notoprodjo Soekito, Sardjono, Indroharto, D. Lumbanradja, and Bustanul Arifin.

[35] Judges also requested a rank and salary regulation independent of that for the rest of the civil service, and proposed to create a special tribunal within the judiciary to deal with issues of judicial discipline and ethics. They insisted moreover that all appointments to higher courts be made from within the professional judicial corps—which would assure the professionalism of the judiciary but would eliminate the possibility of dynamizing the courts through appointments from outside. See "Keputusan Rapat Kerdja para Ketua Pengadilan Tinggi dan Pengadilan Negeri dibawah Pimpinan Mahkamah Agung jang Mewakili para Hakim diseluruh Indonesia," nos. 1 and 2/1966 (Reports of a conference of first instance and appeals court chairmen with the Supreme Court). It is worth adding that since the coup of 1965 some judges have dropped the uniform adopted in the early 1960's and have taken up the black judicial toga again. Prosecutors retain their uniforms. The public prosecution, incidentally, remains independently organized, but has lost its representation in the cabinet and is now directly under the authority of the President.

[36] The draft law on judicial organization and powers proposed by judges to replace Law 19/1964 states in art. 23: "The Mahkamah Agung is empowered to examine whether any regulation of either the Central Government or Regional Government is formally or substantively in conflict with the Constitution or existing statutes." See also "Keputusan Rapat Kerdja . . ." 1/1966.

[37] The attraction of judicial practice in the United States has become even greater in recent years. Since the coup, many judges and advocates— and even some prosecutors and police officials—have seriously considered adopting major parts of American criminal process, especially accusatorial trial procedure. See, for example, Judge Sri Widojati Notoprodjo Soekito,

would symbolize the power of the courts. But basically the wish is as whimsical now as under Guided Democracy, for present leaders are little more willing and politically able than leaders in the past to submit to formal controls.

This disadvantage aside, judges and other law professionals are slightly favored by other changes occurring in the world of Indonesian law. Among the more important developments—failing economic growth, which generally would enhance the significance of lawyers—is an increase in the number of law-trained persons. Another is that lawyers of all vocations are apparently becoming more conscious of their collective identity and interests, though rivalry among the legal professions still dominates their relationships.

Precisely how many Indonesians now hold law degrees is hard to ascertain. The combined output of all major law faculties (including the Military Law Academy) since independence, in addition to those with prewar degrees, now probably exceeds 5,000, in contrast with approximately 300 in 1950.[38] The present number, although small in terms of Indonesia's size and needs, is enough for

"Hukum Atjara Pidana Sebaiknja Menganut Sistim Accusatoir," in the daily *Kompas,* Sept. 2, 1968. Current emphasis on civil rights promotes these views. So does the picture which many Indonesian law professionals have of the prestige and centrality of formal legal roles in America. A new code of criminal procedure is being drafted, but it is not clear how far it will turn away from Continental procedural concepts.

[38] The inadequate statistics I have indicate that of 2,815 judges in Indonesia, 751 have law degrees, as do 1,800 of 3,200 prosecutors. Trained advocates may number between 250 and 350. There are also trained lawyers in the armed forces, civil service, state enterprises, and banks. If the figures in the text are correct, the ratio of lawyers to population in Indonesia is approximately 1:36,000. This compares with about 1:800 in the United States, 1:15,000 in Japan, 1:15,000 in the Malayan peninsula, and a remarkable 1:1,350 in the Philippines. There is no space to analyze even these few statistics, except to point out that they indicate that the relationship between economic development and the size of the professional law community, though a valid one, is qualified by both historical and cultural variables. For the figures on the United States and Japan, see C. Ray Jeffery, with collaboration of E. E. Davis and H. H. Foster, Jr., "The Legal Profession," in F. James Davis and others, *Society and the Law* (New York: Free Press, 1962), p. 350. Little has been said in this essay about the important matter of legal education in Indonesia, and there is no space to do so here. The major law faculties are in the University of Indonesia (Djakarta), Gadjah Mada (Jogjakarta), and Padjadjaran (Bandung); there are several more law schools in Java and the other islands.

some kinds of institutional upgrading to begin. Thus it is now possible to require law degrees for permanent judicial appointments and promotions. The number of graduate lawyers entering the public prosecution also makes it reasonable to demand more rigorous rules of criminal procedure. And in the Ministry of Justice there is a growing interest in the registration and supervision of advocates and notaries, control over whom had practically lapsed in earlier years.

In connection with the growing collective consciousness of lawyers, if it is that, in 1968 a cause célèbre developed in Djakarta which focused public attention upon the entire formal law community, particularly advocates.

Briefly, the matter involved a respected Djakarta attorney of Chinese descent, Yap Thiam Hien, a man known for his professional skill and integrity. His name had been in the news in 1966 as government-appointed defense counsel in the trial of former Foreign Minister Subandrio on charges of complicity in the coup. Near the end of 1967 he appeared in the first instance court of Djakarta as defense attorney for a corporation (P. T. Quick) director accused of passing *tjèk kosong* (literally, "empty checks") backed by inadequate funds. Yap raised a furor by charging that these checks had been made out under duress and by openly accusing a *djaksa tinggi* (prosecutor at the appellate level), a police official with the rank of inspector-general, and two other officials. On December 28, the court decided against Yap's client, and Yap stated that he would appeal.

Yap was suddenly arrested by the police on January 1, 1968, and charged with belonging to a Communist organization, a very serious matter under the New Order.[39] In previous years such arrests had become commonplace, either for political reasons or, sometimes, for ransom. Yap's arrest was evidently intended either to keep him quiet or to retaliate for the accusations he had made. Now, however, the roof unexpectedly fell in on the police.

On January 4, Yap's arrest was reported in the press along with

[39] Yap had belonged to Baperki, an organization of Indonesian Chinese which in the 1960's had moved very close to the PKI. He quit Baperki during that period partly because of its political leanings. While a member, he had been a prominent participant in the debate over Chinese assimilation.

a protest by KASI (Kesatuan Aksi Sardjana Indonesia), a new organization of intellectuals.[40] During the next few days Yap was defended while the police were vociferously attacked for behaving as if the Old Order of Guided Democracy still existed. The protest was joined by university student groups, the new Human Rights Organization, the Indonesian Advocates' Association (Peradin), the Lawyers' Association (Persahi), and an interesting recently formed organization called Servants of the Law (Pengabdi Hukum).[41] They raised issues of civil rights, the rule of law, official *abus de pouvoir*, and procedural justice. General Suharto himself was apparently persuaded to support the position of these groups. By January 6, in record time, Yap was free. He indicated that he would press charges against those who had ordered his detention; the police official and prosecutor whom he had accused in the P. T. Quick trial brought charges against Yap for slander.[42]

[40] *Kompas*, Jan. 4, 1968. *Kompas* is one of the few newspapers actively and consistently concerned with problems of law and civil rights. Significantly it is a minority—Catholic—backed paper. Two similarly inclined dailies from the past were the Chinese supported *Keng Po* (ceased publ. 1958) and its successor *Pos Indonesia* (ceased publ. 1960). Not all minority journals are law-minded, but journals which are tend to be related to minorities. As elsewhere, Indonesian racial and religious minority groups have a special interest in the protection strong formal law may offer.

[41] The Pengabdi Hukum was established in October 1967 by the Djakarta branches of the Judges' Association (Ikahi), the Prosecutors' Association (Persadja), Peradin, and the Human Rights Organization (Lembaga Pembela Hak2 Azasi Manusia). The Association of Police Science Graduates (ISIK) joined on October 10. It is a consultative body whose stated purposes are to strengthen individual rights and the rule of law. See the informative articles by Judge Sri Widojati Notoprodjo Soekito, "Keadilan dan Hak-hak Azasi Manusia," in *Kompas*, Dec. 9, 11, and esp. 12, 1967. Apparently the organization has been weakened by internal rivalry and lack of enthusiastic support.

[42] The slander case, a criminal action, came up for trial in July 1968 and decision was rendered against Yap on October 14, 1968. He was sentenced to one year in jail and denied permission to practice as an advocate, a decision which he immediately appealed and which *may* be revised in the higher court. (*Kompas*, Oct. 15, 1968.) The difficulty in the case was to prove incontrovertibly that the police and prosecution officials had intended to put the squeeze on Yap's former client. From a legal point of view the case was regarded as a critical test of the freedom of advocates to develop the fullest possible defense of their clients through the introduction of arguments, as in the P. T. Quick case, which might affect other parties. See Soemarno P. Wirjanto, "Segi2 Positif dan Menarik dalam Perkara Advokat Yap," in

One well-known lawyer called the Yap case a blessing in disguise for the cause of law.[43] In many ways it was, for it dramatized issues of formal justice whose abuse had long been taken for granted. It is also significant that for the first time members of disparate law professions acted in concert on a matter of professional interest to them all. Even the military lawyer who had opposed Yap in the Subandrio trial spoke in his defense.[44] This last item itself indicates how lawyers have begun to spread throughout national institutions, which does not guarantee the efficacy of formal law, of course, but does strengthen the possibility that legal professions may in time gather influence. Such a development must also depend, however, on the extent to which lawyers perceive a commonality of professional interests and values that more or less transcends (though it cannot entirely override) their specific institutional roles. Along with the reinforcement of formal law values stimulated by the Yap case, it is the stronger professional consciousness which it encouraged that may make the Yap case an important chapter in Indonesian legal history.

Other evidence points in the same direction. The postcoup currency of rule-of-law symbols has, for example, permitted an attempt to restrict *ad hoc* law roles which have developed from reasons of power. One instance may be related to the Yap case, following which President Suharto forbade officers of any of the armed forces (thus including the police) to examine or to interfere in civil cases.[45] Moreover, formal law values draw support from the reactions of an essentially conservative and now rather more secure elite against the abuses of Guided Democracy, and from the shift in official ideological emphasis toward political and economic stability. Awareness may also be growing on the part of political leaders that Indo-

---

Kompas, Sept. 6, 1968. The first instance judge rejected arguments of the defense related to this issue, on the grounds that they were not based on existing law, which Yap's attorneys wanted the court to declare no longer valid.

[43] Jetty Rizali Noor, *Kompas,* Jan. 6, 1968.

[44] *Kompas,* Jan. 8, 1968. Police and prosecution officials, however, tended to be defensive about the case.

[45] *Kompas,* Jan. 18, 1968. President Suharto has emphasized his concern to restore the "original functions" of various parts of the government apparatus, and in this he has won support from high echelons of the police, at least.

nesia is too large, diverse, and complex to try to rule except through more or less impersonal media of governance. If so, it may put a greater premium on formal law roles.

But there are serious limits to the kind of evolution these developments project. They can best be illustrated by focusing again on courts and advocacy, the formal core of the judicial system.

First, because civil administration of the country is in disorder, the judiciary lacks systematic support from a bureaucratic "rule of law." Although there is a natural tendency for judges to emphasize their contribution to an effective legal order—and an equally natural tendency among others to see courts as the center of a legal system—the condition of bureaucratic organization is the fundamental determinant of the character of a legal order. People come into contact more often with administrative offices than with courts, and their picture of how formal law works is usually influenced accordingly. As norms of bureaucratic efficiency and impartiality have declined in Indonesia, because of politicization and lack of economic support, formal law machinery has suffered, and other routes and norms for getting things done have become common. Furthermore, though less important than the last point, courts themselves depend upon bureaucratic services to carry out their decisions fully and correctly, and here they have occasionally been humiliated.

Second, the political system does not yet support strong courts. Political action is often violent because political rules are unsettled, and there is not yet sufficient power anywhere in society to establish them. Failing persistent consensus about institutions and goals, there is little stimulus for the establishment of formal extra-political controls. For this reason judicial hopes for effective powers of review over legislative acts are basically unrealistic. In addition, because concepts of authority and political style are little related to concepts of national law, hardly any ideological basis exists for a powerful institution of review—except the one judges are now creating. The police and prosecution, though suffering from tarnished reputations, remain more central than the courts to the structure of political power, and it follows that they will continue to enjoy higher rewards.

Third, the formal roles of judge and advocate, conceived primarily in the context of a strong private economy, no longer draw support from the economy. Much of our discussion has been concerned with criminal justice. Criminal law and procedure are undeniably critical matters, but they are not the whole of legal development, and the strength of judicial roles will not be found there. Rather the demand for legal skills develops from economic growth and specialization. The model of economic change followed will obviously influence the arrangement of legal roles; independent courts and a strong advocacy are more important in a private than a state economy, though the Soviet example indicates that after a time an administrative economy also creates increasing demands for lawyers' skills, and these demands in turn affect the judicial system as a whole. For the time being, Indonesian trends are toward a mixed economy, in which the private sector may prove to be quite strong. The postcoup encouragement of foreign investment has in a small way stimulated the demand for private attorneys whose services alien corporations must have. Conceivably, foreign investment might have an accelerator effect upon the practice of law as well as upon the economy. But whether courts participate fully in this process depends on two additional factors: whether private and public businesses find judges or fixers more accessible and efficient, and whether the government itself decides that courts are useful instruments for both development and control.

Finally, along with its weak political and economic supports, Indonesia's existing formal judicial structure draws minimal sustenance from social and cultural sources. The judicial system has few positive links with the majority of the people. The advocacy is an urban phenomenon, serving for the most part a specialized clientele, and the same is true of the notariat. Courts are more widespread, but they are not a common or fully legitimate means of settling disputes. Cultural emphases in conflict resolution tend on the contrary to turn people away from government courts.

Avoidance of formal adjudication raises the very important question of how disputes normally are managed. The next part of our discussion attempts to deal with this problem.

PROCESS AND THE SPIRIT OF LAW

In all complex societies there is some spread between formal structure and conventional procedures. In Indonesia, as in many former colonies, lack of such integration is striking. The result is a kind of institutional Gresham's law, in which formal processes tend to be eschewed in favor of more familiar and accommodative ones.

Conciliation

Compromise is everywhere a primary method of dispute settlement. In some societies, however, compromise is more prominent than in others; or maybe it should be put the other way around, that some societies rely more on formal conflict resolution than others. A few of the social variables are clear. Small communities where face to face relations predominate tend to emphasize conciliation and compromise. Conversely, unfamiliar relationships make formal third party decisions more appropriate. Whenever common interests of disputants (and of their friends and neighbors) can be established, compromise is likely. One advantage of private settlement is that the interests of third party "impersonal" dispute-settlers can then be ignored. That is why business corporations in the United States, and elsewhere no doubt, tend to work out conflicts among themselves more often by private agreement than by going to court; [46] a formal case introduces considerations—the public interest, institutional demands of the legal system, interests of the judicial system itself—which seem irrelevant to the immediate concerns of businessmen.

Yet in the United States urbanization, secularization, a corporate economy, and a fairly high level of social and political integration— the latter recently challenged by social developments which have affected the operation and legitimacy of formal processes—have all made official third-party decisions common and legitimate, without of course eliminating private conciliation as a means of solving conflict. Both courts and administrative agencies with judicial functions consequently enjoy adequate support.

Most of Indonesia is on the other side of a formal decision-conciliation continuum. The majority of the population is neither urban nor secular; nor is the economy basically complex or corporate. Social values tend to stress personal though usually guarded contact, communal solidarity, and avoidance of disputes; there is almost no support for the idea that conflict may be functional.

[46] William S. Evan, "Public and Private Legal Systems," in William S. Evan, ed., *Law and Sociology* (New York: Free Press, 1962), p. 180.

Although little quantitative data exists to support the proposition, these characteristics seem more prevalent in Java and Bali than much of the rest of Indonesia. Judges, advocates, administrators, and others frequently claim that certain groups, for example the Bataks of North Sumatra, are more litigious than the Javanese.[47] There are several possible explanations for these assertions. One might follow the ecological distinctions drawn by Geertz in his *Agricultural Involution*. Under the pressure of nineteenth-century commercial agriculture, population increase, and lack of urban outlets for potential Javanese entrepreneurial energies, the irrigated rice fields of Inner Indonesia were cultivated ever more intensely by more people. In the same way more intense effort was directed toward creating surface harmony in the packed village societies. The swidden cultures of Outer Indonesia, which may have had less need anyway to be relentlessly on the lookout for dissonance, were less fully colonialized and more receptive to the entrepreneurial spirit. The rise of trade and a concomitant social individuation outside of ethnic Java and Bali may have diluted values that promote conciliation. Moreover, the spread of Islam in these same areas (partly for the same reasons) and later of Christianity in a few significant pockets, introduced more unequivocal notions of right and wrong, guilt and sin, than the *abangan* traditions of interior Java would recognize.[48]

These distinctions, though possibly valid, should probably not be overdrawn. Compromise, conciliation, the "soft" approach to conflict resolution appear to be common everywhere in Indonesian peasant societies, somewhat less so in the cities, and perhaps least so among

[47] J. C. Vergouwen says "it is a singular trait of a Batak's character to think that he is always in the right and as a consequence he will make an issue over the merest trifle, fighting over swallows' feathers . . . it is called. He is also particularly desirous of gaining the victory in a lawsuit as being the most sagacious party: he suffers a corresponding shame if he loses it." *The Social Organization and Customary Law of the Toba-Batak of Northern Sumatra* (The Hague: Nijhoff, 1964), pp. 377–378. Recently translated from *Het Rechtsleven der Toba-Bataks* (1933), Vergouwen's book is one of the best of the prewar adat law studies. Unfortunately he does not venture an explanation of the Batak traits mentioned above. The question of who is more litigious than who in Indonesia, and why, needs a great deal of research. For the present, lack of statistics is a major stumbling-block.

[48] On the abangan syncretic religious tradition in Java, see C. Geertz, *The Religion of Java* (Glencoe, Ill.: Free Press, 1960).

commercially oriented strata. But in Java and Bali the predilection for conciliation is a compelling and pervasive value of societies turned in on themselves. With a deep sense of relativism or, as Anderson has argued, tolerance,[49] the Javanese are inclined to exceeding care in their personal relations, to caution, diplomacy, reserve, and respect for social status. Every effort is made to avoid personal conflict and, when it occurs, to cover it over by refined techniques of social intercourse, pending the least damaging and humiliating solution.

The style of conflict resolution which these values encourage is one that, in legal terms, pays more attention to procedure than substance. Legal rules and considerations of equity are not of course ignored. Rather they represent parameters which more or less broadly define the outside limits of justice. They are minimum requirements for maintaining the integrity of the social order. But within these limits considerable leeway exists for negotiation, and it is with the possibilities thus made available that conciliation and mediation (used interchangeably here) are concerned. What tends to be emphasized is not the application of given rules, but the elimination of a conflict which may cause social tension or disruption. Those who talk about rules as if they were absolute are likely to be considered obstructors, stubborn trouble-makers, antisocial fools, or worse.

Not much has to be said here about the actual process of conciliation in Indonesian villages and urban *kampung*. In principle it is probably not very different from conciliation in other peasant societies.[50] Many variations occur according to the type of issue involved, social organization, character of political authority, and so on. When a disagreement arises (over a property line, for instance, or redemption of pawned land or an inheritance division) which the disputants have not settled themselves, it may be referred to a close friend, a well-known neighborhood or village elder, or to the

[49] Benedict R. O'G. Anderson, *Mythology and the Tolerance of the Javanese*, Cornell Modern Indonesia Project Monograph Series (Ithaca, N.Y.: Cornell University, 1965).

[50] See, for example, Bernard S. Cohn, "Anthropological Notes on Disputes and Law in India," *American Anthropologist*, 67, no. 6, part 2 (Dec. 1965), 82–122; and Laura Nader, "Choices in Legal Procedure: Shia Moslem and Mexican Zapotec," *American Anthropologist*, 67, no. 2 (April 1965), 394–399.

lurah (village head). Whoever takes the lead may do little more than keep tempers calm and bring the parties together for interminable talk. Ideally, he will try to discover the facts at issue, while at the same time playing down the facts and playing up personal relationships. As Eckhoff suggests, the conciliator tries to "de-ideologize" the conflict, emphasizing shared interests instead—those of the disputants and those of the community.[51] Local figures with influence over the parties may help push them together. The hope is that the disputants themselves will come up with a compromise, but if not, various possibilities will be proposed to them. A strong and influential conciliator may simply lay down a solution and bring pressure to bear on one or all disputants to acquiesce. Throughout the entire process, again ideally, there is usually minimal reference to "rights." That would raise intolerable assertions of absolute standards. When the dust has finally settled, sometimes after weeks or months, no decision occurs, only a coming to terms in which both parties have presumably lost something. Bitterness may remain—not public but private, sometimes leading to revenge—but efforts are made to contain it. The picture publicly drawn in the village is that neither side is right or has won (though private talk may say so); both are wrong for having quarreled and have redeemed themselves by eliminating overt tension. After a very divisive conflict, a ceremony may be held to seal the settlement and cleanse the atmosphere.

Because of the critical influence of personal relationships and shared interests—sometimes more imposed than real—outside interference creates havoc with village conflict resolution. Going out of the village introduces other interests and unfamiliar concerns. A government court, for example, is rarely aware of all the relationships at stake in a local dispute, and it may bring to bear standards alien to custom. Villagers occasionally say that formal courts apply *lain hukum* (different law). In some cases this may actually mean a substantive difference. More often it refers precisely to the court's natural concern with established substantive rules, in which a village group may be much less interested than in simply getting rid of a conflict with minimum social distress. In addition settlements in-

---

[51] Torstein Eckhoff, "The Mediator, the Judge and the Administrator, in Conflict-Resolution," *Acta Sociologica*, 10, nos. 1 and 2 (1966), 148–172.

duced from outside may deny a community whatever benefit of social cohesion might have accrued from resolving issues internally.[52]

The effect of outside political influence is even greater, since it
generally weakens the capacity of villages to handle their own disputes. Villages may be divided to begin with along various religious,
social, and economic lines which make it difficult to settle disputes
across the divisions. When such cleavages are reinforced by external supports, nearly every issue tends to take on huge "ideological" proportions which few village societies are equipped to
handle. This has frequently been the case in Indonesia as political
parties have extended their organizational lines into rural areas.

But the cultural penchant for compromise of personal conflicts remains strong and is not at all limited to villagers. A dispute in
which this writer was involved illustrates how pervasive this value
is at most levels of Javanese society, and how it contrasts with a
legal culture that tends to be concerned with substance and "right."

In late 1960 I agreed to accompany an American visitor on a trip
across Java. In Jogjakarta we registered at the city's largest hotel,
where the events to be related took place. What follows is ex-
cerpted from my field notes, with a few grammatical and clarifying
changes:

After registering, T and I went to our room. T went to the bathroom,
where the toilet was an old-fashioned one with a wall tank and cord.
When T pulled the cord the cover of the tank and the whole mechanism
inside came down (though no water), nearly hit him and crashed onto
the toilet bowl, knocking a huge chunk out of it. T was shaken. I told
the servant about the matter, and the next morning a hotel repairman
came to look over the damage.

During the afternoon, while I sat on the veranda writing and T slept,
a servant came to the room and handed me a note which informed us
that the hotel expected Rp. 5,000 for replacement of the toilet. I was
astonished at this and without thinking everything over went directly
to the hotel office and asked to see the manager. . . . For half an hour
or more he and I argued about the bill. I told him that it was not T's
fault the tank's insides had come down and that had T been hit by the
falling metal, clearly the hotel would have been responsible for damages.
[A hotel of this kind, classified as a "European" type enterprise, is subject

52 Cf. Max Gluckman, *Custom and Conflict in Africa* (New York: Barnes
and Noble, 1967), *passim*, on conflict and social cohesion.

to the civil code.] The manager would not accept this reasoning and said that T had not been hit by the metal and, since such a thing had never happened before, T must be responsible for the damage. . . . Finally I told him that we would not pay the bill, that it was best to take the matter to court, and that I would call Judge S [a friend] . . . to talk the problem over.

[In the course of the next several hours the manager and I met at various times to establish our relative power positions by indicating which influential officials we knew, a game often played in this kind of conflict and one that involves a good deal of bluffing. As it happened, a new element was introduced into the affair when a friend from Djakarta stopped at the hotel and mentioned that not long ago another toilet tank had fallen from the wall in the hotel. When the manager was reminded of this, the situation changed somewhat.]

I finally called up Judge S, fully intending to take the case to court or at least to scare the manager into withdrawing his claim. . . . The judge came to the phone; I told him about the incident, referred to the law on the matter, and made it clear that I thought the hotel was to blame and that I was willing to take the issue to court. Judge S's reaction left me momentarily speechless. He agreed the civil code was on our side. Then he said, "Well, but of course you are willing to pay part of the expenses for replacing the toilet, aren't you? Offer the manager some money in payment of the damages, to show good will, and then come to a settlement somewhere between his demand and your offer." When I recovered my composure I said that T was convinced he was not wrong, and why should he pay anything? Judge S replied, "Yes, of course, but that is beside the point. What is important is that you show good will and settle by *damai* (peace, compromise) if at all possible. Only if the manager demands the full Rp. 5,000 and refuses the offer to damai should you take the case to court."

Later . . . accepting Judge S's advice . . . we offered the manager a thousand rupiah. He carried on a bit but finally accepted without demanding more, we had some tea and small talk together, and the issue was never raised again.

My own automatic strategy and that of Judge S were based on quite different appreciations of what the situation demanded, one of us insisting on legal vindication and the other on peace.

The *perdamaian* (from damai) approach to conflict has other sources of support besides cultural proclivity. In independent Indonesia conciliation and private arbitration have become especially prevalent in commercial circles and perhaps among such minority groups as the Chinese. The sources of this behavior are different from those discussed above, but they are almost as important as qualities of the legal order.

The greater than normal avoidance of government courts by commercial interests is due to considerations of efficiency, utility, and trust. The flight to informal underground procedures in the economy has already been mentioned. In addition the courts themselves have often proved unable to meet demands of the private economy. Although there are exceptions, ethnic Indonesian judges tend to have little interest in commercial law.[53] Few of the older men had an opportunity to work in commercial law in the colony. Most early Indonesian judges, moreover, came from an aristocratic class whose men have had little taste or respect for business; only recently have these values begun to change. After independence, businessmen found the courts inadequate and basically unsympathetic to or uninterested in their problems and needs. This condition grew worse during the period of Guided Democracy when anticommercial biases acquired ideological stature.

Judicial procedures have also discouraged businessmen from using courts. Civil trials are painfully time-consuming; frequently, as a result, financial disputes go to court only if one litigant seeks a delay sufficient to permit continued use of funds or an inflationary reduction of the real costs of settlement. Once pronounced, decisions in commercial cases offer little future legal guidance, partly because poorly paid and personally preoccupied judges have neither time nor inclination to write carefully reasoned conclusions, and also because public policy has been too uncertain to give the judges adequate direction. Finally, since judicial decisions do not always carry their own guarantee of execution, further administrative expense may be required under the table. A comment by

[53] There are several judges of Chinese descent in first instance and appeals courts, though none has yet been appointed to the Supreme Court. Chinese judges are often given responsibility primarily for civil law commercial cases. Similarly, Christian judges sometimes work largely on family law cases under the jurisdiction of the civil code. But these are not hard and fast rules of a division of labor. Among younger judges, a principal difficulty in trying civil law litigation is inadequate familiarity with the Dutch language. Although all the major codes and statutes have been translated unofficially, commentaries are inaccessible unless one knows Dutch.

an older-generation advocate from Bandung sums up some of the problems: [54]

Trials take very long, sometimes three or four years or more. And judges know little about law now and care less. I still write full briefs for my cases, but younger judges often get angry because they take too long to read. . . . Most judges don't know enough about civil law. . . . So apart from the lack of personal satisfaction for me in the courts, it makes no sense for the firms I represent to go to court unless it is absolutely necessary. And not only are the courts difficult, but the whole process of law now is devious. We have to bribe a clerk to deliver the executory documents when a decision is finally rendered. Too many channels have to be used to get anything done, and they all cost money. In all the contracts I write now for my firms, I insert an arbitration clause so that we can avoid the courts. Sometimes I serve on the arbitration panels.

Such difficulties can be ameliorated but hardly solved merely by revision of judicial procedures and attitudes, for the wider problem is as much or more political and administrative.

Private conciliation may have become more prevalent also among Indonesia's approximately three million Chinese, whose attitudes undoubtedly carry over into and are affected by the experience of Chinese commerce. No statistical data are available to prove this assertion, only anecdotal evidence, and conflicts among Chinese do in fact appear in court when other solutions have proved impossible. It is not a matter of Chinese groups rejecting the legitimacy of government courts or the law they apply; these have long been accepted, particularly among *peranakan* (Indonesian born) Chinese. Rather, Chinese suffer the same kinds of legal disadvantage in Indonesia that they do in much of the rest of Southeast Asia, and that unpopular minorities have suffered elsewhere. Administration and courts belong to the majority, whose resentment of the formerly advantaged and still economically strong Chinese has not encouraged solicitude for their position either socially or legally. The problem is complicated by the contempt in which Indonesians are often held by Chinese, particularly those of an older generation which knew colonial conditions. Whatever their attitudes, however, most Chinese tend to doubt that they will be treated with fairness

[54] July 20, 1967.

and dignity in government offices unless they have good personal connections or are prepared to pay, and ample evidence exists to substantiate their fears.

For various reasons, then, conciliation is common throughout Indonesia. Insofar as it represents a cultural bent, it will probably remain—as it has elsewhere in Asia—as permanent a characteristic of Indonesian legal culture as one can imagine. But if there is a measure of general social and economic change, legal culture will also undergo some derivative change. We might beg many questions and ask one: By what process might conciliation begin to give way to formal adjudication in government courts?

Obviously no government will order citizens to submit all their conflicts to formal courts. Nor is it likely that citizens *en masse* will suddenly insist that the courts settle their disputes. But the process, as elsewhere and at other times in history, may involve something in between these two poles.

Conciliation can be an effective means of resolving conflict only when government is either uninterested in the subject matter of a dispute, or is incapable of doing anything about it. In old Java, palace officialdom apparently took notice of village conflicts only if they threatened public order. The case was not much different in the colony, except that the concept of public order was broadened to include more issues. Family law problems, among others, were left by and large untouched. In the independent state, however, the urge of the Indonesian elite toward national integration and "modernization" has extended the standard of relevance to an increasing number of problems in which the government wants to play a part.[55] The power of the central government to press its authority everywhere in Indonesia is limited, but it may grow, and an expansion of judicial authority in some form will (as it has already) accompany it.

A steady extension of national political authority might not by itself greatly affect the place of conciliation, but it will if combined with social change which depends upon sustained government sup-

[55] On the process of expansion of judicial authority over a broader range of legal issues, there is some suggestive material in Dan Fenno Henderson, *Conciliation and Japanese Law: Tokugawa and Modern* (Seattle: University of Washington Press, 1965), vol. 1.

port. Some of the Supreme Court's most significant decisions during the last decade have dealt with claims by individuals to be released from customary obligations and disabilities—for example, with respect to inheritance rights of widows.[56] The Court has been inclined, for ideological and other reasons, to establish the right of widows to inherit from their husbands. It is equally important that these women actively sought revision of customary rules in the first place.

Choice of Jurisdictions

Outside official participation in the settlement of disputes may be sought—and is, it seems, increasingly—for various reasons. It may simply have proved impossible to compromise. Or a disputant may want to harass his antagonist through the trouble and discomfort of going to a formal tribunal. And especially in land and debt cases, one party may seek the advantage of delay. Sometimes enterprising pokrol bambu encourage disputants—having perhaps also encouraged the dispute—to try official recourse on the promise of gain in property or money.

But government civil courts, *pengadilan negeri,* are not the only resort, and may not even be the most obvious one. The alternatives are the bureaucracy, local army officers, Islamic courts, or local political party leaders. One or other of these may indeed actively seek a role in settling local conflicts. The pamong pradja, army, and police are particularly prone to lending a hand in common disputes, not always for partisan reasons, but often because they conceive dispute settling to be a proper part of their responsibilities.

From the point of view of a village, or even an urban disputant, the alternative recourses tend to be differentiated in terms of power rather than formal function; or to put it differently, function follows power. It is not that a government court, for example, is barely recognized as such, but merely that such recognition does not constitute a notion of procedural propriety. Courts also suffer a dis-

---

[56] See R. Subekti and J. Tamara, *Kumpulan Putusan Mahkamah Agung mengenai Hukum Adat* (Djakarta: Gunung Agung, 1961) and D. Lev, "The Supreme Court and Adat Inheritance Law in Indonesia," *American Journal of Comparative Law* (hereafter Amer. J. Comp. Law), 11, no. 2 (Spring 1962), 205–224. These decisions will be taken up again in our discussion of integration.

advantage in that they are further from the perceived center of power than many other offices. Thus if conciliation fails, the next course of action is often to seek out the highest status friend (or friend of a friend) one has, in the hope that his influence will be decisive. The friend is likely to be a member of or have contacts in the bureaucracy, and in recent years the army. Administrative units, moreover, tend to be perceived as sharing power in a functionally undifferentiated way. For this reason offices, commissions, and *ad hoc* committees created now and then in Djakarta or regional capitals, often find themselves deluged with puzzling pleas for help in myriad kinds of impertinent disputes and personal problems. Occasionally an official will try to give such help.

Administrative officials therefore fill an essential role in conflict resolution, one that lends itself to use most naturally wherever bureaucratic conceptions of state are strong. In the nature of this kind of recourse—to officials, army officers, policemen, prosecutors, and so on—coercion of one sort or another frequently plays a significant part in the process of dispute settlement.

Within the judicial world itself, the existence side by side of secular and Islamic courts (*pengadilan agama*) poses another type of jurisdictional problem. Formally there would seem to be little difficulty. Since 1937 the competence of Islamic courts in Java and Madura has been restricted materially to divorce; outside of Java religious tribunals also share jurisdiction over inheritance with civil courts.[57] When a matrimonial case arises among Moslems, there is no disagreement over which court is competent; only the penga-

---

[57] First instance Islamic courts exist in most kabupatèn where there are also pengadilan negeri. One Islamic High Court—*Mahkamah Islam Tinggi*—serves all of Java and Madura, while in Sumatra, Kalimantan, and Sulawesi there are also provincial Islamic appeals courts. Some consideration has been given to the possibility of creating an Islamic chamber in the national Supreme Court. It should be mentioned that the pengadilan agama everywhere in Indonesia lack enforcement powers, for which they must rely upon an "executory declaration" (*executoire verklaring*) from the pengadilan negeri. A hostile pengadilan negeri judge may rule, however, that enforcement —of an inheritance decision by a pengadilan agama outside of Java, for example, or an agreement on inheritance reached before a pengadilan agama in Java—can be obtained only after a proper trial on the merits in the secular court. This has happened on occasion, leading to considerable tension not only between the two courts involved but also between the Ministries of Justice and Religion.

dilan agama can receive it. But in Java every other kind of conflict must go to the pengadilan negeri.

Yet that is not what happens. Most significantly, Islamic courts in Java continue to handle inheritance cases. Often these cases do not really involve litigation, in that the parties merely want advice on how an estate should be divided according to the *faraidl* (division of inheritance) rules. Sometimes, however, there is a conflict, and the Islamic judge is asked to settle it. Legally speaking, he should refer the parties to the pengadilan negeri, and many legalistically inclined Islamic judges actually do so. But frequently the case is accepted. By what is essentially a legal fiction, when a dispute is involved, the pengadilan agama does not "decide" the issue (since it has no formal jurisdiction), but rather delivers a *fatwa*, an advisory opinion. If a claimant is unhappy with the fatwa, he can contest the issue anew according to local adat law in the pengadilan negeri. Depending on the applicable adat rules and the attitudes of local civil judges toward Islam, a claimant may win in the secular court what he lost in the Islamic court. The existence of apparently competing jurisdictions encourages this kind of search for favorable rules.

Normally, however, the fatwa is accepted, and when a contested issue exists the fatwa often seems to be considered a "decision." Furthermore, some Islamic judges also regard their opinions as decisions; this writer has seen written fatwa in which the term *keputusan* (decision) was used rather than fatwa.

Why do many people with inheritance disputes still go to the pengadilan agama, in Java, rather than the pengadilan negeri? In part it is because they assume the pengadilan agama remains formally competent, and some Islamic judges are eager enough to recapture the authority lost three decades ago not to disabuse them of this notion.

Probably more important, those who go to Islamic courts do so because they believe it proper, sometimes in spite of their awareness of formal law. National statutory law is irrelevant in this connection, for the legitimacy of the pengadilan agama derives from the sanction of Islam itself. For the same reason, many Javanese abangan peasants (as well as aristocrats) would not think of going to a pengadilan agama with inheritance problems; and there are occasional reports of families who refuse to recognize the authority of Islamic courts and other religious offices even over matrimonial affairs, creating their own rites instead.

Finally, apart from religious reasons, acceptance of the pengadilan agama also depends to some extent on its usefulness and traditional comforts. Not only are religious courts more efficient than the slow-moving and heavily backlogged pengadilan negeri, but they are also less formal and imposing.[58]

Nevertheless, the influence of the pengadilan agama should not be exaggerated. Most inheritance cases, even in Sumatra, Sulawesi, and other islands, probably do go to the pengadilan negeri, despite its disadvantages, partly because that is where various officials tend to direct litigation once it seems inevitable. But, on the whole, neither court should be given more attention as a dispute settler than local bureaucratic officials and other wielders of power.

The same is true of urban and commercial groups. Here too choice of jurisdiction, broadly conceived, tends to follow identification of relevant power and influence. The bureaucracy, civil and military—the latter increasingly more so than the former—often performs key functions in settling disputes. Not only do men (and groups) in conflict seek support there, but officials with power make themselves available for service. Disadvantaged parties may go to court in search of a better chance. But the common perceptions of power, authority, status, influence, and therefore "competence" are focused elsewhere.

Peasant and Court: The Pokrol Bambu as Law Broker

A peasant who goes to court is not dealing with an entirely unknown element or entering a new and alien world, as some would have it. He is in fact reasonably familiar with this world of officialdom. What is unfamiliar is the procedure. Standards of relevance applied to facts and evidence are likely to be profoundly different

[58] A case in the pengadilan negeri may take years to complete, partly because appeals, which cost very little, are so often made. In the pengadilan agama a few days, weeks, or, rarely, months will elapse from the beginning of a hearing until the issuance of a decision or fatwa. A case may take longer in the Islamic court if a judge attempts conciliation of a dispute. Some Islamic judges, who tend to be older men with primarily religious education and close local ties, are quite effective conciliators, perfectly willing to settle inheritance conflicts outside Islamic legal rules and according to local custom or on any other convenient basis.

for peasant litigant and trained judge. While the latter is interested in those facts pertinent to a specific category of law, the former perceives his conflict in a wider and more complex perspective. Compounding this unavoidable problem, courtroom atmosphere, particularly in large cities, tends to be somewhat stiff and the relationship between litigant and judge full of pitfalls.[59] A few judges, usually those native to an area and commonly recognized as having high status independent of their office, can transcend the narrowly defined context of judicial contact with society at large. They sometimes prove confident enough in their own authority to go outside the formal law to perform judicial functions expected of them; this kind of judge is occasionally able to conciliate disputes in court, as the procedural code requires him to try.[60] But such judges are relatively rare. Furthermore the judicial style may seem odd: the court is part of the bureaucracy but does not work by bureaucratic principles as peasants know them. Thus court sessions are open and public, but judges are often personally inaccessible. Frequently, therefore, people involved in litigation seek out court clerks for

[59] The confrontation between urban judge and peasant may be uncomfortable for both. Sometimes it is a problem of differing world-views that is evident from the beginning as a judge inquires into a litigant's background. For example, in the following situation which occurred on June 28, 1960, the judge was a devout and even politically involved Sumatran Moslem and the litigant an abangan peasant from the kabupatèn of Semarang in Central Java:

Judge: What is your name?
Lit: (Gives name.)
Judge: What is your religion?
Lit: Religion?
Judge: Yes, what is your religion?
Lit: Hmm (with a shrug).
Judge: Well, your religion is Islam, right?
Lit: Islam? Ja (yes), Islam.
Judge: Islam.

That stretched the truth, as the judge undoubtedly knew. If his concerns were thus satisfied, the litigant had already begun the variously placating and manipulating behavior rather common in trial courts, as it is elsewhere in the bureaucracy.

[60] The attempt to conciliate disputes in government courts has become largely *pro forma*. By the time a case gets to the pengadilan negeri, it is usually too far gone to be amenable to compromise, unless the issue was essentially one contrived by outsiders—*pokrol bambu*, for example—without the full understanding of the litigants.

help, on the assumption (often true) that they have great influence over how courts work.

Like the court clerk, the pokrol bambu makes the judicial world more comprehensible to uninformed litigants, and it is not surprising that many successful pokrol bambu are former court clerks.

In his present form, the pokrol bambu probably dates back to the eighteenth or nineteenth century, arising in response to a need for someone capable of dealing with the alien procedures of foreign-dominated legal institutions.[61] As in other colonies—though India and the Philippines, for example, make generalization difficult—the Dutch discouraged Indonesian litigation and professional counsel. The myth of native simplicity eliminated the need for anything so developed as a lawyer. It followed that judges could deal with people's disputes without benefit of an intermediary, who would probably be a trouble-maker.[62] Often, however, litigants were permitted to bring friends to help them in court. The "friends" soon became professionals, performing the service which colonial authorities preferred them not to perform.

There are various kinds of pokrol bambu: honest and dishonest, specialists and generalists, rural and urban, and so on.[63] What is common to all is a lack of a formal law degree and a possession of some knowledge—sometimes much, sometimes little—of how the formal legal system works, often of how it *really* works, rather than a mere understanding of statutes.

To a peasant or lower-class city dweller, high status advocates

[61] The term "pokrol bambu" has derogatory connotations. "Pokrol" derives from "procureur" and though in common parlance it is sometimes used to refer to any kind of counsel, professionals always prefer "advokat." The qualifier, according to one interpretation, refers to the fact that when a bamboo pole is struck it makes a lot of noise, but there is nothing inside.

[62] See J. W. B. Money, *Java*, 2 (London: Hurst and Blackett, 1861), 72–73, 85–86, for a comment praising Dutch discouragement of lawyers for Indonesians. For a similar position on bush-lawyers in the Gold Coast, see excerpts from the Blackall Committee report of 1943 in W. B. Harvey, *Law and Social Change in Ghana* (Princeton: Princeton University Press, 1966), pp. 188–189.

[63] In recent years a distinct breed of pokrol bambu emerged with special knowledge of land law, many of them school teachers working with the Communist peasant front (Barisan Tani Indonesia, now abolished). They defended peasants caught up in land disputes with the government or landowners, free of charge.

are unfamiliar. But pokrol bambu are familiar, and it is for this reason, as well as costs and communications problems, that when counsel is used at all they are preferred to advocates. Pokrol bambu come to their clients in more ways than one as they drum up business. To go to advocates is to be compelled to relate to the formal system, while pokrol bambu often relate the system to litigants in familiar terms of influence and inside contacts.

Pokrol bambu are commonly accused of encouraging litigation and bilking clients, and this is frequently true. (They also do advocates the service of drawing away the barbs usually directed at professional lawyers in most societies.) The pokrol bambu's pitch often is that he knows the judge, prosecutor, police, and important administrative officials, as in fact he sometimes does. He may also claim that special legal tricks will save or gain his client advantages of money or land. Pokrol bambu may or may not actually appear in court; some do who barely understand procedure, and the result is confusion, delay, and angry judges.

In any event, the importance of the pokrol bambu is that he acts as a mediator between two different styles and perceptions of law. He is a kind of law broker who speaks both languages—often literally: Dutch or Indonesian on the one hand, the local language on the other. Like the advocate he maintains a bit of mystery about his skills, but he does interpret the national law and its institutions to those whom he represents, and in reasonably comprehensible terms.

Pokrol bambu have flourished since independence, partly because of an increased volume of litigation and partly because, like fixers, their special skills have been in demand. In time, pressure from advocates for revision of procedural rules to permit only trained counsel in court may weaken the pokrol bambu; so will the establishment of legal aid offices, in which the advocates' association has taken an interest. But so long as there is a wide gap between formal procedures and the common understanding of them, the pokrol bambu's services are not likely to cease altogether.

SUBSTANCE: THE PLACE OF LAW AND LEGAL CHANGE

Indonesian law has undergone a transformation since 1942. It is not merely that new statutes have been promulgated or that the Supreme Court has occasionally departed from colonial jurisprudence. In fact much colonial legislation remains in force, and when parts of it have been abolished or declared valid only as guidelines, they still tend to stick in the minds of lawyers. But the legal system has been infused with new meanings and purposes. The critical difference is that the spirit of the law has changed, even as the letter has sometimes continued to be followed *pro forma.*

What constitutes the new spirit of national law—that is, what are the relevant values, the common cognitions of legal roles, processes, structures, and relationships in the new state—is difficult to say. The problem (for both Indonesia and this writer) is complicated by the existence of diverse religious traditions which harbor different views of law and sometimes justice; the Islamic view of justice, based as it is on a fairly clear idea of God's law, is quite different from the more contingent outlook of abangan peasants in Java. There are also legally relevant social and cultural differences between the various adat traditions. And there are class differences compounded by educational differences, in which among some groups—professional lawyers are one example—imported values form an ideological substratum.

To the extent that formal law had become a social force in Indonesia, it was seriously weakened by the Revolution and by the political turmoil which followed. But in general social and political myths in Indonesia do not consistently support an independent sphere of legal activity which is presumed to define and give order to society; fundamental notions of justice and proper social behavior have little to do with lawyers' law. The next part of our discussion, on concepts of justice and legality, will deal briefly with this point. Yet a concept of impersonal law is inherent in the Indonesian state and may be growing more significant. Moreover, the content of formal law is responding to social and political change, and law is being used within limits to promote change. These matters will be taken up in the concluding parts of the essay.

Justice and Legality

There are two essential questions which can hardly begin to be answered here: What are the basic characteristics of Indonesian conceptions of justice? and, What is the relationship between these conceptions and national law?

Conceptions of justice are everywhere rooted in a desired condition of society. Usually these conceptions are made explicit only when men are confronted by injustice. They can be divided analytically into procedural and substantive components. The former have to do with the style of a legal system; "the rule of law" and "rechtsstaat" are procedural concepts. Substantive justice concerns, in part, what are now called "social rights," and characterizes political and economic arrangements within society. The relationship between procedural and substantive concepts of justice lies in the principles of legitimacy underlying authority in society.

Mention was made earlier of a tendency in dispute settlement to emphasize procedure over substance, to pursue an unhumiliating compromise, rather than a right-wrong decision, in the hope of eliminating conflicts effectively without further social tension. The sources of procedural and substantive justice, however, may be perceived as being identical in a world-view deeply committed to the calm and harmonious ordering of society.[64] The just society here implies the absence of irresoluble conflict, at least, and is achieved first of all by men performing the proper political and social functions of the classes into which they were born. One function of government, in this view, is to maintain the essential correctness of social relationships as a reflection of a greater universal order; successful governance will be manifested in the peacefulness and prosperity of the realm. The just and prosperous society (*masjarakat jang adil dan makmur*) to which Sukarno frequently referred is understood less as a duality of possibilities, each to be pursued independently, than as a kind of causal relationship: prosperity is likely to occur as a mark of the just society.

The just leader in Javanese tradition is basically conservative, a man of studied virtue who has cultivated special powers of mind and body and is incorruptible and passionless in the performance of his duties, which in social terms are conceived as the maintenance

[64] Some but not all of the discussion here is applicable to most Indonesian cultures, but the examples I have in mind are drawn primarily from Java and Bali and from pre-Islamic and pre-European traditions. For fuller and more precise discussions of Javanese values and political traditions, see Soemarsaid Moertono, and Anderson's particularly valuable contribution to this volume. On Bali, see C. Geertz, *Person, Time, and Conduct in Bali: An Essay in Cultural Analysis*, Southeast Asia Studies, Cultural Report Series no. 14 (New Haven: Yale University, 1966).

of harmony among the people. Officials in the independent state often assume responsibility for local dispute settling because excellent governance is understood to consist in a minimum of conflict —which the colonial government also greatly valued; a high rate of litigation is, therefore, unfavorable. When leaders have the necessary qualities of unselfseeking virtue, procedural and substantive justice cannot help but be fulfilled. An inequity in the relationships between men of similar rank should be righted by the king or his official, for otherwise the resulting bitterness would create an undesirable spiritual imbalance in society and, indeed, in the entire universe.[65] There is a standard here for judging the behavior of officials—though not for taking action against them—and it has often been apparent in independent Indonesia. Corrupt officials who are *berat sebelah* (one-sided) in their treatment of men and affairs of government have been condemned not only by intellectuals who spoke of political machination or unlawfulness, which implies recourse, but more quietly by others who regard such behavior as *tidak adil*, not just, and *tidak patut*, unsuitable and inappropriate, without reference to law or politics and without a notion of mundane recourse.

Justice in this view is unitary. It is not understood as the weighing of distinct interests in like cases, as the European goddess of justice does; she stands for a formal, technical, view of justice, the evolution of which depended upon a well-developed concept of private interests. In 1960, at a time of ideological concern for the expression of specifically Indonesian traditions, the goddess was replaced as Indonesia's symbol of justice by a banyan tree inscribed with the Javanese word *pengajoman*—shelter, succor—which connotes paternalistic protection. It is primarily a symbol of substantive justice, one that could be and was translated partially into modern socialist terms. Moreover, it is closely connected not with particular instrumentalities of pursuing justice, but with the indivisible ruler. Finally, it implies less of a concern with like cases than with like persons: the banyan tree, standing before the *kraton*

---

[65] A prewar study of the customary law of crime throughout Indonesia emphasizes the consistent effort in criminal actions to restore the "magical" balance in society. See N. W. Lesquillier, "Het Adatdelictenrecht in de Magische Wereldbeschouwing" (dissertation, State University of Leiden, 1934).

(palace), offers protection to the *rakjat* or little people of the realm. It is a very apt representation of traditional values, though not of realities, relating to justice.

Conceptions of proper social relationships in this perspective help to explain what Indonesian lawyers refer to as a lack of rights-consciousness. It is the result partly of a "nonlegal" view of society, in which the social order is conceived as eternal and essentially uncontrollable, and also of a view of social corporation which leaves little room for the justification of individual interests.

Whether or not all Indonesian societies recognize a *concept* of rights traditionally, all do of course recognize various kinds of rights. Differences exist between the several religious orientations in this respect, and perhaps also between some of the ethnic traditions. Both Islam and Christianity do have concepts of right, the one inherent in the body of Islamic law and the other mainly through its European associations and formal legal provisions. It may also be that the unilineal kinship societies of the archipelago tended to develop, if not concepts of right, at least a greater awareness of rights than the politically organized bilateral societies, as a result of the usually detailed prescriptions (and enforcement) given for intra- and inter-familial relationships and their legal consequences. But this is only a hypothesis, and it is not at all clear that the greater awareness of rights, if such existed, was easily transferred to the independent state. In any event, though the corporate rights of the village, lineage, kingdom, and finally the state take precedence, there are clearly defined rights, among others, of possession and succession almost everywhere in the archipelago. During the colonial period individual property rights grew stronger, as indicated by a decline in village-owned lands, and this trend accelerated after the Revolution under the pressure of both economic and social change.

But at least in Java, and perhaps elsewhere too, men tend not to be oriented to the notion of rights as such. Rather, in the crucial matter of enforcement, personal rights are subordinated in relations between equals to the greater value of social harmony—often enough, at least, to make this generalization a fair one. The principal exception to this tendency occurs when the idea of substantive rights becomes politicized and collective, as it did in the case of land during the 1950's and 1960's. Otherwise one seldom hears from lower-class Indonesians any reference to legal rights. Men do not generally say that they have a right to do something or take something. It is impolite to talk about rights; it connotes selfishness, absoluteness, belligerency, and unwillingness to compromise.[66] One is more likely to encounter the notion of rights among urban intellectuals, professionals, and businessmen, those who tend to be more aware politically and more likely to enter freely into a wide variety of private transactions and associational activities.

Between unequals concepts of right are less meaningful than the compulsion of status. Here it is the attributes of status which are natural, and these attributes have more to do on balance with perquisites than with responsibilities. Traditional concepts of social stratification distinguished between leaders and led first of all not in terms of rights but of relative virtues and appropriate functions. Increasingly, during the years of independence, officials were regarded as having abused their offices, neglected their duties, shown blatant self-concern—in other words, they were regarded as having failed to practice the virtues of good leaders; but they were seldom viewed by common people as having violated anyone's rights. Intellectuals, and particularly lawyers, often made accusations, and after the coup of 1965 a human rights organization was formally established, but such efforts have limited appeal, because the symbols they use have few specific cultural referents. One also seldom sees in court litigants of vastly different social status, and not because disparate status groups have few transactions with one another; the economic traffic is considerable and constant. Rather a peasant simply would not think of suing an aristocrat (old or new), and if it did occur to him, it would seem inappropriate and ineffective. Nor would an aristocrat normally bother to take a peasant

66 Cf. Hahm Pyong-Choon, *The Korean Political Tradition and Law* (Seoul: Hollym Corp., 1967), p. 190: "For a Korean, it is not decent or 'nice' to insist on one's legal right. When a person hauls another person into court, he is in fact declaring war on him. This signifies a complete breakdown of the traditional 'decent' way of solving disputes. He is now resorting to norms made by the state and enforced by the governmental power. He has lined himself up on the side of the bureaucrats to use the power of the state to oppress his fellowman. . . . A person who uncompromisingly asserts his right given to him by the law is an indecent and callous man, a person who lacks the arts of gracious social living, that is, the *virtues*."

debtor or tenant to court; as in other status-oriented societies, the man of high social standing has more powerful instruments than courts—the bureaucracy, police friends, army friends, and so on—at his disposal. In these conditions, men of low status usually find a measure of protection in the collectivity. In independent Indonesia peasant and aristocrat (to use the term loosely here) have in fact faced one another in court as collectivities, usually in litigation between the government and squatters represented (until October 1965) by the Communist peasant organization. But the courts were not capable of solving this conflict and it turned violent. The kind of violent political action that occurred has some basis in traditional social structure and beliefs. In old Java there was no effective redress against the aristocracy except violent political action. Authority could not be challenged through any existing institutions; it could only be influenced and occasionally manipulated. Justice therefore had either to be achieved by violence, which was rarely successful, or restored by the messianic just king, who never came.

In the independent state political action is significant in another way for conceptions of law and justice. The mobilization of religious, ethnic, and even class sentiments has made it impossible to take political legitimacy for granted, with the result that the pursuit of justice has acquired the character of a millenarian quest. As national society is perceived in terms of grand oppositions which leave little room for a common enterprise, the meanings of social and political justice also tend to be cast in terms of the cleavages within Indonesian society. Issues of procedural justice have been subordinated to the imperative of securing substantive claims to legitimate authority. The sources of justice, in the context of ideological conflict, are located in the various religious-social-political aliran, for whose members the just society will approach realization only when their own group assumes unchallenged control of the state. For committed Moslems an Indonesian state governed by non- or anti-Islamic forces, and in which Islamic law is permanently relegated to a private periphery, would be unjust.[67] Among those who come out of the pre-Islamic religious traditions of Java, the threat of an "Islamic State" also conjures visions of terrible injustice.

[67] But there is little agreement within Indonesian Islam on the legal meaning of a "state based on the tenets of Islam." The question has usually been

The same is true of Christians, who as a religious minority have most at stake in a religiously neutral state.

These political conceptions of justice have constricted the applicability of other available procedural notions of justice. The killings which followed the coup of 1965 in several provinces, particularly Central and East Java, become slightly more comprehensible in the light of intense ideological conflict between Moslems and abangan peasants, as well as the economic conflict over land which to some extent was subsumed by and given expression in the religious confrontation. The postcoup paradox of sincere appeals for improved formal justice juxtaposed with silence—with some exceptions—on the treatment of Communist and alleged Communist detainees can also be explained in these terms. Communists are outside the pale. To many men who feel strongly about both formal justice and anti-Communism, therefore, the contradiction is hardly apparent. One can of course cite many similar examples elsewhere in the world where the requirements of procedural and political justice have proved mutually exclusive, and the political conception has usually dominated.

One of several hundred questions that remains now is what bearing these various views of justice have on the problem of legality. What kind of value is placed on obedience to law and on the use of law as an instrumentality of government? Any answer to this question has to be tentative, for we do not know what mix of cultural and political causes led to the general decline of law after the Revolution. Ideological conflict was undoubtedly significant, among other reasons because it made the political system itself appear to be only tentative. But from what has been said earlier one can argue that at the level of national law—village law requires another kind of analysis—political values have little to do with concepts of legality. It is not that men generally feel they should violate laws, which has been the case in revolutionary situations, but that obedience to them is often a question of convenience unconnected with what is right. This does not imply that a government in power is

---

evaded, particularly by Islamic intellectuals who doubt the utility of the *sjariah* (Islamic law) for purposes of development in the twentieth century. Among younger generation Islamic leaders problems of Islamic law appear to have received little more attention.

considered illegitimate, but rather that legitimacy is not dependent on concepts of law.[68] It might be useful to draw a distinction in this connection between "law orientations," based on commonly shared and internalized legal values, as is often the case in highly integrated social systems, and "enforcement orientations." "Orientation" is used here as Weber used it to mean either a positive or negative response to a given norm, but in any case recognition of it.[69] Like much else dealt with in this essay, the two poles define a continuum on which all societies (and within societies different classes and groups) somewhere fall. What is suggested here is that in Indonesian society there generally tends to be less concern with legal rules than with enforcement officials, who are obeyed for reasons not intimately related to acceptance of national law.

National leaders in the independent state regarded the uses of law variously, depending often upon their institutional perspectives and their perception of political priorities. Professional bureaucrats were generally committed to the legal traditions of the colony, and increasingly came under attack as their views of procedural propriety proved inadequate to political conditions and to new demands for substantive justice; hence the charge of "legalism." Political

[68] During the period of Guided Democracy it was not only "rule of law" symbols which faded but the very idea that law was essential to the political order. This point should not be exaggerated, but political leaders, Sukarno among them, tended to ignore legislative functions and even enforcement in favor of other kinds of political activity, often of a symbolic sort. It is noteworthy that during this time also the state gazette and collected statutes (*Berita Negara* and *Lembaran Negara*) fell far behind in publication (and quality of publication) so that new laws and regulations were not known for months in the provinces, and sometimes not at all.

[69] *Law in Economy and Society*, pp. 4–5. An enforcement orientation may fade into a law orientation if enforcement is sustained and the existence of rules is distinguished from the authority of the enforcers—which means, in essence, some internalization of the rules and the values behind them. The opposite process is, of course, also possible; with a breakdown of political order and morality, an orientation to law might deteriorate into an enforcement orientation, and one might argue that this is what happened during and after the Revolution in Indonesia. But this view, perhaps, ignores the relative ease with which social relations continued even when law became less significant. It may be (to offer a hypothesis) that although Indonesian political and social values could accommodate a concept of "impersonal" law, in conjunction with traditionally familiar enforcement institutions— which was the case in the colony—they did not depend upon formal law as a significant integrative mechanism.

leaders and intellectuals who understood development primarily in economic terms also tended to emphasize the advantages of control which legal processes might offer. So did various minority groups, who saw protection in law. During the early 1950's the parliamentary system tended to promote symbols favorable to the "rule of law," even as existing legal processes were being strained, because the language of parliamentarism and the language of formal law were closely related.

Sukarno, as we have seen, was much more concerned with the language of traditional political values, which during the period of Guided Democracy became increasingly explicit. Their effect, along with economic pressure and the struggle for political survival, was to release government officials themselves from any obligation to obey the law.[70] Nor were national leaders particularly weakened by this, but may in fact have enjoyed some advantage, like Sukarno himself, from the appeal to symbols of power more persuasive than anything formal law could offer. What they ultimately sacrificed— apart from their positions, which many lost following the coup— was political and administrative control, the power to do much more than remain in office. Legislative output did not decline drastically, but enforcement was less heeded and became less likely, and the bureaucracy, itself suffering from economic deprivation and lack of moral support, rearranged itself (also in terms that were traditionally comprehensible) the better to take care of its members rather than to execute policy.

Yet the idea of national law is taken for granted as an irrevocable attribute of the state. Within the boundaries of that idea are in-

[70] In much of Asia where bureaucratic political systems developed, governing classes did not regard themselves bound by written laws intended for their subjects. Some of what Eberhard says of China can also be said of Java: "Confucianists always maintained that laws are essentially for the lower classes and should not be necessary for the gentleman. He should be motivated and guided by his concepts of honor and propriety, which are rooted in his concepts of class and class obligations. . . . A true Confucianist is not afraid of deities, ghosts, or spirits, but he is afraid of upsetting the cosmic or social order. Like the religious person, he has his code in his heart, he has internalized his social code. He feels ashamed not only in case of exposure, but even if no one knows of his bad actions—or at least he is expected to feel this way." Wolfram Eberhard, *Guilt and Sin in Traditional China* (Berkeley and Los Angeles: University of California Press, 1967), p. 124.

cluded legal concepts originally taken over from Europe, implanted in formal law roles, and still taught in law faculties. Some of these concepts have proved exceedingly tenacious, despite challenge.[71] The values they imply represent a subordinate part of Indonesian culture; they are in large measure bound up with the notion of the state and are likely to evolve with it.

Secularization

Secularization is one apparent theme of Indonesian political evolution which may strengthen the influence of formal law. "Theme" is meant to suggest not a straight-line development but a tug of war between contradictory forces, complex clusters of conflicting pulls, in which one side seems to be winning but is never completely victorious. One can think of various such oppositions in modern social-legal systems: personal rights versus state authority, centralization versus decentralization, private versus public economic control, and so on.

As the term is used here, secularization refers to changing *national* patterns of political and legal relationships.[72] It does not mean that the influence of religion is rapidly diminishing in Indonesia. Religious bonds remain crucial to social integration (and disintegration) within the several ethnic groups and across ethnic lines as well. Nor is the urban elite fully secular, though it may be coming gradually to depend for its authority upon the achievement of sec-

---

[71] Two rather over-dramatic examples, among many that are available, may illustrate this tenacity. The first has to do with the incongruity of actual status relations and the status concepts inherent in the inherited formal law. There is no question of bringing the law into line with reality, anymore than in most European countries. The notion of legal equality is too much a part of elite doctrine, though it is not very influential in the elite's world-view. The second example involves the problem of black magic (*guna-guna*) which is common throughout Indonesia. There are men, including some lawyers, who feel that the law should make it possible to investigate and settle cases of black magic. But when asked how the matter can be handled, those who worry about it tend to agree with some frustration that it is impossible precisely because of the evidentiary impasse; law or no law, the rule of tangible evidence of a causal relationship between intent and consequence is too deeply imbedded in the legal values of the educated elite to be overthrown. Such matters therefore have to be dealt with outside the formal law altogether.

[72] It might also be applied to changes occurring within Indonesian Islam, but this important matter will not be discussed here.

ular objectives. Rather what is argued here is that a myth of religious and ethnic neutrality is becoming more pronounced in internal political procedures of the state and in cognitive perceptions by leadership groups of the preconditions of national governance.

The legal framework of the Indonesian state is secular, even though common political and legal conceptions may not be. Whatever other consequences it had for Indonesian social and economic history, colonialism established national patterns of social and legal transaction which avoided the danger, pointed out long ago by Maine, of rigid law associated with religion.[73] National unity after independence depended partly upon the maintenance of those patterns and the behavioral norms which they assumed. In addition the inherited legal system has served a passive political function. It represents a status quo advantage for those who oppose the political and legal claims of Islam, for example. This means equally that the status quo cannot be altered radically in favor of other religious or, for that matter, ethnic interests. In essence, any attempt to use the law explicitly for either religious or ethnic purposes—i.e., to institutionalize a sectarian advantage *de novo*—is all but ruled out.[74] It is partly for this reason also that political and ideological conflict in independent Indonesia, which has been over who would be entitled to make law forevermore, could not be contained by existing legal processes; the legal system was predicated on the assumption, no longer valid, that this fundamental issue was already resolved.

Even so, secular legal conceptions and their derivative official roles are as appropriate to many political and social characteristics of national life as they were in the colony. Indonesia is held together not only by nationalism but also structurally by the large commercial cities which dot the archipelago.[75] These cities, whose

[73] Henry Sumner Maine, *Ancient Law* (1861; Boston: Beacon ed., 1963), pp. 74–75.

[74] In reality this gives non-Islamic Javanese views an advantage in fleshing out the legal system. Even so, a symbolic neutrality must be maintained, and by and large it is.

[75] These cities—among them Djakarta, Bandung, Semarang, Surabaja, Medan, Palembang, Padang, Bandjarmasin, and Makasar—and their elites have played a significant integrative role in the independent state. Developed largely by the Dutch, the character of their relationships was determined by the secular concerns of the colony and still tends in that direction. See Norton S. Ginsberg, "The Great City in Southeast Asia," *American Journal*

relations have usually been influenced by trade, have produced a Dutch- (now decreasingly) and Indonesian-speaking elite capable of working together more or less tolerantly for mutual advantage despite cultural frictions. A major prerequisite for the continuing integrity of this national leadership group, however, is that ethnic and religious issues must not be raised too strenuously, and tacit balancing and bargaining possibilities must be admitted with sufficient clarity to all powerful political participants. Even Java's domination of Indonesia must be toned down and made subtle.

The religious, ethnic, and geographical diversity of Indonesia, its inescapable pluralism, requires reasonably neutral political norms to keep the state whole and in relative peace. As different cultures have been thrown into banging contact with one another since independence, ideological politics have strained accommodations to the breaking point. The institutions of national politics have at times tended as much to promote violence, by articulating traditional cleavages, as to contain it. As Sukarno originally conceived it, Guided Democracy was partly an effort to transcend inherently divisive issues in favor of a unifying ideology which would submerge them. It failed. The army's rise to power, immediate causes aside, can be interpreted in this light. Not only is the army Indonesia's most powerful organization, it is also somewhat more capable than others of transcending, or at least containing, traditionally divisive conflict. It is both an integrative institution and, in the perspective of primordial social conflict, relatively neutral.

None of this discussion should be taken to imply that ideological conflict will stop or that eventually it will be contained fully within the evolving legal system. Few legal orders are that complete. At the level of national urban politics, however, one fundamental value of the legal system may be state neutrality toward certain cultural interests, a value supported in the foreseeable future by an insufficiency of central power and authority to enforce anything else. The symbolic emphasis on the "rule of law" since late 1965, however weak legal control is in reality, may reflect this concern to

of Sociology, 60, no. 5 (March 1955), 455–463; also Pauline D. Milone, _Urban Areas in Indonesia: Administrative and Census Concepts_, Institute of International Studies Research Series no. 10 (Berkeley: University of California, 1966).

effectuate a more secular medium of national political and social intercourse.

Integration

The urge to national unity represents the closest thing to a consistent public policy in postrevolutionary Indonesia. Efforts to create a unified state have given rise to intense conflict and to new motivating visions of national society. The latter animus, complicated by competing claims to legitimacy, has been equally evident in ideological and legal activity, both of which are concerned with fashioning appropriate symbolic orders for the new state.[76] Since 1945, "unification"—along with a subtheme of "modernization"—has become the major motif of legal change.[77] Another theme, less explicit, is the expansion of central authority.

In constitutional terms the force of these concerns was manifested in the victory of unitarism over federalism and in the ultimate refusal to implement fully the decentralization law of 1957. It is also evident in the substance and style of all other significant legislation. In the colony differential law was natural. Legal notions from that period were too deeply ingrained to be rejected altogether, and after independence adat especially continued to be paid lip-service, sometimes romantically and sometimes politically, despite the social fragmentation it represents, because it also symbolizes a specifically Indonesian identity. (More subtly, adat is also a symbol of opposition to the expansion of Islam.) But basically, legal diversity, because of the social, political and cultural diversity which it reflects, has been anathema for Djakarta. From the time of the Revolution social differences have not been admitted in new law. The racial criteria which had informed Netherlands Indies

[76] Geertz's discussion of ideology as metaphor can also be applied to law in its nontechnical aspects. See C. Geertz, "Ideology as a Cultural System," in D. Apter, ed., *Ideology and Discontent* (New York: Free Press, 1964). Law does not describe the reality of social relations, but rather is a representation of them, whose acceptance or nonacceptance as social myth determines the validity of the legal order generally.

[77] The fullest and most explicit presentation of such views is in a speech by Supomo in 1947, *Kedudukan Hukum Adat dikemudian Hari* (Djakarta: Pustaka Rakjat, 1959). See also Gouw Giok Siong, "De Rechtsontwikkeling in Indonesië na de Souvereiniteitsoverdracht," in *Weekblad voor Privaatrecht, Notaris-ambt en Registratie,* Feb. 10, 17, and 24, 1968.

legislation were dropped as a matter of public policy. They continued tacitly, however, in the negative form now of discrimination, mainly against Chinese; at the same time an ambivalent reverse policy of assimilation has gathered momentum. But the positive law of independent Indonesia is nearly all nationally applicable, a mark of reluctance to make exceptions for local differences which might contain "separatist" potential and, too, of an ambition to override local and racial differences in favor of national unity. National law is itself symbolic of that unity.[78]

Similarly local institutions which would seem to deny the universality of national authority have been done away with as much as possible. Just as the Java-based pamong pradja was extended to the entire archipelago, in much of which it was unfamiliar and consequently weak, so the national judicial system has been imposed (with more success) in areas where only customary courts had previously had jurisdiction. By 1960, all remaining traditional courts had been abolished and replaced with pengadilan negeri.

Other institutions inherited from the colony have been less easy to deal with because they serve national minorities; the civil registry and the *weeskamer* (guarantor of orphans' estates), for example, have been resented for their exclusiveness, a reminder of special privileges primarily for Europeans, Chinese, and Christians. At times it has been proposed that these extraordinary institutions be abolished, and during the peak years of Guided Democracy, Minister of Justice Astrawinata actually started to move in that direction. But the issue has never been so simple. While concern for integration along with resentment of advantaged minorities might indicate mere abolition, the additional desire for modernization requires, on the contrary, that these institutional services be extended to everyone alike. In the Eight Year Plan of 1960 (itself largely a symbolic enterprise) an earlier Minister of Justice proposed precisely this with respect to the civil registry. Since 1965, this policy has been taken for granted; the expansion awaits funds and energy, but the principle has been established.

[78] The term *hukum nasional* (national law) has two connotations: one meaning exactly that, national in contrast with local law; the other, more prevalent during the last two decades, meaning the law of independent Indonesia as opposed to law originating in the colony.

Efforts to unify matrimonial law reflect similar but far more complex pressures. Chinese and Christians (including Chinese Christians) have sometimes feared that unified personal law might be "leveled down" to the requirements of common Indonesians, perhaps even permitting Islamic influences to creep into their lives.[79] It was this threat more than a denial of legal services which alarmed those who opposed the abolition of institutions like the weeskamer. Islamic groups, on the other hand, have also opposed attempts to unify the law of marriage and divorce, which always represent reformist challenges to such Islamic institutions as polygamy and easy divorce. In 1956, Islamic parties in Parliament defeated a new marriage bill with those objectives. Thus both Christian and Islamic leaders fear the consequences of a unified statute, unless there is some assurance that it will express their religious views. Recently Christian groups, desiring the guarantees of new legislation, took some initiative in proposing the following solution: one basic statute with a few common principles accompanied by separate marriage laws for each major religion (Islam, Catholicism, Protestantism, and Balinese Hinduism) and a mixed marriage law. There is still opposition from some Islamic groups. But even if the laws are eventually passed, the situation will not be greatly different from what it is now and has been since colonial times, except that Islamic and Balinese marriage rules will be "nationalized"—which indeed is one goal of codification. But few fundamental changes will have been worked in family law, in which moreover the major religions will retain fairly complete autonomy. Some law professionals and intellectuals regard separate legislation as a step backward on the road to unity, one that will also make it more difficult to mod-

---

[79] It will be remembered that the major religious groups have quite different formal family law arrangements. While Islamic matrimonial matters are taken care of by the Islamic bureaucracy, now headed by the Ministry of Religion, Christians are served by a civil registry maintained autonomously by the central government. See Huwelijksordonnantie Christen-Indonesiers Java, Minahasa en Amboina (1933), Reglement Burgerlijke Stand Christen-Indonesiers (1933), and the Regeling op de Gemengde Huwelijken [mixed marriages] (1896). On Islamic marriage law, see Th. W. Juynboll, *Handleiding tot de Kennis van de Mohammedaansche Wet* (Leiden: Brill, 1930). Also Nani Soewondo-Soerasno, *Kedudukan Wanita Indonesia dalam Hukum dan Masjarakat* (Djakarta: Timun Mas, 1955), and Cora Vreede-de Stuers, *The Indonesian Woman* (The Hague: Mouton, 1960).

ernize Islamic marriage law. However, given the "neutral norms" argument mentioned in our discussion of secularization—which here results in an apparently contradictory outcome—this is probably about all that can be expected for the present.

A manifestation of the unification theme less obvious to the public appears in the work of Indonesian courts, above all the Supreme Court, which has been subject to the same ideological urges to unity and is freer from the political limitations of legislative bodies. Until recently jurisprudential innovation in the courts has been related mainly to adat, partly because here civil law strictures on judicial interference with written law do not apply. During the late 1950's and 1960's the Supreme Court embarked on two related lines of change with respect to inheritance, which for most Indonesians is governed by adat law.[80] First, widows in Java were recognized, with some qualifications, as heirs of their deceased husbands. The second tack was more radical and created a stir for a time in North Sumatra. Bilateral inheritance rules were extended to the patrilineal Batak of North Sumatra and, furthermore, to all other groups in Indonesia.[81] Women everywhere were accorded a right, not always clearly defined, to inherit property. The reasoning behind these decisions was that, "on the Supreme Court's own knowledge," adat law at the present time everywhere in Indonesia recognizes inheritance and other rights for women. More fundamentally, the decisions reflected the sense of justice and desire for modernization of a large part of the educated urban elite.

With these judgments, the whole edifice of colonial adat jurisprudence began to crumble before the idea of national unity; the decline of colonial conflicts theory naturally followed. Supreme Court judges, partly because of ideological pressure—the hukum revolusi—began to liberate themselves from older judicial norms. Increasingly, they spoke not of discovering adat law but of seeking

[80] See Lev, "The Supreme Court and *Adat* Inheritance Law in Indonesia."

[81] Although Batak leaders protested the ruling in public meetings in Medan, one of which the then Supreme Court Chairman Wirjono Prodjodikoro attended, coming under considerable verbal attack, there are also urban Batak intellectuals and professionals in Medan and Djakarta who disagree with the older traditions and do not feel particularly bound by them. Such judicial decisions, or innovative legislation, would have very little significance did not some initial social support exist for the trends they represent.

out the "sense of justice" of the people and even of applying their own sense of justice. These views favor a nationalization of adat, or rather a subordination of traditional law to nationally oriented legal conceptions and policy directions.[82] In the colony, ter Haar had located the source of adat law in decisions of traditional leaders, in recognition of the close association between law and authority; law, specifically adat law, was thus tied to local communities and their political orders. It is this that has disappeared in presently evolving conceptions of the place of adat law. The determining authority is now the national government, and the fundamental source of law is something very close to the *imperium*.

In recent years courts have also gone beyond adat to examine civil code rules of family law. This development was stimulated by a Supreme Court declaration in 1963 that the civil code would henceforth be regarded only as a guide to the "adat law" of those to whom the code had formerly applied.[83] In the same year a couple of Chinese descent asked the Djakarta pengadilan negeri to validate their adoption of an infant girl from a Hong Kong orphanage. But the law of Chinese adoption, in a statutory exception to common civil code rules, permitted adoption only of boys, on an early (and probably mistaken) assumption that Chinese patrilin-

[82] It is worth mentioning that similar views have been present in Islamic scholarly circles since the first decades of this century, largely as a result of influences from the Islamic reform movement led by Muhammad Abduh. A few Islamic scholars have proposed either that Indonesia create its own madhab or that a freer selection of rules from all existing madhab, rather than that of Sjafi'i only, should be encouraged. Both arguments would favor a further Indonesianization of Islamic law. But these ideas are still of more limited influence in Indonesia than in many other Islamic countries, where family law reform has been relatively rapid in recent decades. The conservatism of Indonesian Islam in this respect is partly due to its continual involvement in political and ideological conflict; any reform concession is made to appear as a surrender of principle to non-Islamic forces. See Hazairin, *Hendak Kemana Hukum Islam?* (Djakarta: Tintamas, 1960), and *Hukum Kekeluargaan Nasional* (Djakarta: Tintamas, 1962); Notosusanto, *Organisasi dan Jurisprudensi Peradilan Agama di Indonesia* (Jogjakarta: Jajasan Badan Penerbit Gadjah Mada, 1963); T. M. Hasbi Ash-Shiddieqy, *Sjari'at Islam Mendjawab Tantangan Zaman* (Jogjakarta: Penerbitan IAIN, 1962); and Mahmud Junus, *Hukum Perkawinan dalam Islam menurut Mazhab Sjafi'i, Hanafi, Maliki, dan Hanbali* (Djakarta: Pustaka Mahmudiah, 1956).

[83] See D. Lev, "The Lady and the Banyan Tree: Civil Law Change in Indonesia," *Amer. J. Comp. Law*, 14, no. 2 (1965), 282–307.

ealism forbade adoption of girls. As the civil code and related statutes were no longer fully binding, the judge in this case—Asikin
Kusumaatmadja, son of Indonesia's first Supreme Court Chairman
and himself now a member of the Court—undertook to examine
whether the old rule remained socially valid. Chinese witnesses
called to court agreed that patrilineal family organization was no
longer so influential among Indonesian Chinese and that adoption
of girls had become permissible.[84] The decision, which followed this
view, explicitly condemned colonial policies of racial distinction
and espoused modern emphases upon equal rights for men and
women.

The integrative thrust of all these decisions, as well as much new
legislation, contains several influences likely to remain for some
time to come. Among them is what is called the "international
standard," which indicates a continuing regard by the national elite
for the judgment of the outside, particularly the European, world.
Another more fundamental influence may be the expansion outward
of Javanese legal views and criteria of social development—bilateral family structure, for instance—via a national political and
legal order dominated by Javanese and others who are often attracted by Java or at least see Indonesia from the perspective of
Djakarta, itself deeply influenced by Java. The ambivalent respect
which other ethnic groups have for Javanese culture tends as much
to promote this expansion as to obstruct it.

So far we have been looking at legal change from the top down.
But what effect do the above decisions or nationally conceived
statutes have on most people? Do they obey, older legal conceptions
to the contrary notwithstanding? Or is national law simply rejected
when it is inconsistent with assumptions made by different social
orders? And finally, are there buffers between local law and national law, protecting the one from insensitivity to tradition and
the other from disobedience and challenges to authority?

---

[84] The witnesses and claimants were careful to argue, however, that in
every respect other than the adoption of girls the old civil code rules were
adequate to Chinese legal needs and values (decision of May 29, 1963,
no. 907/1963 P, typescript). A second decision in this case was necessary
to compel a Djakarta notary to draft an act of adoption (Oct. 17, 1963,
no. 588/63 G, typescript). For the original rule allowing adoption of sons
only, see *Staatsblad* 1917—129, article 5 (1).

The first two questions, which cannot be dealt with at length here, depend in part on the last question, which is a critical one for the analysis of legal systems. In Indonesia, as elsewhere, there are significant buffers, whose effectiveness is made greater by the central government's lack of overwhelming organizational power to enforce its will. This may be an endemic problem in the structure of Indonesian politics; lines of authority stretching out from Djakarta tend to bend and sometimes break not far from the city limits. Countervailing pressures within national administrative and political hierarchies are very strong. Just as the army represents both an integrating and a decentralizing force—local military units defending local interests—so the national judiciary, public prosecution, police, pamong pradja, and so on contain contradictory organizational tendencies. Whereas Supreme Court judges in Djakarta lean toward a perspective that is national, unifying, and uniformizing, judges in the pengadilan negeri (and less so the intermediary pengadilan tinggi) are more influenced by what they understand to be the needs of their local clienteles. Although lower judges may often be sympathtic to new legal trends, many still accuse the Supreme Court of being too strongly inclined toward "Western law" and bent upon ruling into adat law tendencies that are not there. Basically such expressions of discomfort reflect a tension between the momentum of national integration on the one hand and local participation on the other.

Lower courts, however, like administrative units, can be overruled from above. When this happens local interests may protest, as Batak leaders did following the Supreme Court's inheritance decisions. The Court held to its ruling, but this does not mean of course that all groups to which the ruling ultimately applies have relinquished their conceptions of proper family structure and law.

What it does mean is that those who seek change now have an additional resort. This is another facet of the argument made earlier with respect to changing patterns of conciliation. In the past (and still today) a person could in effect opt out of his traditional community through religious conversion, to Islam or Christianity, for example, thus partially redefining his community and his law. In almost the same way now, but in a political rather than a religious dimension, men can opt for the advantages of nationally oriented jurisdictions. Adjudication represents only one of several possibilities here, and a rather limited one at that. Membership in the army, political parties, various kinds of private associations, and other "national" organizations may offer wider and more far-reaching alternatives.

None of this means that a national perspective is winning out overwhelmingly, or that men are fleeing to national institutions at the least provocation. Frequently the opposite is true; local and religious loyalties remain very strong, and in different times and conditions may be as likely to flow as to ebb. Rather, the point is that national institutions and the outlooks they promote are available, and in a period of considerable social change it can be assumed they will be used with more or less enthusiasm. As they are used these institutions cannot help but be influenced over time by demands made upon them to serve local needs and values as well.

THE LIMITS OF LAW

Law, like water, finds its own level. Not only does the level differ from society to society, but it changes within societies. In new states it is less the decline of law than the rise of politics that demands attention. Conflict over economic resources, redistribution of authority and status, and the creation and accumulation of political power are all peculiarly political problems of the first order. Attempts to deal with them through institutions of "impersonal" law, as Ralf Dahrendorf has argued with respect to less explosive issues of labor conflict in industrialized Western countries, cannot be lastingly productive.[85] In some new states legal solutions are also likely to be irrelevant. What is contested, in an important sense, is the existing legal system itself, linked as it is with the structure of political authority, and existing law, which necessarily represents the status quo of economic- and social-resource allocation.

This does not mean that only political order based on a reasonable social consensus is necessary before new states begin to use law as it is used in Europe and North America. The assumption, or the hope, that this will be so is often apparent in analyses of polit-

[85] Ralf Dahrendorf, *Class and Class Conflict in Industrial Society* (Stanford: Stanford University Press, 1959).

ical development in Asia and Africa. But the very term "law" is hypnotically misleading. The uses of law vary enormously among states where powerful legal traditions exist. They will undoubtedly vary as much among new states, depending on degrees of social and political heterogeneity, elite structure, bureaucratic development, and cultural receptivity. But this point aside, a preoccupation with the postcolonial "decline of law," on the part of lawyers and intellectuals in the West and the non-West alike, almost inevitably starts from a conception (or misconception) of the way law works in one society—hence the frequent confusion of legal process with democratic politics and civil rights, because of the prestige of American and English examples—and ignores the extent to which social functions may be served by more than one kind of institution.[86] The evident weakness of formal legal institutions in new states may mean no more than that they happen to be weaker than other institutions. These other institutions may or may not be performing similar functions equally well. Or, of course, all kinds of institutions in a given society may be working equally badly. If so, it makes less sense to focus on the absence of a strong legal system, given differences in legal culture, than on the poor performance of other social and political institutions with deeper indigenous roots. This point applies particularly to analyses of the failure of new states to take advantage of legal institutions as instruments of broad-scale social change. In some states legal institutions may in fact play a significant role in encouraging certain kinds of change, as in the case of the Indonesian Supreme Court's handling of inheritance issues. But for the most fundamental sorts of change law probably is

[86] For example, as the number of practicing advocates indicates, Englishmen rely much less than Americans on the use of the judicial system for dispute settlement, though it is unlikely that there are proportionately more disputes in the United States than in England. While in the United States there is a strong tendency to pull major social and political issues into legal channels, this is much less true of England. Brian Abel-Smith and Robert Stevens mention that "if possible, constitutional issues in England are settled outside the courts as political or social, rather than legal questions. . . . Even civil liberties, traditionally thought of in connection with the common law, insofar as they are protected, are protected primarily by political and social pressures rather than by any activities of the courts" (*Lawyers and the Courts* [Cambridge: Harvard University Press], p. 1).

always of limited value, though in some societies less so than in others.[87] Where cultural myths and values have emphasized means of social-political regulation and intercourse other than an autonomous sphere of law, legal institutions are consequently less likely to develop the kind of independent power they have in a few European countries and the United States. Even the emergence of powerful bureaucratic establishments, essential to strong legal systems, cannot alone create common positive orientations to legal processes, especially, for example, when patrimonial values also remain strong.

But in itself the presence or absence of a strong legal system and a cultural emphasis upon legal process says little about the quality of social and political life. This does not render law less interesting as a focus of research or less important as a potential social resource, but it does put it in the more humble and dependent place in social life where it belongs.

What I hope to have shown in this essay is that the social scientist's main contribution to understanding legal institutions will come primarily from the broader perspective he brings to law as it is linked to essential bases of political authority, economic behavior, social structure, and culture. Nowhere are these relationships made clearer than in new states, where inherited legal institutions are compelled to adapt to fundamentally changed social circumstances.

---

[87] See the discussion of the Soviet failure to restructure family relationships in Central Asia through legal institutions, in Gregory Massell, "Law as an Instrument of Revolutionary Change in a Traditional Milieu: The Case of Soviet Central Asia," *LSR*, 2, no. 2 (1968), 179–228.

Afterword:
The Politics of Meaning

✧✧✧✧✧✧✧✧✧

Clifford Geertz

1

One of the things that everyone knows but no one can quite
think how to demonstrate is that a country's politics reflect the
design of its culture. At one level, the proposition is indubitable—
where else could French politics exist but France? Yet, merely to
state it is to raise doubts. Since 1945, Indonesia has seen revolution,
parliamentary democracy, civil war, presidential autocracy, mass
murder, and military rule. Where is the design on that?

Between the stream of events that make up political life and the
web of beliefs that comprises a culture it is difficult to find a middle
term. On the one hand, everything looks like a clutter of schemes
and surprises; on the other, like a vast geometry of settled judgments. What joins such a chaos of incident to such a cosmos of
sentiment is extremely obscure, and how to formulate it is even
more so. Above all, what the attempt to link politics and culture
needs is a less breathless view of the former and a less aesthetic
view of the latter.

In the chapters of this book, the sort of theoretical reconstruction
necessary to produce such a change of perspective is undertaken,
mainly from the cultural side by Anderson and Abdullah, mainly
from the political by Lev and Liddle, more or less evenly from both
by Sartono. Whether the subject be law or party organization, the
Javanese idea of power or the Minangkabau idea of change, ethnic
conflict or rural radicalism, the effort is the same: to render Indonesian political life intelligible by seeing it, even at its most erratic,

as informed by a set of conceptions—ideals, hypotheses, obsessions, judgments—derived from concerns which far transcend it, and to give reality to those conceptions by seeing them as having their existence not in some gauzy world of mental forms but in the concrete immediacy of partisan struggle. Culture, here, is not cults and customs, but the structures of meaning through which men give shape to their experience; and politics is not coups and constitutions, but one of the principal arenas in which such structures publicly unfold. Thus reframed, determining the connection between the two becomes a practicable enterprise, though hardly a modest one.

The reason the enterprise is immodest, or anyway especially venturesome, is that there is almost no theoretical apparatus with which to conduct it; the whole field—what shall we call it? thematic analysis?—is wedded to an ethic of imprecision. Most attempts to find general cultural conceptions displayed in particular social contexts are content to be merely evocative, to place a series of concrete observations in immediate juxtaposition and to pull out (or read in) the pervading element by rhetorical suggestion. Explicit argument is rare because there are, as much by design as neglect, hardly any terms in which to cast it, and one is left with a collection of anecdotes connected by insinuation, and with a feeling that though much has been touched little has been grasped.[1]

The scholar who wishes to avoid this sort of perfected impressionism has thus to build his theoretical scaffold at the same time as he conducts his analysis. That is why the authors in this book have such diverse approaches—why Liddle moves out from group conflicts and Anderson from art and literature; why Lev's puzzle is the politicization of legal institutions, Sartono's the durability of popular millenarianism, Abdullah's the fusion of social conservatism and ideological dynamism. The unity here is neither of topic nor argument, but of analytical style—of aim and of the methodological issues the pursuit of such an aim entails.

These issues are multiple, involving questions of definition, verification, causality, representativeness, objectivity, measurement,

---

[1] Perhaps the foremost, as well as the most uncompromising, practitioner of this paratactic approach to relating politics to culture is Nathan Leites. See especially his A Study of Bolshevism (Glencoe, Ill.: Free Press, 1953), and The Rules of the Game in Paris (Chicago: University of Chicago Press, 1969).

communication. But at base they all boil down to one question: how to frame an analysis of meaning—the conceptual structures individuals use to construe experience—which will be at once circumstantial enough to carry conviction and abstract enough to forward theory. These are equal necessities; choosing one at the expense of the other yields blank descriptivism or vacant generality. But they also, superficially at least, pull in opposite directions, for the more one invokes details the more he is bound to the peculiarities of the immediate case, the more one omits them the more he loses touch with the ground on which his arguments rest. Discovering how to escape this paradox—or more exactly, for one never really escapes it, how to keep it at bay—is what, methodologically, thematic analysis is all about.

And it is, consequently, what, beyond the particular findings concerning particular subjects, this book is about. Each study struggles to draw broad generalizations out of special instances, to penetrate deeply enough into detail to discover something more than detail. The strategies adopted to accomplish this are again various, but the effort to make parochial bodies of material speak for more than themselves is uniform. The scene is Indonesia; but the goal, still far enough away to sustain ambition, is an understanding of how it is that every people gets the politics it imagines.

2

Indonesia is an excellent place to take up such a quest. As heir to Polynesian, Indic, Islamic, Chinese, and European traditions, it probably has more hieratic symbols per square foot than any other large land expanse in the world, and moreover it had in Sukarno (who it is a mistake to think was untypical in anything but his genius) a man both wildly anxious and supremely equipped to assemble those symbols into a pandoctrinal *Staatsreligion* for the newformed Republic. "Socialism, Communism, incarnations of Vishnu Murti," a newspaper call to arms cried in 1921: "Abolish capitalism, propped up by the imperialism that is its slave! God grant Islam the strength that it may succeed." [2] "I am a follower of Karl Marx . . . I am also a religious man," Sukarno announced some decades

---

[2] Quoted (from *Utusan Hindia*) in Bernhard Dahm, *Sukarno and the Struggle for Indonesian Independence* (Ithaca, N.Y.: Cornell University Press, 1969), p. 39.

later, "I have made myself the meeting place of all trends and
ideologies. I have blended, blended, and blended them until finally
they became the present Sukarno." [3]

Yet, on the other hand, the very density and variety of symbolic
reference has made of Indonesian culture a swirl of tropes and
images into which more than one incautious observer has merely
disappeared.[4] With so much meaning lying scattered openly around
it is nearly impossible to frame an argument relating political
events to one or another strain of it which is totally lacking in
plausibility. In one sense, seeing cultural reflections in political activities is extremely easy in Indonesia; but this only makes the
isolation of precise connections that much more difficult. Because
in this garden of metaphors almost any hypothesis discerning a
form of thought in a piece of action has a certain logic, developing
hypotheses which have truth as well is more a matter of resisting
temptations than of seizing opportunities.

The main temptation to be resisted is jumping to conclusions
and the main defense against it is explicitly to trace out the sociological links between cultural themes and political developments
rather than to move deductively from one to the other. Ideas—
religious, moral, practical, aesthetic—must, as Max Weber, among
others, never tired of insisting, be carried by powerful social groups
to have powerful social effects; someone must revere them, celebrate them, defend them, impose them. They have to be institutionalized in order to find not just an intellectual existence in society but, so to speak, a material one as well. The ideological wars
which have wracked Indonesia for the past twenty-five years must
be seen not, as they so often have, as clashes of opposed mentalities
—Javanese "mysticism" versus Sumatran "pragmatism," Indic "syncretism" versus Islamic "dogmatism"—but as the substance of a
struggle to create an institutional structure for the country that
enough of its citizens would find sufficiently congenial to allow it to
function.

[3] Quoted in Louis Fischer, *The Story of Indonesia* (New York: Harper,
1959), p. 154. For a similar statement from a public speech of Sukarno, see
Dahm, p. 200.

[4] For an example, see Herbert Luethy "Indonesia Confronted," *Encounter*,
25 (Dec. 1965), 80–89; 26 (Jan. 1966) 75–83, along with my comment
"Are the Javanese Mad?" and Luethy's "Reply," *ibid.*, Aug. 1966, pp.
86–90.

Hundreds of thousands of political dead testify to the fact that nowhere nearly enough did, and it remains a question how far they do so now. Organizing a cultural hodgepodge into a workable polity is more than a matter of inventing a promiscuous civil religion to blunt its variety. It requires either the establishment of political institutions within which opposing groups can safely contend, or of the elimination of all groups but one from the political stage. Neither of these has, so far, been more than marginally effected in Indonesia; the country has been as incapable of totalitarianism as of constitutionalism. Rather, almost every institution in the society—army, bureaucracy, court, university, press, party, religion, village—has been swept by great tremors of ideological passion which seem to have neither end nor direction. If Indonesia gives any overall impression, it is of a state manqué, a country which, unable to find a political form appropriate to the temper of its people, stumbles on apprehensively from one institutional contrivance to the next.

A great part of the problem, of course, is that the country is archipelagic in more than geography. Insofar as it displays a pervasive temper, it is one riven with internal contrasts and contradictions. There are the regional differences (the rhetorical combativeness of the Minangkabau and the reflective elusiveness of the Javanese, for example); there are the faith-and-custom "ethnic" divergences among even closely related groups, as in the East Sumatran "boiling pot"; there are the class conflicts reflected in the nativistic movement material and the vocational ones reflected in that of the struggle for a workable legal system. There are racial minorities (Chinese and Papuans); religious minorities (Christians and Hindus); local minorities (Djakarta Batak, Surabaja Madurese). The nationalist slogan, "One People, One Country, One Language," is a hope, not a description.

The hope that the slogan represents, however, is not necessarily unreasonable. Most of the larger nations of Europe grew out of a cultural heterogeneity hardly less marked; if Tuscans and Sicilians can live together in the same state and conceive of themselves as natural compatriots, so can Javanese and Minangkabau. Rather than the mere fact of internal diversity, it has been the refusal, at all levels of the society, to come to terms with it that has impeded

Indonesia's search for effective political form. The diversity has been denied as a colonial slander, deplored as a feudal remnant, clouded over with ersatz syncretisms, tendentious history, and utopian fantasies, while all the time the bitter combat of groups who see in one another rivals not merely for political and economic power, but for the right to define truth, justice, beauty, and morality, the very nature of reality, rages on virtually unguided by formal political institutions. By acting as though it were culturally homogeneous like Japan or Egypt instead of heterogeneous like India or Nigeria, Indonesia (or more exactly, I suppose, the Indonesian elite) has managed to create a near anarchic politics of meaning outside the established structures of civil government.

This politics of meaning is anarchic in the literal sense of unruled, not the popular one of un-ordered. As each of the essays in this volume shows in its own way, what I have elsewhere called "the struggle for the real," the attempt to impose upon the world a particular conception of how things at bottom are and how men are therefore obliged to act, is, for all the inability thus far to bring it to workable institutional expression, not a mere chaos of zeal and prejudice. It has a shape, trajectory, and force of its own.

The political processes of all nations are wider and deeper than the formal institutions designed to regulate them; some of the most critical decisions concerning the direction of public life are not made in parliaments and presidiums; they are made in the unformalized realms of what Durkheim called "the collective conscience" (or "consciousness"; the useful ambiguity of *conscience* is unavailable in English). But in Indonesia the pattern of official life and the framework of popular sentiment within which it sits have become so disjoined that the activities of government, though centrally important, seem nevertheless almost beside the point, mere routinisms convulsed again and again by sudden irruptions from the screened-off (one almost wants to say, repressed) political course along which the country is in fact moving.

The more accessible events of public life, political facts in the narrower sense, do about as much to obscure this course as to reveal it. Insofar as they reflect it, as of course they do, they do so obliquely and indirectly, as dreams reflect desires or ideologies, interests; discerning it is more like interpreting a constellation of symptoms than tracing a chain of causes. The studies in this book therefore diagnose and assess, rather than measure and predict. Fragmentation in the party system bespeaks an intensification of ethnic self-consciousness; enfeeblement of formal law, renewed commitment to conciliatory methods of dispute settlement. Behind the moral quandaries of provincial modernizers lie complexities in traditional accounts of tribal history; behind the explosiveness of rural protest, enthrallment with cataclysmic images of change; behind the theatrics of Guided Democracy, archaic conceptions of the sources of authority. Taken together, these exercises in political exegesis begin to expose the faint outlines of what the Indonesian Revolution in fact amounts to: an effort to construct a modern state in contact with its citizens' conscience; a state with which they can, in both senses of the word, come to an understanding. One of the things Sukarno was right about, though in fact he had something rather different in mind, was that it is, this Revolution, not over.

3

The classical problem of legitimacy—how do some men come to be credited with the right to rule over others—is peculiarly acute in a country in which long-term colonial domination created a political system that was national in scope but not in complexion. For a state to do more than administer privilege and defend itself against its own population, its acts must seem continuous with the selves of those whose state it pretends it is, its citizens; to be, in some stepped-up, amplified sense, *their* acts. This is not a mere question of consensus. A man does not have to agree with his government's acts to see himself as embodied in them any more than he has to approve of his own acts to acknowledge that he has, alas, himself performed them. It is a question of immediacy, of experiencing what the state "does" as proceeding naturally from a familiar and intelligible "we." A certain amount of psychological sleight-of-hand is always required on the part of government and citizenry in this in the best of cases. But when a country has been governed for two hundred years or so by foreigners, it is, even after they have been displaced, a yet more difficult trick.

The political tasks that loomed so formidable as independence was reached for—ending the domination of outside powers, creating leadership cadres, stimulating economic growth, and sustaining a sense of national unity—have indeed turned out to be that and more since independence has been gained. But they have been joined by another task, less clearly envisaged then and less consciously recognized now, that of dispelling the aura of alienness from the institutions of modern government. Much of the symbol-mongering that went on under the Sukarno regime, and which has been moderated rather than ended under its successor, was a half-deliberate attempt to close the cultural gulf between the state and society that, if not altogether created by colonial rule, had been enormously widened by it. The great crescendo of slogans, movements, monuments, and demonstrations which reached a pitch of almost hysterical intensity in the early sixties was, in part anyway, designed to make the nation-state seem indigenous. As it was not, disbelief and disorder spiraled upward together, and Sukarno was destroyed, along with his regime, in the collapse which ensued.

Even without the complicating factor of colonial rule, however, the modern state would seem alien to local tradition in a country like Indonesia, if only because such a state's conception of itself as a specialized instrument for the coordination of all aspects of public life has no real counterpart in such a tradition. Traditional rulers, and not only in Indonesia, may have been, when they could manage it and were so inclined, despotic, arbitrary, selfish, unresponsive, exploitative, or merely cruel (though, under the influence of the Cecil B. DeMille view of history, the degree to which they were has commonly been exaggerated); but they never imagined themselves, nor did their subjects imagine them, to be executives of an omnicompetent state. Mostly they governed to proclaim their status, protect (or, where possible, enlarge) their privileges, and exercise their style of life; and insofar as they regulated matters beyond their immediate reach—which was commonly very little—they did so only derivatively, as a reflex of concerns more stratificatory than properly political. The notion that the state is a machine whose function is to organize the general interest comes into such a context as something of a strange idea.

So far as popular reaction is concerned, the results of that strangeness have been the usual ones: a degree of curiosity, a degree more of fear, heightened expectancy, and a great deal of puzzlement. It was to such a confusion of sentiment that Sukarno's symbol-wielding was a failed response; but the various matters discussed in this book are others, less concocted so less ephemeral. In them, one can see in concrete detail what being abruptly confronted with the prospect of an activist, comprehensive central government —what de Jouvenel has called "the power-house state"—means to a people used to masters but not to managers.[5]

It means that the received concepts of justice, power, protest, authenticity, identity (as well, of course, as a host of others these essays do not explicitly treat) are all thrown into jeopardy by the requirements, or seeming such, of effective national existence in the contemporary world. This conceptual dislocation—the putting into question of the most familiar frames of moral and intellectual perception and the vast shift of sensibility thereby set in motion— forms the proper subject of cultural studies of new state politics. "What this country needs," Sukarno once said, in a characteristic burst of linguistic syncretism, "is *ke-up-to-date-an.*" He didn't quite give it that, merely gestures toward it, but they were gestures graphic enough to convince all but the most provincial of Indonesians that not just the form but the nature of government had changed and that they had, in result, some mental adjustments to make.[6]

4

This sort of social changing of the mind is a great deal easier to sense than to document, not only because its manifestations are so various and indirect, but because it is so hesitant, shot through with uncertainty and contradiction. For every belief, practice, ideal, or institution that is condemned as backward, one, often the same one and by the same people, is celebrated as the very essence of contemporaneity; for every one attacked as alien, one,

[5] Bertrand de Jouvenel, *On Power* (Boston: Beacon Press, 1962).

[6] The quotation is from Sukarno's letters attacking traditionalist Islam, written while he was in prison exile in Flores, *Surat-surat Dari Endeh*, eleventh letter, August 18, 1936, in K. Goenadi and H. M. Nasution, eds., *Dibawah Bendera Revolusi*, 1 (Djakarta: Panitia Penerbit Dibawah Bendera Revolusi, 1959), 340.

again often the same one, is hailed as a sacred expression of the national soul.

There is, in such matters, no simple progression from "traditional" to "modern," but a twisting, spasmodic, unmethodical movement which turns as often toward repossessing the emotions of the past as disowning them. Some of Sartono's peasants read their future in medieval myths, some in Marxist visions, some in both. Lev's lawyers waver between the formal dispassion of Justice's scales and the sheltering paternalism of the banyan tree. The publicist whose career Abdullah traces as an example of his society's reaction to the challenge of modernism, editorializes simultaneously for the restoration of "the genuine Minangkabau *adat* [custom]," and for headlong entry "unto the path of *kemadjuan* [progress]." In Java, Anderson finds "archaic-magical" and "developed-rational" theories of power existing side by side; in Sumatra, Liddle finds localism and nationalism advancing *pari passu*.

This undeniable, commonly denied, fact—that whatever the curve of progress may be, it fits no graceful formula—disables any analysis of modernization which starts from the assumption that it consists of the replacement of the indigenous and obsolescent with the imported and up-to-date. Not just in Indonesia, but throughout the Third World—throughout the world—men are increasingly drawn to a double goal: to remain themselves and to keep pace, or more, with the twentieth century. A tense conjunction of cultural conservatism and political radicalism is at the nerve of new state nationalism, and nowhere more conspicuously so than in Indonesia. What Abdullah says of the Minangkabau—that accommodating to the contemporary world has required "continuing revision of the meaning of modernization," involved "new attitudes toward tradition itself and [an unending] search for a suitable basis of modernization"— is said, in one manner or another, throughout each of our essays. What they reveal is not a linear advance from darkness to light, but a continuous redefinition of where "we" (peasants, lawyers, Christians, Javanese, Indonesians . . .) have been, now are, and have yet to go—images of group history, character, evolution, and destiny which have only to emerge to be fought over.

In Indonesia, such bending backward and forward at the same time has been apparent from the beginning of the nationalist movement and merely grown more marked since.[7] Sarekat Islam, the first really sizeable organization (its membership increased from approximately four thousand in 1912 to approximately four hundred thousand in 1914), appealed at once to visionary mystics, Islamic purists, Marxist radicals, trading-class reformers, paternal aristocrats, and messianic peasants. When this commotion disguised as a party came to pieces, as it did in the twenties, it separated not into the "reactionary" and "progressive" wings of revolutionary mythology, but into a whole series of factions, movements, ideologies, clubs, conspiracies—what Indonesians call *aliran* (streams)—seeking to fasten one or another form of modernism on to one or another strand of tradition.

"Enlightened" gentry—physicians, lawyers, schoolteachers, sons of civil servants—attempted to marry "spiritual" East and "dynamic" West by fusing a sort of cultic aestheticism with an evolutionary, *noblesse oblige* program of mass uplift. Rural religious teachers sought to transform anti-Christian sentiments into anticolonial ones, and themselves into links between urban activism and village piety. Muslim modernists tried at once to purify popular faith of heterodox accretions and work out a properly Koranic program of social and economic reform. Left-wing revolutionaries sought to identify rural collectivism and political, peasant discontent and class struggle; Eurasian half-castes to reconcile their Dutch and Indonesian identities and provide a rationale for multiracial independence; Western-educated intellectuals to reconnect themselves to Indonesian reality by tapping indigenous, antifeudal (and to some extent anti-Javanese) attitudes in the interests of democratic socialism. Everywhere one looks, in the fevered days of the nationalist awakening (ca. 1912–1950), someone is matching advanced ideas and

[7] For the history of Indonesian nationalism, on which my remarks here are but passing commentary, see J. M. Pluvier, *Overzicht van de Ontwikkeling der Nationalistische Beweging in Indonesië in de Jaren 1930 tot 1942* (The Hague: van Hoeve, 1953); A. K. Pringgodigdo, *Sedjarah Pergerakan Rakjat Indonesia* (Djakarta: Pustaka Rakjat, 1950); D. M. G. Koch, *Om de Vrijheid* (Djakarta: Jajasan Pembangunan, 1950); Dahm; George McT. Kahin, *Nationalism and Revolution in Indonesia* (Ithaca, N.Y.: Cornell University Press, 1952); Harry Benda, *The Crescent and the Rising Sun: Indonesian Islam under the Japanese Occupation, 1942–1945* (The Hague and Bandung: van Hoeve, 1958); W. F. Wertheim, *Indonesian Society in Transition* (The Hague and Bandung: van Hoeve, 1956).

familiar sentiments in order to make some variety of progress look less disruptive and some pattern of custom less dispensable.

The heterogeneity of Indonesian culture and that of modern political thought thus played into one another to produce an ideological situation in which a highly generalized consensus at one level —that the country must collectively storm the heights of modernity while clinging, also collectively, to the essentials of its heritage— was countered on another by an accelerating dissensus as to what direction the heights should be stormed from and what the essentials were. After Independence, the fragmentation of the elite and the active sectors of the population along such lines was completed as the society regrouped into competing *familles d'esprit,* some huge, some minute, some in between, which were concerned not just with governing Indonesia but with defining it.

Thus, a paralyzing incongruity grew up between the ideological framework within which the formal institutions of the would-be power-house state were constructed and operated and that within which the overall political formation of the, also would-be, nation took shape; between the "blended, blended, and blended" integralism of Guided Democracy, the Pantjasila, Nasakom, and the like and the "boiling pot" compartmentalization of popular sentiment.[8] The contrast was not a simple center and periphery one—integralism in Djakarta, compartmentalism in the provinces; but it appeared, and in not very different form, on all levels of the political system. From the village coffee shops where Sartono's peasants laid their small plans to the bureaus of Merdeka Square where Anderson's "ministeriales" laid their larger ones, political life proceeded in a curious kind of double-level way, in which a rivalry, again not

[8] For the state ideology of the Republic until the mid-sixties, see Herbert Feith, "Dynamics of Guided Democracy," in Ruth T. McVey, ed., *Indonesia* (New Haven: HRAF Press, 1963), pp. 309–409; for popular divisions, Robert R. Jay, *Religion and Politics in Rural Central Java,* Southeast Asia Studies, Cultural Report Series no. 12 (New Haven: Yale University, 1963); G. William Skinner, ed., *Local, Ethnic and National Loyalties in Village Indonesia,* Southeast Asia Studies, Cultural Report Series no. 8 (New Haven: Yale University, 1959); and R. William Liddle, *Ethnicity, Party, and National Integration* (New Haven: Yale University Press, 1970). The rather schizoid political atmosphere thus created can be sensed in the debates of the constitutional convention of 1957–1958; see *Tentang Dasar Negara Republik Indonesia Dalam Konstituante,* 3 vols. (Djakarta?, 1958?).

just for power but for the power above power—the right to specify the terms under which direction of the state, or even mere official existence, is granted—went on, wrapped in the generous phrases of common struggle, historic identity, and national brotherhood.

That is, political life proceeded in this way until October 1, 1965. The bungled coup and its savage aftermath—perhaps a quarter of a million dead in three or four months—brought to open view the cultural disarray fifty years of political change had created, advanced, dramatized, and fed upon.[9] The wash of nationalist clichés soon clouded the scene again, for one can no more stare at the abyss than at the sun. But there can be very few Indonesians now who do not know that, however clouded, the abyss is there, and they are scrambling along the edge of it, a change of awareness which may prove to be the largest step in the direction of a modern mentality they have yet made.

5

Whatever social scientists might desire, there are some social phenomena whose impact is immediate and profound, even de-

[9] The death estimate is that of John Hughes, *The End of Sukarno* (London: Angus and Robertson, 1968), p. 189. Estimates range from 50,000 to a million; no one really knows, and the killing was on so grand a scale that to debate numbers seems obtuse. Hughes' account of the coup, the massacres, and the ascendency of Suharto, though not very analytic, is probably as reliable and even-handed as any. For other discussions, from varying points of view, see R. Shaplen, *Time out of Hand* (New York: Harper, 1969); Daniel S. Lev, "Indonesia, 1965: The Year of the Coup," *Asian Survey*, 6, no. 2 (1966), 103–110; W. F. Wertheim, "Indonesia Before and After the Untung Coup," *Pacific Affairs*, 39 (1966), 115–127; Basuki Gunawan, *Kudeta: Staatsgreep in Djakarta* (Meppel: Boom en Zoon, 1968); Justus M. van der Kroef, "Interpretations of the 1965 Indonesian Coup: A Review of the Literature," *Pacific Affairs*, 43, no. 4 (Winter, 1970–1971), 557–577; E. Utrecht, *Indonesië's Nieuwe Orde: Ontbinding en Herkolonisatie* (Amsterdam: van Gennep, 1970); Howard Palfrey Jones, *Indonesia: The Possible Dream* (New York: Harcourt Brace Jovanovich, 1971); Lucien Rey, "Dossier on the Indonesian Drama," *New Left Review* (March–April 1966), 26–40; A. C. Brackman, *The Communist Collapse in Indonesia* (New York: Norton, 1969). To my mind, the literature on the coup, right, left, and center, has been marred by obsessive concern with the exact roles of Sukarno and of the Indonesian Communist Party in the immediate events of the plot (not unimportant issues, but more important for understanding the moment than for understanding the country), at the expense of its meaning for the development of Indonesian political consciousness.

cisive, but whose significance cannot effectively be assessed until well after their occurrence; and one of these is surely the eruption of great domestic violence. The Third World has seen a number of these eruptions over the twenty-five years it has been coming into being—the partition of India, the Congo mutiny, Biafra, Jordan. But none can have been more shattering than the Indonesian, nor more difficult to evaluate. Since the terrible last months of 1965, all scholars of Indonesia, and especially those trying to penetrate the country's character, are in the uncomfortable situation of knowing that a vast internal trauma has shaken their subject but not knowing, more than vaguely, what its effects have been. The sense that something has happened for which no one was prepared, and about which no one yet quite knows what to say, haunts these papers, making them read, sometimes, like the *agon* of a play with the crisis left out. But there is no help for this: the crisis is still happening.[10]

Of course, some of the outward effects are clear. The Indonesian Communist Party, on its claims the third largest in the world, has been, at least for the present, essentially destroyed. There is military rule. Sukarno was first immobilized, then, with that controlled, relentless grace the Javanese call *halus,* deposed, and has since died. The "confrontation" with Malaysia has ended. The economic situation has markedly improved. Domestic security, at the cost of large scale political detentions, has come to virtually the entire country for almost the first time since Independence. The flamboyant desperation of what now is called the "Old Order" has been replaced by the muted desperation of the "New Order." But the question, What has changed? is still, when it refers to the culture, a baffling one. Surely, so great a catastrophe, especially as it mostly occurred in villages among villagers, can hardly have left the country un-

---

[10] The fact that no one predicted the massacres has sometimes been instanced as an example of the futility of social science. Many studies did stress the enormous tensions and the potential for violence in Indonesian society; moreover, anyone who announced before the fact that a quarter of a million or so people were about to be slaughtered in three months of ricefield carnage would have been regarded, and rightly, as having a rather warped mind. What this says about reason faced with unreason is a complicated matter; but what it does not say is that reason is powerless because not clairvoyant.

moved, yet how far and how permanently it has been moved is impossible to say. Emotions surface extremely gradually, if extremely powerfully, in Indonesia: "The crocodile is quick to sink," they say, "but slow to come up." Both writings on Indonesian politics and those politics themselves are permeated right now with the inconfidence derived from waiting for that crocodile to come up.

In the history of comparable political seizures, however (and when one looks at the history of the modern world, they are easy enough to find), some outcomes seem more common than others. Perhaps the most common is a failure of nerve, a constriction of the sense of possibility. Massive internal bloodlettings like the American or the Spanish civil wars have often subjected political life to the sort of muffled panic we associate with psychic trauma more generally: obsession with signs, most of them illusory, that "it is about to happen again"; perfection of elaborate precautions, most of them symbolic, to see that it doesn't; and irremovable conviction, most of it visceral, that it is going to anyway—all resting, perhaps, on the half-recognized desire that it do so and to get it over with. For a society, as for an individual, an inner catastrophe, especially when it occurs in the process of a serious attempt to change, can be both a subtly addictive and a profoundly rigidifying force.

This is particularly so (and here the analogy—which, as public disasters refract through private lives, is not entirely an analogy—with individual response continues) when the truth of what has happened is obscured by convenient stories, and passions are left to flourish in the dark. Accepted for what they were, as terrible as they were, the events of 1965 could free the country from many of the illusions which permitted them to happen, and most especially the illusion that the Indonesian population is embarked as a body on a straight-line march to modernity, or that, even guided by the Koran, the Dialectic, the Voice in the Quiet, or Practical Reason, such a march is possible. Denied, by means of another cooked-up ideological synthesis, the half-suppressed memory of the events will perpetuate and infinitely widen the gulf between the processes of government and the struggle for the real. At an enormous cost, and one which need not have been paid, the Indonesians would seem to an outsider to have now demonstrated to themselves with convincing force the depth of their dissensus, ambivalence, and disorientation. Whether the demonstration has in fact been convincing to the insiders, for whom such revelations about themselves must inevitably be terrifying, is another question; indeed, it is the central question of Indonesian politics at this juncture of history. For all their before-the-storm quality, the studies in this volume contribute, if not an answer, at least a sense of what the probabilities are.

However great a disruptive force the massacres may (or may not) have been, the conceptual matrix within which the country has been moving cannot have changed radically, if only because it is deeply embedded in the realities of Indonesian social and economic structure, and they have not. Java is still spectacularly overcrowded, the export of primary products is still the main source of foreign exchange, there are still as many islands, languages, religions, and ethnic groups as there ever were (even, now that West New Guinea has been added, a few more), and the cities are still full of intellectuals without places, the towns of merchants without capital, and the villages of peasants without land.[11]

Lev's lawyers, Abdullah's reformers, Liddle's politicians, Sartono's peasants, and Anderson's functionaries, as well as the soldiers who now police them, face the same range of problems with about the same range of alternatives and the same stock of prejudices as they did before the holocaust. Their frame of mind may be different— after such horrors it is hard to believe that it is not—but the society within which they are enclosed and the structures of meaning which inform it are largely the same. Cultural interpretations of politics are powerful to the degree that they can survive, in an intellectual sense, the events of politics; and their ability to do that depends on the degree to which they are well grounded sociologically, not on their inner coherence, their rhetorical plausibility, or

---

[11] It should perhaps be remarked that the external parameters have also not changed very much—China, Japan, the United States and the Soviet Union are still more or less where and what they were, and so, for that matter, are the terms of trade. If so-called outside factors seem to have been slighted in favor of so-called inside ones throughout this volume it is not because they are considered unimportant, but because in order to have local effects they must first have local expressions, and any attempt to trace them beyond such expressions to their sources would, in studies of this scale, soon get out of hand.

their aesthetic appeal. When they are properly anchored, whatever happens reinforces them; when they are not, whatever happens explodes them.

So what is written here is, if not predictive, still testable. The worth of these essays—the authors of which may or may not agree with my interpretation of their findings—will, in the long run, be determined less by their fit to the facts from which they are derived, though it is that which recommends them to our attention in the first place, than by whether they illumine the future course of Indonesian politics. As the consequences of the last decade appear in the next, we shall begin to see whether what has been said here about Indonesian culture is penetrating or wrongheaded, whether it enables us to construe what happens in terms of it or leaves us straining for understanding against the grain of what we thought was so. Meanwhile, we can only wait for the crocodile along with everyone else, recalling, as a bar to the sort of moral presumptuousness that neither Americans nor Indonesians are at this time very well positioned to affect, what Jakob Burckhardt, who perhaps deserves to be called the founder of thematic analysis, said in 1860 about the dubious business of judging peoples:

It may be possible to indicate many contrasts and shades of difference among different nations, but to strike the balance of the whole is not given to human insight. The ultimate truth with respect to the character, the conscience, and the guilt of a people remains for ever a secret; if only for the reason that its defects have another side, where they reappear as peculiarities or even as virtues. We must leave those who find pleasure in passing sweeping censures on whole nations, to do so as they like. The people of Europe can maltreat, but happily not judge one another. A great nation, interwoven by its civilization, its achievements, and its fortunes with the whole life of the modern world, can afford to ignore both its advocates and its accusers. It lives on with or without the approval of theorists.[12]

12 J. Burckhardt, *The Civilization of the Renaissance in Italy* (New York: Modern Library, 1954; orig., 1860), p. 318.

Glossary

abangan	nominally Moslem in orientation, influenced by pre-Islamic beliefs
adat	custom, customary law
adjar	a sage (pre-Islamic)
akal	intellect, mind, reasoning faculty
alam	world
Aldjam'ijatul Waslijah	a modernist Islamic organization
aliran	(1) current, flow, trend
	(2) distinctive politico-religious tradition
balai	hall, council hall; nagari governing council (Minangkabau)
Bapost	Badan Penuntut Otonom Sumatera Timur— Body to Demand East Sumatran Autonomy
bid'ah	heresy, deviation from Islamic orthodoxy
bupati	regent
chatib	Islamic functionary, mosque official
dalang	puppeteer, narrator in wajang (qv)
demang	district chief
désa	village
djaksa	public prosecutor
djaksa tinggi	public prosecutor at the appellate level
djihad	Holy War (see perang sabil)
djimat	talisman, charm against danger
DPR	Dewan Perwakilan Rakjat—People's Representative Council, Parliament
dukun	magician, healer, seer
dunia madju	the modern world
fatwa	decision or opinion handed down by an Islamic court
gamelan	Javanese orchestra

Gerindo	Gerakan Rakjat Indonesia—Indonesian People's Movement
Gestapu	Gerakan September Tiga Puluh—September 30th Movement
guru	teacher, especially in mystical sense
hadji	pilgrim returned from Mecca
halus	smooth, fine, civilized
haram	prohibited, forbidden by Islam
HIR	Herziene Inlandsch (Indonesisch) Reglement —Revised Native Regulation
HKBP	Huria Kristen Batak Protestan—North Tapanuli Batak Church
hukum	law
hukum revolusi	law of the revolution
idjtihad	striving to attain truth by reasoning (akal)
ilmu	knowledge, science
imam	Moslem religious leader
iman	belief in God (Allah)
JSB	Jong Sumatranen Bond—Young Sumatran Union
kabupatèn	regency
kafir	infidel, unbeliever (in Islam)
kampung, kampuang	village; lower class neighborhood in a city, often inhabited by migrant villagers
kasar	crude, coarse, uncivilized
kasektèn	magical power
KASI	Kesatuan Aksi Sardjana Indonesia—Indonesian Intellectuals' Action Union
kaum	(1) village religious official (Islamic) (2) group, class of people
Kaum Kuno	traditionalists
Kaum Muda	younger group, progressives, modernists
Kaum Tua	older group, conservatives, traditionalists
kemadjuan	progress
kemenakan	nephew
Kitabullah	Book of God, the Koran
kjai	(1) Moslem scholar or sage (2) term of respect, particularly used for head of pesantrèn (qv)
kramat	(1) sacred, magically powerful (2) holy man, saint

kraton	palace, court
KRSST	Kebangunan Rakjat Simalungun Sumatera Timur—Awakening of the Simalungun People of East Sumatra
kuntji	key
landraad (pl. landraden)	secular court of first instance (see pengadilan negeri)
lapau	coffee house
laras	(1) one of two rival political traditions in Minangkabau (2) Dutch-created federation of nagari in Minangkabau
luhak	district in Minangkabau
lurah	village headman
madhab	school or doctrine of Islamic law
madrasah	Islamic school
Mahkamah Agung	Supreme Court
makrifat, makrifattullah	highest (mystical) knowledge
malim	Islamic religious expert or official
mamak	mother's eldest brother who heads Minangkabau family
Masjumi	Madjelis Sjuro Muslimin Indonesia—Council of Indonesian Moslem Associations
mufakat	consensus
murid	pupil
nafsu	desire, instinctive drive
nagari	village republic in Minangkabau
naql	established religious authorities (Moslem)
ndaru, andaru	radiance of royalty
negara hukum	state based on law
negari	royal capital or state in Java
ngèlmu	knowledge, usually esoteric
ngèlmu kadigdajan	traditional art of combat
NU	Nahdatul Ulama (Moslem Scholars' Party)
Nur Muhammad	Light of Muhammad
officieren van justitie	public prosecutors (for European courts)
pamong pradja	regional administrators, the core of the civil service
pamrih	(concealed) selfish motive

Parkindo	Partai Kristen Indonesia—Indonesian Christian (Protestant) Party
Partindo	Partai Indonesia—Indonesian Party
pasisir	coastal areas (especially the north coast of Java)
patih	grand vizier; also, deputy of a bupati (qv)
pengadilan agama	Islamic court
pengadilan negeri	court of first instance (secular)
pengadilan tinggi	court of second instance (appeals)
penghulu	(1) adat chief in Minangkabau
	(2) mosque official in Java
pepatah adat	adat aphorisms
Peradin	Persatuan Advokat Indonesia—Indonesian Advocates' Association
peranakan	Indonesia-born foreigner (usually refers to Chinese)
perang sabil	Holy War (see djihad)
Persahi	Persatuan Sardjana Hukum Indonesia—Indonesian Lawyers' Association
pesantrèn	rural Islamic school
pidato adat	adat speech
PKI	Partai Komunis Indonesia—Indonesian Communist Party
PNI	Partai Nasional Indonesia—Indonesian National Party
pokrol bambu	bush lawyer
prijaji	Javanese aristocracy, ruling literati, higher officialdom
PSI	Partai Sosialis Indonesia—Indonesian Socialist Party
pusaka	heirloom, regalia
pusat	center
raad agama	religious council (Islamic)
radja	(1) sovereign, king, in Java
	(2) viceroys in Minangkabau coastal areas
radjah	sacred texts or compounds of characters, figures, designs, inscribed on paper, earthenware or other material

rakjat	the people, the masses, the common people
rantau	fringe territories of Minangkabau; marantau—to go outside Minangkabau; perantau—one who travels outside Minangkabau
Ratu Adil	The Just King
rechtsstaat	state based on law
rodi	government corvée
SAAM	Sarekat Adat Alam Minangkabau—Adat Association of the Minangkabau World
sakato alam	consensus of the people, in Minangkabau
santri	(1) student, usually in an Islamic school (2) devoutly Moslem
satria	knight, warrior
sénapati	commander-in-chief
sjariah, sjarak	Islamic Law
SOBSI	Sentral Organisasi Buruh Seluruh Indonesia—All-Indonesian Federation of Labor Unions
SOKSI	Sentral Organisasi Karyawan Sosialis Indonesia—Central Organization of Socialist Functionaries of Indonesia
suku	group of kinsmen related by descent from a common mythological ancestor, in Minangkabau
suwita	system of patron-client relationships traditionally extending throughout Javanese society
tambo	traditional Minangkabau chronicle
taqlid	unquestioning acceptance of the word of religious teachers
tarékat	mystical brotherhood, usually Sufist
tasauf	mysticism, mystical doctrine
tédja	radiance emanating from man of power
tjantrik	pupil, usually of sage
tjikal-bakal	village founders
topèng	mask
tuanku laras	head of nagari federation, created by the Dutch
ulama	Islamic religious teacher
ummat	the community of Islamic believers
volkschool (pl. volkscholen)	three-year elementary government school in the Dutch colonial period

wahju	divine royal radiance, sign of royalty
wajang, wayang	shadow-play, type of drama
wajang bèbèr	story-telling illustrated by picture-scrolls
wali	Islamic saint
wedana	lower-level district officer, under the bupati (qv)
wilde scholen	unaccredited (nationalist) private schools
wong tjilik	the common man, the common people

Index

343

Culture and Politics in Indonesia

Designed by R. E. Rosenbaum.
Composed by Vail-Ballou Press, Inc.,
in 10 point linotype Caledonia, 3 points leaded,
with display lines in monotype Bulmer.
Printed letterpress from type by Vail-Ballou Press
on Warren's 1854 text, 60 pound basis,
with the Cornell University Press watermark.
Bound by Vail-Ballou Press
in Columbia book cloth
and stamped in All Purpose foil.

Library of Congress Cataloging in Publication Data
(For library cataloging purposes only)

Holt, Claire.
  Culture and politics in Indonesia.

  Includes bibliographical references.
  1. Indonesia—Politics and government—Addresses, essays, lectures. 2. Indonesia—Civilization—Addresses, essays, lectures. 3. Political sociology—Addresses, essays, lectures. I. Title.
JQ762.H6   320.9'598   78-162538
ISBN 0-8014-0665-X